THE DRUG HANG-UP
America's Fifty-Year Folly

Books by Rufus King:

Gambling and Organized Crime
The Drug Hang-up: America's Fifty-Year Folly

THE DRUG HANG-UP

America's Fifty-Year Folly

by RUFUS KING

CHARLES C THOMAS • PUBLISHER

Springfield • Illinois • U.S.A.

Published and Distributed Throughout the World by

CHARLES C THOMAS · PUBLISHER
Bannerstone House
301-327 East Lawrence Avenue, Springfield, Illinois, U.S.A.

1972, by RUFUS KING

ISBN 0-398-03071-5 (paper)

Library of Congress Catalog Card Number: 75-39810

First Printing, 1972
Second Printing, 1974

Printed in the United States of America
BE

Library of Congress Cataloging in Publication Data

King, Rufus, 1917–
    The drug hang-up.

    Bibliography: p.
    1. Narcotic laws–U.S.–History. I. Title.
KF3890.K5   344'.73'0545   75-39810

ISBN 0-398-03071-5 (paper)

Contents

THE DRUG HANG-UP
America's Fifty-Year Folly

"The oppression of crowns and principalities is unquestionably over, but the more frightful oppression of selfish, ruthless, and merciless majorities may yet constitute one of the chapters of future history."

—Peter S. Grosscup
Judge, U. S. District Court, Illinois
1894

"I had to operate courts for sixteen years in a way that I cannot justify. I could not help realizing in the course of my experience that the legal approach to drug addiction has become just about the most absurd and vicious operation that man can imagine."

—John M. Murtagh
Justice, New York Supreme Court
1971

■ ONE

Senator Hughes's Friendly Anger

■ IN THE EARLY 1960's, after a forty-year freeze, the drug-abuse pattern in America commenced to shift. Users took up new substances like LSD and revived markets for old substances like cocaine. Marijuana became important for the first time. There were notable changes in the make-up of the drug-using community; citizens with "advantages" began turning up as offenders, many of them not yet fully adult.

Similar shifts were noted in other Western countries. In England, for example, which had also been through a stable era of about four decades, but one characterized by virtually no problem, London youngsters began taking up pot, and the addict population grew from the low hundreds toward the low thousands.

The forces accounting for such changes in the relation between people and chemicals, in America and elsewhere, seem as complex as the sum of all the other problems of our times. Everything from the growing ill repute of cigarettes and the high cost of alcohol to increased leisure and the general discontent of our younger generations may play a part. And coinciding with these forces—or perhaps contributing to them—has been a Pandora release of new substances; the development of new drugs, new derivatives, and simplified production methods has created varieties of abuse unheard of a few years ago, while drug abusers

1

now appear curious and sophisticated enough to stay close behind each new step taken by the laboratory pioneers.

Simultaneously in the early 1960's America's national response to the drug-abuse problem began coming under critical scrutiny. Alternatives to bare criminal repression were explored. So-called dangerous drugs were entrusted to the control of an agency with scientific orientation, the Food and Drug Administration, rather than to the tough Narcotics Bureau in the Treasury Department. Education was urged, and even private research in drug-abuse areas began encountering less official discouragement. New stress was laid on rehabilitation. The Supreme Court applied the Bill of Rights to knock out criminal penalties for merely being a drug addict.

A detailed account of all this will be presented in the ensuing narrative. But to put what follows in perspective, it must be noted that the pattern has now been frozen again. And though enforcement proponents were compelled to make a few concessions, America has been brought almost full circle back to 1920. To stem what former FDA Commissioner Dr. James Goddard calls "the Niagara of chemistry . . . the chemistry of trauma, psychosis, and death," we have reinstated the federal criminal apparatus with powers that make yesterday's tyrannies look almost beneficent.

On October 27, 1970, a week before the national elections, President Nixon took time from his campaigning to pay an unusual visit in the nation's capital. At his insistent urging, Congress had rushed out a sixty-one page drug bill titled Comprehensive Drug Abuse Prevention and Control Act of 1970, and instead of the customary White House ceremony, the President took this bill to a downtown office building, where the Department of Justice maintains headquarters for its Bureau of Narcotics and Dangerous Drugs, for the official signing.

There he met Attorney General Mitchell and BNDD Director Ingersoll, the latter a former police chief, in a room decorated with trophies from Ingersoll's raids, to deliver a fight talk (which also reached anyone exposed to the national news media that day). Congress had been requested to act, the President said, because drugs were a major cause of street crime in the United States and, besides, their use was alarmingly increasing among young people. But now the federal government was going to move, and move very strongly in the field: "We can deal with it. We have the laws now. We are going to go out and enforce those laws." Calling for public support, the President seemed to be inviting citizens to stir up panic instead of giving calm backing for the federal effort:

> And I urge all who may be listening to this signing ceremony to remember that in every home in America, in every school in America, in every church in America, over the television and radio media of this country, in our newspapers, the message needs to get through, that this nation faces a major crisis in terms of the increasing use of drugs, particularly among our young people.

Secretary Richardson of HEW, personifying the government's medical, scientific, and educational forces, attended the ceremony as a spectator but did not participate. This was the final act of an internal struggle that had been instrumental in unseating Richardson's predecessor, Secretary Finch, and which had climaxed earlier in the year when a dozen senators, led by Senator Harold Hughes, tried first to substitute a soft-line education and rehabilitation bill for the Administration's law-enforcement measure, and then, failing that, to tack it on the latter by amendment.

When HEW Assistant Secretary Roger Egeberg told Hughes the Nixon Administration opposed his bill ("Drug Abuse and Drug Dependence Prevention, Treatment, and Rehabilitation Act of 1970") and, in effect, wanted no changes except an enlargement of the repressive powers conferred on the Attorney General, Hughes—"not understanding how you and Secretary Finch could relegate this to the Department of Justice"—responded (referring to drug-traffic victims):

> I regret I feel this passion, but they have been relegated to dying in the street forever, and I want to get them out. I need your help to do it. I am angry, it is obvious. I am angry that the Department says they have everything they need, when everything in the country indicates it isn't being done. So, I will continue to be angry. I hope it will be a friendly anger as we try to work out these problems that we have between us.

In the end the Hughes forces lost to a move that merely added a token enlargement of the government's existing mental-health efforts; Secretary Finch lost to Attorney General Mitchell; and President Nixon's problems in this area were worked out by solutions borrowed straight from President Harding.

Every effort has been made in the telling of this long tale, starting from the beginning of America's involvement with drugs, to be as accurate and dispassionate as possible. But the subject is so inflamed these days that even the fairest statements are liable to be denounced as slanted to some particular viewpoint, while incontestible matters of fact (smoking pot, for example, does *not* lead specially to heroin) keep getting lost in controversy.

But anyway I *do* have a viewpoint. America has scarcely done anything right about drug problems since somewhere around the year 1912, and even then our spokesmen at the Hague Opium Convention, and our lawmakers at home, were moving onto shaky ground. We have been misled at practically every turn—misguided in the basic effort to control personal indulgences by criminal repression, often out of step with the rest of the world, wrong in tolerating so much *federal* domination of the field, and mistaken to some degree in nearly every current appraisal. We have been perennially victimized by unscrupulous exploitation of drug issues in the arena of politics.

And at the same time there are indeed new challenges and new dimensions in today's problems, calling for accurate, coolheaded responses. We should be striving to eliminate old misconceptions, to come up with right answers, to avoid repeating old mistakes. Instead we seem bent on escalating this persistent national problem into a full-blown national disaster. The 1970 drug-control bill, administered by hard-nosed enforcement officials, may well achieve no less than that for us.

So perhaps a few traces of something like the good Senator's friendly anger may creep into my story. Perhaps as it unfolds they may even be found not unforgivably amiss.

■ TWO

From Our Pusher Ancestors
to the First Prohibitionists

■ GENERATIONS of viewers-with-alarm on the American drug scene have excoriated the nonaddicted peddler. What predator could be more vicious than this exploiter of human misery, this merchant of death on the installment plan?

But looking only a little further back, we find our European forebears, aided by not a few Yankee partners, deliberately addicting ancient, honorable China to the very drug we now fear most.

As was true of most rulers in the seventeenth century, Chinese emperors were more alarmed by the smoking of tobacco among their subjects than by the abuse of opium, both of which got their start in that era. Opium, brought to China by Arab traders about 1200 A.D., had long been favored for medicinal purposes. But the practice of smoking opium remained unknown until the late sixteenth century, when Spanish or Portuguese merchants introduced tobacco into the Flower Kingdom and taught its cultivation and use.

There may be poetic justice in the picture as now, at long last, we are coming to see it: for between the two it is tobacco, not opium, which is the killer. During the three centuries China has been struggling unsuccessfully with the opium problem forced on her by "foreign devils," Western societies have sacrificed millions of their own people by encouraging tobacco smoking. There is

5

almost certainly a relationship between these divergent selections of vice and the fact that death rates from cancer and cardiac involvement are considerably lower among most Oriental peoples than in the tobacco-saturated West.

The opium poppy, *papaver somniferum,* was cultivated so long ago in Asia Minor that the precise locale of its discovery and development is unknown. It is described in Sumerian tablets now more than 5,000 years old. Egyptologists have found references to opium in the chronicles of that land, and the Greeks knew the plant well—references to its medicinal value are found in Greek writings of the Homeric era, nine centuries before the birth of Christ. Opium brought westward by Arab traders was used as medicine throughout the Christian and Islamic worlds for nearly a millennium before it first appeared in India, in the ninth century A.D., and, as we have just noted, first reached China sometime after 1200.

While it is possible that the drug was eaten by some medieval citizens who found it made them feel good even when they were not suffering from anything requiring medicine, there are no records of such indulgent use, either in the Orient or the West, until the turn of the seventeenth century, and then the first problem is supposed to have arisen when someone discovered that opium fumes, inhaled with smoke from burning tobacco, were better even than the effects of the New World novelty puffed by itself.

This was what happened in China. Some authorities say the Dutch on Formosa first mixed opium in their smokes "to counteract the malaria that abounds in the jungles of the Island," and that the practice spread to the mainland through Amoy. In any event, at about the time the Chinese were learning how to light up, India was becoming a substantial opium producer, and a steady traffic from India to the Chinese market soon developed. Early in the eighteenth century, official Chinese edicts began prohibiting all use of tobacco, and in 1729 Emperor Yung Cheng issued the first imperial ban on opium, prescribing severe penalties, including death for opium-shop proprietors, to stamp out the habit.

But in those days China was weak, while our lusty occidental forebears were contemptuous of "natives" and greedy for profit. This was the era of clipper trade, with tea, silks, spices, and Chinese artifacts moving in great volume to markets in Europe and America. The Western demand for Chinese items soon became so large that trade balances began heavily favoring

China, and payments had to be made in specie. Moreover, the Chinese refused to open their markets to barbarian merchantmen. One of the devices principally relied upon to rectify this unfavorable situation was cultivation and promotion of the opium traffic.

India was always the principal source for the China market. Opium cultivation had been made a monopoly by the Great Mogul early in the eighteenth century, and on his defeat by Lord Clive in 1757 the monopoly was taken over by the British East India Company. Thereafter British merchants dominated the trade, and despite the Chinese prohibition on smoking, opium imports into that country, which had stayed at the level of 200 to 300 spice chests (150 pounds each) per annum, began to soar: to 1,000 chests in 1776, to over 5,000 in 1800, and to a yearly average of 17,000 in the 1820–1830 decade.

Succeeding Chinese emperors continued to resist this influx, banning all importation of opium in 1880 and extending the death penalty to its use. But they were no match for the pressures generated by British traders, backed up by the French, the Dutch, the Portuguese, and some adventuring Americans. Canton harbor, approached through the Portuguese concession at Macao, was the principal gateway for the import traffic. To avoid embarrassment, inbound merchant ships unloaded outside the harbor into depot vessels anchored there, or directly into smaller coastal craft, some of which were actually owned by corrupt Chinese officials.

In 1839 Emperor Tao Kwang sent a personal emissary, Commissioner Lin Tse-hsu, to Canton to clean up the situation. Lin first appealed directly for help to Queen Victoria, who had come to the British throne two years earlier at the age of eighteen:

> We have heard that in your Honourable Barbarian Country the people are not permitted to inhale the drug. If it is admittedly so deleterious, how can your seeking profit by exposing others to its malific power be reconciled with the decrees of heaven? You should immediately have the plant plucked up by the very root. Cause the land there to be hoed up afresh, sow the five grains and if any man dare again to plant a single poppy, visit his crime with condign punishment. Then not only will the people of this Celestial Kingdom be delivered from an intolerable evil, but your own barbarian subjects, albeit forbidden to indulge, will be safeguarded against falling a prey to temptation. There will result for each the enjoyment of felicity.
>
> We have reflected, that this noxious article is the clandestine

manufacture of artful schemers under the dominion of your honourable nation. Doubtless, you, the Honourable Chieftainess, have not commanded the growing and sale thereof.

There is no record of a response from Her Majesty. After increasingly hostile negotiations, Lin persuaded the British Superintendent of Trade at Canton, Captain Charles Elliot, to order all local European merchants to surrender their existing stocks of opium, and on April 3, 1839, they turned over 20,283 chests, having a claimed value of over £2 million.

However, the merchants continued receiving new supplies which had been en route, and in a series of confrontations involving outrages on both sides the British authorities were soon induced to declare war. The degree of American involvement is suggested by the fact that following the surrender to Lin, a resolution presented in the U.S. Congress denounced him as a "robber baron" and called for U.S. support for a punitive military expedition. The engagement which followed was known as the First Opium War, and was fought in two installments between 1840 and 1842. British forces first captured Chusan and exacted the cession of Hong Kong plus an indemnity of $6 million; but this was repudiated by the Chinese, whereupon the British resumed the attack with a formidable armada dispatched from India, seized half a dozen major cities, and exacted concessions in what came to be known as the Treaty of Nanking, including the opening of Canton, Shanghai, and other ports, and an indemnity of $21 million.

In 1843 the British insisted on further treaty concessions, and the following year American interests, represented by Commissioner Caleb Cushing, negotiated an agreement which put American merchantmen on an equal footing with the British—except that the American treaty excluded U.S. citizens who engaged in the opium traffic from the protection of their government. Chinese resistance was soon further undermined by the accession of a very weak emperor, Hien-feng, who took the throne in 1850, and although the central government continued to ban imports and publish edicts against opium smoking, the India trade kept flourishing (50,000 chests in 1850; 85,000 in 1860), and at the same time local cultivation of the poppy was launched in many areas of China by corrupt provincial viceroys.

In the troubled years which followed, China was torn by civil war (the Taiping Rebellion), and in 1856, magnifying a trivial episode involving disrespect for the British flag, the British and the French once more declared war. Again the

Chinese were easily bested, and under the new treaty, negotiated at Tientsin in 1858, not only the British and French victors but also the Americans and Russians extracted new concessions, one of which was full legalization of inbound opium shipments.

Chinese defiance continued, but to little avail. When foreign emissaries were refused access to Peking, the British renewed hostilities (in 1860), captured the capital city, forced the emperor to take to his heels, and burned the Imperial Summer Palace.

Although American clipper ships had always figured largely in the general China trade, the American share in the opium traffic was not very great at the outset and, as has been noted, the U.S. government early commenced an official campaign, through Commissioner Cushing, to discourage American participation. In 1834 the East India Company had relinquished its absolute control of British trade, however, and thereafter the company's monopoly of Indian opium in the Calcutta market also became somewhat relaxed. American traders had tried to bring opium from Persia, unsuccessfully because of the vastly superior quality of the Indian product, and had been identified with a small traffic from Turkey (which led Commissioner Lin to believe Turkey must be an American colony).

But commencing in the 1840's, as new British traders moved in, their American competitors were also able to obtain more of the drug directly from Calcutta sources, American firms handled shipments openly, and some of the sleek opium clippers working along the China coast flew the Yankee flag. Moreover, according to British accounts, it was U.S. Minister William B. Reed who, in 1858, first suggested restoring opium to the Chinese tariff schedules as a legal commodity because he "had become an advocate of the legalization of the trade from witnessing the abuses to which its contraband character gave rise."

It would be unfair to imply that meanwhile no one in London protested this poisoning of helpless China with "foreign mud." In 1783 opium was denounced as "a pernicious article of luxury which ought not to be permitted but for the purpose of foreign commerce only." The East India Company shed tears, for home consumption, about how it lamented the spread of nonmedicinal uses of the drug, and how it would gladly curb the market "in compassion to mankind" if it could do so without merely relinquishing the profitable trade to foreign competitors. In Parliament the opium monopoly was attacked as "utterly inconsistent with the honour and duty of a Christian kingdom."

But Calcutta remained the dominant source for supplies. The

East India Company clung to its control of Indian production until the company was dissolved in 1857. And long thereafter India under British control still continued to be the world's prime source of opium—without official restrictions until 1908.

It was estimated that by 1880, after twenty years of legalized importing, 2 per cent of the Chinese population was addicted to opium smoking, and that Chinese domestic production amounted to at least three times the volume of the import traffic, the latter having nevertheless risen steadily until it reached an annual average in the range of 100,000 chests. Succeeding Chinese emperors, beset by internal chaos and vainly clinging to the attitudes and values of the old Celestial Empire, continued to protest and to issue new edicts forbidding abuse of the drug—but with no effect. Corruption was universal; Chinese functionaries allegedly often made as large a share of the fabulous profits through their "squeeze" as foreign traders took for themselves.

The official attitude in Washington, although continuing to deplore this exploitation of China, did not altogether prevent participation in the trade by Yankee merchantmen through most of the balance of the nineteenth century. Several great American fortunes are supposed to have had their roots in China opium profits. And although bilateral opium agreements prohibiting exploitation of the traffic by American nationals were early negotiated with other countries in the Far East, commencing with the United States-Siam Pact of 1833, no such restrictions were agreed to with China until 1880, and Congress did not implement the Chinese commitment with express sanctions until 1887.

Chinese authority continued to disintegrate, and her drug problem kept growing. In 1894 opium comprised 14 per cent of China's total imports. By 1900 an estimated 27 per cent of the adult male population was addicted in some degree. Even though domestic growth of the poppy was now tolerated in every province of the empire, the traffic supplied from British-controlled production—and still carried on in part by smugglers to avoid the Chinese duties—continued to be a major factor. One report fixed total Chinese consumption in 1900 at 22,588 *tons* of the smoking preparation, and attributed at least a seventh of this total to the Indian source.

Americans learned about opium smoking from Chinese imported to build railroads, and from the large contingent of U.S. missionaries in Asia, but the habit was not spread much by these contacts. What plunged the U.S. government suddenly into the drug scene—overseas rather than at home, and the *federal* government instead of local authorities—was the chain of events that started with the famed explosion in Havana harbor in 1898.

Avenging the *Maine,* Uncle Sam emerged as a colonial power. Although Cuba and the United States were allies in driving out the Spanish oppressor, the United States found itself in a nasty operation against the Filipinos, who ungratefully resisted U.S. designs to liberate them. When the Hero of San Juan Hill became president in 1901, the Philippine insurgents had just been subdued and Civil Governor W. H. Taft in Manila was discovering, among other things, that he and his Philippine Commission faced a runaway opium problem.

The Spaniards, in a system devised in 1843, had auctioned contracts to individual opium wholesalers who then set up their own distribution outlets, which nominally only provided the drug to Chinese inhabitants but actually promoted opium eating and smoking to some extent among natives of the islands as well. In the chaotic insurrection years, local merchants took over from the contractors and the habit spread further. Taft proposed reinstating the Spanish system, which stirred protests from everyone, led by the newly entrenched merchants and den proprietors but soon echoed in an uproar among outraged moralists in the United States. The Yankee conscience was prickling over America's high-handed ways with its own Chinese immigrants as well as over the broken promise of Philippine liberation; some salve could be found in sparing new U.S. colonials what the "perfidious British" had so long forced on China; and besides, there were no vested interests in the United States, as there were in London, to defend opium profits.

In 1902 Congress expressed the mood of the country in a sweeping prohibition against any sales by U.S. traders of guns, liquor, or opium to natives on Pacific islands who had no "civilized government" of their own to protect them.

Taft backed down and commissioned a special Opium Investigating Committee to study ways in which the problem was being handled in the Far East. The Committee, which took two years to observe and digest (while the Philippine situation worsened), seems not to have enjoyed its sojourn in China, and wrote the Chinese off: "There are no outdoor games in China, or indeed any games except in a gambling sense. Absolute dullness and dreariness seem to prevail everywhere. As these two demons drive the Caucasian to drink, so they drive the Chinese to his opium."

Most favored was the Japanese approach, and the Committee

cannot be faulted for its choice; but its recommendation was to follow the Japanese model in Formosa, designed to deal with a situation closely paralleling that in the Philippines, and not the total-prohibition policy enforced by the Mikado among his own people. Japan had taken Formosa from China in 1895, assuming control of 3 million inhabitants, 6 or 7 per cent of whom were addicted to eating or smoking opium. Recognizing that prohibition would be cruel and unworkable, the Japanese authorities set up a government opium monopoly and a licensing system for opium shops and opium users. Progressive restrictions on licenses, plus education, treatment facilities in ten government hospitals, and low pricing to keep smuggling at a minimum, were aimed at wiping out abuse of the drug "in perhaps thirty years." In 1900 there were 1,107 Formosan opium shops catering to 169,064 licensed users. The system was not working perfectly, but the Committee found it "humane and apt."

In Japan itself, for reasons the Committee set forth at length the native population, and even the eight thousand Chinese residents, were "practically proof against the vice. . . . The Japanese to a man fear opium as we fear the cobra or the rattle-snake, and they despise its victims. China's curse has been Japan's warning, and a warning heeded." Thus the Japanese prohibition was successful because it had been applied not as cure but as a preventative, accepted by a people whose reverence for authority was legend, and supported by strongly held popular views.

The Philippine Investigating Committee's report was printed and circulated in Washington, but Congress seems to have missed or ignored its nuances. In 1905 the U.S. lawmakers took matters out of the hands of the Philippine Commission by slipping a proviso into the Philippine Tariff Act of that year to the effect that Philippine authorities might take measures at once "for the suppression of the evils resulting from the sale and use of the drug" (on which, otherwise, a moderate import duty was laid by the Act), but that in any event after March 1, 1908, only the government could import opium in any form, and all nonmedic-inal uses would be unlawful.

Thus it came to pass that from the Olympus of democracy there emanated, in 1905, a decree almost as arbitrary—and almost as futile—as those which the Dragon Throne began issuing in 1729. Efforts were made in the Philippines in the intervening three years to register and license addicted users and to prepare for the prohibition deadline; but when it came the entire traffic quickly went underground, and Americans soon had their first taste of big-scale clandestine drug operations.

Meanwhile, American diplomats, who were being especially well received in Peking at this time because of Secretary Hay's insistence on the "open door" policy, pressed the Chinese to take stronger measures to deal with their own drug traffic. In 1906 the Chinese government launched a ten-year program, forbidding by edict all further consumption of opium and all cultivation of the poppy. A six-month period was allowed for users to break off their habits, following which any backslider would be executed. And now the British agreed—at last—to reduce their exportation of Indian opium at the rate of one-tenth of the then-existing volume for each of the succeeding ten years, provided the Chinese made at least parallel reductions in domestic production and consumption.

The Chinese effort had surprising apparent effects. Poppy fields were destroyed, dens were closed, and smoking was repressed. By 1909 Chinese opium production was reportedly reduced by 80 per cent, causing severe economic distress in some of the producing regions. By 1913 smoking had been so curtailed that the British agreed to terminate further shipments from India, ahead of the ten-year schedule.

But Chinese smokers in large numbers seem to have turned to manufactured drugs, principally morphine and heroin. By treaties in 1902 and 1903, respectively, Great Britain and the United States undertook to limit their shipments of manufactured opiates to China to legitimate medical supplies. These obligations were indifferently enforced, however, and a route was left open to the China market via transshipments in Japan.

Visible above an allegedly large smuggled flow, China's *declared* imports of morphine jumped from an average of 19,766 ounces per year in the decade from 1898 to 1907 to an annual average of 478,629 ounces between 1915 and 1920, with a record high of 600,228 ounces in 1917. Japan's declared morphine imports (much of it supposedly going on to China via smugglers) reached totals of 558,812 ounces in 1916 and 880,000 ounces in 1920.

It was not until 1920 that U.S. authorities took vigorous steps to choke the flow of morphine passing to the Far East by transshipment and by transit routes from American ports.

Returning for a moment to 1906, American zeal and concern over the Philippines led the United States to take further steps. Speaking through President Roosevelt, the U.S. government proposed that all powers concerned with the international opium traffic should meet and consider cooperative measures to put an end to it. Out of this overture came the Shanghai Conference, convened on February 1, 1909, and attended by representatives of China, Great Britain, Austria, Hungary, France, Germany, Italy, Japan, the Netherlands, Persia, Portugal, Russia, and the United States. At Shanghai the groundwork was laid for the Hague Convention of 1912, to which we shall soon return following different threads of this narrative.

■ THREE

The Sensible Century and Mr. Harrison's Tax Act

■ IN MANY WAYS America must have been a relaxed and comfortable place in her first dozen decades—if one disregards the plight of black compatriots and the sufferings of the war that released them from slavery. The frontier heritage nurtured self-reliance, and if Americans were not always right in their convictions, they seemed generally righteously serene about them. The family was the family, and father was head of it. Country and flag were objects of simple adoration. The dollar remained truly worth one hundred cents, with only moderate attraction for tax collectors. The good were good and were rewarded with opportunity, if nothing else; the bad were very bad and deservedly wound up shaven, garbed in stripes, and wearing balls and chains. Thrift and simple virtue in this world assured everlasting bliss in the next.

Nineteenth-century Americans were for the most part relaxed about personal indulgences, too. Most towns had their amiably tolerated drunks and a complement of ne'er-do-wells who squandered their lives harmlessly in pool halls and saloons. Snuff and tobacco were accepted—for men only, and not including the diabolical cigarette—but those curious strictures were also embraced without controversy. Moralists decried the evils of gambling, card playing, and Sabbath breaking more than the personal ingestion of toxic substances. Opium remained one of the most important medications available to practitioners of the healing arts; opium eating was beginning to make small inroads as an indulgent habit, but in most of America cigarettes continued to be viewed with more opprobrium than any form of the opium habit.

When morphine, a derivative of opium, was isolated by German pharmacists at the turn of the nineteenth century, it was found to have superior analgesic qualities and was soon universally relied upon for the relief of pain. In an error they have repeated with new substances since, doctors hailed morphine as a nonaddicting substitute for opium, and some recommended it unreservedly as a cure for both alcoholism and the opium habit. Codeine, another valuable opium alkaloid, was isolated a few years later, and in 1845 Alexander Wood invented the first practical hypodermic syringe.

As the nineteenth century progressed, eating-opium could be bought in grocery and candy stores, and the promoters of patent medicines, including even "soothing" preparations for children, took to loading their products with the drug. Nostrums were widely promoted to cure victims of alcoholism or the drug habit—and this was indeed what they would do, by substituting addiction to the medicine itself. A few marginal physicians, predecessors of the odious "scrip doctors" who sold drugs and prescriptions to anyone for what the traffic would bear after the advent of prescription controls, bolstered their practices by inducing addiction among patients of sufficient means so that once they were hooked they might happily continue "treatment" indefinitely.

It was the Civil War, however, that gave the American addiction rate its big boost. In those bitter years, morphine and the new syringe proved a blessed substitute for inadequate battlefield ministrations, and opium was always in short supply because it was an effective antidote for the ubiquitous dysentery which afflicted soldiers under both standards. In the years following Appomattox, addiction became tolerantly known as "the army disease."

So it would not be proper to suggest that drug abuse in this permissive era was insubstantial. In the 1880's one observer estimated that 4 per cent of the population of the United States used some kind of opiate for nonmedicinal purposes. There were simply no controls. Patients introduced to the needle by their doctors could carry on with self-administrations, if they chose, merely by addressing themselves to the neighborhood chemist for supplies. (There was another limitation on popular use of the needle, however, and that was lack of knowledge about antiseptic procedures until the turn of the twentieth century. The portrayal of user-victims as covered with abcesses might not have been an atypical distortion in Lord Lister's day and before the advent of antibiotics.)

If drug use was not really approved by society, addiction was nonetheless regarded merely as a personal weakness similar to overindulgence in alcohol, and no efforts were made—or dreamed of—to impose penal restrictions. By the 1880's, enlightened medical men were beginning to speak out, warning that opium was claiming people "who crave the effect of a stimulant, but will not risk their reputation for temperance by taking alcoholic beverages," and that drug victims "have not come from the ranks of reckless men and fallen women, but the majority of . . . [whom] are to be found among the educated and most honored and useful members of society."

Opium received attention in the famed works of Coleridge and De Quincey, and its use by American figures like Edgar Allan Poe was well known. But the best measure of how drugs were accepted in England and America is provided by the most admired hero of Victorian literature—himself the creation of a medical man—who relaxed at the Baker Street flat after his bouts with Professor Moriarity by summoning Dr. Watson to prepare him a needle.

Heroin was isolated in 1898, again by a German, and once more this new poppy derivative was hailed by much of the medical profession not only for its very real therapeutic advantages over other drugs in dealing with bronchial and pulmonary problems, but also as the long-sought nonaddicting substitute for morphine. And during all this era, of course, doctors quite apart from the reprehensible few already mentioned who intentionally addicted patients to build up their practices, made many addicts simply because the opiates *were* good medicine, soothing, calming anxieties, and arresting pain in situations where medical practitioners had no other effective way to deal with their patients' problems.

Estimating the addict population at any given time, and even the composition of the addict community, easily degenerates if one does not specify careful reservations. Authoritative pronouncements can be found to buttress almost any thesis about any period. It has been noted that one accepted estimate of the pre-1900 drug-using population was 4 per cent of the nation, or

2.5 million persons based on the 1890 census. This seems high, perhaps because (like some of the figures being offered today) it may have included those who had merely tried some addicting substance as well as true addicts. The two most respected authorities on the subject, who made a retroactive examination in 1924, concluded, figuring from the amounts of opium and opiates known to have been imported and distributed, that before World War I America was sustaining an addict community (to the opiates only) of not more than 100,000.

Whatever the figure, it was agreed by most observers that in those days addicted persons were mostly middle-aged and that a substantial preponderance were women. If there was a regional weighting it was toward the South, and if any class groupings were significant they would *not* have been lower, underprivileged, or minority. As one eminent physician of the period observed, "Thousands of women were addicts of opiates, with no thought of wrong-doing, who would have gone on their knees to pray for a lost soul had they seen cigarette stains on the fingers of a daughter."

Lord Lister is credited with the classic comparison: "Opium soothes; alcohol maddens." In turn-of-the-century America, while their fellows were being incapacitated in ever larger numbers by drink, drug users, able to maintain their supplies without difficulty and at modest expense, generally pursued normal callings and posed no problems for society. People in responsible positions—the most-told tale being that of a New York Central engineer who never missed a run in more than two decades while he was a heavy user of morphine—carried on normally in useful lives.

There are several reasons why drug addiction (though I should repeat now and then that alcohol, nicotine, coffee, and tea are honest-to-goodness drugs by *every* definition, too), escaped the early missionary fury against drink which eventually swept the United States into the Prohibition experiment. Demon Rum not only disabled, but it unforgivably disabled people of the working classes, whose fidelity to the twelve-hour day was essential to America's emergence as a great industrial power. Drugs had no such threatening potential. Opium smoking, associated with laziness and nonproductivity in the Far East, *was* inhibited by high duties laid on in the 1880's, by a law prohibiting manufacture in the United States after 1887, and by a total ban on imports for the smoking use after 1909. Smoking also received a setback in the public view in the early 1900's when it became associated to some extent with the so-called criminal classes. But this probably had the effect, among others, of inhibiting adventurous youngsters who might otherwise have tried it, driving them instead to the differently frowned-upon cigarette. The "opium den" was a dime-novel fantasy for most good citizens, while the saloon, and in cities the corrupt and corrupting saloon-keeper, were conspicuous targets.

Opium had singularly important medical uses, as we have noted, and a substantial number of addicts had acquired the habit in the course of medical treatment. Drugs were cheaper than spirits, so maintaining a habit imposed little hardship on the user or those dependent upon him. And finally, as has also been noted, when heroin was isolated in 1898 there followed a period in which the medical profession itself proclaimed this new discovery as promising all the benefits of morphine without attending disadvantages—as, in fact, a reliable cure for addiction.

We have not yet said anything about cocaine, and it deserves only passing mention in relation to the opium problem because, in the first place, cocaine is not addicting, in terms of compulsion to use, the tolerance phenomenon, and withdrawal symptoms—although official propagandists now distort this classic definition. Nor is cocaine even habituating to the same degree as tobacco. It is a product of the coca plant, long known to Indians of South America who chewed its leaves to reduce fatigue and to induce mild euphoria. The pure drug was first isolated in 1883 and was widely used in medicine until more effective substitutes became available. Coca-leaf flavoring, with the secret formulas long since changed to delete all traces of the drug, has made the plant better known to soft-drink fans throughout the world than to drug abusers.

Unlike the opiates and alcohol, cocaine is a stimulant. Ingested by sniffing or injection, it produces manic excitement, and used persistently it is capable of causing delusions. Cocaine sniffing, like opium smoking, came to be associated in the public mind with prostitutes and criminals, and never made much significant penetration into the American population at large, although it will reappear in our story in a surprising renaissance in the decade just past.

There is another touch of poetic justice in the China-Philippines story that was unfolded in the last chapter, for it was primarily the Far East involvement that led the *federal* government to get mixed up in drug-use repression on the home front. Decreeing prohibition for the Philippines and trying to mobilize

the international community to impose abstinence on China may
not have been responsible for all the excesses of the Eighteenth
Amendment, although I would not rule out a possible connection.
But the controlling force of these episodes in saddling the United
States with its own federal drug police is scarcely open to doubt.
And much of America's unique difficulty with drug problems
in the ensuing decades seems directly attributable to this misguided commitment of national power in dealing with matters
which chiefly affect only individual citizens' body chemistry.

U.S. preoccupation with opium in China after the turn of the
century coincided handily with the push of American commercial
interests to break up spheres of influence and open Far East
markets to all comers. Humanitarian sentiments ran high in the
American electorate, and so did lusty self-assurance about America's new role as a world power. U.S. involvement was deepened
in the Philippine struggle, and when the Philippine Commission
began implementing the opium prohibition Congress had specified, American authorities became more concerned about conditions on mainland Asia because of the inbound smuggling traffic
that soon flourished.

When the Shanghai Conference, summoned by President
Roosevelt, was convened in 1909, American delegates came with
resolutions calling for cooperation to end the traffic, but the
colonial powers restricted themselves to expressions of high
resolve and discussions of gradual reductions. Nonetheless, the
stage was set for the Hague Conference, also proposed by
Roosevelt, and convened by the Netherlands government three
years later.

Again at the Hague, the American delegation played a leading
role, vigorously supported by the Chinese, in pressing for immediate sanctions to restrict production and end trafficking. In
the Hague Opium Convention of 1912, the result of the Hague
Conference, each signatory committed itself to impose controls
on domestic production of opium and opium derivatives (none
of the parties except China and Persia being opium producers)
and to take steps to restrict domestic consumption of the drug
strictly to controlled channels and legitimate medical uses (no
one, again excepting China, having a large domestic-consumption
problem).

As might have been expected, the Hague Convention had, at
the outset, little international effect, although the U.S. delegation
credited itself with a humanitarian coup and further meetings
were called in 1913 and 1914 to try to induce wider acceptance

of the Hague principles. Ratifications came so slowly that it was not until the aftermath of World War I that the Convention became a vital force, and then only because the document was incorporated, largely at U.S. insistence, into the Paris treaties.

But because America had been so strongly committed to the purposes of the 1912 effort, and because, as will be described in the next chapter, the United States was beginning to lose its perspective on the home front, Congress in 1914 enacted the Harrison Narcotic Act, which stood as the basic federal drug law for the next fifty-six years. The Harrison Act was not in any sense a prohibition statute, but rather a mild regulatory measure consisting of registration and record-keeping requirements to which a moderate federal tax was added in 1919. Its avowed purpose was to bring the domestic drug traffic (including cocaine) into observable channels. As one of its chief supporters, Dr. Hamilton Wright, who had been a member of the Hague delegation, explained:

> It is designed to place the entire interstate traffic in the habit-forming drugs under the administration of the Treasury Department. It is the opinion of the American Opium Commission that it would bring this whole traffic and the use of these drugs into the light of day and thereby create a public opinion against the use of them that would be more important, perhaps, than the Act itself.

The heart of the Act as it emerged in 1919 was an excise tax, at the modest rate of one cent per ounce, on opium, coca leaves, and their derivatives, the tax to be evidenced by stamps affixed to the package or container in which the drug first entered domestic commerce—that is, by the importer, manufacturer, producer, or compounder. Other provisions were logically drawn to facilitate collection of this tax. It was made unlawful for anyone to purchase, sell, dispense, or distribute drugs except from the original stamped package, and unlawful for anyone to deliver or give away drugs except pursuant to a written order from the recipient prepared on special forms supplied by the Treasury Department.

Similarly, to bring the traffic into observable channels and facilitate collection, the Act required everyone whose vocation involved the handling of narcotic drugs and cocaine (hereafter we shall ignore the wholly illogical inclusion of cocaine, as has nearly everyone else for the past fifty years)—importers, manufacturers, wholesalers, druggists, doctors, dentists, researchers—to register with the Treasury Department and to pay an occupational tax graduated from $1 to $24 per year. Each registrant was required to keep appropriate records, and these records were made available by law to Treasury representatives and other law-enforcement officers for inspection.

Note that the Harrison Act imposed no standards as to quality, labeling, or packaging comparable to those prescribed in the federal Food and Drug Act of a few years earlier. And note further that it imposed no restrictions of any kind on who might register and deal in the drugs, so long as the records were kept and the taxes paid. It required a far stretch indeed to make of this bland federal revenue law the fearsome instrument of repression it was soon to become. But stretch there was. And that is the sad—sometimes incredible—part of the narrative to which we come next.

■ FOUR

Hysterical Beginnings

■ PEOPLE who had a direct stake in turning the American drug problem from a minor social concern into a major law-enforcement commitment fifty years ago, and in keeping it that way ever since, have always been few in number. Their success started with some lucky breaks—lucky for them, that is, not for the national welfare or for, so far, almost three generations of their countrymen.

As has been noted, at the outset there was no popular swell, like the anti-saloon movement, against evils inherent in drugs. Even the medical profession, with few exceptions, hailed the advent of each new narcotic as a welcome addition to its scanty armory. U.S. leadership in attempts to repress opium in the Far East led to the Hague Convention which in turn was a major factor in inducing Congress to pass the Harrison Act. But in the latter action other forces came into play, one generated, unlikely as it now sounds, by a famous rivalry in the elite "Four Hundred" of New York society.

In 1911 William K. Vanderbilt, grandson of the renowned Commodore and a towering figure among New York socialites, divorced his first wife and, after an appropriate interval, married Ann Harriman Sands. Also after a seemly interval, the first Mrs. Vanderbilt married O. H. P. Belmont. And soon the second Mrs. Vanderbilt and Mrs. Belmont became cutthroat rivals. The ladies jousted for prominence in their own circles and for attention in the society pages of the New York press, but Mrs. Belmont gained a telling advantage by espousing the cause of the suf-

23

fragettes, thus making a place for herself in the news coverage
on front pages as well.

Seeing her rival thus featured in accounts of the not-so-gentle
campaign waged by the fair sex for the electoral franchise, Mrs.
Vanderbilt (and, as it turned out, her attorneys—lawyers doubled
for public relations consultants in 1912) cast about for a cause
with which she could win similar recognition. And what she hit
upon was repression of narcotic drugs.

As Mrs. Belmont's distaff revolt tied into other major trends
in American life—the economic emancipation of women, the
decline of the paternal-protector image, the disillusionments of
war—so Mrs. Vanderbilt's crusade against drugs picked up un-
deserved momentum because of mounting pressures behind the
Prohibition drive. Described by one observer as "a famous lady
who had time on her hands, money in the bank, and rivalry in
her heart," she organized anti-narcotics committees, led marches
up and down Fifth Avenue (with news coverage that must have
produced despair in the camp of her rival), and, thanks to the
bottomless reservoir of Vanderbilt funds, launched telegram and
letter campaigns to lawmakers in Albany and Washington on the
theme that helpless people of the lower classes had to be protected from "this poison."

Partly as a result of such efforts, just before World War I the
State of New York enacted the first repressive anti-narcotic law
in America, and, for that matter, the world's first, if one disregards the unique situation in the Far East. Known as the
Towns-Boylan Act, the New York law, which became effective
July 1, 1914, aimed at all nonmedicinal trafficking and use,
with substantial criminal penalties. A *New York Times* editorial commended Mrs. Vanderbilt for her part in developing this
legislation; but apparently her publicists had overplayed it, for
Representative Boylan, the House cosposor, thereupon announced that he gave full credit for initiating the bill to Dr.
Charles B. Towns, stating that if Mrs. Vanderbilt had helped at
all it had only been by acting as an "agitator."

Nonetheless the cause was carried on among her followers
with zeal. Ladies as unfamiliar with opium as their counterparts
today are with LSD joined her crusade to save lost souls and
rack up society-page credits for sharing in the good work. More
action committees were formed, more letter and telegram campaigns were organized, and delegations waited upon editors,
ministers, and teachers. A permanent national organization, the
White Cross, was launched to broaden the scope of the campaign.

However, these socialite crusaders, most of them New Yorkers, might have had less effect had it not been for other greater events shaping the nation's history in this era. The 1914 Harrison Tax Act was neglected, and even the drive for national prohibition and the suffragette movement were pushed into the background, as America drifted into her first Great War. Long before the United States actually entered the hostilities, Germany's goose-stepping legions began to be depicted as Hun, Boche, and Antichrist. German cruelty, German immorality, and the terrifying reach of the German grand design for world conquest emerged as focal points for all America's fears and fantasies.

Vague warnings of danger of national enslavement by drugs blended with fuzzy notions about spies, saboteurs, and an imminent German invasion of the New World—and suddenly the harmless, pitied victim of the drug habit emerged as the menacing dope fiend, tool of German malevolence. The campaign to reduce trafficking in drugs rapidly picked up overtones of patriotic fervor.

In New York a minor war was waged under the Town-Boylan law against cocaine (the intoxicating and debilitating effects of heavy cocaine use being more obvious than those of the opiates). It was reported in the press that "cocaine poisoning" produced insanity and that the drug was being widely sold to school children. Harlem was supposed to be so full of dangerous child addicts that good citizens were urged to stay out of it. One 1916 estimate purported to establish that there were 200,000 highly dangerous drug fiends roaming the streets of New York City, not only lurking among the criminal classes but ranging through the entire "upper world" as well.

Extra emphasis was given to such reports from a curious direction: opponents of Prohibition pointed to the suddenly discovered menace of drug enslavement as a foretaste of what would happen when the threatened curtailment of beverage alcohol took effect. By 1917 increasing numbers of civic leaders and responsible citizens were calling for federal intervention and strict federal controls to stop the drug traffic. In that year the first caches of illegal drugs were seized by Treasury agents (and Treasury then started the deceptive practice, continued ever since by drug-law enforcers, of announcing each seizure in terms of how many millions of dollars the contraband substances might have been worth if they had been sold at maximum prices in the illegal market).

Also in 1917 the first narcotic agent was caught and convicted for taking a large bribe.

Estimates of the addict population in New York City alone

jumped to 300,000. Heart-rending details of addiction among women and young children were unfolded. Simultaneously it was revealed that drug peddlers were concentrating their efforts on military camps, producing many soldier addicts. In April 1918 *The New York Times* reported that a murder victim—who, they implied, paid with his life for the disclosure—had told the authorities how German agents were actively engaged in smuggling drugs on a large scale into army training centers. The Treasury Department announced officially that it had discovered addiction to be spreading all over the country, and that new addicts were being found in alarming numbers among young soldiers. In August 1918 the press reported details of another German plot to furnish drugs in the camps.

Again the good ladies moved in: it was rumored that the fiendish enemy had agents prowling around schoolyards offering candy to innocent tots; the candy was, of course, loaded with dope, so any child unfortunate enough to eat a piece would immediately return to its family as a confirmed and dangerous "heroin maniac." This news prompted a committee of congressional wives in Washington to issue a series of national appeals to all mothers to teach their children never to eat anything tendered by a stranger and, if possible, to do their extra bit for the war effort by bringing their broods home from school for lunch every day.

On the editorial page of *The New York Times* for December 18, 1918, a bare month after the end of hostilities, there was offered the following "blood-curdling story of German fiendishness," purportedly relayed to the *Times* from a reputable source in Iceland:

> Into well-known German brands of toothpaste and patent medicines —naturally for export only—habit-forming drugs were to be introduced; at first a little, then more, as the habit grew on the non-German victim and his system craved ever-greater quantities. Already the test had been made on natives in Africa, who responded readily; if the German Staff had not been in such a hurry German scientists would have made their task an easy one, for in a few years Germany would have fallen upon a world which cried for its German toothpaste and soothing syrup—a world of "cokeys" and "hop fiends" which would have been absolutely helpless when a German embargo shut off the supply of its pet poison.

In this period (1918–19) it was authoritatively reported and widely believed that drug abuse had shifted its point of incidence and overnight had become a great threat to young people; 70 per cent of known addicts were discovered to be under twenty-five years of age; children in the New York public school system were allegedly turning up in their classrooms completely stoned.

And still the interlinking coincidences go on: even the full-blown drug hysteria which had developed by the end of the war might have subsided and been forgotten along with other wartime excesses had it not fitted perfectly into the empire-building ambitions of a brand-new Washington agency, the ill-famed Prohibition Unit. Created in the Treasury Department to enforce the Volstead Act against the liquor traffic, it naturally also received the task of enforcing the tax provisions of the Harrison Act.

Cop-and-robber law enforcement was a new field for the federal government in 1919. Wartime security had been assured by the military services, revenue collection had been primarily the responsibility of the Coast Guard, and only a small handful of federal officers policed federal enclaves and saw to the enforce-ment of federal laws in such special areas as counterfeiting. Even in the case of out-and-out criminal prohibitions like the Mann Act (outlawing interstate transportation of women for immoral purposes), the detecting and apprehending of offenders was left mainly to local authorities, who then turned the culprits over to the Department of Justice for prosecution. Treasury's Internal Revenue Service was newborn: though an emergency federal income tax had been imposed briefly at the time of the Civil War, the first regular federal levy on incomes dated only from the law which followed ratification of the Sixteenth Amendment in 1913.

So now the U.S. Treasury took up where Mrs. Vanderbilt and the wartime Cassandras had left off. A fanatical crusade was launched against drug users by the T-men. While some Prohibi-tion Unit agents began shaking up the populace with roughneck searches, catch-all roadblocks, and end-to-end inspections of passenger trains in search of contraband liquor, others set out to badger everyone connected with narcotic drug use. In 1918 the Narcotics Division reported that it had *dropped* charges against (that is, instituted and then terminated—or, in other words threatened) 14,701 persons registered under the Act. In 1919 the figure was 22,595, and in 1920 it jumped to 47,835.

Press rumors about addicts in the armed forces and "dope fiends" coming home from the services to menace their com-munities now took on the dignity of official Treasury pronounce-ment. At the same time, dirty work formerly credited to German agents began being attributed to Orientals working out of sinister opium dens and organized in "tongs." Japan was officially accused of fostering the trade in morphine with China (which her government was indeed permitting, mostly via transshipments) for the supposedly quite realizable purpose of conquering that mass of humanity in short order when the drug had sapped China of her will to resist. It was agents of the Yellow Peril who now reportedly prowled about American schoolyards handing out dope to children. Arrests of drug offenders with heavy epicanthic folds were pushed for first-page coverage. T-men even took to making raids on foreign ships lying at dockside in New York.

In April 1919 a special committee appointed by Prohibition Commissioner Roy A. Haynes and headed by G. C. Keith, his deputy in charge of narcotics enforcement, made its own official assessment of the situation. It reported that there were 1.5 million "victims of the drug habit" in the United States, that no part of the country was without its quota of addicts, and that the problem was ballooning everywhere. It also noted that since only three states—New York, Massachusetts, and Texas—had followed the federal lead in enacting drug-control legislation at the state level, the full burden of the anti-drug campaign would have to be borne by federal authorities.

According to this Treasury group, heroin costing $12 to $15 per ounce at wholesale through legal channels brought five times that price on the black market, and it was claimed that the addict population was now younger because of the large numbers of young men returning from military service enslaved to the habit. It was also disclosed that 80,000 potential draftees had been rejected because they were drug addicts during the brief period of wartime conscription, and that an alarming number of medical doctors, commissioned directly into the services, had themselves turned out to be "drug fiends."

Dr. Royal S. Copeland, New York City Health Commissioner, made headlines by estimating that there were some 8,000 young addicts loose on the streets of his city and warning that with legitimate supplies of drugs cut off, this small army would be "likely to break out violently when the narcotic hunger becomes stronger," since "if the victims are permitted to roam about without the drugs they become dangerous."

In a statement released on June 12, 1919, the Secretary of the Treasury reported that the United States was consuming ten to sixty times as much opium per capita as any other nation; that the number of opium users was somewhere between 200,000 and 4 million, and "probably more than" a million; and that dope peddlers had set up their own elaborate national organization to procure and distribute their illicit wares. He warned that the drug problem would inevitably grow more acute as the enforcement of Prohibition compelled persons who had been dependent on alcohol to comfort themselves with dope.

Commissioner Copeland chimed in again, observing to the press that drug addiction "is born in the underworld and is the twin brother of every crime in the great categories of violence"— this time evoking a mild rejoinder from Deputy Police Commissioner Carlton Simon, who asserted that of the 250,000 addicts known by his Department to be currently using drugs in New York City, no more than 15 per cent were to be found in the "criminal class."

Schoolchildren were once more reported to be nodding at their desks under the influence of drugs. There were press accounts of very young tots being turned into fiends by dope peddlers so that they could then be used as agents to induce other kindergartners to take up $5- or $10-dollar-a-day drug habits.

A substantial increase in the number of arrests for general crimes in New York City in 1919–20 was labeled a "crime wave" and attributed to the drug problem, and the latter was described in every reference as "growing" and "increasing." The Knights of Columbus launched a national crusade with the announcement that they had discovered there were indeed at least 4 million addicts in the country. A sharp increase in addiction was announced in Brooklyn; the campaign waged by Scotland Yard to combat London's drug traffic, centering of course in Limehouse, was luridly described; drugs were said to have been distributed on a large scale to high school girls in Denver; and Pennsylvania reported in, with an addict population estimated to be 30,000— it was said that in Pittsburgh alone some 5,000 addicts were spending $25,000 per day for heroin. Alarming stories of sales of drugs to young schoolchildren came from El Paso and Rochester, and someone made headlines with a new estimate, that 30 per cent of all residents in the New York metropolitan area were addicted.

Meanwhile, raids in Chinatown and spectacular disclosures about sinister Oriental peddlers went on apace. Meanwhile, also, patterns of corruption kept unfolding, as the temptingly greater and greater profits of drug trafficking took their toll: one Treasury agent caught taking hefty bribes in 1917 has already been mentioned; scandal hit the Chicago Narcotics Division office in 1919, and several Treasury officials were indicted there as a result; a former Deputy Collector was charged with extortion and diverting cocaine into illegal channels in 1920. Other police officials and local officers were accused of taking bribes, or of active participation in the traffic as partners in peddling rings, and even the Canadian Mounties caught two of their famous Redcoats directly involved in drug trafficking.

Early in 1923 it was estimated—on the basis of an alleged addict population of a million, 85 per cent of whom were stated to be confirmed criminals—that the drug traffic was costing the nation more than $1.8 billion per year.

But even in these early days, a few counterforces began to appear. The Narcotics Division was reorganized within the Bureau of Internal Revenue to make it an independent subagency distinct from the free-swinging Prohibition Unit, and as we shall see in the next chapter, it turned from broadside attacks to narrower assaults on the so-called clinics, and particularly on the medical profession. Since the T-men had now been in the field for several years, moreover, it no longer looked good to let the problem continue to appear to be completely out of control, as if their valiant efforts had had no effect. So Treasury sponsored one of the most careful and responsible analyses ever made of the situation, the Kolb-DuMez study of 1923–24, carried out by the Public Health Service, which officially shrank the nation's addict population to no more than 110,000.

In April 1923 Governor Al Smith tried to help calm the situation:

> Agitating the community and increasingly forcing itself upon our attention is the narcotic drug evil. I am convinced that part of the agitation on this subject is due to the sensationalism of certain types of newspapers and magazines. Lurid, sensational articles, intended to inflame the imagination of young people and to make the whole subject mysteriously and morbidly attractive, have led to the prevalence of a belief that the use of narcotic drugs is much more general than it really is.

In October President Coolidge told a federal law-enforcement conference:

> The national laws and the laws of most of the States regulate the sale of narcotic drugs. . . . Their use is, in part, perhaps, due to physical disease, and, in part, to lack of moral stamina, but their abuse is almost wholly a result of violations of the law. If the law can be enforced, medical science would very soon rid the country of this menace.

On the same occasion Attorney General Daugherty, of Teapot Dome fame, told the gathering, with respect to enforcement of the Volstead Act, "All questions of 'individual liberty,' 'inalien-

able rights,' and states rights are foreclosed. There is no guar-
antee of any liberty except the law."

Prohibition Commissioner Haynes, no longer concerned with
the Harrison Act (the new Narcotics Division was headed by
Colonel L. G. Nutt) took a moderate tone:

> While I am most appreciative of the great arousal of the people
> on the question of narcotics, I am at the same time thoroughly
> convinced that there is no great increase in the use of narcotics
> in America. Nothing can be gained by magnifying real conditions
> (neither would it be right to do so), nor by hiding real conditions.
> Conditions are bad enough as they are, but not as bad as some try
> to depict.

It is a little surprising, looking back now at the excesses and
disruptions of the early 1920's and the strains of the Great Depression, that drug addiction did not more closely match the
inflated figures of the day. Terrible as the problem has been
during succeeding years, conceivably it could have been much
worse. Moreover, though it must be clear to anyone who has read
this far that I have little use for the hard-fisted repressive policies
which were grafted onto the Harrison Act in this period, there is
not much question that repression worked effectively for some—
maybe for many—Americans. As with the Eighteenth Amendment, when Uncle Sam threw his full authority into the balance, a significant number of dabblers with drugs, like many
topers, must have simply renounced their indulgences.

I might not be offering so forthright a concession, softening
some of my own arguments, were it not for a critically important
related problem of our times: What are we going to do ultimately
about tobacco? Federal repression of the cigarette traffic would
doubtless commit us to running much of this same painful course
over again. But it might save many Americans, including im-
periled youth, from afflictions no opiate ever caused—carcinoma,
cardiac failure, and fatal pulmonary susceptibility to our polluted
atmosphere.

The two related dogma which have characterized the "official
line" on drugs, espoused by federal authorities for more than
half a century, are that everyone connected with the drug traffic
should be clapped into prison for maximum terms, on the one
hand, and that anyone who cannot cure himself of his addiction
must be permanently isolated from society in a sort of leper
colony, on the other. Both these viewpoints were strongly expressed by nonfederal spokesmen as early as 1923, and, curiously,
it was a policeman who held forth on the merits of the life-quar-

antine measure and a doctor who called for Draconian criminal
sentences. Dr. John W. Perilli, a prominent New York physician
and trustee of Bellevue Hospital, stated his convictions as follows:

> I believe we should handle the drug problem from a practical
> viewpoint and in a drastic manner. If the nations of the world
> agree to limit the supply of drugs, and if Great Britain places a
> ban on opium, or at least limits the supply to a minimum, I am
> sure great gains in the fight on the evil will be made. Licensing
> the manufacturers of drugs will also help in the war on narcotics.
> It will prevent illicit vendors from gaining a plentiful supply, and
> will keep out of the field manufacturers whose sole aim is to
> furnish dope for addicts and, at the same time reap a harvest. I
> am confident that if a Federal statute were enacted, and if that is
> not feasible, State laws, giving the drug vendors a sentence, as
> habitual criminals, of from forty years to life, that there would be
> mighty little dope peddling.

Deputy Police Commissioner Simon, of New York City, expressed
the other view:

> We believe that if the narcotic problem could be attacked by the
> establishment all over the United States of correctional hospitals,
> with a long period of after treatment in camps or colonies, with
> outdoor work and vocational training, that within a few years
> narcotic addiction would be entirely eliminated as a public menace.

Commissioner Simon advocated that those who might not be
cured in such a program should be "isolated indefinitely in
institutions similar to those provided for mental defectives or
inebriates."

Yet as early as 1919, four years before these statements and at
the height of the hysteria, a number of more humane medical
men had begun concerning themselves with the plight of the addict who had been able to obtain drugs at trifling cost and without difficulty but suddenly found his sources of supply blocked
by the police. These men proposed the establishment of so-called
narcotic clinics, manned by public-health authorities or private
doctors, where addicts could apply for drugs to tide them over
until the anticipated chaos of transition had subsided, when
either the addict could be withdrawn and cured, or some sensible
provision could be made to take care of his drug dependency. A
pioneer in this program was Commissioner Copeland, some of
whose comments have already been noted. His first clinic, in
New York City, was opened in April 1919.

■ FIVE

Enforcers Versus Healers

■ ALL IN ALL, the medical profession does not come off looking well in this story. America's drug problem has been attributable partly to the doctors on several counts: to their irresponsibility in the use of addicting and dangerous substances for medical purposes; to flagrant abuse of the prescribing privilege by a few (a *very* few); to repeated error in acclaiming discoveries like morphine and heroin as nonaddicting drugs; and to the failure of most practitioners to embrace the notion that addiction is pathological so it falls within the purview of the Hippocratic Oath. But there have been extenuating factors. If the doctors lacked courage in standing up for the right, it must be said for them that to have resisted the overbearing attacks launched against them by their government in the early 1920's would have required them to be very courageous indeed.

There is no question that in the Harrison Act Congress intended to make a wide exception for the use of controlled drugs by legitimate practitioners. That is what the law said, from 1914 to 1970, in so many words: "Nothing contained in this chapter shall apply to the dispensing or distribution of any of the drugs . . . to a patient by a physician, dentist, or veterinary surgeon . . . in the course of his professional practice only." The last word—"only"—was inserted because of the so-called scrip doctors whose abusive practices have already been noted.

Accordingly it was assumed in the early days of the Act that legitimate practitioners would not be affected by the new control patterns, beyond the simple obligation to register and keep rec-

33

ords. And it was further assumed by most proponents that the main effect of the federal law would be precisely to bring addiction problems more into view, and hence more easily within the reach and control of the medical profession.

But that is not what happened. It quickly became apparent in the hysterical atmosphere which prevailed at the end of World War I that *someone* would have to make provision for the addict population—whatever its numbers really were—when the free-and-easy sources of supply were suddenly dried up. It was for this purpose that Dr. Copeland opened his clinics in New York City and called for the establishment of similar facilities throughout the state; and simultaneously, clinics and dispensaries of various kinds were opened elsewhere around the country in cities where addict populations were large—New Orleans, Chicago, Jacksonville, San Francisco, Los Angeles—a total of nearly forty.

But they came almost immediately under attack. Copeland was accused by fellow doctors of intensifying the problem by giving out drugs too freely, and he responded by complaining bitterly that the medical community was giving him no support and was merely dumping the whole crisis in his lap. It was charged elsewhere that clinic facilities attracted "fiends" and other criminal types to the communities where they operated, and that they were simply "gratifying the cravings" of weak-willed persons who would otherwise be compelled forthwith to give up their evil habits.

This clinic controversy, which has been raging ever since, was inflamed by a misunderstanding, or intentional distortion, which has not yet been fully straightened out. There is little question that in the administration of some of the narcotic facilities much harm *was* done by handing out drugs carelessly to addicted persons for self-administration, or by writing prescriptions for large amounts for the addict to fill for himself. When this occurred, drugs were badly abused by the recipients and were diverted to others in the newly born illegal market. Such irresponsible dispensing was attacked as "ambulatory" treatment, i.e., giving out drugs for uncontrolled personal consumption as contrasted with administering or providing regulated dosages directly at the narcotic facility under the supervision of clinic personnel. Early in 1920 an American Medical Association committee recommended that "ambulatory treatment of drug addiction, as far as it relates to prescribing and dispensing of narcotic drugs to addicts for self administration at their convenience, be emphatically condemned."

But the word "ambulatory" was simultaneously pounced upon by the enforcement-minded faction as denoting a policy of leaving addicted persons at liberty in the community instead of locking them up in hospitals or prisons. So when responsible authorities deplored giving out drugs too freely, irresponsible enforcers claimed this was a mandate to put all the addicts they could round up behind bars.

Subsequently the medical spokesmen themselves contributed to this ambiguity, at least partially because it soon became clear that ministering to "ambulatory" addicts *without* the convenience of merely prescribing or handing out drugs was burdensome and unrewarding for the general practitioner. In 1921 the AMA Council on Health and Public Instruction created another committee which reported much more emphatically:

> Your Committee desires to place on record its firm conviction that any method of treatment for narcotic drug addiction, whether private, institutional, official, or governmental, which permits the addicted person to dose himself with the habit-forming narcotic drugs placed in his hands for self-administration, is an unsatisfactory treatment of addiction, begets deception, extends the abuse of habit-forming narcotic drugs, and causes an increase in crime. Therefore, your committee recommends that the American Medical Association urge both Federal and State governments to exert their full powers and authority to put an end to all manner of such so-called ambulatory methods of treatment of narcotic drug addiction, whether practiced by the private physician or by the so-called narcotic clinic or dispensary.

Then the committee added the following ambivalent paragraph:

> In the opinion of your Committee, the only proper and scientific method of treating drug addiction is under such conditions of control of both the addict and the drug, that any administration of habit-forming narcotic drugs must be by, or under the direct personal authority of the physician, with no chance of any distribution of the drug of addiction to others, or opportunity for the same person to procure any of the drug from any source other than from the physician directly responsible for the addict's treatment.

This 1921 recommendation was adopted verbatim by the AMA House of Delegates in 1924. It remained the official AMA position for years thereafter and will turn up again in our narrative, still causing trouble in the late 1950's.

In July 1919 Dr. Copeland, in the thick of the feud, set up a system for registering all the addicts who were then under treatment through the New York clinics (the number had already grown to 7,000), and issued to each one a dosage card on which had to be indicated each prescription or administration. Local doctors were sharply warned not to administer or prescribe narcotics to addicts except on presentation of a dosage card, and soon the police began to make arrests for violations of this edict —on technically doubtful ground, perhaps, but with attending publicity calculated to intimidate doctors and druggists, and plainly having that effect.

In August 1919 the New York authorities tried to establish facilities where addicts could be isolated in a drug-free environment (a concession to the "hard" anti-ambulatory school). John D. Rockefeller offered to contribute a building for the purpose, but by this time the public was so fearful of "fiends" and "maniacs" that no site could be agreed upon. A proposed location in the Pelham Bay area of the Bronx aroused such a storm of local protest that it had to be rejected; then plans were announced to develop a hospital at Seaview on Staten Island, with the same result; and finally efforts were made to treat narcotic addicts at Riverside Hospital in New York, until other Riverside patients went on strike and so disrupted the hospital that the narcotics project had to be abandoned. In December 1919 the New York City Council threatened to cut off all funds for all of Dr. Copeland's facilities if he did not at once abandon any further ideas about thus congregating dangerous dope fiends where they might break out and harm the citizenry.

Besides pushing the idea that addicted persons could only be dealt with in total confinement, the enforcement authorities and a large segment of the medical profession, echoed by the press, also kept stressing the twin notions that drug addiction was a mere weakness of character which could be overcome by righteous and right-thinking people (an idea which, when reflected in medical-school teachings, has produced disproportionately large numbers of addicts among three generations of doctors) and that drug addiction and criminality were inseparable, that addiction always suggested latent criminality in those who had not yet run afoul of the law, and that it induced all manner of crimes among those who were "hooked." In short, strong forces converged to create around the addict a complete mythology supporting the "fiend" appellation.

Obviously if the clinic concept were allowed to develop and spread, T-men and local police authorities would be left without much responsibility except controlling any abuses that might grow up around the edges of the clinic administrations, not the much larger national prohibition commitment they envisaged.

Therefore, as might have been expected, the heaviest attack was launched by the Treasury. Dr. Charles E. Terry, the most authoritative chronicler of this period, described what happened to the clinics as follows:

> As in all pioneer movements, they underwent a period of experimentation in which mistakes were made which, eventually, according to their proponents, might have led to valuable findings and encouraging results. Here again, however, the interpretations and enforcement procedures originating in certain regulations of the Department of Internal Revenue in its administration of the Harrison Narcotic Act resulted in their closing before their development could bear fruit through practical administrative and medical procedures. They were declared illegal, and closed.

It is generally agreed that Dr. Copeland's units in New York were among the most poorly run. No adequate records were kept, drugs—including nonaddicting cocaine—were freely handed out, and prior to the abortive dosage-card effort no precautions were taken to see that the same addict did not present himself repeatedly, even at the same clinic, to accumulate supplies. Yet unfortunately the New York experiment received disproportionately more publicity than others which were reportedly far more successful, notably those operating in Louisiana and California. Copeland was forced to terminate his operations on January 5, 1920, in a storm of recriminations and controversy. Summing up the experience, and reflecting prevailing attitudes of the day, one of Copeland's associates, Dr. S. Dana Hubbard, wrote:

> The clinic is not the solution—but it aids in bringing the secretive addict out of his lair. He becomes friendlily disposed and, deprived of his supply, he is willing to be cured. . . . No doubt, with suitable organization and funds to institutionalize and adequately and properly care for them, not only to effect withdrawal of drugs, but to rehabilitate by several months aftercare in the open country, together with efforts to get the individuals away from bad and demoralizing associates, into new and more useful environments, many will revert to useful and normal lives.
>
> Many of these addicts have never had a square deal, and only need a fair chance to change their ways. Already many of them have been returned to useful lives, and many more can be revamped with proper and necessary help.

Clinics elsewhere throughout the United States were forced to close in 1921–22, with the exception of one at Shreveport, Louisiana, which held out until 1923. Doctors and public-spirited citizens who had inclined to view the plight of the addict as a medical problem were overwhelmed; those who shouted that the only solution was criminal repression won the day. Although Treasury itself had called for assistance from local authorities in relieving addicts caught without their supplies in 1919, the Commissioner of Internal Revenue's annual report for 1920 reveals a reversal of attitude (and a new tone which must have been hard at first for medical professionals to appreciate, as coming from mere tax collectors):

> As a temporary expedient to relieve this seemingly critical situation a number of narcotic clinics or dispensaries were established. Some of the so-called clinics that have since been established throughout the country without knowledge or sanction of this Bureau apparently were established for mercenary purposes or for the sole purpose of providing applicants with whatever narcotic drugs they required for the satisfaction of their morbid appetites. Little or no attempt was made by some of these private clinics to effect cures, and prominent physicians and scientists who have made a study of drug addiction are practically unanimous in the opinion that such clinics accomplish no good and that the cure of narcotic addiction is an impossibility unless accompanied by institutional treatment. Steps are now being taken to close these clinics, which are not only a menace to society but a means of perpetuating addiction. In many cases their continued existence constitutes a flagrant violation of the law.

Behind this official assault was the conclusion, propounded dogmatically by the federal fiscal authorities, that drug addiction was a *curable* condition. The Prohibition Bureau's regulations of this period began with the statement: "It is well-established that the ordinary case of addiction will yield to proper treatment, and that addicts will remain permanently cured when drug addiction is stopped and they are otherwise physically restored to health and strengthened in will power."

Moreover, a small but strident segment of the medical community went further even than the tax authorities in heaping abuse on addicts and beating the drums for a total-prohibition crusade. In 1921 a member of the American Medical Association's Committee on Narcotic Drugs, purportedly speaking officially for the Association, was quoted in a widely circulated Treasury publication as follows:

> The shallow pretense that drug addiction is a disease which the specialist must be allowed to treat, which pretended treatment consists in supplying its victims with the drug which has caused their physical and moral debauchery . . . has been asserted and urged in volumes of literature by the self-styled specialists.

The vice that causes degeneration of the moral sense, and spreads through social contacts, readily infects the entire community, saps its moral fiber, and contaminates the individual members one after another like the rotten apples in a barrel of sound ones.

Thus what had commenced as a controversy within the medical profession evolved into a relentless attack upon the medical community, carried on by police authorities whose leadership and direction came directly from Treasury officials in Washington. Doctors were hounded and bullied, and a campaign was launched to drive them away from the addict altogether.

One of the few dissenting voices which managed to make itself heard was that of a medical doctor who happened also to be a Member of Congress, Representative Lester D. Volk of New York. In January 1922 he spoke out:

It seems to me that the untutored narcotics agents of this great Government . . . might have been better employed than in taking sides in a medical controversy involving the broad subject of what will or will not constitute the proper medication in the treatment of addiction. Yet this was done, and I am sorry to say is now being done by our Government, and will continue to be done until the end of time unless some protesting voice is raised against undue interference by lawyers, policemen, and detectives in the practice of medicine, and furtherance of its research and study.

There has developed a tendency in carrying out the objects of the Harrison law to substitute for the provisions of the Act arbitrary administrative opinions expressed in rules and regulations which amount to practically a repeal and nullification of the law itself.

As a substitute for open discussion of known medical facts there has been set up a propaganda for the incarceration of all drug users, their treatment by routine methods, and complete elimination of the family doctor. An undeniable effort is now being made whereby physicians are to be denied any discretion and power in the prescribing of narcotic drugs and to force all those addicted to the use of these drugs into hospitals exploiting questionable "cures."

But such warnings were of little avail. The agents carried on unchecked, attacking those who disagreed and continuing their campaign to drive the doctors into full retreat. How this was accomplished—the episode to which we now turn—is perhaps the most remarkable of any we shall encounter in this saga: Treasury officials and the Attorney General of the United States succeeded in playing an out-and-out trick on the U.S. Supreme Court.

SIX

Dr. Behrman, Dr. Linder, and the High Court

■ THE EXEMPTION which Congress wrote into the Harrison Act for medical practitioners has already been set out. So long as doctors were shielded by this clear provision, police authorities could not get at the addict who turned to them for help, while, on the other side of the coin, if addicts were able to find relief at the hands of doctors or public-health authorities, the illicit trafficker would have a scant market and little to keep his prices up. Thus cops and pushers found themselves identically interested in squeezing the addict by cutting him off from possible help as a patient, and have maintained a de facto partnership ever since.

The federal Act, as was to be expected with a measure so innovative, gave rise to questions which needed to be resolved by court tests. But especially in testing criminal sanctions, which was what the agents wanted at this time, the government has a degree of control because it can pick and choose in initiating prosecutions that are likely to be appealed and thus become ruling cases. This was clearly an important factor in what happened with the doctors. Recall the astonishing number of 47,800 reported federal violations by *registered* persons where the charges had been used merely as threats and then dropped. The first cases actually prosecuted were selected by waiting for offenders with medical degrees but whose abuses in the administration of drugs were most flagrant and outrageous, that is, the worst of the "scrip doctors."

The initial interpretation was given by the Supreme Court on the same day in 1919 that the justices handed down their divided opinion (five to four) affirming the constitutionality of the Act itself. The constitutional case was *United States* v. *Doremus,* in which the Court found the tax to be valid even though obviously imposed for purposes other than the raising of revenue. The doctor case was *Webb* v. *United States.*

It was clear from the record that Dr. Webb had been making no effort to practice his profession conscientiously with respect to addicts who applied to him; on the contrary, he simply sold prescriptions by the thousands, indiscriminately to all comers, for fifty cents apiece. On this state of facts, the Attorney General had taken the unusual procedural step of posing a certified question to the High Court (perhaps to make quite sure, among other things, that the issue would get there first in Dr. Webb's case rather than via the appeal of some less culpable offender). The certified question was:

> If a practicing and registered physician issues an order for morphine to an habitual user thereof, the order not being issued by him in the course of professional treatment in the attempted cure of the habit, but being issued for the purpose of providing the user with morphine sufficient to keep him comfortable by maintaining his customary use, is such order a physician's prescription under exception (b) of §2?

Now note how this question is itself a misrepresentation: by no stretch could what Dr. Webb had been doing be fairly characterized as a prescription to a patient "to keep him comfortable by maintaining his customary use." But the Court, doubtless outraged by the underlying facts and responding to popular hysteria which was then at crescendo, answered: "To call such order for the use of morphine a physician's prescription would be so plain a perversion of meaning that no discussion of the subject is required."

The next doctor case had the additional advantage, from the government's viewpoint, of involving a Chinese, Dr. Jin Fuey Moy, thus capitalizing on the then-current association of all the evils of the drug traffic with the mysterious Orient. Dr. Jin was also an out-and-out peddler, having given prescriptions for morphine by the gram to anyone who made application, at the rate of a dollar per gram. Upholding his conviction in an opinion rendered in 1920, the Court said of the crucial exempting language:

> Manifestly the phrases "to a patient" and "in the course of his professional practice only" are intended to confine the immunity of a registered physician, in dispensing the narcotic drugs mentioned in the act, strictly within the appropriate bounds of a physician's professional practice, and not to extend it to include a sale to a dealer or a distribution intended to cater to the appetite or satisfy the craving of one addicted to the use of the drug.

And now the stage was set for the trick. The doctor selected, likewise a flagrant violator, was named Behrman, a name made dubiously famous in immediately succeeding years because, after the government pulled it off, medical doctors were rounded up in large numbers by means of what came to be known as the "Behrman indictment." And that is were the trick lay: though Behrman was proved to have given a known addict, at one time for use as the addict saw fit, prescriptions for 150 grains of heroin, 360 grams of morphine, and 210 grams of cocaine (which the court reckoned would be enough for about 4,000 doses), the indictment against him was drawn so as to omit any accusation of bad faith, and to recite, on the contrary, that this "treatment" was for the purpose of curing the addict.

Thus, the validity of the indictment was made to depend on a holding *that prescribing drugs for an addict was a crime regardless of the physician's intent in the matter.* If it were wrong for Dr. Behrman to give such great quantities while really intending to deal with the symptoms of addiction in the course of an attempted cure, as the charge alleged, it would be wrong for the most conscientious doctor to give *any* amount of any addicting drug for the same purpose.

The United States District Court in which Behrman was arraigned sustained a demurrer, which meant, in effect, that the District Judge declined to be taken in by any such nonsense and found the indictment faulty. But the government invoked a special statutory right to appeal directly to the Supreme Court. And there the District Judge was reversed and the government prevailed.

It is noteworthy, in passing, that in this maneuver, as sometimes elsewhere, the American Medical Association seems to have been lined up on the side of the enforcement authorities. In 1921, besides throwing its weight on the wrong side of the "ambulatory" argument and, by implication, sponsoring intemperate attacks on drug addicts as malefactors rather than patients, through a special committee the AMA called on Department of Justice officials in Washington to confer "as to the practicability of obtaining decisions from the United States Supreme Court which will remove existing uncertainties as to the meaning and application of the provisions of the Harrison law." That might have been all right if the Association had held out for honest test cases fairly brought. But when Solicitor General Beck exhorted the Court to expedite its consideration of the *Behrman* case, he was authorized to invoke the authority of the AMA as calling for this particular clarification, and thus by implication supporting the government's position.

The *Behrman* decision was not unanimous—and in that far-off day divisions among the justices were exceptional and not, as recently, the rule. (Remember, in the same connection, that the Act itself had been upheld in *Doremus* only by a five-to-four divided court.)

The majority in *Behrman* detailed the flagrant facts, clearly relying upon them to justify its opinion. The dissenting minority consisted of three: Justice Holmes, who wrote for them, and two other heavyweights, Justices Brandeis and McReynolds. The dissent is a good example of Holmes's terse genius. In its entirety it reads:

> It seems to me wrong to construe the statute as creating a crime in this way without a word of warning. Of course the facts alleged suggest an indictment in a different form, but the Government preferred to trust to a strained interpretation of the law rather than to the finding of a jury upon the facts. I think the judgment should be affirmed.

The *Behrman* decision was handed down March 27, 1922, whereupon the Narcotics Division launched a reign of terror, threatening doctors who had anything further to do with drug addicts, and sending a goodly number of recalcitrant practitioners off to prison with the *Behrman* formula. Any prescribing of drugs for an addict, unless he had some other ailment that called for treatment with narcotics, was likely to mean trouble with the Treasury agents. The addict-patient vanished; the addict-criminal emerged in his place. And so instead of policing a small domain of petty stamp-tax chiselers, Treasury was able to expand its drug-law enforcement until the prison population began to swell with thousands of felony drug convictions each year.

Far more than in the parallel campaign against liquor, the

typical victim of this war on drug users often tended to be a respected member of his community until the T-men caught him. In cases that went all the way to trial, the ratio between arrests and convictions remained notably low, indicating abusive use of the indictment processes: in 1920, 3,477 arrests produced 908 convictions; in 1921, 4,014 arrests produced 1,583; at the peak, in 1925, 10,297 federal arrests produced 5,600 convictions. And while we are recording figures, note another surprising one: in a 1928 census of federal prisoners (in federal institutions), in the very heyday of Prohibition, there were two prisoners serving sentences for narcotic offenses for every one incarcerated for liquor-law violations. Drug offenders constituted one-third of the total federal prison population (2,529 out of 7,138; the numbers are small because many federal convicts were then farmed out to state institutions, but the ratio is typical).

Reacting to abusive practices by Treasury "special employees," a prominent physician wrote in 1922:

> There is a criminal element in the ranks of the "addict" that would be criminals in the church or in the Masonic fraternity or elsewhere, and the courts of justice should make searching investigations into the indictments brought against physicians or others for alleged violations of the narcotic drug act when the charges are based on the testimony of this element. Give any one of them into my hands for 48 hours, and I can make him swear in any court, with a good face, too, that he had just witnessed the battleship *Maine* riding at anchor at the corner of State and Adams, with Washington at the helm, "Bob" Evans lashed in the rigging, and Woodrow Wilson in the hold stoking. A promise of a continuation of the drug, or a threat to discontinue it, is sufficient. Many physicians in the United States have been dealt with on just such unreliable evidence.

But returning to the mainstream of our narrative, the *Behrman* ruling soon found a challenger. In 1924 Dr. Charles O. Linder, completing a lifetime of honorable practice in Spokane, Washington, was induced by one of Treasury's addict stool-pigeons to write a prescription for four tablets of cocaine and morphine. (At the trial the doctor claimed she told him she was in great pain from a stomach ailment, and that her regular physician was unavailable; she swore she had disclosed to him that she was a drug addict.) Several Treasury agents thereupon descended on his office on a Saturday afternoon, stamped through his waiting room crowded with patients, and broke in on him in the midst of a consultation. After a rough-and-tumble search of the premises, they dragged him off to jail. He was indicted in the *Behrman* formula, convicted, sentenced, and lost his intermediate appeal to the Circuit Court. But Dr. Linder persisted. In the Supreme Court his conviction was reversed and he was completely vindicated.

The opinion in *Linder* v. *United States* (April 13, 1925), unanimous this time, was written by Justice McReynolds, one of the dissenters three years earlier in *Behrman*. It sets forth at length what became the controlling interpretation of the federal law:

> The enactment under consideration levies a tax, upheld by this Court, upon every person who imports, manufactures, produces, compounds, sells, deals in, dispenses or gives away opium or coca leaves or derivatives therefrom, and may regulate medical practice in the States only so far as reasonably appropriate for or merely incidental to its enforcement. It says nothing of "addicts" and does not undertake to prescribe methods for their medical treatment. They are diseased and proper subjects for such treatment, and we cannot possibly conclude that a physician acted improperly or unwisely or for other than medical purposes solely because he has dispensed to one of them, in the ordinary course and in good faith, four small tablets of morphine or cocaine for relief of conditions incident to addiction.

In the *Linder* opinion, moreover, the Court returned to, and carefully circumscribed, its decisions in *Webb* and *Jin Fuey Moy*, pointing out that both earlier cases must be narrowly limited in application to the facts which were involved in each. Then it dismissed the *Behrman* case (and blasted the *Behrman* indictment) in the following strong disclaimer:

> This opinion related to definitely alleged facts and must be so understood. . . . The opinion cannot be accepted as authority for holding that a physician who acts bona fide and according to fair medical standards, may never give an addict moderate amounts of drugs for self-administration in order to relieve the conditions incident to addiction. Enforcement of the tax demands no such drastic rule, and if the Act had such scope it would certainly encounter grave constitutional difficulties.

Note that the Court extends itself even to the extreme position of endorsing the giving of "drugs for self-administration," as well as drugs administered under the control of a physician. This is vigorous language, for a pronouncement from the the High Court, leaving no doubt that further assaults upon the medical profession in the *Behrman* formula were intended to be denounced.

Yet by 1925 strong language from the Court was not enough to change the pattern. The trick had worked. The medical profession had withdrawn completely from the field, and the doctors never permitted the addict to reapproach them. The peddler had moved in and taken over, and his profits soared as enforcement efforts kept reducing his competition and driving his customers ever deeper into the underworld, where they were easy prey. Even in the 1960's, four decades after *Linder,* Narcotics Bureau regulations advising doctors and pharmacists of their rights in dealing with addicts continued to ignore what the Supreme Court had so plainly said, and still relied on the discredited language of *Webb* v. *United States:*

> An order purporting to be a prescription issued to an addict or habitual user of narcotics, not in the course of professional treatment but for the purpose of providing the user with narcotics sufficient to keep him comfortable by maintaining his customary use, is not a prescription within the meaning or intent of the Act; and the person filling such an order, as well as the person issuing it, may be charged with violation of the law.

■ SEVEN

Dr. Ratigan's Lonely Battle

■ IT WAS in the three years between the *Behrman* case and Dr. Linder's vindication that the Narcotics Division commenced the unworthy practice, carried on by federal authorities ever since, of recruiting informers and agents provocateurs from the addict community for money rewards or, not infrequently, for immunity from prosecution and an assured supply of drugs. Drug-enforcement officials have always denied the charge that their "special employees" are provided with drugs, but the consensus of all nonintimidated reports from the addict community, plus simple common sense, provide evidence to the contrary. The addict-turncoat is of little use to his law-enforcement masters if he is suffering withdrawal symptoms, so he must have his periodic "fixes" regularly one way or the other, either with drugs from seized supplies or else by the criminal act of purchasing in virtual partnership with the enforcement agents.

In these years also, the Division commenced reporting its prowess in the dubiously relevant and slightly sadistic measure of how many years' imprisonment it had inflicted on lawbreakers; for example, for 1925–26, "6,797 years, 11 mos., 10 days," and for 1926–27, "7,088 years, 10 mos., 10 days."

This was the formative period in which patterns were set. Federal agents arrogated to themselves not only the image of gallant saviors holding evil forces at bay, but also that of the nation's only "experts" able to inform a timorous public about the nature of the problem, its severity, and how it should be dealt with. In 1924 the American Medical Association knuckled under

47

again, establishing a special committee to repeat the 1921 finding that addicts could be treated only when they were locked up in total confinement (the old distortion of "ambulatory"), and officially recording its "firm conviction" that any kind of treatment for drug users without compulsory isolation "begets deception, extends the abuse of habit-forming narcotic drugs, and causes an increase in crime." Medical authorities even began parroting the dogma that addiction itself was somehow connected with weakness of character and latent criminality.

But above all, the official campaign played into the hands of peddlers and the nascent drug rings. Whenever law-enforcement efforts were increased in a particular community, the black-market price of drugs—and the peddlers' profits—increased too. Thus patterns were set in this era in which more than a few corruptible individuals on the law-enforcement side joined forces directly with peddlers to share in the golden flow of cash generated by the traffic. A venal federal narcotics agent or local drug-squad officer could work wonders in protecting and immunizing his peddler-partners, arresting competitors who might turn up to challenge their arrangements, diverting seized drugs back into the traffic, and even making high-level contacts himself with notoriously shy smugglers and overlords of the traffic.

The Narcotics Division now began suggesting to its worried public that it was at last bringing the situation under control. Official estimates of the addict population dropped from the millions of 1919–20 and the manageable 200,000 of 1923 on downward to a stable range of 60,000 to 75,000 by 1925. Thereafter for four decades federal spokesmen allowed no serious tinkering with this total. Admittedly during World War II, when international shipping, and therefore smuggling, was drastically curtailed, the total dropped; but for the most part the T-men contented themselves all those years with talk of *threatened* increases, especially when they went periodically to Congress for larger appropriations to carry on their good work.

As has been related, the repudiation of the *Behrman* case and the denunciation of the government's repressive policies by the Supreme Court in *Linder* in 1925 had almost no effect, notwithstanding that the *Linder* case immediately became the supreme law of the land and has, for that matter, remained the final word on the meaning of the Harrison Act and the proper limits of drug-law enforcement until the revisions of 1970. The Narcotics Division and its successor, the Narcotics Bureau, never relented. If mere official misstatements in the guise of Treasury regulations did not always suffice, a menacing call from the federal agents, coupled if necessary with open threats of prosecution, would usually prevail when a doctor dared minister to an addict.

As practitioners of the healing arts moved into their Golden Age, emerging as one of the softest, most conservative, and richest groups in America, it is small wonder that few of them have chosen to stand up to this harassment or deigned to trouble themselves with the unpleasant and unrewarding task of treating the afflictions of drug addicts, although once again it must be conceded in fairness that there was a hard fist behind the verbal menace when agents warned doctors to stay in line. Not a few of the latter had been packed off to serve time in prison before Dr. Linder's victory. And to see how little the victory really meant, let us move forward a decade to the story of Dr. Thomas P. Ratigan, Jr.

If this were a work of fiction, I would present Dr. Ratigan very much as he played his part in real life—only I would substitute a victorious ending. I believe he was right, and had he emerged as conqueror instead of near-forgotten martyr, America might well have been turned back toward dictates of common sense in the 1930's, avoiding most of the errors and excesses of three succeeding decades.

The locale of the action was Seattle. Ratigan grew up there as one of eleven children in the family of an inconspicuous civil servant in the City Treasurer's office. Though crippled in a street accident while he was working as a downtown newsboy, he put himself through college and medical school, receiving his M.D. in 1925.

In 1931, after the usual residencies and service on the staff of a local medical clinic, Dr. Ratigan went into practice for himself, opening a clinic which he called the Public Health Institute. And here the tale might also bear modifying slightly, for even in mid-Depression Seattle and starting from humble antecedents, our doctor-hero should not have advertised his services. In those days Seattle boasted a dentist who had changed his Christian name to "Painless" so he could promote himself as "Painless Parker," and it was not unusual for West Coast practitioners to insert self-laudatory squibs in telephone directories, but even in this company Dr. Ratigan overreached. Local newspapers began carrying advertisements describing his Institute as "A Clinic for People of Moderate Means," assuring prospective patients that the quality of his services was unquestioned and consultations were free, and displaying competitive price lists, such as $1.00 for a blood test, forty cents for a urine test, $2.00 to treat varicose veins, and $2.00 for nonsurgical attention to hemorrhoids.

Possibly the general public did not respond to these attractive prices. We do not know his motives at the outset, but it was in this period that Dr. Ratigan began ministering to a large proportion of Seattle's addicts. Consistently with his expressed determination to provide medical attention for people who could not afford to patronize his more orthodox colleagues, he charged $1.00 for each clinic visit by an addict, although he subsequently claimed that more than half of his administrations were given gratis to those who were without funds.

Of vital importance, Dr. Ratigan scrupulously observed the cardinal distinction, confused by the medical profession and distorted by the Narcotics Division, between ambulatory in the sense of being afoot and at liberty, and ambulatory meaning provided with drugs for self-administration. Addicts who presented themselves at the Public Health Institute received an appropriated dosage by injection. At no time, except for patients whose addiction was genuinely related to pain associated with other illness, did Dr. Ratigan permit addicted persons to take drugs or prescriptions for drugs off the premises.

Reference has already been made to the way the Treasury Department picked and chose its test prosecutions. With the emphatic pronouncements of the *Linder* case standing as the law of the land, the Narcotics Division, reorganized in 1930 as a full-fledged Treasury bureau, had to be careful lest it expose itself to further judicial reprimand or give the courts a chance to put an end to its doctor-baiting altogether. Accordingly, in the period after 1925, cases where Treasury went all the way in prosecuting medical men involved only the most flagrant abuses. And even in some of these, when the convictions reached federal appellate courts the reviewing judges cited *Linder* and reversed, holding that the accused doctor was protected in the exercise of his medical discretion by the Harrison Act exemption.

So in a way the most impressive tribute to Dr. Ratigan's determination and good faith came from his arch-enemy and ultimate nemesis, the Narcotics Bureau itself. By early 1932 the Public Health Institute was well known in Seattle and was beginning to attract addicts from other areas. The Bureau, with its minute surveillance of drug and prescription records, not to mention its informant connections, must inevitably have known of this operation from its inception; yet for several years, apart from petty harassing tactics that came to light later, the authorities made no move to challenge Ratigan. The first blow fell in May 1934, by which time it must have been clear to the federal men that Ratigan was becoming a threat to the foundations of their empire, so that action could no longer be deferred.

The federal marshal who arrested Dr. Ratigan on this first occasion was more considerate than the crude gang of T-men who had taken Dr. Linder in Spokane under similar circumstances a decade earlier. He permitted the doctor to finish consultations with several patients before leading him away. The indictment charged illegal sales of morphine in seven counts. Bail was set at $2,500, then reduced to $1,500, and—since he was always accused of profiteering—it seems significant that the doctor remained behind bars several days before his family and friends could raise the latter amount. At the time of his arrest, local Bureau agents announced to the press that records in their possession showed Ratigan had, over the past two years, dispensed the equivalent of more than 100,000 standard doses of morphine (a suspicious way of presenting the matter because anyone really addicted, with a developed tolerance, would require several times whatever a "standard dose" might be).

Ratigan's attorney was one of Seattle's most eminent, John F. Dore, who had just completed a two-year term as mayor. A demurrer to the indictment, based on Dr. Linder's case, was held under advisement for two months by the District Judge; when it was denied, Ratigan, who had been at liberty on bail and carrying on his operations, surrendered and pleaded not guilty, insisting that he had always acted in good faith and that whether a particular patient needed narcotics or not was purely a question of medical opinion.

The government's case against Ratigan was essentially that he had administered hypodermic injections to addicts "to satisfy their cravings." At his trial the key witness was one Thomas O'Malley, brought to testify from jail, where he was being held on a disorderly-conduct charge, and who discredited himself by admitting that he had been given a shot of morphine by a City Hospital physician that morning. His story was that prior to his arrest he had been receiving injections in Dr. Ratigan's anteroom twice daily over an extended period. The Bureau's district supervisor testified that according to Ratigan's purchase records (and the fact that he had kept them accurately was not questioned) the clinic had purchased enough morphine between June 1932 and March 1934 to give 219,600 "normal doses" of the drug.

Ratigan admitted that he had been treating 7,000 addict patients per year, in all cases administering the drug by hypodermic on the premises. The government called investigators who testified that they had placed the clinic under surveillance and had observed "known narcotic addicts" entering and leaving repeatedly over a long period. Four leading physicians then paraded through the witness box, each affirming that in his opinion the amount of narcotic drugs used by Dr. Ratigan was "in excess of that used in the ordinary routine of medical practice." This was of course scarcely open to question: Ratigan's recorded purchases of morphine for the two-year period—without any distorting speculation about "dosages"—totaled 54,900 half-grain tablets.

The doctor took the stand again in rebuttal to insist that he had only administered morphine "to ease pain when the patient needed it to restore him to normal." The government countered with additional testimony from the chairman of the Narcotic Research Department of the Washington State Medical Society, who gave his opinion as an expert that no one need have any disease to be an addict, and that addiction was a condition which could be cured. Under cross-examination this witness admitted, nonetheless, that there was no place in the state where addicted persons could go for treatment or to "undergo cure."

On October 14, 1934, the jury found Ratigan not guilty, whereupon the prosecutor made an angry statement to the press charging that Ratigan received $10 per injection and was a mere drug peddler. The doctor's comment on the verdict was, "The jury decided that the doctor is the judge as to who should have morphine and who should not."

The harassment of Ratigan continued, of course. A fair application of the federal constitutional protection against double jeopardy might have suggested that once brought to trial and acquitted for administering drugs to addicts in a manner which was fully disclosed to the jury, Ratigan should not have been prosecuted again for the same offense arising out of the same facts. But a few months later, in April 1935, Ratigan was in jail again.

The complainant who put him there this time was a federal narcotics inspector, and the charge was assault arising out of a street fight which had allegedly taken place directly across from the clinic. Bail was set at the surprising figure of $10,000, and Ratigan was held "incommunicado."

While he was thus silenced and out of the way, the federal officers told their version: two of them had been patrolling the business district "in a search for narcotics addicts" and happened to find themselves near the clinic. Suddenly Ratigan appeared, coming toward them with a camera to take their picture. The agents said they protested, whereupon without further provocation Ratigan struck one of them with such force that the agent's wrist was fractured.

In due course lawyer Dore was reached, located his client, had the bond reduced to a more reasonable $1,000, and got him out. Dr. Ratigan's account of the incident for which he had been arrested was different. According to a contemporary news report:

> Dr. Ratigan's release brought for the first time his story of the fight with two agents in front of his office, and disclosed a battle in the office yesterday when Miss Bernadette Ratigan, the physician's 91-pound sister, struck the wall after Warner [one of the city detectives] assertedly knocked Dr. Ratigan into a corner.

The federal agents and city officers who arrested Ratigan had descended on the clinic together, and when the doctor attempted to telephone his attorney, he was knocked down by Warner. The press stories noted that "Dr. Ratigan does not have full use of one leg."

Ratigan claimed that the federal agents had been shadowing him and watching his office continuously, and that on numerous occasions they had accosted his patients, threatening them with prison if they entered the clinic. He wanted pictures of the agents to support a proposed action to enjoin this interference, and said that his able-bodied younger brother had pursued the agents several times trying to photograph them. He claimed that on the occasion in question he had been rushed and knocked prostrate on the street.

The assault case was finally dropped because Ratigan found an impressive witness to give the Bureau's agents the lie: a nurse at City Hospital, where the factured wrist had been treated, was willing to testify that the injured complainant had told her he had been hurt in a fall which had nothing to do with the alleged assault.

But a heavier blow was struck in October 1935. Federal agents again appeared at the clinic, arrested Ratigan and three patients who were with him, and then arrested twelve more as they arrived. All the patients were arrested "for questioning." Ratigan was allowed to summon his attorney this time, but when the lawyer arrived he was told to keep still; when the attorney protested he too was arrested—for disorderly conduct.

The bond was $2,500. Ratigan was indicted in thirteen counts for administering narcotics to one George Morey, a forty-four-year-old "government informer" who had been to the clinic approximately thirty times. When bond was posted, the doctor told the press: "I give seven or eight addicts daily treatments. I am not ashamed of it. It is in the course of my regular practice. The present enforcement of laws by narcotics agents is wrong. It tends not only to create more addicts, but also creates criminality among them."

During preliminary legal maneuverings Ratigan kept his clinic operating, but now the Bureau opened a new line of attack, trying to cut off his supply of drugs by threatening the pharmaceutical houses from which he bought. And in this connection he was arrested again on another charge—refusing to turn over his purchase records to Bureau officers.

Ratigan's trial on the Morey indictment began a week after this later arrest and its accompanying new blast of damaging publicity. Three addict-informers bore the burden of the government's case: Morey, who told of receiving injections and also claimed that he had once bought a small phial of a narcotic solution from the doctor for $3.00; a Mrs. Sowers, who said she had received treatments merely by asking for them and paying the price of $1.00 each; and her husband, a third-offender burglar, brought in from an Oregon jail to give his testimony.

The agents claimed the doctor had purchased 134,100 half-grain tablets of morphine in the year ending October 8, 1935. Seattle physicians again testified that they used far smaller amounts than this in the course of their practices. The prison doctor from McNeil Island Penitentiary said that the only workable cure for addiction was compulsory withdrawal, although he admitted on cross-examination that he had never seen an addict cured by this method whose cure could be described as permanent. On Ratigan's behalf, other addict-witnesses testified that he had given them injections only after a thorough initial physical examination and that in addition he had required each of them to sign an affidavit affirming their addiction.

In his own defense, Ratigan insisted that the informers who had testified against him had obviously been given drugs just before taking the stand. He admitted that he had treated addicts who came to him for narcotics, providing they were suffering from withdrawal symptoms or other physical symptoms, and avowed that he would continue to do so. He also admitted that he charged $1.00 per treatment, whereas other physicians in the community charged $3.00 or $5.00 for similar administrations.

He explained that he was treating a large number of addicts by giving them morphine in his office each morning before they went to work and again in the evening after they had fulfilled the obligations of their jobs. Asked about his refusal to let the federal agents examine his files, he responded:

> Narcotics agents used to come to my office and look over my records, taking down the names of addicts. Then they went to the places where addicts worked, called them from their tasks, and interviewed them. After that, the employers would say to the addicts: "We don't want you around here anymore," and the addicts would be thrown into the street to shift for themselves.

Countering the charge that he was making large profits, Ratigan claimed that only half his patients could afford to pay anything. Ninety-nine per cent of all addicts, he told the court, are poor people who cannot afford $2.00 per prescription at drugstores. The maximum injection he gave patients was worth $3.00 at current legitimate prices, whereas the same amount of morphine on the black market would cost at least $30.00.

He was adamant about never having permitted addicts to take drugs out of the clinic premises:

> The only logical way of preventing more persons from becoming addicts is for physicians to administer to the addicts and not permit the patients to receive any morphine for self administration. The addicts who have morphine in their possession are the ones who create more addicts. The number of addicts will increase greatly year after year until some definite system of treating them is adopted by the entire medical profession.

Dr. Ratigan estimated that he had treated as many as thirty to forty addicts per day, admitted that he had bought a total of 194,000 half-grain tablets during the preceding year, and said he had administered all but the 5,000 tablets seized by the agents at the time of his arrest. The drugs cost him $15.50 per thousand half-grain tablets in bulk, and he explained that he charged $1.00 per treatment regardless of the amount of drug administered, and that depending on the degree of addiction he would give one, two, or three injections per day and administer from one to as much as five and a half grains of morphine per treatment.

The press made much of the prosecutor's summation, including an assertion that dope traffic was the largest single industry in the United States, supposedly amounting to $2 billion per year. Ratigan was described in a fist-pounding tirade as the biggest dope peddler in the city, "catering and pandering" to addicts' appetite for drugs, and not acting in good faith within the bounds of legitimate professional practice as a physician. The fact, probably true, that Ratigan had been dispensing more drugs than all the other physicians in Seattle and Portland combined was stressed. From somewhere the government came up with a figure of $77 per day as Ratigan's profit, and he was charged with "earning money on the misery and slavery of unfortunate addicts."

This time, on August 20, 1936, the jury came back with a verdict of guilty on all counts. Ratigan, now thirty-nine, was still ready to fight. He announced that he would continue his work "until the Supreme Court says what I am doing is wrong." Referring to the maximum possible cumulative sentence, he jibed, "Sixty-five years in the penitentiary should satisfy the three years' craving of narcotic agents for a conviction. Conviction by twelve people means nothing to me as to what is good medical practice."

But the real sentence imposed on him was a harsh seven years, plus a fine of $10,000. The prosecutor begged the judge not to release him on bond until he had surrendered his narcotic license and turned over his supply of drugs to the federal authorities, but the judge concluded reluctantly that he had no power to impose such a condition. In announcing the sentence he told the doctor that the crime of which he had been convicted was "one of the most, if not the most, hideous of crimes against society."

When released on bond pending his appeal, Ratigan told his friends: "I am not through, by a long way. I have the solution to the narcotics problem and I am carrying it out. I am proud of my conviction. If administering morphine to confirmed addicts is a crime, I am a criminal." During the appeal he sought to carry on, but now he was attacked from yet another quarter. The Washington State licensing authorities set a hearing to revoke his license to practice medicine, obliging him to bring an action in the local courts for an injunction to hold off the proposed revocation until his federal conviction had been finally disposed of.

Meanwhile the Bureau kept pressing its attack on Ratigan's suppliers, circulating official bulletins to every pharmaceutical house and drug dealer in the United States warning against selling drugs to him without first consulting the Bureau. Ratigan countered with a suit in the District of Columbia. By this time he must indeed have been tired of lawyers, and running low on resources even if he *had* made profits from the clinic.

He was summarily denied relief against the Bureau in the

District of Columbia suit. In February 1937 the U.S. Circuit Court affirmed his conviction, and in June of the same year the Supreme Court—his final resort—denied review. His last effort was a petition for rehearing in the High Court, but this too was promptly denied.

In Seattle that summer mass meetings were held to support Ratigan's cause. Members of the Washington Legislature and, interestingly, officials from the State Narcotic Farm, where addicts were supposed to be sent for treatment, assailed the federal government and spoke in support of his position as "the only intelligent viewpoint." An investigator from the Narcotic Farm reported to one of these meetings that he had made a thorough review of all the clinic's work with drugs and had not found a single person for whose addiction Ratigan could in any way be held responsible. The main theme of Ratigan's supporters was that if drug addicts could get their supply of drugs at cost there would be no illegal peddlers, and that since there would then be no significant recruiting of new addicts the problem would tend to disappear in a single generation as the existing addict population died off. But the meetings came to little. No one seemed willing or able to continue the struggle on the local scene.

Ratigan surrendered in June 1937 and was sent to the McNeil Island penitentiary. In a final interview he described himself as "a martyr to the 100,000 suffering dope addicts in the United States . . . a pleasure I had not anticipated." But even at this juncture he stuck to his convictions: "My solution to the narcotics problem, by administering to addicts, is the only real solution and will be adopted in the future."

In May 1938 a blue-ribbon panel of medical doctors, specially appointed by the Governor, revoked Ratigan's medical license.

Ratigan was not considered for parole, and even after he had served his full term there were obstacles to his release. First, he could not pay the fine which had been imposed, and thus he was held an additional thirty days; then, reportedly, he refused to sign a pauper's oath upon discharge, so his good-behavior credits were revoked and he was sent back to McNeil Island and detained there for two more months.

In 1953 this tortured healer turns up again, suing the local Medical Service Bureau and the county and state medical societies; in 1954 he challenged the panel which had revoked his right to practice medicine, to have his license reinstated. His suits were dismissed, and reinstatement of his license was denied on the cruel ground that any right of court review he might have had at the time of the revocation was long forfeited because it had not been prosecuted earlier, while he was still in the penitentiary.

The story ends with a brief obituary in 1961. In his last decade Dr. Ratigan had survived as an unlicensed and ignored private tutor, occasionally lecturing on chemistry, nutrition, or the drug problem. But he was never forgotten in one quarter. As late as the mid-1950's his persecutor of twenty years, the Federal Narcotics Commissioner, was still assuring congressional committees that Ratigan's license would stay revoked: "He has taken the medical board into court several times. *I am sure he will not get his license back.*"

■ EIGHT

Congressman Coffee and His Slender Company

■ SEEKING means to convey a true picture of the distortions supported for so long in the United States by overbearing federal narcotic authorities, it occurs to me that besides detailing a few chronicles like Dr. Ratigan's, I might stress the point another way: in only a few pages here, before telling about Congressman John Coffee, I can note *all* the significant critics of Narcotics Bureau policy from the beginnings of the reign of terror, at the close of World War I, until the American Bar Association and American Medical Association made their joint challenge at the end of the 1950's.

One of the first of these was Dr. Ernest S. Bishop, a highly respected senior member of the profession in New York, and an acclaimed authority on drug addiction. From the outset he objected to the oppressive way in which Treasury agents had set about enforcing the Harrison Act, remonstrating that Congress had never intended a prohibition measure, and that associating addiction with crime would tend both to create a black market and to lead adventure-seekers to take up drugs.

Dr. Bishop was indicted in January 1920 for a technical infraction of the Harrison Act. An indictment is merely a formal accusation of the commission of a crime, authorized by a twenty-four-member grand jury on a one-sided presentation by prosecuting officials—if the government wants to indict someone, grand

59

jurors almost never resist. But ordinarily (and in deference to some clear constitutional precepts), an indicted person is arraigned promptly, and if he pleads not guilty he is soon thereafter brought to trial. In Dr. Bishop's case the authorities simply left the indictment hanging as a threat, to discredit and silence him, for more than three years, until the matter had become a national scandal. By the time he succeeded in having it quashed, Dr. Bishop was growing old, was ill, and was never able to resume the fight.

When the clinic programs of the early 1920's came under federal attack, as has already been described, no one really arose to battle vigorously in their defense, and indeed their two most prominent New York sponsors—Dr. Royal S. Copeland (who later served nearly three terms in the U.S. Senate) and Dr. S. Dana Hubbard—eventually did about-faces and meekly joined the chorus of abuse being heaped on "ambulatory" treatment.

The last holdout was Dr. Willis P. Butler, parish physician in Shreveport, Louisiana. After general medical practitioners of the Shreveport area had been driven out of the picture by federal indictments returned against four of them, and after clinics in New Orleans, Alexandria, and elsewhere in the state had been shut down at the insistence of Treasury agents who brought pressure through the Louisiana State Board of Health, Dr. Butler carried on alone, supported only by the city council (quaintly named Police Jury) of Shreveport. His clinic, which also flouted accepted standards of the day by taking venereal cases, continued treating addicts until early in 1923, when he was curtly summoned to the office of the U.S. Attorney and there told by federal narcotic agents that they had been sent specially to close his clinic "because it was the only one left in the United States."

This show of authority—in the inflamed atmosphere of 1923—so intimidated Dr. Butler that he agreed to terminate his work, sadly recording thereafter that of the hundred-odd incurable cases he was obliged to abandon, a number promptly landed in city jails or the state penitentiary, some died, and most, forced to patronize drug peddlers, quickly "reached a condition of wretched poverty."

If one were to name a single grand old man on the American drug scene it would assuredly be Dr. Lawrence Kolb, whose career and personal experiences embrace the whole epoch. It was Dr. Kolb, then a young physician in the U.S. Public Health Service, who with A. G. DuMez made the classic 1924 study which, as noted earlier, brought the estimated addict population of the

nation down to a reasonable figure (110,000) and helped somewhat to damp the hysteria of preceding years. He also organized
and headed the first staff at the U.S. Public Health Service Hospital, then called the U.S. Narcotic Farm, at Lexington, Kentucky.

But Dr. Kolb, like other eminent public servants whom we
shall meet later, never faced the fury of an onslaught by the
Narcotics Bureau because he was held sternly in check in his
official positions in lifelong federal employment. It was only
after he retired from the Service, with the rank of Assistant Surgeon General and so many professional honors that he was unassailable, that Dr. Kolb was able to speak out, in stinging articles such as his 1956 *Saturday Evening Post* feature entitled
"Let's Stop This Narcotics Hysteria" and in his valedictory book,
which appeared in 1962.

The protesting voice raised in 1922 by doctor-lawyer-congress-
man Lester Volk has already been quoted here; he—like Coffee
a dozen years later—found his remonstrances wholly futile, ignored alike by his colleagues on Capitol Hill and by the executive
establishment at the other end of Pennsylvania Avenue.

In the early thirties a prominent Los Angeles physician, E. H.
Williams, who had a national reputation as a writer, lecturer, and
authority in the drug field, and two associates were prevailed
upon to take over treatment of a small group of addicts who
had been receiving help from Los Angeles City public-health authorities. All three doctors were promptly indicted, tried, and convicted on the testimony of a government addict-informer who
had been surreptitiously included among the city patients. On
appeal, the conviction of one of Dr. Williams' co-defendants was
reversed (with a scalding rebuke from the court for the tactics
employed by the Narcotics Bureau), but in his own case the
record was left standing because of a technical default on the
part of his attorneys.

Subsequently Dr. Williams tried to establish a nonprofit organization, the World Narcotics Research Foundation, to encourage studies aimed at dissipating some of the ignorance and
confusion surrounding the problem. Bureau agents countered
this effort by contacting persons potentially interested in the
Foundation and warning them that the venture was "in for trouble with Uncle Sam" and that it was a "criminal organization."
Why criminal? Because of Dr. Williams' Bureau-engineered conviction, still remaining on the books solely because of a technical
lapse.

Also in the mid-thirties, a retired businessman in Seattle,

Everett G. Hoffman, doubtless aware of Dr. Ratigan's contemporaneous activities, took on the Narcotics Bureau with speeches and articles specifically challenging the bland official assertions that there were only some 300 addicts in the Seattle area and that the addiction situation was well in hand. Hoffman insisted that the number was more like 3,000, and charged collusion among enforcement agencies to distort the facts. Warnings began to reach him that if he did not desist he was likely to be framed by the federal men. He proceeded with his campaign until February 1938, when he was subpoenaed to appear before a federal grand jury. He was interrogated in such a way that it became clear an attempt was being made to establish a criminal charge against him. Grand jury proceedings are protected by secrecy, and Mr. Hoffman never disclosed the details of what happened, but the experience was enough to quiet him; he caused the Bureau no more serious embarrassment.

And a final good name on the roster: at this writing one combatant of long standing remains very much in the fight, Dr. Alfred R. Lindesmith, whose doctorate is in sociology and whose unassailable base has long been increasingly important faculty posts at Indiana University. Lindesmith first occupied himself with the drug scene in the early thirties, bringing to his studies a Phi Beta Kappa background, a mixture of fine scholarship and articulateness, and a no-nonsense determination to observe carefully and talk about what he saw. Lindesmith's own books, *Opiate Addiction* (1947) and *The Addict and the Law* (1965), are landmark statements, while thanks to his good offices the Indiana University Press was for many years the main—and sometimes the only—publishing outlet for outspoken critics of official Narcotics Bureau dogma.

The first attack on Lindesmith came in 1939, shortly after his initial appearances in professional journals as a dissenter. A bureau agent went to members of the Indiana University Board of Trustees, and then to the president of the University, with a somber warning that Lindesmith was connected with a "criminal organization." Although he was then only a very junior faculty member, his president—in the happy atmosphere of those days where academic freedom was taken for granted—smartly dispatched the government man to face the young professor himself, whereupon it quickly came to light that the allegedly criminal organization was none other than the World Narcotics Research Foundation then being organized by Dr. E. H. Williams, whose own story we have just told, and that Lindesmith's "criminal association" consisted of exchanges of correspondence with the eminent Dr. Williams.

The following year, when Lindesmith published an article entitled "Dope Fiend Mythology," the Bureau responded with a twenty-seven-page answer, purportedly authored by a San Francisco judge but transparently scrabbled together from prior Bureau pronouncements. The latter work, entitled "Lindesmith's Mythology," was subsequently reproduced in great quantities by the Treasury Department at U.S. taxpayers' expense and handed out for years to discredit Lindesmith and as an authoritative statement of Bureau policy.

This second assault on the professor stirred unfavorable comment from observers whose connection with the press and public life could not be blinked. So he received another official visit, this time from a higher-ranking Bureau spokesman (who will appear in person a few chapters hence) dispatched from Washington. Lindesmith was informed, by way of grudging apology, that the mission of the Narcotics Bureau was to make certain that only "right information" reached the public, and thus the Bureau was obliged to respond when anyone disseminated "one-sided" views.

And that is the full list, bringing us to the Honorable John M. Coffee, a member of Congress from the state of Washington who served five terms in the House, arriving as a freshman in 1937 at the time the Ratigan fight was reaching its climax in his home state. He deserves special attention in this narrative for four reasons: he came on the scene at the moment when *someone* should have picked up Dr. Ratigan's failing cause; he was serving, with increasing importance, precisely where the Bureau should have been called to account—in the Congress of the United States; what he undertook to do was so right, and his statements so faultlessly reasoned and presented, that no one has made a better case before or since; and his efforts, through the entire ten years of his incumbency, *failed, incredibly, to pick up a single supporter.*

Coffee was an able lawyer who had moved into politics through local offices in the city of Tacoma. He was a Democrat, so he belonged to the party which had firm control of both houses of Congress most of the time, but he got short shrift even from his own leadership.

His vehicle was a House Joint Resolution, first introduced in April 1938, calling for a review and evaluation of the narcotic-drug situation by the U.S. Public Health Service. Had this ever passed it would have turned medical authorities like Dr. Kolb loose to examine the policies of the Bureau, appraise their effects, and speak out freely with congressional protection. Had the resolution ever so much as reached the hearing stage, it might have provided a forum for both private and official critics of the Bureau to raise questions about its activities. But though re-introduced by Coffee in subsequent congresses, the measure never found a single parallel sponsor in the Senate and never survived being bottled up, year after year, in its reference committee.

Coffee's first line of attack, addressed to a nation just pulling out of the Great Depression, was economic. Quoting the American Association on Drug Addiction, an ad hoc organization which had sprung up in the Pacific Northwest to support Ratigan, he estimated that the annual cost of addiction to American tax-payers was $2,735,000,000, or approximately $80 per family. Said Coffee:

> It is claimed that this is a needless burden imposed on the people, not by conditions inherent in the problem of drug addiction, and not by the operation of law, but by the mistaken interpretations of law made by the Federal Narcotics Bureau. If this claim is justi-fied, the Narcotics Bureau stands as the costliest Bureau or gov-ernmental department in the world, and the Commissioner of Narcotics ranks as far and away the costliest man in the world.

Brushing aside attempted bans on importation (with the ob-servation that preventing the smuggling of products of such small bulk must always encounter "obvious extreme difficulties"), Coffee then leveled his attack on the federal law:

> In examining the Harrison Special Tax Act we are confronted with the anomaly of a law designed (as its name implies) to place a tax on certain drugs, and raise revenue thereby, resulting in reducing enormously the legitimate importation of the drugs in question, while developing a smuggling industry not before in existence. That, however, is only the beginning. Through opera-tion of the law, as interpreted, there was developed also, as coun-terpart to the smuggling racket, the racket of dope peddling; in a word, the whole gigantic structure of the illicit-drug racket, with direct annual turn-over of upward of a billion dollars.
>
> Incidental effects were the persecution of perhaps a million vic-tims of the diseased condition known as drug addiction, the great majority of whom had been law-abiding, self-respecting, self-sup-porting citizens, but who now became human derelicts and were thrust by thousands into jails and prisons simply because they could not legally secure the medicine upon which depended their integrity of mind and body.

Good lawyer that he was (and, happily, at this writing, is), Congressman Coffee stressed the full importance of the Supreme Court decisions, culminating in the *Linder* case, already described. The issue could not be framed better than this:

> The Narcotics Bureau ignores these decisions and assumes authority to prevent physicians from even the attempt to cure narcotic addicts unless the patients are under forced confinement. The addicts number, by the very lowest estimate, at least 100,000. The institutions that will receive them as patients are almost non-existent. It follows that the prohibitory mandate of the Narcotics Bureau effectively denies treatment to the vast majority of narcotic addicts. It is believed that this is the first instance in all history of the denial of medical treatment to a class of citizens of whatever status or capacity. The fact that the Supreme Court has declared that narcotic addicts are diseased and proper subject for medical treatment makes the action of the Narcotics Bureau peculiarly paradoxical.

Further on the matter of involuntary treatment in incarceration, Coffee carried the argument as follows:

> Addiction, once developed, is a very chronic condition. It is admitted by the authorities, including the narcotics commissioner, that very few "cures" result from incarceration for a 1-year period. It has been suggested that a 5-year segregation is the least that can be expected to restore the average addicts. The idea of incarcerating even a hundred thousand, let alone a million, unfortunates for a term of five years is rather startling—especially considering that they are sick people, for the most part of average respectability and moral status, not markedly handicapped by their infirmity.

The alternative he urged was simply to allow the Harrison Act to operate "as was designed," and to bring victims of drug addiction under medical supervision so they could be supplied with whatever medicine they might need, at slight cost, through legitimate channels:

> Morphine which the peddler sells for a dollar a grain would be supplied, of pure quality, for 2 or 3 cents a grain. The peddler, unable to meet such a price, would go out of business—the illicit narcotic drug industry, the billion-dollar racket, would automatically cease to exist. . . . Almost as certain is it that the army of narcotics derelicts would be reduced to the vanishing point. Courts would cease to be crowded with delinquents who owe their downfall to the necessity of meeting the dope peddlers' exhorbitant demands. Jails would be emptied; Federal prisons would lose a quarter or a third of their population.

The Congressman concluded with a challenging question:

> Why should persons in authority wish to keep the dope peddler in
> business and the illicit drug racket in possession of its billion-dollar
> income? It will be obvious, I think, that this is the really signifi-
> cant question at issue. . . . If we, the representatives of the people,
> are to continue to let our narcotics authorities conduct themselves
> in a manner tantamount to upholding and in effect supporting the
> billion-dollar drug racket, we should at least be able to explain to
> our constituents why we do so.

But as has already been noted, not a single colleague so much
as acknowledged Coffee's efforts. None of the committees which
should have been concerned ever called a hearing. And Narcotics Commissioner Anslinger, having the congressional situa-
tional so well in hand, made only oblique attacks on Coffee in
Geneva, through the League of Nations. In 1939 when the Opium
Information Committee passed a resolution calling for a world-
wide review of legal and economic aspects of drug addiction,
Anslinger took the opportunity to attack all such studies and to
excoriate their proponents on the ground that drug addiction is
a criminal condition, not an affliction, and that the addict must
accordingly be treated as a criminal regardless of economic or
social consequences, which should not be taken into consideration. Coffee responded:

> The Commissioner holds persistently to his view in opposition
> to all recognized medical authorities and to the opinions of humani-
> tarians in general. He has repeatedly characterized the narcotic
> addict as a major criminal of America. In support of this strange
> claim, the Commissioner advances a curious argument. He cites
> fingerprint records which show more recidivists among narcotic-
> law violators than among any other types of criminal. This, in his
> view, establishes the narcotic addict as the major criminal of the
> country.
> If you accept this reasoning, the same table reveals vagrancy as
> the second major crime, with prostitution, drunkenness, and suspi-
> cion bracketed in the same category. . . . The valid interpreta-
> tion of the table is not that the narcotic-law violator is a major
> criminal, in any proper sense of the word—the contrary being the
> fact accepted by all competent criminologists—but that addicts
> are arrested again and again for purchasing the drug that their
> infirmity makes essential to their well-being; and that dope ped-
> dlers violate the statutes with every sale.

In 1940 Coffee also challenged Anslinger on his official estimates of the addict population:

Reference should be made to another pronouncement of the Narcotics Bureau that is equally misleading and even more ridiculous. This is the assertion that the number of drug addicts in this country has been reduced to an astonishing degree in the past 15 years or so. This appraisal might be dismissed with the statement that no one else who is entitled to an opinion on the subject pretends to have any accurate knowledge as to how many addicts there were 15 years ago or how many there are now. Perhaps it is worthwhile, however, to examine the Commissioner's claims in brief detail, because he appears to regard the alleged reduction in the number of addicts as giving strong support to the methods of operation of his Bureau, which we have criticized—and which we continue to criticize.

Coffee addressed an inquiry to Dr. Lawrence Kolb, then Assistant Surgeon General, who we have already identified. Dr. Kolb responded by a letter written in February 1940 to which the Congressman referred as follows:

> In this letter, Dr. Kolb quotes the estimate of the Bureau of Narcotics that there are 1.53 addicts per ten thousand of the population (or about 20,000 addicts in all), and adds that, whereas no survey available is absolutely reliable, "from the information we do have, I am inclined to believe that we still have at least 100,000 to the various opium preparations and cocaine." That would be at least five times the number estimated by the Narcotics Bureau. . . .
>
> It is obvious that the Bureau's claim . . . has no standing in the eyes of the physician who, because of his long familiarity with the subject and his recent experience in charge of the Federal Narcotics Hospital at Lexington, Ky., may be regarded as the foremost authority in this particular field. . . . Suffice it that this flagrant misrepresentation is of a piece with other pronouncements —as to criminality of addicts, cures of addicts, and so forth—that have come from the Bureau.

Finally, Congressman Coffee attacked the Bureau position that addicts could only be benefited by incarceration. He pointed out that prisoner-patients reported to be "cured" upon their discharge were merely not taking drugs when released, "somewhat as a duck kept in a dry pen is not swimming." And this is a typical Coffee peroration:

> Let me repeat that this legislative body has no direct concern with the question of curability of disease to which we have just adverted. What does concern us, however, is the fact that the United States Government in establishing the hospital at Lexington, and a second one at Ft. Worth, Texas, as authorized by action of

the Congress, recognizes narcotic addiction as a disease, subject to medical treatment. It is perhaps immaterial, but not without interest, that the Supreme Court has explicitly voiced the same view; whereas the Commissioner of Narcotics holds stubbornly to the view that the addict is not a sick man, but a criminal, and by his ruling makes it impossible for the medical profession outside institutions to offer treatment or aid to victims of this officially recognized malady. . . .

Questions of the number of addicts, the criminality of addicts, the curability of addicts, are matters for the statistician, the Department of Justice, the medical profession. But the matter of flouting Federal law—the supplanting of statutes enacted by the Congress with rulings of a minor Bureau of the Treasury Department—is something of vital concern. That the edicts of one man should take precedence over congressional enactments and clear decisions of the Supreme Court is an anomaly worthy of attention.

But does this anomaly obtain? I answer, unqualifiedly, yes. That is the actual situation which has obtained throughout the ten years of the existence of the Bureau of Narcotics. One man, the Commissioner in charge of that Bureau, has persistently interpreted the Harrison Special Tax Act, the statute governing the distribution of narcotic drugs, in a way clearly at variance with the terms of the Act itself, and in defiance of the interpretation of the Supreme Court of the United States.

But that is all there was. To have been so forcefully and articulately right was not enough. Congressman Coffee's ten-year campaign against the Bureau received little attention from the general press, no support on Capitol Hill, and no acknowledgment in other quarters. He was defeated for re-election in 1946, and it was another full decade before anyone else on Capitol Hill cast so much as a quizzical eye upon the Anslinger empire.

■ NINE

Mephistopheles and Pot

■ FOR ALL THAT he is an amiable gentleman at close range, Harry Jacob Anslinger, who ran the U.S. Narcotics Bureau for more than three decades, may well stand in our history as one of the most tryrannical oppressors of his fellow citizens ever to be sustained in public office by this republic. Like his counterpart John Edgar Hoover, Anslinger built an impregnable empire within the federal structure by portraying himself to members of Congress, and to their electorates back home, as an indispensable defender against the forces of evil. But of the two, Anslinger was far more recklessly fanatical, and while Hoover created a law-enforcement agency that has developed incomparably high standards for itself and its imitators, Narcotics Bureau agents have been widely scorned among professionals as irresponsible persecutors often unworthy of the authority of a federal badge.

It will be recalled that the federal government first became concerned with drugs quite haphazardly, from U.S. efforts to curb trafficking at the international level plus the fact that the Hague Convention committed signatories to control domestic drug use as well. Chance similarly brought Commissioner Anslinger into the picture as narcotics czar. A native Pennsylvania Dutchman, with hairless pate, gravel voice, and taurine neck, Anslinger came indirectly from a promising career in the U.S. Foreign Service. His first State Department assignment, at the outbreak of World War I, was as liaison to the Efficiency Board of the War Department's Ordinance Division, and from this he

69

was posted in 1918 as an attaché to the American legation at The Hague. He remained in Holland until 1921, participating on the peripheries of the American delegation to Versailles, then served two years as vice consul at Hamburg. In 1923 he was elevated to the rank of consul and dispatched to La Guaira, Venezuela, whence he was transferred to Nassau in the Bahamas to head the U.S. Consulate there.

In the latter post, Consul Anslinger negotiated successfully with British authorities to dry up an immense flow of bootleg liquor moving in from the West Indies, and it was this diplomatic achievement that brought him to the attention of the beleaguered Prohibition authorities in Treasury. As a result, he was borrowed from the State Department and brought back to Washington to become chief of the Division of Foreign Control in the Treasury Department's Prohibition Bureau, advancing three years later, in 1929, to the post of Assistant Commissioner of Prohibition. (Note this close personal link, which tends to strengthen the theory, heretofore advanced, that federal drug-law enforcement policies were significantly shaped at the outset by parallels in the experience with Prohibition.)

Early in 1930, scandal touched the office of Deputy Commissioner L. G. Nutt, whose province had been enforcement of the narcotic laws. A federal grand jury found that his agents in New York had grossly falsified their records by reporting city police cases as federal arrests, and further suggested a possibility of outright collusion between federal officers and prominent illegal traffickers. In the shakeup which followed, Nutt was removed and Assistant Commissioner Anslinger, having up to that time had nothing to do with the narcotic side of the Bureau's operations, was given an interim appointment to Nutt's post. At this juncture, however, perhaps partly to quiet criticism, Congress acted on a reorganization measure which took drug control out of the Prohibition Bureau altogether and created an independent Bureau of Narcotics in the Treasury Department. President Hoover named Anslinger to fill the new office of Commissioner of Narcotics on August 12, 1930.

We shall hear much of Harry Anslinger in the rest of this narrative, even in the period after 1962, when the combined determination of President Kennedy and his Attorney General brother sufficed to push him out of the commissioner post. For not only has he dominated every area of drug-law enforcement on the home front with overbearing energy, he has at the same time similarly dominated most policy deliberations on the international scene, and this latter power he continued to wield with unabated vigor until early 1970. Heading the U.S. delegation to the old League of Nations Opium Advisory Committee and that of its successor, the United Nations Commission on Narcotic Drugs—and every significant special conference and convention on the subject since the Hoover regime—has always been Commissioner Anslinger.

Nor has he ever lost his diplomatic, if somewhat heavy-handed, touch in playing the power of his connections in Washington skillfully in concert with his thundering voice at Geneva and the U.N. compound in New York. Whenever he sought to propagate some new dogma or win additional concessions at home, delegates and plenipotentiaries from the high contracting parties would soon be heard chorusing support in their international convocations, while he achieved notable changes in the attitudes and policies of sister nations by brow-beating their delegates in international gatherings with support in the form of Anslinger-inspired statements from U.S. officials or sometimes even made-to-order congressional resolutions.

As commissioner he always fought to win, sometimes not by Marquis of Queensbury rules and seldom gracefully. He tended to respond to criticism with vituperative roars. And for a quarter of a century, from his assumption of office in 1930 until he was finally obliged to soften his stand slightly in the late fifties, he opposed all public discussion aimed at enlightening Americans about the drug problem or exploring alternatives to his overbearing policies, on the ground that anything akin to education or open-mindedness would aggravate the situation and stir the curiosity of potential new victims. Those who questioned his Bureau were denounced as "self-styled experts," bleeding-hearts, ax-grinders, and "meddling do-gooders."

But on the other hand, despite its modest resources no agency in Washington responded faster than the Bureau of Narcotics to any hint of a request or solicitation of a favor from Capitol Hill— or from less important sources. If a congressman wanted to regale some backwater constituents with tales about the war on dope (and the congressman's heroic role in it), the Bureau would oblige with a script; if a high school civics class wrote for information, it would receive a sheaf of handouts and possibly a follow-up call or visit from a local Narcotics Bureau office; and if someone in the entourage of a Personage chanced to become addicted, arrangements could sometimes be made for sheltered treatment without fear of embarrassing attention from drug authorities.

The Narcotics Bureau was always a one-man domain. The only lieutenant to emerge with stature in his own right was Malachi Harney, whose distinction lay not in softening any of the Bureau's hard-to-swallow fixations but in promulgating them with notably more wit and grace than his chief. When it became obvious that Anslinger, like Hoover, had no intention of retiring in the usual tradition to make a place for a subordinate, Harney jumped into the nominally higher post of Assistant Secretary in charge of all Treasury law enforcement (nominal with respect to asserting authority over the Bureau, at least), and went into retirement from there.

The Marijuana Tax Act, which became law on August 2, 1937, and which suddenly brought *cannabis sativa* into the opium-coca "narcotic" pattern, is perhaps the strongest illustration of Commissioner Anslinger's extraordinary powers—and of how abusively he sometimes contrived to wield them. Certainly the launching of a full-blown federal prohibition against this unimportant garden weed will long remain a high-water mark of national fatuity; and the way the Act was slipped through Congress highlights the Commissioner's amazing adeptness at steering federal lawmakers in whatever direction he chose, although there are other achievements—scaring much of the world witless over the allegedly unique menace of heroin, innovating savage mandatory minimum penalties, imposing international travel restrictions on drug addicts—that may merit equal honors as monuments to unwarranted frenzy and panicky misdirection.

The North American marijuana plant is a weakling member of the great botanical family of Indian hemp, from which comes the best of natural fibers for twine and rope as well as, in other variants, stronger preparations known as bhang and ganja, and (in pure resin) hashish or charas. The active ingredient in marijuana, from the strain *cannabis sativa,* is indisputably a drug, and a hallucinogen at that, but it is not addicting, and in the strength encountered when smoked as "pot" it is at most no more than mildly intoxicating. The impact of the drug in its entire range of potencies is comparable to that of alcohol: a few susceptible individuals seem to lapse into temporary panic or mild psychotic episodes, some alterations of perception and motor coordination attend its use, and repeated intoxication with the stronger extracts has been inconclusively associated with insanity.

Ganja and hashish are believed to have been identified and used as both medicaments and ceremonial intoxicants in the Middle East several millennia before the birth of Christ. Cannabis was long a mainstay among soothing and healing elixirs and is still used in medical practice where doctors remain cool-headed, as in Great Britain. Traditionally hashish was eaten and ganja was ingested after being brewed into a tea. Like opium, the milder marijuana (which bears the same relation to hashish that beer does to hundred-proof spirits) came to be smoked only after the world learned the ritual of combustion-inhalation from the enjoyment of tobacco. Pot smoking was taken up in Europe at the end of the eighteenth century, although for many years it did not achieve much popularity outside of small avant-garde circles. The practice (and the plant: *cannabis sativa* was not indigenous to the western hemisphere) subsequently reached the West Indies from Europe or Africa, and was thereafter widely embraced in Latin America and Mexico. But marijuana made no significant appearance in the United States until after World War I.

In the 1920's, use of the drug in this country was confined to blacks who came from or were influenced by the Caribbean, and to Mexican-Americans. It was early viewed with suspicion because of total ignorance about it in most quarters, the general climate created by Prohibition, association with these lowest of foreign minorities, prejudice against cigarettes, and the dim idea that it was somehow capable of being bracketed with opium smoking.

Sinister associations also derived from a half-remembered legend of the Moslem world, about a secret society in the Middle Ages which allegedly partook of hemp in connection with its efforts to eliminate false prophets of Allah by murder—its leader was named Hashishin, from which were supposedly derived both "hashish" and "assassin."

British authorities in India, worldly about such things, arranged long ago for a special commission to make an elaborate study of all aspects of drug use of Indian hemp. The commission's report, submitted in 1894, concluded, in essence, that moderate indulgence produced no significant mental or moral injuries, caused no physical damage, and aroused no more compulsion to excesses than beverage alcohol, with which ganja tea was favorably compared. Other authorities in the intervening years have generally reached similar conclusions, though differentiating the pure and potent hashish (which, the Indian commission suspected, might have had some connection with little-understood "madness" in Indian asylums) from the milder and more innocuous marijuana for smoking (usually consisting of the seeds, leaves, and stalks of the female plant, dried and broken up into combustible shreds).

Nonetheless, and without reliable current data to go on, several states along the Mexican border enacted marijuana-prohibition laws in the early thirties. And at this juncture there appeared on the scene a fanatical father-and-son team who played somewhat the same role in whipping up hysteria about marijuana as Mrs. Vanderbilt had played with respect to opium and cocaine a quarter of a century earlier.

The marijuana crusaders were Earle Albert Rowell and his son Robert. Father Rowell had been campaigning against the "weed of madness" since the mid-1920's, asserting in pamphlets and from lecture platforms that the deadly "reefer" destroyed will power, perverted and corrupted all moral standards, induced the commission of violent crimes, and inevitably led to insanity. Mental hospitals were being filled with marijuana victims, he warned. Each person enslaved to this terrifying new addiction was driven forthwith to make smokers of others, thus spreading the evil in a chain reaction. Moreover, the nation was about to be engulfed in a holocaust of industrial accidents and highway mishaps caused by marijuana intoxication.

Son Rowell joined at the peak of the campaign, helping his father lecture up and down the land, and aiding him in personally destroying fields of hemp whenever they happened to chance upon the sinister crop. It must be added in fairness, however, that the Rowells kept sounding one note of likely truth in their zealous campaign against marijuana which has not been repeated since with the intensity it deserves. As a side issue, they vociferously disapproved the use of alcohol and tobacco, and they hammered on the point that habituation to smoking tobacco very often preceded smoking of the sinister "joint." They warned that in allowing itself to be enslaved by the merchandisers of cigarettes, the nation was setting itself up for an inevitable ultimate takeover by peddlers of the reefer (now being seriously programed, incidentally, by high-priced Madison Avenue talent for some of the tobacco giants). In short, they argued that tobacco addiction was a bad thing because it could nourish an appetite for "something stronger."

The Narcotics Bureau moved into the campaign in the mid-1930's, throwing the authority of the United States government behind the alarming, if ridiculous, proposition that marijuana smoking was causing many violent crimes such as assault, rape, and murder. Intervention by the federal tax agency was suddenly imperative to head off an unprecedented crime wave. And of course this new menace was having its most sinister effects on innocent young people, including teenagers and moppets in schoolyards. Even the traffic-accident theme was played, note-worthy in this context in relation to its cynical reappearance, thirty years later and with far more eclat, when the focus had shifted to amphetamines and other pep pills.

Credit for pushing Commissioner Anslinger and the Treasury Department into this quixotic partnership with the Rowells and other fanatics of the period must doubtless go in some part to his rival, Director Hoover, a few blocks down the street in Justice. By the middle thirties the FBI had acquired a place in the public eye that made its chief a national figure of demigod proportions. Compared with the spectacular closing of the Lindbergh case, shoot-outs against characters like Karpis and Dillinger, and the G-men's dramatic gallery of public enemies, Anslinger's battles against dope rings and drug fiends were becoming tame stuff. Though the Treasury men continued—as always—to upstage Hoover on the international scene (where they were beginning to make headway building up the Mafia bugaboo), Anslinger was sorely in need of a new "angle" at home. And immediately at hand was the commotion being raised by the Rowells, with the prospect of attracting much headline attention in an official campaign to stamp out their "weed of madness." Moreover, it soon became apparent that legislation on the subject would attract favorable notice and put Anslinger back in the limelight on Capitol Hill.

So in the 75th Congress several marijuana bills were intro-duced, all proposing to extend the Narcotic Bureau's authority. The one which became law was H.R. 6385, sponsored principally by Representative Robert L. Doughton, chairman of the House Ways and Means Committee. At the hearings, in the spring of 1937, a brilliant young Treasury counsel, Clinton M. Hester, set the stage, but the performance was essentially Anslinger's, and the support he marshaled for the bill was typical. In lieu of expert analysis or scientific findings, the Committee was told that marijuana was a monstrous Mr. Hyde having none of the off-setting virtues of Dr. Jekyll; that in antiquity it had disrupted the Moslem world by driving Hashishin's army of fanatics to murder viciously and at random throughout the Middle East; and that a Treasury study conducted by his Bureau proved that the drug was being used widely by high school students who smoked it in cigarettes—with effects characterized as "deadly."

The record was loaded with newspaper clippings and lurid accounts of individual crimes allegedly caused by marijuana intoxication, together with free-swinging references to "experts" from other lands. For example, Dr. J. Bouquet, a Tunisian, had found in his studies (not otherwise described) that the use of cannabis caused crime, produced addiction, and resulted in sterility—and also that it induced blind rages in his subjects, inevitably causing mental deterioration and leading ultimately to insanity. For window dressing, a puzzling selection of career government employees was paraded to the stand: a chemist-consultant to the Department of Agriculture who said that poisonous concentrations of marijuana caused mental and physical deterioration in dogs; a chemist from the Treasury Department who described the hemp plant and how it was cultivated and harvested; a botanist from the Department of Agriculture who informed the Committee about the commercial uses of hemp; and a government veterinarian who assured the Committee that marijuana had no valid medicinal uses for animals.

There was a surprising opposition witness. We have seen how often the American Medical Association tended to knuckle under in the early controversies over the opiates, and we shall see the good doctors strike their colors again in subsequent chapters. But at the House marijuana hearings, the official AMA spokesman, Dr. William C. Woodward, took a determined stand against the bill, insisting that no scientific evidence had been adduced about the dangers of the drug, that prior representations of the AMA position had been distorted, and that cannabis actually had valid medical uses and might well be found to have even more in psychiatric therapy. Dr. Woodward challenged the Committee, demanding to know why inquiry had not been made of the Bureau of Prisons whether there were in fact any persons convicted of marijuana-induced crimes in custody, why the Children's Bureau had not been consulted about the charge that youngsters were smoking marijuana cigarettes and the Office of Education about alleged spreading of the habit in schools, and how it happened that spokesmen from the Division of Mental Hygiene and the Division of Pharmacology of the Public Health Service had not appeared. He related scornfully that at the two federal narcotic farms there was not a single record of any marijuana or cannabis addiction ever having come to the attention of the medical staffs of these facilities.

This scrappy spokesman urged the Committee to leave the marijuana problem to local authorities, at least until some reputable scientific basis for federal control was discovered. But like others in the path of the Anslinger steamroller, he was flattened. His testimony touched off a barrage of hostile questions from Committee members, and he had obviously little persuasive effect.

The marijuana bill sailed through the House, and when it reached the Senate, Hester and Anslinger put on the same show more briefly, entertaining the Senate committee with additional hair-raising stories about specific crimes supposedly caused by the drug. But on one point Anslinger took a square position which is particularly noteworthy in the light of subsequent developments: he had told the House committee, in response to a direct question, that there was absolutely no connection between the use of marijuana and addiction to opium and coca products: "No, sir; I have not heard of a case of that kind. I think it is an entirely different class. The marijuana addict does not go in that direction." And when he came to the Senate hearing he was even more emphatic, insisting that marijuana users were "an entirely new class," totally unrelated to any part of the opium traffic: "The opium user is around 35 to 40 years old. These users are 20 years old and know nothing of heroin or morphine."

Congressional sponsors pulled out all stops. Representative Hamilton Fish, for example, who was also pushing for a ban on cannabis imports, told a nationwide audience: "Marijuana is used largely in the form of cigarettes, which cause delusions and produce insanity and often lead to atrocities that only a drug-soaked mind could conceive. Marijuana is a sinister drug that has only recently become available and popular among the younger element."

The Senate also acted in docile and unanimous compliance with the Bureau's wishes, and President Roosevelt signed the Act into law on August 2, 1937.

■ TEN

The Weed of Madness and the Little Flower

■ BUT CONTRARY to expectations (and the apprehensions of responsible people like Dr. Woodward) marijuana did not emerge as much of a challenge even for Mr. Anslinger's men when the public furor subsided after passage of the 1937 Act. Reefer smoking remained a minor indulgence of poor black and Mexican-American groups, spreading from this stratum no further than a few small coteries of far-out intellectuals and jazz musicians. Only recently, commencing in the latter 1960's and in the company of other far more significant shifts in American values and attitudes, has marijuana begun to fulfill some of the dire prophecies about its widespread use heard a quarter of a century ago. And this lag is all the more puzzling because "grass" has always been so much easier to obtain than the opiates or cocaine. It grows in any temperate climate, the only limitation being that the farther away from the equator it is cultivated the less potency it develops; and it requires no elaborate processing— mere drying, crumbling, and do-it-yourself rolling.

Many explanations have been offered for the recent upswing in all forms of drug abuse. It is urged, for example, that the current "hippie" generation reflects a fundamental rejection of aggressive, self-assured competitiveness, which has long made dominant American groups prone to addiction to alcohol, in favor of passivity, disengagement, and an inclination to "tune out," which

78

is fostered by the use of marijuana and other hallucinogenic, soporific, and depressant chemicals. It is also pointed out that the forces of so-called organized crime were slow to take up distribution of marijuana because it is by no stretch addicting enough to enslave its victims like opium, and because the profits from marijuana trafficking remained comparatively small—so that markets have not been expanded and large supplies have not been available until recently. Or perhaps the Rowells were right and the phenomenal success of cigarette promotion since World War II, coupled with what might be called a cancer backlash, is inducing the widespread switch.

But whatever the reasons for its delayed popularity, marijuana smoking is now regarded by most Americans as the Number-One Drug Problem, at least in the sense that it has actually emerged as a reality in the experience of millions, whereas no one even suggests widespread contact with heroin—except scare propaganda *about* heroin and its few hundred thousand consumer-victims. The spread of marijuana use is also of foremost importance in compelling some re-evaluations of today's policies and prejudices, which is the *raison d'être* of this book. So it seems appropriate to jump briefly out of chonological sequence to unfold the rest of the marijuana story in a straight progression of its own from this point.

As has been indicated, the cannabis family yields two intoxicating substances which though chemically the same are poles apart in their strength. That is the first confusion—and a sometimes intentionally fostered distortion—which clouds the subject. In the early literature and the occasional early records of cannabis abuse or alleged addiction, references were to the pure resin, hashish, and not to the milder forms of smokable shreds or drinkable tea. But moreover, even bearing in mind this reservation—which puts the American reefer right out of most of the early controversies—there are still pointblank contradictions as to whether hashish itself, although admittedly a strong intoxicant and hallucinogen, is actually damaging, crime-inducing, or in any traditional sense addicting.

As has already been suggested, anything transpiring on the international drug scene since 1930 is suspect as a measure of the honesty and validity of Anslinger's promulgations, since he dominated most international deliberations after that date like an overbearing schoolmaster. But cannabis (and here for a moment we are talking only about the pure drug hashish, or charas) had received some attention before Anslinger's time. At the original Hague Conference in 1912, where the Opium Convention was drafted, the delegates noted "the question of Indian hemp," referring to the British findings of 1894 and recommending that the matter be studied to determine whether cannabis was being abused in any way so as to require internal legislation or international agreement. After the war, in 1923, the South Africans raised a question about it again before the League Advisory Committee, and in the ensuing two years the views and experience of all member nations were solicited.

In 1924–25, at the plenary Second Opium Conference, the Egyptian delegate, pointing out that his government had been trying to stamp out "hashishism" since 1884 and that "illicit use of hasish is the principal cause of most of the cases of insanity occurring in Egypt," urged that the drug be brought into the control and prohibition pattern already established for opium. He added: "I earnestly beg all the delegates to give this question their best attention, for I know the mentality of Oriental peoples, and I am afraid that it will be said that the question was not dealt with because it did not affect the safety of the Europeans." As a result of this needling, the drug—defined to include only the fruiting tops of the plant from which resin can be extracted, or the extracted resin—was added to the proscribed categories. Several governments insisted, nevertheless, that hashish had not been found to be harmful in any form, and others simply ignored all requests for data and refused to cooperate.

Matters rested there until 1933, by which time Delegate-Commissioner Anslinger was firmly established on the scene. The International Advisory Committee's report for that year contains the folowing U.S.-oriented item:

> A smuggling trade in cigarettes containing Indian hemp ("marijuana" cigarettes) appears to have sprung up between the U.S.A., where it grows as a wild plant freely, and Canada. It may well be that, as the control over the opium and coca derivatives makes it more and more difficult to obtain them, recourse will be increasingly had to Indian hemp for addiction purposes, and it is important that the trade in Indian hemp and its products should be closely watched.

By the time the Advisory Committee held its next biennial meeting, in 1935, the U.S. Bureau's campaign was taking shape at home, so the Committee was treated to a lengthy harangue from the U.S. delegation, revealing that habitual use of marijuana had suddenly become widespread in this country and that there was an alarming relationship between "addiction" to Indian hemp in this form and criminality.

The Egyptians jumped in to support the U.S. request for more stringent measures, but the Indian representative objected on the ground that hemp drugs had been tolerated in his country for centuries, and further that cannabis in its milder forms (ganja and bhang) were intimately connected with prevailing Indian social and religious customs. Several European governments, led by Poland and Switzerland, voiced objection to any prohibitory action because there was "no thorough study available of Indian hemp particularly from the medical and scientific standpoint." Responding to this, a subcommittee of the League Advisory Committee was named to make a full evaluation, with authority to conduct its own research if that proved necessary.

But note the timing. The League subcommittee assembled in 1935 only to choose a panel of experts and to commission the preparation of a bibliography; when it convened to go to work in 1936, it served mainly as a sounding board for the American viewpoint, presented through an American expert, Dr. Treadway, that cannabis (and now we are talking about all forms, including marijuana smoking) *might* be physiologically harmful, *might* produce insanity, *might* be addicting, and *might* directly cause crime. In 1938, when the subcommittee met again to receive various reports, it played up a laudatory account of the new U.S. Marijuana Tax Act which had been passed the preceding year, and its own recommendations sounded a novel theme: it called for research into the relation "between cannabis addiction and addiction to other drugs, especially heroin." Somewhere, possibly from the questions put to him at the hearings on the U.S. Act in 1937, Anslinger had picked up the notion that marijuana smoking might be discredited by depicting it as a "stepping stone" to other forms of addiction. So—presto!—this new line is immediately parroted by the captive international body.

But events of more consequence than our narcotic commissioner's campaign against pot smoking preoccupied the League of Nations after 1938, and neither the Advisory Committee nor its subcommittee on Indian hemp met again.

Even after the onset of World War II, which is universally believed to have broken up smuggling rings and sharply reduced the availability of the opiates in the United States, there was no great upswing in marijuana smoking. Hysteria about the reefer menace subsided, and although the Narcotics Bureau continued to fulminate, total marijuana seizures remained in the range of

a scant truckload or two per year (a trifling amount when it is
noted that the concentration of the active cannabis ingredient in
marijuana is about the same as the concentration of nicotine in
cigarette tobacco), and convictions for marijuana offenses remained substantially below the comparable figures in other drug
categories.

Research which might long ago have begun to dissolve myths
and answer basic scientific questions about marijuana and its
effects on human beings was consistently frustrated in the United
States because researchers could not obtain permits to possess
and use the drug for experimentation (the issuing authority
being, of course, the Bureau of Narcotics). This virtual blackout
on research has, incidentally, been relentlessly maintained almost
to the present; and typical of the say-anything dishonesty of
Commissioner Anslinger and his successors is the current explanation that medical science could never have found out very much
about the effects of marijuana in past years anyway, because the
strength of various preparations from different plants might have
varied; that all the Bureau itself could have furnished for distribution to researchers was stale material seized in raids; and that
only now—since 1966—is there some prospect of definitive results
because, thanks to a U.S. federal grant, laboratory scientists in
Israel have produced and synthesized the active marijuana ingredient (THC). Had the scientific community looked similarly
askance at research on unstable and unsynthesized molds, for
instance, we would still be waiting for penicillin and its multi-
fold blessings. Moreover, this display of bland cynicism comes
not only from contemporary law-enforcement people but from
Public Health Service officials in the National Institute of Mental
Health—of whom one might have expected more.

One public figure who stood out among his contemporaries as
a man not to be trifled with was Fiorello H. La Guardia, who found
himself directly embroiled in the marijuana controversy as mayor
of New York. Instead of playing up to hysterical press suggestions that the juveniles in his city were about to launch marijuana-induced orgies of theft, sex, and murder, he turned to the
New York Academy of Medicine for advice. The Academy, after
reviewing existing literature and conferring with city officials,
recommended that the Mayor authorize a two-part study—first
to evaluate the current effects of marijuana in the community,
and second to test the drug's effects on human beings under
controlled laboratory conditions. A blue-ribbon committee of
doctors and public officials was thereupon organized, and the so-
called La Guardia study got under way in 1939.

The sociological investigation was carried out by a team of New York police officers who were detached from their other duties, specially trained, and assigned to report directly to the committee. Over the course of almost two years they observed, interviewed, investigated, and carefully assembled an accurate picture of the situation in New York City. They found marijuana smoking to be centered in Harlem and in one other midtown section occupied by the newly immigrated Latin-Americans. Users were characteristically in their twenties, and marginally employed or without jobs. Distribution was accomplished through hundreds of retail peddlers and locations known as "tea-pads," where a reefer could be smoked on the premises.

Smokers generally agreed that using marijuana made them feel better and seemed to produce no ill effects, and further that there was no discomfort—nor even much difficulty—in discontinuing the habit at will. There was no evidence suggesting that addiction to heroin or other opiates had any sequential relation to marijuana smoking, no evidences of marijuana-induced sexual aberrations or eroticism, and nothing to substantiate a causal relationship between smoking and the commission of crimes. Outside the saturated areas, the Mayor's investigators found virtually no use of marijuana in high schools or junior high schools, and no observable connection between juvenile delinquency and such smoking as they did find. So the final conclusion in this branch of the inquiry was that "publicity concerning the catastrophic effects of marijuana smoking in New York City is unfounded."

The study of physiological and psychological effects was conducted with volunteer prisoners in a hospital ward at one of the city's hospitals. Observation of each subject ran over a period of several weeks, and a total of seventy-seven were used, forty-eight who had had previous experience with the drug and twenty-nine who had not. Dozens of tests were administered, and the results recorded and calibrated were far too detailed to be given here. But in substance, what emerged was a pattern of effects, responsive symptoms, and behavior covering ranges roughly approximating those which would have been covered in testing similar administrations of alcohol or tobacco smoke. Some subjects were excited, made nervous, or lost motor coordination. Some who had never used the drug had flash reactions of nausea or panic. Almost all experienced dizziness, light-headedness, and feelings of euphoria, although occasionally the responses were anxiety or ill-tempered antagonism. As the effects of the drug wore off, always within a few hours of its administration, the subjects became drowsy and were usually very hungry and thirsty.

Nine single experiences (nine episodes, not nine subjects) characterized by the observers as psychotic reactions were recorded, all involving acute anxiety, disorientation, and irrational behavior. Six of these were temporary and ended before the effects of the drug had worn off; two of the remaining three were identified with factors other than the drug—"prison psychosis"; and although it was speculated that marijuana might have brought on the other recorded case, it turned out that the subject was an epileptic and that his reaction may well have coincided with an epileptic seizure. Careful tests of IQ, learning ability, memory, and emotional responsiveness showed up-and-down irregularities in relation to the administration of the drug, but no results that could be characterized as a significant pattern.

In sum, the clinical studies showed no permanent alterations in basic personality structure, but minor variations in peripheral aspects while the subjects were intoxicated.

Even before the La Guardia study was released, Anslinger began to shoot at it. Responding to a preliminary description published in the *American Journal of Psychiatry* by two participating doctors in 1942, he wrote:

> Of course, the primary interest of the Bureau of Narcotics is the enforcement aspect. From this point of view it is very unfortunate that Doctors Allentuck and Bowman should have stated so unqualifiedly that the use of marijuana does not lead to physical, mental or moral deterioration.

The Narcotics Bureau allegedly brought heavy pressures to bear in trying to suppress the report (a charge that can be accepted as valid in the light of similar in-fighting to be detailed in following chapters), and the Committee's findings were in fact held up nearly three years before being made public.

The blow at Doctors Allentuck and Bowman had been open, in the form of a letter signed by Commissioner Anslinger himself. The blow at the La Guardia Report, when the latter finally made its appearance, was underhanded, published as an editorial in the *Journal of the American Medical Association* (the AMA having once again abandoned its own professional brethren, in the New York Academy this time, to execute one of its turntails for the Bureau). But the text was pure Anslinger:

> For many years medical scientists have considered cannabis a dangerous drug. Nevertheless, a book called "Marijuana Problems" by the New York City Mayor's Committee on Marijuana submits an analysis by 17 doctors of tests on 77 prisoners and, on this

narrow and thoroughly unscientific foundation, draws sweeping and inadequate conclusions which minimize the harmfulness of marijuana. Already the book has done harm. One investigator has described some tearful parents who brought their 16 year old son to a physician after he had been detected in the act of smoking marijuana. A noticeable mental deterioration had been evident for some time even to their lay minds. The boy said he had read an account of the La Guardia Committee report and that this was his justification for using marijuana. He read in *Down Beat*, a musical journal, an analysis of this report under the caption "Light Up Gates, Report Finds 'Tea' a Good Kick."

A criminal lawyer for marijuana drug peddlers has already used the La Guardia report as a basis to have defendants set free by the court. . . . The book states unqualifiedly to the public that the use of this narcotic does not lead to physical, mental or moral degeneration and that permanent deleterious effects from its continued use were not observed on 77 prisoners. This statement has already done great damage to the cause of law enforcement. Public officials will do well to disregard this unscientific, uncritical study, and continue to regard marijuana as a menace wherever it is purveyed.

There was more. But the above is a good sampling—and remember that this nonsensical frothing, which could not conceivably have come from anywhere but the Bureau, was making its appearance under the prestigious AMA *Journal* masthead.

Nor is that the end of the matter: as part of its response to the currently revived interest in marijuana, the new Bureau of Narcotics and Dangerous Drugs, successor to the Treasury Bureau, has reprinted this 1945 editorial and is broadcasting it *today* as part of its package of handouts designed to defend the old Anslinger line.

After the New York Academy studies and the La Guardia Report the blackout on research imposed by the Narcotics Bureau became almost total. Reputable scientists would not risk being pounced upon by federal or state agents for working with the drug obtained from illegal sources (and possession for *any* purpose was a crime under the laws of a number of states, anyway); and cop-trained officials in the Bureau unhesitatingly pronounced even the facilities of great hospitals and leading universities inadequate for the conducting of responsible experiments, and hence unworthy of a Treasury license. The number of Treasury-approved projects dropped from eighty-seven in 1948 to eighteen in 1953, and to six in 1958.

■ ELEVEN

Smearing Mary Jane

■ IN THIS ENFORCED vacuum marijuana continued to be portrayed as a national menace calling for heroic responses from the drug-police camp. And that brings us to a brief look at Commisioner Anslinger's famous annual reports. From the early 1920's the Narcotics Division and its successor, the Narcotics Bureau, prepared a single document each year to serve as its report to the U.S. Congress and at the same time to fulfill the reporting obligations of the United States as a party to the International Opium Convention and subsequent treaties. This lent itself to the bootstrap operations we have already observed—whatever the Bureau said to Congress could subsequently be cited in Geneva and New York as the official U.S. position vis à vis the international community, and vice versa; that is, whatever the U.S. Commissioner might say as an international delegate was thus fed right back to Congress as gospel from the high contracting powers.

These double-barreled reports are titled "Traffic in Opium and Other Dangerous Drugs" and there is nothing else like them in all the annals of U.S. bureaucratic publishing. Year after year they scolded, grumbled, and exhorted, leaning heavily on bold-face capitalization, torrents of italics, and turgid hyperbole. They innovated such shabby reporting tricks as measuring the T-men's prowess by adding all prison sentences imposed on persons they had arrested (already mentioned—the 1933 total was 3,248 years, 10 months, 18 days), and reckoning the value of contraband seizures in exaggerated estimates of what they might have brought at top-dollar retail prices on the illicit market. Although the Government Printing Office does not encourage embellishing illustrations in official reports, these documents were always laced with photographs: criminal types posed where they were caught, mug shots of unattractive Bureau targets, and revolting portraits of alleged victims of the traffic.

Instead of statistical analysis, the reports leaned heavily on anecdotal items like the following:

> On the night of November 4, 1947, at Chicago, Ill., a narcotic agent, after negotiating with an intermediary, Ralph Hicks, for the purchase of five pounds (2 kilograms, 268 grams) of marijuana for a total of $500 was taken to a point near the intersection of Loomis and Polk Streets where AGREDANO appeared with the marijuana. When the agent attempted to place him under arrest, AGREDANO drew a pistol and the agent was compelled to shoot him, the bullet going through his left arm and penetrating the chest cavity. AGREDANO died of these wounds on November 5, 1947.

It is noteworthy in connection with this otherwise insignificant —and typical—account that Treasury tax collectors were never intended to be armed, and that Narcotics Bureau agents only received special authority to carry guns from Congress in the Narcotic Control Act of 1956.

The following year, the Bureau solemnly chronicled this as a marijuana case:

> On June 30, 1948, at Cleveland, Ohio, James Buchanan was arrested by police of that city for the murder of a 60-year-old East Cleveland widow. After questioning by police detectives he admitted his participation in the crime and also accused an accomplice. Buchanan admitted having participated, during the previous 6 months, in the brutal attack of 16 women for the purpose of robbing them of their money. He stated further he wanted the money to buy wine and reefers (marijuana cigarettes) which he would consume at the same time. Before venturing out to commit their atrocious crimes, Buchanan and his partner would fortify themselves with wine and marijuana. Buchanan was 24 years of age at the time of his arrest, married, and the father of three children.

To give the full flavor of these singular documents—remembering that they are official publications of an agency of the United States government and at the same time formal communications addressed by the government to other nations, is a task which, though tempting for what it reveals about Anslinger and his

Bureau, would require more than the compass of this volume. When anyone, no matter how clumsy or obscure, published something that supported the Bureau's official line, the report would note it and sometimes devote pages to commendation of the author and quotations of favorite passages.

When one Pablo O. Wolff, for example, who later became the World Health Organization's resident expert on marijuana thanks to vigorous U.S. sponsorship, published an alarmed monograph on marijuana in Latin America (where the drug has always been regarded with sanguine calm), the Bureau hailed it as "a painstaking review of information on the abuse of cannabis," and "a much-needed compilation of current knowledge in one volume":

> His consideration of the relationship between marijuana and delinquency and criminality throws important light on this phase of the subject.
> He has been completely impartial, which is the basic requirement for all scientific investigation. His extensive study of hashish (marijuana) intoxication in many countries has enabled him to give a well-rounded picture of the destructive action of marijuana on both character and intelligence.

Even federal judges were patronized. In the 1949 report, this second-rate Treasury agency set forth the following, captioned "The Sound Policy of a United States District Judge":

> In two recent cases, one involving narcotic drugs and the other marijuana, Hon. William T. McCarthy, United States District Judge, of Boston, Mass., let it be known that certain types of violators could expect no leniency in his court. . . .
> In the marijuana case . . . Judge McCarthy stated: ". . . After all, opium or any of its derivatives—and this is not one—have a therapeutic value. They bring consolation to the sick and dying; they make their last days on this earth comfortable. But marijuana has no therapeutic value whatsoever. It has been responsible for the commission of crimes of violence, of murder and of rape. Those are two major tributaries that flow from the use of this marijuana. I don't say misuse of it. It has no value of any kind. . . . I don't like to be harsh in cases, I would rather be kindly, but I have a job to do, and I have a fixed, determined viewpoint in these narcotic cases."

The same report then details, for the information of Congress and the U.N., some "Crimes Associated with Marijuana":

> On August 23, 1949, at San Jose, Calif., a 19-year-old youth was arrested for the unlawful possession and cultivation of mari-

juana. The marijuana, which was found growing in the flower garden of his residence, was admittedly for his own use. In a statement to the arresting officers this boy stated that he had read in the public library a copy of the Mayor's Report on Marijuana Problems. Because it gave him the definite impression that marijuana was not harmful or habit-forming, he decided to try smoking it. He stated further that as far as he was concerned the Mayor's Report is erroneous on practically all points. He said he had to have marijuana now and that was why he had been growing it.

David Eugene Ash was arrested at Amarillo, Tex., in the early morning of September 11, 1949, by State and county police officers for operating a vehicle while under the influence of drugs (marijuana). Ash had backed a large dual-wheeled truck over the top of a parked passenger automobile and overturned the truck. A quantity of marijuana was found on his person at the time of his arrest.

Ash is a member of a notorious family and has a long criminal record, including convictions for theft, receiving and concealing stolen property, and affray. He has two sisters who are married to notorious narcotic addicts and criminals. Each of the sisters was sentenced in 1949 to serve one to seven years for violation of the Kansas State narcotic law. He has two brothers who each have long criminal records.

The total of seizures of bulk marijuana reported by the Bureau for the nation for the year 1949 was, incidentally, less than a thousand pounds, and total seizures of marijuana cigarettes were approximately twenty pounds.

Members of Congress have always seemed to relish Mr. Anslinger's themes, and pronouncements emanating from the Bureau were sometimes topped by echoes from Capitol Hill. As public anxiety about drug addiction peaked again in the early fifties, the Bureau found a champion in Congressman Hale Boggs, who took up the witless refrain that the courts were really responsible for drug trafficking because they were meting out sentences of insufficient severity. The remedy for this, according to Anslinger and Boggs, was greatly increased penalties with mandatory minimums (provisions *requiring* sentencing judges to impose punishment of at least a specified number of years' imprisonment), and the Congressman introduced a bill for this purpose, quickly emulated by other lawmakers in both houses, in the 81st Congress in 1950.

This so-called Boggs Act failed to pass on the first round, but it was reintroduced in the 82nd Congress and acquired so much momentum that it was reluctantly embraced by the Kefauver Committee, becoming law in 1951 as one of the latter's legislative proposals. Drum-beating for tougher sentences for all dope-connected convictions somewhat eclipsed the marijuana issue in the Kefauver proceedings, but the new penalties were attached to marijuana offenses as a matter of course, without any question or opposition.

Kefauver noted that marijuana was coming into the country from Mexico in "a tremendous flow," observed that more and more young people were using it, and accepted the Bureau claim that there was a causal or sequential relationship between marijuana use and addiction to the more damaging drugs:

> The path to addiction ran practically the same throughout the testimony from young addicts. In their own vernacular, Mr. Dumpson put it this way: "They say they go from sneaky Pete to pot to horse to banging." In ordinary language, this describes the popular sequence—drinking wine, smoking "reefers" or marijuana cigarettes (sometimes starting at the age of 13 or 14) then sniffing or "snorting" heroin, finally injecting it directly into the vein.

Again in 1955–56, when the Daniel Committee conducted its hearings and sponsored even more severe penalties and higher mandatory minimums in the Narcotic Control Act of 1956, marijuana was carried along into the new pattern with only glancing attention. The Senate investigators noted that Mexico was still the source of a great volume of marijuana, that not only civilian users but also U.S. servicemen stationed at military installations near the border went across frequently to get drugs, and that "juveniles also cross with ease."

Even Commissioner Anslinger was momentarily outdone by the zeal of some of the questioning:

> *Senator Daniel.* Now, do I understand it from you that, while we are discussing marijuana, the real danger there is that the use of marijuana leads many people eventually to the use of heroin, and the drugs that do cause them complete addiction; is that true?
>
> *Mr. Anslinger.* That is the great problem and our great concern about the use of marijuana, that eventually if used over a long period, it does lead to heroin addiction. . . .
>
> *Senator Daniel.* As I understand it from having read your book, an habitual user of marijuana or even a user to a small extent presents a problem to the community, and is a bad thing. Mari-

juana can cause a person to commit crimes and do many heinous things; is that not correct?

Mr. Anslinger. That is correct. It is a dangerous drug, and is so regarded all over the world. . . .

The Commissioner explained that cannabis had been withdrawn from medical use after 1937 because it had no therapeutic advantages and was dangerous, "with the likelihood that it might cause insanity." Then followed this exchange:

Senator Welker. Mr. Commissioner, my concluding question with respect to marijuana: Is it or is it not a fact that the marijuana user has been responsible for many of our most sadistic, terrible crimes in this Nation, such as sex slayings, sadistic slayings, and matters of that kind?

Mr. Anslinger. There have been instances of that, Senator. We have had some rather tragic occurrences by users of marijuana. It does not follow that all crimes can be traced to marijuana. There have been many brutal crimes traced to marijuana. But I would not say that it is the controlling factor in the commission of crimes.

Senator Welker. I will grant you that it is not the controlling factor, but is it a fact that your investigation shows that many of the most sadistic, terrible crimes, solved or unsolved, we can trace directly to the marijuana user?

Mr. Anslinger. You are correct in many cases, Senator Welker.

Senator Welker. In other words, it builds up a false sort of feeling on the part of the user and he has no inhibitions against doing anything; am I correct?

Mr. Anslinger. He is completely irresponsible.

In 1948 the United States government and the Narcotics Bureau—full synonyms in this context—had launched a campaign in the U.N. Commission to consolidate all existing international drug agreements into a new Single Convention. Year after year the Bureau reports scolded and exhorted to move this project along, and commencing in the middle fifties they began to bear down on cannabis:

Cannabis was the most widespread drug of addiction, geographically. The problem of cannabis was emphasized because it sometimes serves as an introduction to addiction to other drugs and because of increased traffic, particularly in Asia, Africa, Central

and South America. India made outstanding progress towards prohibiting cultivation and use of cannabis. Seizures of cannabis in
the United Kingdom in the first quarter of 1957 exceeded the
total quantity seized there during the entire year 1956. Egyptian
authorities destroyed cannabis and cannabis preparations in all
pharmacies. Lebanese authorities destroyed more than 5,000,000
square meters of clandestine cannabis plantations and continued
their program of suppression. . . .

Heading a new parade of episodes in 1958 under the caption
"Narcotics and Crime" came the story of one Joe Padilla Franco,
an amiable alcoholic by his own description, who bought three
marijuana cigarettes from the Green Ladder Bar in Roswell, New
Mexico, drank some beer, smoked two of the joints, and some
time later woke up to recall that he had stabbed a three-year-old
girl to death, whereupon he fled to Mexico. When apprehended,
Joe told the authorities that the whole thing had been like a
dream, and that he "believed he would not have killed the child
if he had not smoked the marijuana." In the following year, the
Bureau's official gallery of horrors featured this:

> On June 22, 1958, about 2:30 A.M., two officers of the San Fran-
> cisco Police Department noticed Joe Ross William Callegos, a
> Mexican, constantly blowing the horn of the automobile he was
> operating in downtown San Francisco. When the officers told
> Callegos that horn blowing at that hour was very annoying, Cal-
> legos sped away from them, on the wrong side of the street, com-
> pletely disregarding traffic lights at two intersections.
> The officers pursued and finally overtook Callegos, who tried to
> throw away a marijuana cigarette. As one of the arresting officers
> picked up the cigarette, Callegos struck him and kicked the officer
> in the face and stomach as they handcuffed the defendant, who be-
> came so violent that the officers had to put cuffs on his feet to sub-
> due him. During questioning Callegos appeared to be under the
> influence of a narcotic drug. Two marijuana seeds were found in
> one of his pockets.

How surprised and proud this Mexican Joe must have been if
he ever learned that his horn-blowing and seed-carrying had
been thus officially reported in such vivid detail by the U.S.
Treasury department to Congress and by the U.S. government to
the United Nations!

■ TWELVE

Balancing the Grass Account

■ SOME DAY, when dispassionate historians begin to sift through this drug story, credit for reversing the swing of the pendulum may go to the marijuana chapters. For by the early sixties it began to appear that Anslinger might have overreached, and that President Lincoln's aphorism about all of the people all the time was still a working theorem in matters of common sense and simple justice.

A handful of federal judges, life-appointed and reachable only by the sanction of impeachment, began calmly defying mandatory sentencing provisions when marijuana offenders came before them (*ten years* for a saxophone player caught for the third time with a joint in his pocket?). Juries began coming in with speedy "not guilties" in cases where the defense raised no shred of reasonable doubt but the prosecution was trying for five- or ten-year mandatory minimums for marijuana offenses. Even a few courageous prosecutors began turning open-and-shut marijuana cases into lesser offenses like vagrancy or malicious mischief.

And querying voices began to be heard, some of them ringing with great authority. President Kennedy's Ad Hoc Panel on Drug Abuse reported in 1962 that the evidence connecting marijuana with sexual offenses and other anti-social and criminal acts was "very limited," that none of the elements of true addiction was present in marijuana use, and that it is generally only a "spree" drug, concluding that "the hazards of marijuana use have been exaggerated" and that "long criminal sentences imposed

93

on an occasional user or possessor of the drug are in poor social perspective."

The dean of all American authorities, our enduring hero Dr. Lawrence Kolb, commented mildly that though marijuana, if used excessively, might conceivably cause criminally inclined persons to commit crimes, "its potency as an instigator of crime has not been measured or demonstrated in the United States because of its limited use." Then he added, "The tendency to credit a narcotic as the cause of physical, mental, and social disasters is so great in the United States that marijuana-induced crimes are often reported in the press and by police-trained people when there is no causal relation of marijuana to the crime."

In November 1963, following the White House Conference on Narcotic Drugs, the President's Advisory Commission on Narcotics and Drug Abuse sharply distinguished marijuana from the addicting categories, chided both the official and scientific communities for the great dearth of accurate knowledge about the field, scoffed at the Narcotics Bureau's insistence that high penalties and mandatory minimums were an effective deterrent, and concluded unequivocally:

> The present Federal narcotics and marijuana laws equate the two drugs. An offender whose crime is sale of a marijuana reefer is subject to the same term of imprisonment as the peddler selling heroin. In most cases the marijuana reefer is less harmful than any opiate. For one thing, while marijuana may provoke lawless behavior, it does not create physical dependence. This Commission makes a flat distinction between the two drugs and believes that the unlawful sale or possession of marijuana is a less serious offense than the unlawful sale or possession of an opiate.

In 1966 the New York County Medical Society officially classified marijuana as a mild hallucinogen, insisting that there was no credible evidence proving its use to be associated with crimes of violence in the United States.

In 1967 President Johnson's Commission on Law Enforcement and Administration of Justice questioned the entire impact of the Marijuana Tax Act:

> The Act raises an insignificant amount of revenue and exposes an insignificant number of marijuana transactions to public view, since only a handful of people are registered under the Act. It has become, in effect, solely a criminal law, imposing sanctions upon persons who sell, acquire, or possess marijuana. . . .
> Marijuana is equated in law with the opiates, but the abuse

characteristics of the two have almost nothing in common. The opiate produces physical dependence. Marijuana does not. A withdrawal sickness appears when use of the opiates is discontinued. No such symptoms are associated with marijuana. The desired dose of opiates tends to increase over time, but this is not true of marijuana. Both can lead to psychic dependence, but so can almost any substance that alters the state of consciousness.

On the relation between marijuana and crime, the Law Enforcement Commission noted absolute differences of opinion: that marijuana is a major cause of crime and violence, on the one hand, and that it has no association whatsoever with crime, and only a marginal relation to violence, on the other. The Commission suggested that since marijuana tends to release inhibitions, its effects depend primarily on the individual and on immediate circumstances, so that "it might, but certainly will not necessarily or inevitably, lead to aggressive behavior or crime."

Of the Bureau's singsong line that marijuana leads to other drugs, the President's Commission said:

> There is evidence that a majority of the heroin users who come to the attention of public authorities have, in fact, had some prior experience with marijuana. But this does not mean that one leads to the other in the sense that marijuana has an intrinsic quality that creates a heroin liability. There are too many marijuana users who do not graduate to heroin, and too many heroin addicts with no known prior marijuana use, to support such a theory. Moreover there is no scientific basis for such a theory.

In the other camp, however, neither these questionings nor the mounting challenges in the scientific literature and popular press softened Commissioner Anslinger or the man who succeeded him in 1962, Henry L. Giordano, a career Bureau deputy. As late as 1968 Commissioner Giordano was still telling congressional committees the wholly misleading truth that large enough doses of marijuana (laboratory saturation of animals) have been shown to cause temporary psychoses, and that for predisposed persons a small amount can have dangerous effects. When he insisted to Chairman Dodd of the Senate Juvenile Delinquency Subcommittee that marijuana was proved by "recent studies" to have been the first step in the progression to heroin for 80 per cent of all drug addicts, the Senator backed him down:

> *Chairman Dodd.* I do not know just how to understand that. Does that mean that in some people there is a physical or chemical disposition to the use of heroin as a result of using marijuana?

Mr. Giordano. No. What that means is that marijuana use on the part of certain people using marijuana leads them to something stronger which may end up being heroin. A recent study in California indicated that of individuals arrested in 1960 involving marijuana use, that by 1965, one out of eight had progressed to heroin. Now, as to whether there is something significant in the makeup of marijuana that automatically leads to heroin, the answer is, "No." Association in the drug culture is a partial reason. People get into the abuse area and when they are looking for something stronger, the next thing may be heroin.

But Giordano then switched facilely to another old line (and remember this is 1968, not 1920):

Within the last few years we have witnessed a dramatic increase in the abuse of marijuana throughout the United States and primarily among young people. Our reports indicate that 42 per cent of the marijuana users coming to the attention of law enforcement officers in 1967 are under the age of 21.

Simultaneously the Bureau began defending its policies by sounding a new alarm: the appearance in illicit channels of substantial amounts of hashish and synthetic cannabis essence (THC), described as potent new forms of marijuana. Giordano struck out at those who questioned existing marijuana laws in lumbering (and inconsistent) terms fully worthy of his predecessor:

There has been some criticism of this penalty structure, particularly with regard to the penalty for possession. Some persons feel that this sentence is unduly harsh as applied to mere users of marijuana or youthful experimenters. However, this is not the manner in which the law is applied. Our thrust is aimed at the trafficking element and our conviction statistics bear this out. In 1967 about 60 per cent of all our marijuana defendants had previous criminal records, usually for serious crimes. Their average age was 28 years. Nearly 70 per cent of all of the cases were for sales violations. The remaining violations were for possession, but this does not mean that the individuals involved were not traffickers.

And under Giordano the Bureau enlarged its training school (to indoctrinate local police authorities), continued its propaganda via agent-lecturers, and intensified its barrage of Treasury-endorsed pamphlets designed to promote its "hard" enforcement line.

Meanwhile, on the international scene Mr. Anslinger, who retained his post at the U.N. until 1970, pressed ahead. In 1954 the WHO Expert Committee had ordained that the use of cannabis can no longer be justified for any legitimate medical purpose. In 1955 Dr. Wolff, the American protégé who had by then become chief of the Addiction Producing Drugs Section of WHO, reported categorically that marijuana smoking "eventually leads the smoker to turn to intravenous heroin injections" and that cannabis was dangerous from all viewpoints, physical, mental, social and criminological. This in turn provided a basis for the U.S.-led campaign to bring cannabis within the scope of the proposed new all-inclusive Single Convention.

When the Single Convention was finally adopted and approved by the U.N., marijuana was included as if it were in exactly the same addicting class as opium. Anslinger thereupon promptly reversed his field and used the Single Convention (which the United States did not ratify until 1967) as supporting authority for increased anti-marijuana propaganda and enforcement activities on the home front.

Simultaneously the definition of drug addiction itself was altered by the World Health Organization, primarily to accommodate U.S. insistence that stimulants like cocaine, and hallucinogenic—"mind-altering"—substances could rightly be embraced in that invidious term. In place of the classic tripartite definition based on habituation, tolerance, and withdrawal symptoms (to which the League Narcotics Commission had early added, again partly in response to U.S. pressure, "detrimental to the individual or society"), there was substituted, by the subservient WHO Expert Committee, an open-ended description of "drug dependence" which could be applied to *any* substance believed to have adverse physiological or psychological effects and which attracted human users. This helped lay the groundwork, incidentally, for the more recent U.S. crusade against "dangerous drugs" and "drug abuse."

Thus on this front, too, the scientists yielded meekly to the enforcers. At the 1961 session of the U.N. Commission, for example, when an INTERPOL (police) representative began scolding commentators from the Netherlands who had dared make the heretical suggestion that cannabis addiction was no worse than alcoholism, the WHO spokesman jumped in to support him, pointing out that under the new definition adopted by the Expert Committee cannabis was definitely an internationally controlled substance, with the "added danger that cannabis abuse is very likely to be a forerunner of addiction to more dangerous addicting drugs."

The U.N. Commission has gone on excoriating "unauthoritative statements minimizing the harmful effects of cannabis and advocating that its use be permitted for non-medical purposes," repeating Anslinger's old saws that the drug causes violence, is injurious to health, and is associated with the use of other drugs, including heroin, and exhorting all governments to greater efforts to eradicate marijuana traffic and combat suggestions that cannabis in any form might be relatively harmless.

In the sixties England experienced an increase in marijuana smoking comparable, on a smaller scale, to that observed in the United States. Late in 1968 a panel of distinguished doctors and citizens, headed by Lady Wootton of Abinger, made a report based upon an exhaustive study which had been commissioned by the Home Secretary. The Wootton Committee (actually a subcommittee of the Advisory Committee on Dangerous Drugs which was established under the Dangerous Drugs Act of 1965), after holding hearings on all aspects of the subject, rejected suggestions that cannabis should be entirely removed from control or legalized in the United Kingdom; but at the same time it distinguished cannabis sharply from traditionally addicting narcotics, suggested that dangers allegedly associated with it had been exaggerated, and found that (at least in connection with smoking and other moderate uses) there was neither any substantial progression from cannabis to other drugs nor any noteworthy relation between cannabis use and the commission of crimes.

The Wootton report urged that penalties relating to cannabis be sharply reduced, that *all* possession not connected with selling be dealt with summarily as a "trifling" offense (maximum fine £100 or four months' imprisonment), and that possession of small amounts should not be regarded as serious enough to merit any punishment other than a small fine. The report also noted that cannabis preparations and derivatives ought still to be recognized as legitimate drugs, available for medical treatment as well as research, and urged principal reliance upon a campaign to reduce nonmedical use of the substance by education.

Needless to say this study attracted attention and stirred activity in Washington. On Capitol Hill there flowered a variety of proposals to soften federal possession penalties and to set up marijuana study commissions, along with a spate of research-appropriation bills. Elaborate evaluation projects using animal and human subjects have been launched by the score, some under sponsorship of the new Bureau of Narcotic and Dangerous Drugs, the National Institute of Mental Health, and even the armed forces. Large sums have been poured into efforts to simplify laboratory procedures for synthesizing THC. Led by Gallup, professional and amateur surveyors have produced dozens of statistical analyses measuring the extent of marijuana use in every affected segment of American society.

This commotion quickly reached state lawmakers and local enforcement agencies as well. Bills to reduce marijuana penalties for first-offense possession, but sometimes offset by *increases* in penalties for selling, have been introduced in nearly every recent session of every state legislature. Led by New York, California, and Illinois, over half the states have cut possession penalties from felony to misdemeanor levels (with a record low of seven days *maximum*, plus attending a course on drugs, in Nebraska). Local prosecutors and drug squads have sometimes been surprisingly forbearing with first-offender teenagers, although local judges have sometimes also gone on handing out incredible exemplary sentences (ten and twenty years if other factors, such as anti-war activities or long hair, play an aggravating role).

In June 1970 Congress tied the Marijuana and Health Reporting Act to the 1970 general hospital construction appropriations bill signed by President Nixon after he had vetoed a much more generous grant and allotment measure (on the grounds, among others, that federal efforts should be "redirected—away from emphasis on additional hospital beds" toward "facilities for ambulatory care, long-term care and rehabilitation—alternatives to hospitalization"). The marijuana rider contained a congressional finding designed to freeze the status quo—"Notwithstanding the various studies carried out, and research engaged in, with respect to the use of marijuana, there is a lack of authoritative information involving the health consequences of using marijuana"—and then went on to oblige the Secretary of Health, Education, and Welfare to report annually "current information" on the health consequences of using the drug, and any recommendations he might have for new legislation.

The Secretary's subsequent reports have backed and filled harmlessly over the subject: marijuana may or may not cause mental illness, is only a "minor contributor" to major crimes and violence, is perhaps only associated with hard-drug use rather than directly causative of it—and whether smoking it produces an "antimotivational syndrome" (causing youngsters to grow long hair and "drop out") is a question which "remains to be answered."

But there has been no comparable timidity—or honest carefulness—in other quarters, including the halls of Congress itself. A free-swinging Senate investigation of alleged massacres of Vietnamese civilians by U.S. troops at Songmy made headlines by suggesting the whole thing happened because our men were stoned on pot. The Vice President warned solemnly: "In our opinion marijuana is dangerous. It is not just the grown-up equivalent of alcohol. . . . We must have the courage to stand up and say to our children, 'No, pot is not the equivalent of whisky.'" Lieutenant Calley's defenders tried to weave pot smoking into his case, and Congress and the Pentagon have continued a noisy dialogue about the use of cannabis in the armed forces (while, as we shall see later, the whole GI establishment is supposed to be steeped in heroin, and Polaris crewmen are alleged to take LSD trips to relieve their boredom).

President Nixon, pushing one of his remarkable White House sessions in which media officials have been exhorted to dramatize drug problems in fiction episodes (this one was for thirty-five TV producers, in August 1970), revealed that *he* had new evidence showing marijuana to be harmful and dangerous. Federal forces have remained as aggressive as ever, with highly publicized raids and quasi-military games like "Operation Intercept," which tried literally to seal and screen the entire Mexican border for a short period. The Mexican government, which acknowledges no drug problem of crisis proportions among its own people, has been bludgeoned and bribed (upward of $1 million in aircraft, equipment, and direct aid) into "Operation Cooperation," aimed at restricting marijuana cultivation on her own soil. Federal pot arrests are rising in number and, worse, victims are being spied upon and jailed in all corners of the nation.

In the Comprehensive Drug Abuse Prevention and Control Act of 1970, mentioned in the first chapter, marijuana fared badly. Congress listed it specifically in the classification reserved for substances most addicting (in the new nomenclature, having "high potential for abuse"), least useful ("no currently accepted medical use in treatment in the United States"), and most dangerous ("lack of accepted safety for use . . . under medical supervision"). This classification automatically calls into play the stiffest penalty structure and most repressive regulatory powers ever conferred on drug-law enforcers.

Authority to reclassify substances is placed not in any medical or scientific hands, but *in the Attorney General*. In other classifications the Attorney General is required to ask for a "scientific and medical evaluation" from the Secretary of Health, Education, and Welfare. But in the case of marijuana, Congress got around this by providing that no scientific or medical factors need be considered "if control is required by United States obligations under international treaties." (Recall Anslinger's successful coup in pressuring signatories of the 1961 Single Convention into including control requirements for cannabis.)

The full sweep of the federal enforcement powers conferred on the Attorney General by this formidable Act will be detailed when we return to assess its impact on other drugs and drug abuses, but we must note one more provision aimed specially at pot. The Act created yet another Commission on Marijuana and Drug Abuse, wholly political in composition and orientation (two senators, two congressmen, and nine presidential appointees, required to be in partisan balance but not otherwise qualified). This commission, set up in 1971 with ex-Governor Shafer of Pennsylvania as chairman, is charged with pronouncing anew on every one of the old marijuana themes. Its membership includes several people who appear elsewhere in these pages—liberally inclined Senators Hughes and Javits offset by a pair of law-and-order congressmen, an eminent pharmacologist who served on President Kennedy's Ad Hoc Panel on Drug Abuse in 1962, and Dr. Henry Brill, long-time leader of the official U.S. campaign to obscure and discredit British success in minimizing drug-abuse problems. Dozens of new studies have been commissioned by this group. Scores of witnesses have been heard. But no one expects it to do more than lament, exhort, affirm most of the status quo—and perhaps call for more research. If this prediction about the Commission's findings sounds pessimistic, here is one of President Nixon's own forecasts:

> As you know, there is a commission that is supposed to make recommendations to me about this subject, and in this instance, however, I have such strong views that I will express them. I am against legalizing marijuana. Even if this commission does recommend that it be legalized, I will not follow that recommendation. . . . I do not believe that legalizing marijuana is in the best interests of our young people and I do not think it's in the best interests of this country.

One of the new federal Bureau's most stalwart apologists, Dr. Edward R. Bloomquist, has lately turned his attentions to marijuana, assailing it as causing, in the new nomenclature, a drug-abuse pattern which includes psychological dependence, some tolerance, and undesirable side effects, and as being capable of altering perception and causing paranoid symptoms. Dr. Bloomquist adorns the pages of medical journals with references to high school students who go about saying, "I know it won't hurt me; I read about it in the library and I know," and with speculations that marijuana might cause a user to "enter a motor vehicle and . . . plow through a crowd of pedestrians." He inclines to dwell on the alleged effects of the drug on sexual responses— "releasing restraints," making the experience of orgasm "more prolonged and more intense," but at the same time asserts it is "no cure-all for impotence."

In one of his summations Dr. Bloomquist refers to President Lincoln's warning that as a nation of free men the United States will never be destroyed except by itself—"We must live through all time, or die by suicide." This, he says (now quoting Dr. B), "painted a clear picture of how drug abuse can become a national menace—a menace that clouds men's moods and deludes their thoughts."

At the risk of giving a competing author too much notice, I am constrained to go one step further in this exposure of subversion. Dr. Bloomquist is currently in print with a treatise which relies for authority on, among others, two persons identified only as attorneys but who are in fact members of the legal staff of the U.S. Narcotics Bureau itself. And his publishers note with pride that more than half a million of his reprints have been distributed to interested persons in response to requests, which is true— because the Bureau reprinted some of his pronouncements at U.S. taxpayers' expense and scattered them wherever they might have propaganda value.

Similarly distributed over the country at taxpayers' expense (to facilitate collection of a federal excise tax which no one has ever been allowed to pay) have been other reprints such as an article by a Massachusetts judge who decided one of the recent marijuana test cases in the Bureau's favor, and who concludes:

> No foreign enemy poses a greater danger to our nation than a self-imposed danger of permitting drug use to become part of our culture, and no outside force would be more destructive. Young and old must join in a common effort to remove this cancerous growth from our society, and, further, to devote all their talents and resources toward reversing the forces which would lead inexorably to the end of civilization.

Likewise handed out broadside is a slick booklet prepared by former Commissioner Giordano which attributes to marijuana such symptoms as illusions, delusions, and sensory derangements, which warns that effects of the drug on the nervous system and brain "are undoubtedly the most profound and constitute the greatest problem for the user," which says marijuana can produce psychotic episodes, and which claims that habitual use "is definitely associated with criminality, violence and insanity." Giordano, a one-time pharmacist, talks about habituation to marijuana in terms of "craving," and revives the possibility that there may be an ominous tolerance phenomenon. Pot smokers, says he, "will go to great lengths" to obtain their supply. And he warns that another dangerous aspect of habitual marijuana use "is the pattern of graduation to narcotic addiction": smoking pot develops a taste for "drug intoxication," which in turn leads many people to the use of more potent drugs—even heroin.

Further, as might be expected, the Giordano tract relies heavily on the 1961 Single Convention and on the fact that "on the advice of the Expert Committee on Dependence-Producing Drugs of the World Health Organization" marijuana was placed in a special category with heroin as being a drug "particularly liable to abuse and to produce ill effects." Thus Americans cannot now back out of their lunatic prohibition campaign against this mild substance at home because of the treaty obligation—and must keep faith with everyone abroad who was bullied into including marijuana in the Single Convention by U.S. spokesmen in the first place.

Finally, the American Medical Association has once more struck its standards and backed off. Shrugging the experience of centuries, the research and evaluations of recent decades, and the dozens of responsible studies currently under way, the AMA made headlines with a press release in April 1971 headed "Research Shows Pot Smoking Harmful":

> CHICAGO—Smoking marijuana caused serious psychological problems in 38 patients, and adversely affected the nervous systems of the heaviest smokers, reports an article in the current (April 19) *Journal of the American Medical Association.*
>
> A five-year study in human beings of effects of marijuana smoking, conducted by two Philadelphia scientists, offers documentation of significant impairment, researchers declared.
>
> Medical science for some years has suspected that pot smoking could cause more harm than realized or acknowledged. Heretofore this had been only a theory, in that it could not be substantiated by sound research in human beings. . . .

The paper thus ballyhooed as, at last, the conclusive final word resulting from "sound research" was the work of two child psychiatrists who picked over several hundred cases referred to them for therapy over a five-year period to come up with thirty-eight—twenty boys and eighteen girls between the ages of thirteen and twenty-four, including a dozen who came after being arrested for marijuana offenses. These patients had *told* the psychiatrists (that is, revealed "by history") that they smoked pot at least twice a week, were not on anything else such as speed or LSD, and had no psychiatric problems until shortly after they started using the drug. The authors did not trouble with formal neurological examinations, but observed that a few among the group staggered, had hand tremors, and went about "overshooting exits on turnpikes" and "misjudging traffic lights and stop signs at intersections." An undisclosed number were also not very good at catching baseballs or hitting basketball nets with basketballs.

Most of their subjects "consistently showed very poor social adjustment, poor attention span, poor concentration, confusion, anxiety, depression, apathy, passivity, indifference, and often, slowed and slurred speech." Altered consciousness, inability to bring thoughts together, paranoid suspiciousness, and regression toward an infantile state "were all very common." Sexual promiscuity was found to be "frequent," while the incidence of unwanted pregnancies and venereal diseases was "high." Interference with personal cleanliness, grooming, dressing, and study habits or work ("or both"), they reported, was "marked." If anything was left to be desired as to the personal cleanliness or grooming of any of the thirty-eight *before* they became smokers, the bad characteristics "were always markedly accentuated following the onset of smoking."

In one subgroup "a clear-cut diagnosis of psychosis was established." Some—"several"—were suicidal. But in some who were not so apathetic, the doctors observed that hyperactivity, aggressiveness, and a type of agitation "were common." After these generalizations the work, which fills in toto only seven AMA *Journal* pages in thus settling all questions about the subject, gets down to cases such as the following (paraphrased):

A1, 17 and female, smoked daily for a year before treatment and daily for another year while she was seeing the doctors, lost her memory and perception, thought she was a great actress, and finally tried suicide while remaining in a "pleasant mood" during and after the (suicide) effort.

A2, a 17 year old boy "seduced homosexually after an older man gradually introduced him to marijuana smoking," thought he was Messiah, but returned to normal when he was hospitalized and marijuana (and presumably the older man) were withdrawn.

A3, a 14 year old boy became, after 8 months of smoking, an active homosexual.

A4, 16, female, became preoccupied with political issues, rebelled, dropped out, and tried suicide (she had been "a quiet and socially popular girl" before smoking).

B1, 24, husband, became paranoid and impotent after two months of daily use, but returned to normal when he stopped.

B2, was a 20 year old cum laude son in the family business, until 6 months of smoking made him impotent, unambitious, and deluded into believing that he headed simultaneously both the Mafia and the KKK.

B3, 18, male, because of 3 years' smoking became preoccupied with astrology, vegetarianism and yoga; he also thought he was God; he couldn't be persuaded to quit pot, so he has "moved to the west coast and continued his unproductive, aimless life, supported financially by his parents."

B4, 19, male, smoked for 4 months and thought he could communicate with animals and was the Messiah; he continued to make high grades in school, but only "on the basis of sheer momentum of accumulated academic experience"; he shunned family and friends but went back to them upon cessation of smoking.

And so on. In the "C" category there was only one case, a popular sixteen-year-old with a B average who, a psychological tester said, might commit asocial and/or anti-social acts prior to becoming depressed in the future. The two "D" category cases were bright, neat honor-roll youngsters who began wearing old, torn, dirty clothes and dropped out of college, although one gave up pot, got his motivation back, and is now a preprofessional student. In the "E" category thirteen unmarried girls, every one virtuous before smoking, showed an "unusual degree of sexual promiscuity, which ranged from sexual relations with several individuals of the opposite sex to relations with individuals of the same sex, individuals of both sexes, and sometimes, individuals of both sexes in the same evening." Seven of the thirteen became pregnant (one or more times), four got venereal infections, five took up lesbian activities, and three tried suicide—all having lost their sexual inhibitions "after short periods of marijuana smoking."

At the end of this recitation, the AMA authors blame "equivocation by authorities in speech or writings on the innocence or dangers of marijuana," and scold parents for permissiveness:

> Several of our patients had parents who talked to the adolescent of their own curiosity about the effects of marijuana, without emphasizing its dangers, or emphasized the discrepancies in the law, without insisting that the youngster must not use marijuana or other drugs because of the serious effects that would occur. We have found that equivocation by the parents has contributed to eventual drug experimentation.

And in summation they wipe out all competing experience and conflicting authority in a single paragraph:

> We are aware that claims are made that large numbers of adolescents and young adults smoke marijuana regularly without developing symptoms or changes in academic study, but since these claims are made without the necessary accompaniment of thorough psychiatric study of each individual, they remain unsupported by scientific evidence. No judgment on the lack of development of symptoms in large, unselected populations of students or others who smoke marijuana can be made without such definitive · individual psychiatric history-taking and examination.

But let us get on to other episodes. Even in this lengthy discussion, I have barely skimmed the cynicism and hypocrisy of the marijuana story. As this is being written, for example, the mighty Treasury and Justice Departments have launched a new joint campaign to collect the old $100-per-ounce tax from persons convicted of possession within the past six years (the period of limitation) and before the Marijuana Tax Act was repealed in 1970—so possession offenders can be met at the prison gates on their release with huge (and headline-making) tax bills. Nor have I begun to catalogue all the distortions about marijuana fostered by those who have had a stake in repressing its use. Indeed, were I as free-swinging as some of the hard-liners I might construct a plausible theory that anti-marijuana pressures are coming from promoters of its natural competitors, tobacco and alcohol. There is evidence of this in the reported grumbling among brewers and bartenders. But *someone* has to draw a line somewhere.

Indisputably marijuana smoking has become very important in the United States. But respressive efforts have helped make it so. Estimates of the number of smokers are as widely varied as those which characterized the opium hysteria in 1919–21. All seem to agree that no fewer than a million—perhaps five or six million—

are occasional users on a more than single-experiment basis. Estimates of the number of regular or habitual pot smokers range from a few hundred thousand to well over the million mark.

Marijuana has unquestionably overflowed its old confines in slums and ghettos, spreading into schools and threatening to saturate "respectable" middle-class communities. Youngsters who used to make themselves sick trying cornsilk and purloined tobacco behind the barn now *do* have many counterparts retching over a daring few puffs at a joint. And where the habit penetrates, behind it comes the narcotics officer, armed with extraordinary powers, enforcing exorbitant penal statutes, and availing himself of all the most odious gutter tactics of police work, informers, bought convictions, entrapment tricks, the use of phony indictments to coerce cooperation—and far too often simple, unvarnished frame-ups. Moreover, especially since pot money is not "dirty money," like the proceeds of heroin pushing, the traffic— also far too often—must certainly nurture simple, unvarnished corruption as well.

The only bright spot is that if this nightmare grows a little worse, as the concerted efforts of our lawmakers and law enforcers seem to promise it will, then it may, one day, God willing, wake us up.

■ THIRTEEN

Chairman Kefauver and the Mafia Myth

■ RETURNING to the main strands of the narrative, as World War II approached, estimates of the addict population promulgated by the Treasury Department kept shrinking—demonstrating, of course, Treasury's effectiveness in enforcing the federal law. But as the curve continued downward it began to look as if the federal agency might be working—or at least talking—itself out of an important part of its job. Soon after Harry Anslinger assumed command in 1930, the official figure had been stabilized at around 60,000, with threatened undulations upward when the Bureau sought appropriations, and claimed declines when the efficacy of the T-men's performance was in question.

It is important to remember that because there was no contact between addicts and society other than arresting police, and because of a blackout on nonofficial information about the situation, the Bureau could assert virtually anything it wanted, with little fear of challenge. Even so, there were some apparent inconsistencies. For example, female addicts outnumbered males two or three to one at the time the Harrison Act was passed (when more valid estimates *could* be made), and this ratio had seemingly reversed itself by the end of the thirties. Similarly, white addicts had greatly outnumbered nonwhites for at least a full generation under federal controls, until suddenly the official majority turned black. And with each periodic hysteria about increases in addiction among youths there would have had to be large inputs of new addicts early in their lifespans, with the result that tens or even hundreds of thousands of female, white, and aging victims must simply have vanished conveniently when they were no longer wanted in the count.

Nor are arrest and prosecution figures very enlightening: federal cases reached a high plateau in the 1925–30 period and then curved sharply downward (from around 7,000 per year to around 3,000), while state and local authorities, emerging more prominently on the scene after 1930, accounted for a moderately increasing number of cases until the 1950's and then suddenly produced a skyrocket curve (5,000–6,000 in 1945; 33,000–35,000 by 1955). But the latter figures are unreliable because of inadequate and irregular reporting techniques, and the picture is additionally confused, after 1937, by the inclusion of marijuana cases.

In any event it is a virtual certainty that between 1940 and 1945, while war disrupted most of the globe, there was a marked decline in whatever the true level of addiction might have been, although the Bureau did not risk discounting its own importance too much, and brooked no speculation in which the figure ever got below 30,000. By 1948 Commissioner Anslinger was officially promulgating a ratio of one addict per 3,000 in the population, bringing the total back up to 45,000. Yet at this point observers began to comment on the fact that no great postwar increase in addiction had developed, and to make the heretical suggestion that drug addiction might not be so great a national hazard after all.

So the Bureau went into action. Anslinger and other spokesmen announced that addiction was once again alarmingly on the upswing and that, as always, young people were in danger of being enslaved in great numbers. Through Bureau reports and Treasury handouts, old dogma about the addict were refurbished —that "criminals use dope as a substitute for courage," that "one of the most remarkable features of the personality of the criminal addict is his tendency to induce others to become addicts," and that addicts "derive real pleasure from inducing others to follow the same vice" and are "no more useful to the community than a case of smallpox." In his familiar left-hand-right-hand pattern, U.S. Commissioner Anslinger reported to Congress and his home audience what U.N. Delegate Anslinger had himself told the international body about an alleged Japanese plot (related in 1948 but actually referring to a prewar episode):

. . . a document submitted by the representative of the United
States giving full information on the factory built by the Japanese
authorities in Mukden for the purpose of manufacturing narcotic
drugs to be distributed to the inhabitants of Manchuria. . . . Because narcotic drugs constituted and may constitute in the future a
powerful instrument of the most hideous crime against mankind,
the Commission recommended to the Economic and Social Council that steps be taken to insure that the use of narcotics as an
instrument of committing a crime of this nature be covered by the
proposed convention on the prevention and punishment of genocide.

The Bureau warned that drug addicts should not be paroled
or put on probation like other convicts because "cure of addiction
in no way includes any degree of cure with respect to the pre-
dominant criminal tendencies." And it was asserted that all the
old illicit sources which had flooded the American market before the war were opening up again and that new bases, notably
India and Hong Kong, were also becoming important. In 1949
the official line included this:

The Bureau has noticed during the past few years an alarming
increase in the number of young persons, those in their teens and
early twenties, arrested for violation of the federal marijuana and
narcotic laws in New York, Chicago, and San Francisco. . . .
There also have been an increasing number of these young narcotic
offenders who admit starting the use of narcotics with marijuana,
then after a short while changing to the more powerful narcotics
such as heroin, morphine and cocaine.

And now the Bureau began pushing a new notion, that at this
time the threatening increases in the drug traffic were due to
soft-hearted judges and ought to be met by drastic increases in
the length of sentences imposed on convicted drug-law offenders.
The idea that long prison sentences are per se an effective
deterrent is an oversimplification which has been fought by
enlightened penologists since the turn of the century. Besides
assaulting the discretion (and, indeed, the integrity) of the
judiciary, it grounds in the patent distortion that longer terms
meted out to those who have run the whole course of detection,
apprehension, prosecution, and conviction will deter other *potential* offenders. Planners of crime worry about *being caught.*
Police—including Anslinger's dope cops and their successors
today—deter crime by making apprehension swift, accurate,
and certain, not by cutting corners or beating the drums for
savage punishments. Instead of allowing judges to fit sentences

to the circumstances of each offender as well as to his offense, and instead of giving comparatively new rehabilitation aids like presentence investigation, probation, and parole a chance to play their parts in the process, the thrust of this Anslinger-originated nonsense was to force the hands of the judges indiscriminately in all cases by reviving statutory mandatory minimums.

This was the T-men's new campaign, and to some extent the entire aftermath of attacks on judges in general, and latterly on Supreme Court justices in particular, for "coddling" criminals, may be traceable to this badly motivated beginning.

In 1950, on the eve of the Kefauver investigation, the Bureau shifted emphasis slightly to report that the "rising increase" in the use of narcotics by youngsters now involved primarily "young hoodlums." The nation was responding to the newfound menace of juvenile delinquency, and accordingly the official line was modified:

> The Bureau is giving particular attention to this disturbing situation and is convinced that the majority of the young persons encountered in the narcotic traffic are of the hoodlum type and not school children. When arrested for a narcotic violation many of these young persons are found to have prior arrests for violations other than narcotics.

And by 1950 the harsh-punishment theme was being sounded insistently:

> Stiff penitentiary sentences for convicted purveyors of narcotics would assist materially in checking this increased use of narcotics by young persons since it would not only remove those persons from the traffic for a considerable period of time, but would act as a deterrent to others who might contemplate engaging in this nefarious traffic.

Contemporaneously the Bureau missed no opportunity to stir up excitement at the state level. Witness the following, from an alarming report by a Special Study Commission in New Jersey:

> When the present narcotic menace first arose, Governor Alfred E. Driscoll was one of the first Chief Executives of any State in the country to take action. . . .
> The United States is fortunate in having as its leader in the fight against the illicit narcotic traffic one man who stands out like a beacon, the outstanding authority in the world on the subject and the finest type of public official, Commissioner Harry J. Anslinger of the Federal Bureau of Narcotics. The Commissioner

and his associates are career men dedicated to their work and completely unselfish in their devotion to duty.

When this Commission commenced its work, the first thing that was done was to solicit the assistance and advice of the Commissioner and the members of his department. The response was immediate, and the subsequent efforts to aid us were completely unselfish and untiring. The citizens of our country are fortunate in having Commissioner Anslinger lead this fight, and we wish gratefully to acknowledge the fatherly assistance which he has given to us.

The tough-penalty campaign bore fruit on Capitol Hill in 1950, as we have already related in the marijuana chronicle, when one of Anslinger's strongest supporters, Congressman Hale Boggs, introduced his bill to increase all drug-offense penalties, with mandatory minimums of two years for a first offense, five years for a second offense, and ten (to twenty) for third and subsequent repetitions. The Bureau immediately endorsed this as being "of material assistance in the fight against the narcotic traffic."

When the Kefauver Committee (Special Senate Committee to Investigate Organized Crime in Interstate Commerce) got under way the following year, Commissioner Anslinger was one of its earliest official witnesses. He testified that his Bureau's enforcement of the narcotic laws for the past generation had reduced the problem by half, but went on immediately to warn that there had been recent marked increases in addiction, "mainly among young hoodlums." He told the Committee that addicts always tend to make more addicts, and avowed that most addicts "cannot be cured by any means presently known."

Interestingly, in view of what we shall see in a moment about his proprietorship of the Mafia, on this first Crime Committee appearance Anslinger said that the distribution of illegal drugs in the United States was being accomplished "sometimes by individuals, but more generally by organizations of greater or less complexity." Some individuals were simply associated in the relation of buyer and seller, and sometimes they were in a common conspiracy to distribute drugs, but he explained how they might shift from one organization to another "and intermittently in and out of the traffic."

Not a word about Mafia. He said that characters like "Waxey" Gordon, "Legs" Diamond, and "Lepke" Buchalter dipped into narcotics from time to time, along with (the only Italian in the roster) "Lucky" Luciano.

At the time of this testimony, the underworld organization which had been receiving most attention, and which currently most fascinated and terrified the general public, was Murder, Inc., and—sure enough—Anslinger told the Committee that Murder, Inc., was not only an interstate but actually an inter-country and intercontinent drug-pushing organization, "obtaining its supplies in China and distributing them from New York throughout the country, particularly to the Southwest." He said his Bureau estimated that Murder, Inc., "smuggled into this country and distributed enough narcotics to supply one-fifth of the entire addict population."

After giving the senators some typical Bureau anecdotes— "shot to death while sleeping in his mother's home," "blood on the seat and brain tissue on the dashboard," "killed by a shotgun blast before the eyes of his 15-year-old daughter"—Anslinger concluded that the narcotics traffic feeds on the slow murder of its customers, and urged as his principal recommendation that increasingly severe sentences should be imposed on all drug offenders, with, typically, a bootstrap reference to statements he himself had planted in various international proceedings: "Both the League of Nations and the United Nations have recommended more severe sentences as one of the best methods to suppress the traffic."

As a result of this testimony and subsequent hammering on the same theme, the Kefauver Crime Committee adopted the reintroduced Boggs bill as one of its own recommendations in 1951, and the 82nd Congress enacted it. So instead of *maximum* sentences of up to two years for most drug offenses and increased maximums only for repeaters, federal judges found themselves compelled to give *at least* two, five, and ten years (two to five, five to ten, and ten to twenty) for each succeeding conviction in a drug category, with, moreover, no possibility of using the alternatives of suspended sentence or parole for second and subsequent offenses, though such devices remained available for all other convicted defendants, including traitors and murderers. The American Bar Association and other concerned groups fought the Boggs Act, but to no avail. In 1951 anything that made lawmakers look tough in the view of their frightened and confused constituents was sure-fire; there was not so much as a murmur of dissent in either house as this lamentable measure went through.

Without denying that the Kefauver hearings had *some* worth, at least in dramatizing the broad significance of so-called orga-

nized crime to American TV viewers, it must be noted, nonetheless, that (a) not a single Crime Committee recommendation
except the Boggs Act became law (until Attorney General
Kennedy picked three or four up, without attribution, a dozen
years later); (b) the Committee uncovered nothing which was
not already documented, and often stale besides, in some police
file or newspaper morgue; (c) arch-villains like Costello and
Accardo were virtually created for their roles by Committee-
initiated publicity before being presented on the screen; and
(d) after a seemly wait for the "heat" to subside, many of the
same operations were revived in the same locales, often with the
same underworld figures apparently in control.

I have doubtless assumed a heavy enough burden by arguing
in these pages that the American drug experience reflects so
much folly and fraud. But I do not back away from the inference
that related areas, including much of the crime-control spectrum
and especially the "organized crime" field, are similarly tainted.
The unfolding of the Mafia story—which I believe to be largely
fiction—illustrates this.

"Mafia" is supposed to be an acronym from a cry of protest
that arose spontaneously all over Sicily on March 30, 1282, when
a French soldier of the then-occupying forces raped a young
bride in a church in Palermo on that day (and no other). Its
existence as a force in American life was first suggested in 1893,
to justify the lynching of a dozen Italians by a New Orleans mob
after they had been found not guilty in a trial for murdering
a popular New Orleans police officer named David Hennessy,
who had died in the arms of his faithful lieutenant, Billy O'Con-
nor, murmuring, "They got me, Bill." The wily Sicilians thereupon stayed out of sight so successfully that their next significant appearance anywhere on the scene was in Cleveland in
1928, where a group of twenty-three persons, most of them
obviously Italian and described as "alleged Mafia leaders," were
arrested in a downtown hotel, found to be in possession of firearms, and made the subject of a group photograph.

Again there was a long lapse, punctuated only by a few
Sunday-supplement references to "Black Hand Societies" in immigrant ghettos, until the late 1940's, when Mafia stories began
to turn up once more. But this time the sinister Italian conspiracy emerged as the exclusive creature of the Narcotics
Bureau. The Mafia concept suited the Bureau ideally as a backdrop for its own image-building. It had mysterious foreign roots,
overtones of danger and violence, and an exotic quality akin to

that of the Chinese tongs, which had been so successfully (and undeservedly) associated with opium dens a quarter century earlier. And indisputably there *were* identifiable Italian-Americans more or less prominently connected with criminal enterprises throughout the country. Many had drifted into bootlegging and learned how to operate in the so-called rackets during the 1920's when, as recent immigrants, there were not many comparable opportunities available to them in the upperworld.

The Mafia provided Commissioner Anslinger with another answer to Director Hoover, whose FBI was still upstaging competing enforcement agencies by glamorizing *individuals* as wartime master-spies, communist agents, and candidates for its Ten Most Wanted list. Obviously a full-blown international secret society, played up as an evil adversary that the Bureau had to battle constantly, offered propaganda advantages surpassing those of even the most glamorous single malefactor.

In this connection it is noteworthy that Hoover and his G-men scorned the Mafia and deprecated all suggestions that there was any such thing until the early 1960's, when Attorney General Kennedy unearthed Joe Valachi and took the concept away from Treasury by renaming it Cosa Nostra. After that a total and impenetrable monopoly of all revelations about Cosa Nostra was maintained by Justice's FBI for nearly a decade, until some protesting citizens of Italian ancestry forced Attorney General Mitchell to drop the entire matter forthwith—whereupon their leader was felled in a 1971 on-camera shooting that was as improbable, bizarre, and police-dominated as the 1963 Ruby-Oswald execution in Dallas. But the ramifications of *that* are indeed beyond the compass of these pages.

As has been noted, at the beginning of the Kefauver hearings Anslinger not only made no references to the Mafia, but pointedly credited the illicit drug traffic to persons and organizations with non-Italian names and no ties to tiny Sicily. Throughout its early proceedings, the Crime Committee itself talked about the "mob" or the "crime syndicate," and played no favorites as among Irish, Jewish, Italian, or, for that matter, melting-pot overlords of crime. But the seeds were being sown, and the Mafia story was taking shape largely from Narcotics Bureau revelations.

Anslinger's anecdotes of Bureau conquests, alluded to a few pages back (brain tissue on the dashboard, remember?), turned up verbatim in the Kefauver Committee's famous Third Interim

Report early in 1951, and according to the Bureau, as quoted by the Committee:

> It is almost inevitable that the Mafia should take an important part in American criminal rackets. Here is a nation-wide organization of outlaws in a sort of oath-bound, blood-cemented brotherhood dedicated to complete defiance of the law where personal advantage or interests are concerned. Here is a more or less permanently established network, an organized maze of underground conduits, always ready and available when racket enterprise is to be furthered. The organization is such that a member in one part of the country can, with perfect confidence, engage in any sort of illicit business with members in any other section of the country.

Observing that it was very difficult to obtain any reliable data about Mafia operations, the Senate Committee produced the 1928 Cleveland group picture as "one notable concrete piece of evidence." It deemed ominously significant the fact that one of the Italians who had appeared in that photograph twenty-three years earlier, and who had been revealed to the Committee "by the experts" to be a top Mafia leader, was unable to give a satisfactory explanation of his presence at the Cleveland gathering when interrogated by Chairman Kefauver two decades later. It also deemed significant its discovery that virtually all witnesses of Italian extraction denied knowledge of the Mafia, denied being members of it, and sometimes openly ridiculed the notion, which denials the Committee characterized as "patently absurd."

At this point, the Kefauver Committee put itself on record as "inclined to agree with the opinion of experienced police officers and narcotics agents" that the Mafia dominated the American crime scene, with extensive international ramifications:

> The Mafia is a secret conspiracy against law and order which will ruthlessly eliminate anyone who stands in the way of its success in any criminal enterprise in which it is interested. It will destroy anyone who betrays its secrets. It will use any means available—political influence, bribery, intimidation, etc., to defeat any attempt on the part of law enforcement to touch its top figures or to interfere with its operations.

Anslinger could scarcely have asked for more.

But when the Crime Committee's Final Report came out a few months later it contained a central section on drugs tuned to near-hysteria, and it restated virtually every item of Bureau cant even more strongly:

The illegal traffic in narcotic drugs exemplifies organized crime at its devastating worst. It represents one of the great tragedies of our times, especially when it preys upon young people who are ignorant of the effects of drug addiction not only upon themselves as individuals but upon family and society as a whole. Addiction resulting from an ignorant or depraved attempt to obtain temporary pleasure is an inexcusable tragedy. Drug addiction is a form of contagious disease with a high recurrence. . . .

Against this backdrop of tragedy, the picture of the dope peddler promoting drug addiction in order to create new customers is nothing short of revolting. . . . In the past 24 months, America has been jolted to its foundations by the discovery that youngsters, especially in the larger cities, are using narcotic drugs, many to the point of addiction. New York, Chicago, Baltimore, and Washington, D.C. saw big increases in the number of underaged drug users coming to the attention of the police. In a large number of cases, these young people were engaging in crime for the sole purpose of supporting their drug habit.

The Committee recounted (and this is still 1951) the sad stories of a nineteen-year-old boy who threw away a scholarship at an eastern university because of drugs, a midwestern freshman who dropped out in his first semester and stole money from the mails—"all because of dope," a group of collegians who grew marijuana in their backyard, and girls in their late teens with narcotic habits who admitted resorting to prostitution "rather than endure the horror of going without drugs." From Harlem came reports that 50 per cent of all members of youthful street gangs smoked marijuana, including youths of thirteen; indeed, even some nine-year-olds had reportedly been approached by peddlers attempting to have them take drugs.

On the Mafia, the Final Report summed up in these fulsome terms:

Experienced enforcement officers believe that the present influx of heroin from abroad is managed by the Mafia with Charles "Lucky" Luciano, notorious gangster, vice king, and racketeer, deported convict, now resident in Italy, as the operating head. . . . Worldwide in scope, the Mafia is believed to derive the major source of its income from the distribution and smuggling of narcotics. An undercover agent of the Treasury Department's Bureau of Narcotics testified at length before the Committee just after his return from an extended assignment in Italy. Asked whether Luciano is the kingpin of the Mafia, the agent responded that if "Lucky" isn't the kingpin, "he is one of the Royal Family," that he receives large sums of money from American gangsters and that he certainly wields influence in Mafia policy matters.

The only area in which Bureau control of the Kefauver findings slipped a little was in the matter of public education.
Anslinger's violent insistence that any dissemination of public
information about drugs would stir up curiosity and cause addiction was resisted by the Committee, which recommended a
cautious program to inform people of "true facts." Responsibility
was placed on the nation's educators, who were exhorted to
start information programs in the schools, and although there
were no immediate changes, this marked a turning point; gradually in the following decade, there were the beginnings of a
few serious assaults on Bureau-fostered ignorance about the drug
problem.

The Committee recommended that Commissioner Anslinger's
force of agents be doubled and that his Bureau's appropriations
be substantially increased. Even the communist menace was
given a drug tie-in in the Final Report. Although, it noted, most
nations were willing to help control the production of opium
poppies, "there is some doubt as to the attitude of Communist
China"; and moreover, when the United States representative on
the U.N. Commission (Anslinger, of course) called attention to
heroin manufacture in Communist China, "the Russian delegate
tried unsuccessfully to have his remarks stricken from the
record."

■ FOURTEEN

Lawyers, Doctors, and
Senator Daniel

■ THE DECADE of the fifties, following the Crime Committee investigation which opened it, saw some more heavyweight matches. In prior years the Bureau had been challenged only by individuals, Linders and Ratigans and Lindesmiths—and by solitary Congressman Coffee. But now some important national groups began stirring themselves. The legal profession, through the American Bar Association, began taking an interest in drug-law enforcement, and for the first time raised questions about Commissioner Anslinger's empire. The American Medical Association waxed bolder than it had at any time since World War I, and appeared almost ready to step in and assert some of its prerogatives. There were whisperings of rebellion in the ranks of the Public Health Service. At one point it even looked as if Congress might take a critical new look. And the hitherto inviolate Treasury agency began coming under sporadic fire from enlightened sectors of the press.

In 1952 a skillful free-lancer, Alden Stevens, drawn to the subject by the plight of a friend caught in addiction, attacked the Bureau head-on in a popular journal under the title "Make Dope Legal." At the same time a dean of the medical profession, Dr. Hubert S. Howe, and two eminent colleagues, Dr. Herbert Berger and Dr. Andrew A. Eggston, began campaigning for re-establishment of control of drug addiction by medical practitioners, and the latter team persuaded the New York Academy of Medicine to adopt a reform proposal which became known as the Berger-Eggston Plan.

A parade of articles and tracts followed: "Should We Legalize Narcotics?," "We're Bungling the Narcotics Problem," "How Much of a Menace Is the Drug Menace?," "The Dope Addict— Criminal or Patient?," "This Problem of Narcotic Addiction— Let's Face It Sensibly," and (from the great Lawrence Kolb), "Let's Stop This Narcotics Hysteria!" The Bureau countered with a stream of handouts and reprints of its own, patronizing anyone who appeared to be a spokesman for its viewpoint and using the prestige and resources of the Treasury Department to disseminate favorable material by inundating the country with pamphlets. Commissioner Anslinger joined the fray, contributing statements and articles and participating in the authorship of two books, *The Traffic in Narcotics* (with William F. Tompkins) and *The Murderers* (with Will Oursler).

In 1954 the American Bar Association created a special Committee on Narcotics, and early in 1955, on recommendation of this body, the ABA House of Delegates passed a resolution calling on Congress to re-examine the Harrison Act and make a full review of federal enforcement policies developed under it. Notwithstanding that the Kefauver investigation had terminated only three years before, the U.S. Senate responded with astonishing alacrity. The Bar Association action was taken February 21, 1955, and *on the same day* Senator Price Daniel of Texas introduced S. Res. 60, to authorize the Senate Judiciary Committee "to conduct a full and complete study of the narcotics problem in the United States, including ways and means of improving the Federal Criminal Code and other laws and enforcement procedures dealing with possession, sale, and transportation of narcotics, marijuana and similar drugs."

The special subcommittee which the resolution proposed was to have subpoena powers and authority to hold hearings anywhere in the United States. By moving so fast, Senator Daniel assured control of the ensuing investigation for himself, since the initiating sponsor is customarily named chairman. His resolution passed the Senate on March 18.

Though in retrospect it seems clear that challengers of the Bureau never had much of a chance—and quite possibly that Anslinger chose Daniel and called *all* the shots from the outset —there was, or appeared to be, spirited in-fighting, in the beginning, over the way the investigation was to be set up and staffed. Friends of the ABA and others who hoped the sub-committee might throw fresh light on the subject tried to see to it that there would be representation of neutral and in-quiring viewpoints. But they were outmaneuvered. The Senator, it soon appeared, was mainly interested in building a record in Texas to further the campaign which he planned to make for the governorship of that state (and did make, successfully, the following year). Originally there were two other members, fair-minded Senator O'Mahoney of Wyoming, who was pre-vented from taking an active role because of illness, and Senator Welker of Idaho; subsequently Senators Eastland of Mississippi and Butler of Maryland were added.

The post of counsel went to a mild Capitol Hill hanger-on, kin and protégé of a venerable House chairman. But in the critical job of chief investigator, from which the real power was wielded, there turned up a Daniel fellow Texan, W. Lee Speer, with eighteen years of service in the Bureau of Narcotics, oblig-ingly loaned to the subcommittee by Commissioner Anslinger.

It was obvious from the first moments of the opening hearings, on June 2, 1955, that Anslinger had been hard at work, and that anyone who hoped the investigation might truly illuminate the drug scene was going to be disappointed. Senator Daniel began with the chairman and counsel of a special committee that had been hastily set up in the *Canadian* Senate on February 24, 1955 (note the date), to inquire into the narcotic drug situation in Canada, particularly with respect to Vancouver, B.C., where efforts had recently been made to treat addicts noncriminally through a modified clinic system.

As Anslinger watched, beaming, the Canadian visitors read statements which so parroted dogma of the U.S. Bureau that it sounded suspiciously as if they had been written in Washington, with interpolations such as: "Especially to Commissioner An-slinger, may I say one word to you, that he is considered by us as one of the greatest authorities, you, Commissioner Anslinger, on the narcotic drug problem in the entire world." This Canadian recitation set the tone. Addicts are criminals ("the majority had criminal records before becoming involved with drugs") and mere incarceration was not enough ("the only practical and re-alistic solution to the problem is the compulsory isolation and quarantine of the addict population in suitable treatment and rehabilitation facilities"). The Canadians reported that the Vancouver Chief of Police had recommended putting all drug addicts on a remote island for treatment "which would include a work program."

In 1952, with the advent of the Eisenhower administration, the Treasury Department had initiated a move to tighten its lines of control over drug-law enforcement within the federal bureaucracy itself. Informal meetings were set up between Commissioner Anslinger and second-echelon representatives from State, Justice, H.E.W., and Defense (the latter because of alleged concern over addiction among U.S. troops in Korea). In 1954 this consultative group was transformed into a formal Interdepartmental Committee on Narcotics; the same spokesmen continued to meet and the venture was still dominated by Treasury, but the group was now even more valuable as another echo of the Bureau's official line.

So the first witness after the Canadians was the chairman of this interdepartmental committee, an Assistant Secretary of the Treasury. After appropriate homages to Anslinger ("uniquely qualified to provide you with accurate information concerning all phases of the narcotics problem"), he affirmed the current official estimate that the addict population of the country was only about 50,000, and then picked a middle course between discounting notes of hysteria, on the one hand, and leaving any impression that the Bureau had not been doing its job with maximum efficacy, on the other:

> Popular indignation has been understandably aroused over reports that the illicit drug traffic has extended to youngsters of school age. I believe that the experts who will testify on this point will bring out the fact that reports of any large number of such cases have not been substantiated; yet the fact that any at all exist is shocking, and amply justifies the public's determination to correct such a situation.

Then Anslinger himself described how his Bureau had reduced addiction from one in 400 persons before the Harrison Act to one in 1,500 persons at the end of World War I, and currently to about one in 3,000—or the previously given total of 50,000 to 60,000. He reported that his name-and-address list of "active" addicts had grown to 28,514, with approximately 1,000 new names being added each month, coupled with the inconsistent assertion that every user of illicit drugs came inevitably to the attention of some police authority within two years after acquiring his habit. He provided last-digit figures for each major city—New York, 7,937; Los Angeles, 6,975; Chicago, 1,896; etc.—and stated that addiction among adolescents had been a major problem after World War II but had reached its peak in 1951 and had since significantly abated.

Although most addicts "are likely to be well-schooled in crime before they turn to drug addiction," the rest, he avowed, inevitably turn to vice, shoplifting, and petty thievery to assuage their cravings, and thereafter quickly graduate to "major crimes." Accordingly, penal institutions provide the only answer, to "make us safe from criminal drug addicts and drug peddlers by keeping these undesirable people off the streets and out of further criminal activity." As for treatment programs not depending on confinement: "The American Medical Association, the National Research Council, the United Nations Commission on Narcotic Drugs, and other authorities on the subject of addiction have stated that drug addiction cannot be cured by ambulatory means."

When it was pointed out to the Commissioner, in questioning, that a contemporaneous study done for the Attorney General of California had found a total of no fewer than 20,000 addicts in that state alone, he responded:

Now, that committtee that made that report made a guess. They made a guess based on the number of arrests, figuring that so many peddlers had so many customers. Well, you get into fantastic figures when you try that sort of thing. . . . That report on California, I must say, was probably based on the number of arrests multiplied by a given figure which, after all, is not accurate. We are giving you accurate information, Senator, that has come to our attention, come to the knowledge of the authorities, city, state, and Federal, up to this time.

In the questioning he was also able to play up another main theme—that heroin production was being officially encouraged in Red China "to cause destruction and deterioration among people in the free countries to which this drug is being sent."

At one point there was a notable disclosure of the Bureau's *real* attitude toward persons who are merely addicted, as opposed to the usual protestations that federal authorities only go after big-time peddlers:

Now, we often find the courts will say, "Well, now, I have here this poor drug addict. He only peddles to take care of himself." Well, I hope the honorable Senators are not taken in with that sort of thing, because that addict will peddle a capsule or he will peddle a kilo or a thousand ounces or a ton if he can. Now, 70 percent of those we send to prison are addicts. . . . You should make no distinction, and I will be challenged on this plenty, and you will hear a lot of testimony to the contrary.

From this opening the Daniel Subcommittee embarked on a junket, holding hearings in Philadelphia, New York, Los Angeles, San Francisco, Chicago, Detroit, Cleveland—and, of course, Austin, San Antonio, Ft. Worth, Houston, and Dallas. Hundreds of witnesses, consisting mostly of an interminable parade of law-enforcement officers, filled a record of more than 8,000 pages. The Subcommittee circularized prosecutors, sheriffs and police chiefs in every major city it did not visit.

Woven through volume after volume of anecdotal material and dire warnings were two tough themes: even the severe mandatory sentences prescribed by the Boggs Act were insufficient, since the solution to all problems was stiffer punishment for all offenders; and addicts who could not otherwise be imprisoned were nevertheless "contagious" and ought to be removed from normal contacts with society unless and until they cured themselves. In the hundreds of pages of testimony heard in Texas, smuggling on the Mexican border was highlighted out of proportion, and marijuana came in for exaggerated condemnation.

■ FIFTEEN

New York, September 1955

■ IN THE MIDST of all this, a day and a half were set aside by the Daniel Subcommittee to give critics and dissenters a hearing. Although most of the witnesses came from Washington, this session was held in New York, because congressional hearings held out of the capital usually receive less notice from the official community and the national media.

Dr. Hubert Howe opened the session, asserting that opiate addiction is seldom curable, that no program would succeed if it simply filled larger penal institutions with more addicts, and that imprisoning addicts for any period less than life only brings them into contact with other addicts and criminals, thus defeating its own purpose. When Dr. Howe observed that persons who believe addicts under the influence of opiates to be dangerous are totally misled—probably because of common familiarity with the effects of alcohol—he was interrupted:

> Senator Daniel. Doctor, what about those addicts who commit heinous crimes such as murder for pay, and robbery and burglary, and take the drug in order to get them into a mental state in order to preclude worry about what they are doing?

> Dr. Howe. Well, that has been stated, but there is no definitive evidence that anything like that occurs as far as opiates go. Opiates are sedatives. If they take enough of them they put them to sleep.

When he said addiction is a disease which should be cared for

125

by doctors, "but doctors have been scared away by the Federal Bureau," he was interrupted again:

Senator Butler. Doctor, is it your testimony that an addict who has a supply of drugs sufficient to keep him from experiencing pain and suffering that he would experience without that drug could be a useful citizen and pursue a normal occupation?

Dr. Howe. In a great many instances that is the fact. We see it right now. . . . There is evidence in all countries of that, that given a small amount of drugs, enough to prevent withdrawal symptoms, many of these individuals—and there is even further than that, there is medical evidence that suggests that some psychopathic individuals are better off with the drugs than they are when you take them away from them. . . .

Senator Butler. Would you say the alcoholic is much more of a potential threat to society than the addict?

Dr. Howe. No question about it. That goes without question.

Senator Daniel. Well no, Doctor, you might have said something a moment ago that you did not mean exactly as it was said, that the drug addict, when he had his heroin or his morphine, that he then is restored to a normal situation as far as he is concerned, and, therefore, he can go about his business just as anyone else.

Dr. Howe. That is right.

Senator Daniel. Now, is that an accurate statement?

Dr. Howe. That is right . . .

Senator Daniel. Which is right, I do not know? I hope we will have enough statistics here to help us clear up the matter. But now, if you have two people with the same mental faculties, one under enough heroin or morphine to take care of his addiction, and the other person not addicted at all, not under the influence of any type of opiate, what would be his mental faculties as compared with a person, a normal person, without any opiates?

Dr. Howe. Well, he is quiet, he is comfortable, and he wants to be let alone. He will do his job; he has no enemies or anything . . .

Senator Daniel. Doctor, would you let the individual under the influence of an opiate, for instance, drive automobiles? Today a person under the influence of alcohol would not be permitted to do that.

Dr. Howe. No.

Senator Daniel. What about the person under the influence of heroin or morphine?

Dr. Howe. Well, of course, if he had enough to put him to sleep, he wouldn't. But the ordinary dose, they could drive an automobile just as well as anybody else could.

Senator Daniel. If they had the ordinary minimum dose?

Dr. Howe. That is right.

Senator Daniel. To make them comfortable? You think it would be safe to put them out on a street to drive an automobile?

Dr. Howe. I certainly do.

As we noted earlier, Dr. Howe had been associated with the New York Academy proposal to provide drugs to addicts by direct administration in something like clinic facilities; this was anathema to the Bureau, and the senators got on him about it before the doctor brought it up:

Senator Butler. There has been some evidence here that some people become addicts simply to keep the addict comfortable or keep him company, or just to get in the swim, so to speak. Now, if it becomes generally known that addiction would be aided, and anybody who becomes an addict can always be kept in the happy and comfortable position of being satisfied, wouldn't you have a great tendency on the part of the addict to induce others to come in by simply saying, "Well, here it is a wonderful thing and a wonderful sensation, and there is no harm, you don't take any chances now. You can come in and keep this going, and live in this beautiful state all your life at public expense." Doesn't that multiply your addicts?

Dr. Howe. No. Let me tell you the answer to that, which is this: We believe very decidedly that if you afforded all the present addicts their drugs through a doctor, they cannot get it any place else, that that would, to a large extent, destroy the black market. If you undersell them, if there is no profit at all in narcotic drugs, the black market cannot live and thrive. You say, "Oh, well, they will make new ones." Well, they can't live much on trying to induce—

Senator Butler. I know you may drive the black market, but the addict who talks to his brother or his sister or some member of the family and says, "This is a wonderful sensation," let us put the profit motive out of it—here is a man who wants to live in this limbo, or whatever you want to call it—

Dr. Howe. Where is he going to get his drugs?

Senator Butler. . . . and induces him to become an addict, with the assurance that he will never suffer the pains of the lack of the opiates.

Dr. Howe. May I ask you this: Where will they get their drugs?

Senator Butler. He would get it from your clinics, would he not?

Dr. Howe. No, he wouldn't. Nobody could get that unless they had had a hospital examination and been referred to a clinic and told how much he could have. That is what was brought up—

Senator Butler. Doctor, is it not a fact that you would give to the addict—you would not give him enough to make him come back every 4 or 5 hours, you would give him enough for every 20 hours. If he wanted to share that with his little brother, he could probably do that.

Dr. Howe. Well, that is a matter of administrative detail. On the whole, the idea would be, to start with anyway, probably to give everyone of them by hypo. He would have no drug. He could not spread it around to anybody else, and we believe that there are certain ways that these drugs can be made to last longer, that you can give him one hypo a day, just as we have insulin, that lasts over several periods, and he could—you see, that could quite easily be done. He would go to a clinic once a day, and he would get enough drugs to keep him comfortable for 24 hours.

Senator Butler. If he shares that with his neighbor—

Dr. Howe. How can he share it with his neighbor when it is in his arm? . . .

Senator Daniel. We are going to let you go right on. The only reason we have asked you these questions is to try to develop the entire picture, and I want you to know that we are certainly going to question the witnesses who oppose this view the same way we are questioning you.

Dr. Howe. I welcome them. It is not that I am trying to insist that this is the thing to do. If anybody else can suggest anything better, I am glad, but nobody that I know of has come up with anything except "Put them in jail; cut their heads off; do anything." Now, of course, as I have frequently said, that would be one good way to get rid of tuberculosis. If you took everybody with tuberculosis and put them in a gas chamber, there would be no tuberculosis.

Senator Daniel. The one thing the Chairman is prepared to agree with you on is that we are not solving the problem of drug addiction in this country today as we should.

After more peppering, Dr. Howe came to the basic rationale behind the New York Academy proposal:

Many people recoil with horror at the suggestion of furnishing low-cost drugs to addicts, even under the best system of supervision which our Government can devise. For those of us who want to pass laws prohibiting everything undesirable, and many Americans seem to, it is a thoroughly startling idea. The public has yet to grasp the fact that addicts are dangerous when they are without their drugs, not when they are with them. They do not realize that in Britain this problem has been solved. The question, therefore, clearly is: Why should we have narcotic laws, the practical effect of which is to force people to rob, steal, proselyte, and prostitute, in order to support their habit, especially when the need for criminal activity can be prevented for a few cents worth of drugs per addict, per day? . . .

One may also consider that, after 40 years of the Harrison Act, the addict still obtains his drug, unless he is in the strictest form of incarceration.

We are not saying to give the addicts more drugs. We are simply advising a different method of distribution. The Government says he cannot get it legally; therefore, he has got to steal and rob, and so on, in order to get it.

Well, he gets it, but we believe there is a better method of distribution than that. We are not in any way advocating that they get more than they need. But every addict gets his drug right now. As I say, unless he is in jail, every addict gets his drug, and many of them get it in jail, at least they do in New York.

Why not let him have his minimum requirement under licensed medical supervision, rather than force him to get it by criminal activities, through criminal channels? We now have, in the narcotic black market, a matchless machine for the manufacture of criminals. Isn't it about time we looked over the horizon to see how the problem has been solved elsewhere?

But the senators kept snapping away at him. How could anyone respond to psychiatric guidance or other treatment while he was under the influence of opiates? How could an addict on drugs hold a job? Who would hire him, knowing he is an addict? If an addict gets a job, isn't he likely to go on pushing dope— "or would your plan just supply everybody?" What about cocaine and marijuana?

> *Dr. Howe.* I do not think that amounts to much. In the first place, the black market in cocaine here in New York anyway amounts to very little now because it is too expensive. Sure, you will have marijuana, and you will have alcohol, and you will have some of these other things, but I do not think—I think these can be controlled. Marijuana is not an addicting drug. They like it. Many people have told me they prefer it to alcohol because they get about the same effect, and it is cheaper. They can get a good drunk for fifty cents, and it costs them more than that to get the same effect through alcohol.

Senator Daniel. But it is habit-forming.

Dr. Howe. No, it is not.

Senator Daniel. Marijuana?

Dr. Howe. No, it is not a habit-forming drug. Neither is cocaine. . . .

Senator Butler. But the main prop of your plan is the ability of
these addicts to be employed profitably?

Dr. Howe. That is right.

Senator Butler. And I seriously doubt—

Dr. Howe. That is right.

Senator Butler (continuing) . . . that that is a reality.

Dr. Howe. That could—that is a reality, and I am sure that it
would work.

Senator Daniel. While they were still on the drug?

Dr. Howe. That is right, while they were still on the drug, an ordinary amount. We often have difficulty in telling—somebody
would send an addict up to me—is he on drugs or isn't he? He
comes in, he is perfectly normal in every way that I can see.
You examine him and you find that he has some scars on his
arm. You do not know whether he is taking drugs freely or
whether is is not. . . .

Senator Daniel. Doctor, what would be wrong with isolating these
addicts, like you do those who have leprosy or those with mental
illnesses? Your program would call for a new set of laws in the
country, both state and Federal. What would be wrong with a
new set of laws that would follow your suggestion on not brand-
ing them as criminals, if that is all that they have ever done,
but getting them in some kind of an institution or farm or something where they cannot spread their addiction to other people,
and where you can try to do all these things about treating
them and rehabilitating them?

Dr. Howe. Well, they have talked of all kinds of Devil's Islands
and everything else for these people. But you must realize, as
I say, that addicts are not a homogenous group. They are everything from doctors and lawyers and ministers and everything
else all the way down, and I do not think you could very well
establish a Devil's Island and put them all there. What they
need is to be gotten back into society, gotten back where they
can hold down jobs.

Senator Daniel. The incurable ones?

Dr. Howe. Sure, sure. They can work. What did all these clinics say? They furnished them with their drugs; they all worked. They supported their families. The minute that the clinics were closed up, the whole thing disappeared. They went back underground; they got their drugs, they lost their jobs, they were put in jail, and they died in jail, and all that kind of thing. But they worked perfectly well in each one of these.

Following Dr. Howe an outspoken judge told the Subcommittee:

Common sense and experience dictate that habits cannot be controlled or cured by the criminal law. As Mr. Bumble in Charles Dickens' *Oliver Twist* said, "If the law supposes that, the law is an ass." . . . One thing I believe is that the medical profession is ahead of the law. They proceed on the basis of individual diagnosis and treatment and not mass-prescription. . . . I say it is a medical problem. Turn it over to the doctors, and if you give them the authority to do so, then their laboratories will go to work, they will try to find cures and use the money that you now use—that you waste, not use—that you waste in law enforcement, use it for education.

Then the Subcommittee heard Dr. Eggston, for the Medical Society of the State of New York, who supported the Academy plan and urged the establishment of narcotic service clinics to distribute drugs free of charge, with proper safeguards and in connection with rehabilitation efforts. A spokesman for the American Bar Association followed, endorsing the dissenters:

For 40 years we have been looking for ways to make the existence of the narcotic drug addict just as tough as possible. For 40 years we have asked only what new penalties, what new police techniques, might make it easier to catch him and lock him up, whether as an ordinary criminal or, more recently, in connection with some more or less sincere efforts at rehabilitation in confinement. I believe that this entire approach is open to grave question as a practical matter, and that it happens to be illegal, and very likely unconstitutional besides.

After more of this, Commissioner Anslinger took the stand leading his rebuttal team, which was headed by Surgeon General Leonard Scheele. With few exceptions, career officials in the Public Health Service have stayed in line behind the Narcotics Bureau in matters pertaining to drug addiction, since disagreement with Anslinger's pronouncements was always sure to be rebuked. Depending on the seriousness of the heresy, the retaliation could be by informal protests from top-echelon Treasury officials to their opposite numbers in the offending agency, by formal communications about the impropriety of criticizing a sister arm of government—with copies lodged in the offender's all-important personnel file—or by threats, abuse, or even budgetary pressures from the Commissioner's stable of compliant congressmen and senators. So it was not surprising that on this important occasion the Surgeon General had come to New York with a half dozen of his PHS staff to defend the Bureau.

Disclaiming much knowledge of the subject, Scheele related the background of the federal hospitals and gave bland generalities about addiction. More therapy was needed but could not be provided because of personnel shortages; there was a dearth of research about drugs and addiction; and rehabilitation programs should always be followed up by effective aftercare. He told the Subcommittee that "addicts make addicts," that although addicted persons are sick their addiction is usually a manifestation of some "personality or character disorder," and that treating addicts should be primarily the responsibility of local officials who should mobilize local resources to control the problem courageously, scientifically, and humanely.

Even so, when the senators began pushing him too hard, they got resistant answers:

> *Senator Butler.* What I am getting at basically is this: There are certain sanctions in the law now. Would it be wise to relax those sanctions and treat these people as sick people or would it be wise to increase those sanctions? Would it be wise, for instance, if you had a man who had been in the institution, and after repeated trips went back to addiction, to permanently incarcerate a man or what would be the situation?

> *Dr. Scheele.* I suspect there is a practical side of the whole problem that would lead one to say that such a person might just as well be incarcerated. On the other hand, as physicians, we always take a hopeful outlook. In the treatment of many forms of mental illness, and narcotic addiction falls in this category, we are not necessarily successful even though we would like to be successful in our first contact with the patient.

Next, the Public Health Service doctors testified together. When it became apparent that, though guarded in their expression, these eminent and expert careerists were unwilling merely to chorus disapproval of Dr. Howe and the New York Academy, Senator Daniel turned on them: "I will say to you frankly, Doctor, that I am disappointed that this group, after all the years of work and study with drug addicts, does not have a more definite position" Then he and Senator Butler and the Committee's counsel subjected them to an afternoon of what amounted at times to bullying cross-examination, which Senator Daniel concluded with a little speech:

> Gentlemen, I tell you that, after sitting through two more days of hearings here, I am convinced that we are never going to lick this problem of the drug traffic until we get the addicts off the streets of this country. They have got to be taken off the streets, and I know it is hard. Some of the enforcement officers think it is best to get them in the jails temporarily, and the different States have passed those kinds of laws. I would like to see us at the same time that we set up our laws to take them off the streets, set up some place to have them go and get a chance for treatment, and then if they won't take it, and you cannot do anything with them, then, it seems to me, it is just as humane to put them in some kind of a colony or some kind of farm or institution like you do mental patients. . . .
>
> Any other comments, gentlemen? I think you see that what this Committee is driving at and what kind of information we would like to have now has been brought out in the discussion, and I am sure you have some papers, studies, and other things that would be of help to us; and if we have not asked for them specifically, we will appreciate your volunteering them or any other information that would be helpful to the Committee.

Reference has already been made to the scrambling that had gone on in Canada to line up support from that country for the U.S. Bureau's chief themes. After the PHS group stepped down, a doctor from British Columbia was called to relate how a proposal for legal sale of drugs to addicts in Vancouver had been rejected, after study, for fear that with any form of legal distribution the illicit traffic would not only continue but might increase. However, when this witness was pressed on his position with respect to so-called clinics, Anslinger's hand suddenly showed through in a way that might have been amusing in some less serious context:

> *Senator Daniel.* What were your findings as to the actual practice in the clinics that have been attempted in the various countries, Doctor? I would like your conclusions as to the operation of these clinics . . .
>
> *Dr. Stevenson.* Yes, sir. My information . . . is one of your own documents, so that while it is here it is simply copied or taken from your own official documents; perhaps one of your own

witnesses from the United States might be a more suitable person to give that evidence. But at least it is listed here, and it is
available if you wish it read into the record, sir.

Senator Daniel. I am thinking now about page 6 of your report.
Is this a conclusion of your Committee based on your study of
these clinics there on page 6 of your report where you say: "The
chief defects of these earlier narcotic 'clinics' might be listed as
follows—" Is that your conclusion after having studied all of the
information you could obtain concerning the clinics?

Dr. Stevenson. No. Those statements are made in that booklet
published by the United States Government entitled "Narcotic
Clinics in the United States."

Senator Daniel. Did you agree with those findings after your study?

Dr. Stevenson. Well, I had no reason for disagreeing with them.
They were stated as facts . . .

Senator Daniel. Well, let me take up these points here just to see
if you found similar experiences from other countries or similar
reports from other countries . . .

Dr. Stevenson. I don't know any other country that has had clinics.
This refers entirely to the United States. As a matter of fact,
I do not know any country at all that has had clinics except the
so-called clinics that were in the United States in 1919–23. I
think that is a misuse of the word "clinic," too, but that is a side
line.

Commissioner Anslinger thereupon addressed the Subcommittee himself, lumping his adversaries together in a characteristic performance:

Mr. Chairman and honorable Senators, the proposal of the
proponents is, in fact, a proposal for the United States Government to sell poison at reduced prices to its citizens. Now, that is
—narcotics are labeled as poisons all over the world, by treaty.
Our traditional policy since 1912 has been to oppose legalized sale
of narcotics. . . .
Those clinics were closed by the action of the medical authorities, the recommendation of the medical authorities and by the
State legislature. In one year of operation—now, mind you, the
proponents say, "Well, we didn't have time enough." Well, that is
nonsense. They were in existence for five years. In one year of
operation we seized in the illicit markets 75,000 ounces of narcotic
drugs. Today we will only seize about 6,000 ounces, without
clinics. . . .
The Chief of Police of Shreveport said, "Well, this is very simple

for me. When I have a burglary in the town, I just go down to the clinic at 4 o'clock when they get their customary supply." Most of those addicts were selling to other addicts who would not appear at the clinic.

Senator Daniel. Just a moment, Commissioner Anslinger, you say this was the Chief of Police of Shreveport?

Mr. Anslinger. Yes, sir.

Senator Daniel. Did he say these were addicts on free drugs who were committing crimes?

Mr. Anslinger. Were committing crimes. There were thieves from all over the area, and the record will show that many criminals came in from Texas to get their supply at the Shreveport clinic.

Senator Daniel. To get their supply of dope?

Mr. Anslinger. Yes, sir; and it was—the people of Shreveport demanding that those clinics be closed. . . . Now, as to the question of crime, in Formosa, the only place where they actually made a study, Dr. Tu of the University of Taipeh made this study, and he showed that criminality—of the crimes committed in Formosa at the time these monopolies or the legalized sale of drugs were in effect, 70 per cent of the crimes were committed by opium smokers who got their narcotics at Government shops at very cheap prices a few cents a day; whereas only 30 per cent of the crimes that were committed were committed by nonsmokers. Now, these proponents just skirt this question of opium smoking. Well, the active principal in opium smoking is morphine, an opium alkaloid, and are we now to establish opium dens throughout the country? We just about got rid of opium dens in the United States. . . . Now, they also brush marijuana and cocaine aside. You know, cocaine was the big drug of addiction before the Harrison Act. Why, it was sold across the country. . . .

You do not see cocaine addiction, but if you are going to make narcotics available to these addicts, why, you have got to consider the cocaine addict, although we have been able to get rid of cocaine addiction principally through international effort and the acts of the government in Peru in closing down illicit factories. I do not know what they say, they just say nothing about marijuana or how it is to be handled; they just avoid that.

Once again, Anslinger had ready for the Subcommittee's records a resolution which had been adopted by the compliant United Nations Commission on Narcotic Drugs, wherein the Commission, after a string of preambles, noted "that in the

treatment of drug addiction, methods of ambulatory treatment
and open clinics are not advisable." Anslinger then noted, "That
was just two months ago; and that question was examined by the
Commission on Narcotic Drugs and by the Opium Advisory
Committee of the League of Nations for some 25 years now, and
this is the result of the opinion of world experts, and this is
world authority talking."

Then he followed with another typical play. Some time before, two prestigious quasi-governmental bodies in Washington,
the National Research Council and the National Academy of
Sciences, had established a joint committee on drug addiction
and narcotics. Of course, no such official committee could be set
up without including in its membership the Commissioner of
the federal Bureau, and, naturally, in such a group Anslinger
could be expected to have great influence in proselytizing his
views. This was indeed the case. In October 1954 the joint committee had adopted a resolution which suggested even in syntax
that it had probably come directly from the Commissioner's
desk:

> The Committee disapproves a policy of legalization of administra-
> tion of narcotics to addicts by established clinics or suitably desig-
> nated physicians because:
>   1. It is impossible to maintain addicts on a uniform level of
> dosage;
>   2. Ambulatory treatment of addiction is impossible and has
> been so judged by the American Medical Association and other
> informed groups;
>   3. The clinics would facilitate the production of new addicts by
> increasing drug availability; and
>   4. The policy is contrary to international conventions and na-
> tional legislation.

Now Anslinger put this resolution into the record not once but
twice, repeating it in full, first as an action of the National Research Council and then again as an action of the National
Academy of Sciences.

When he had finished, Senator Daniel (who sometimes addressed him as "Doctor" on the basis of an obscure honorary
degree) whirled him into the following elephantine two-step:

> *Senator Daniel.* Doctor, on this last point here, before you leave
> the international picture, this last point says the policy is "con-
> trary to international conventions and national legislation." Is it
> your opinion that in order for this country to change its present
> policy and set up a clinic system of legalized narcotics for

addicts to maintain their comfort, that we would have to revoke some of our treaty obligations?

Mr. Anslinger. You would have to have a completely new international system, completely new treaties, because the treaties from 1931, the treaties of 1936, 1946, 1948 and 1953 do not contemplate the non-medical or quasi-medical needs or legitimate needs. The word "legitimate" does not appear in those treaties. . . . In 1925, when the word "legitimate" crept into the 1925 convention, the American delegation walked out at the League of Nations because they refused to participate in any discussion which contemplated the legalized sale of poison to citizens. . . .

Senator Daniel. Can you give us some ideas as to how many state laws would have to be changed in order for these clinics to operate?

Mr. Anslinger. All of them. Forty-eight.

Senator Daniel. Forty-eight?

Mr. Anslinger. Yes, sir; they do not contemplate that.

Turning to the situation in England (which we shall come to soon), Anslinger lashed out:

Mr. Anslinger. Now, I think there were some statements made here yesterday about the disappearance of the black market in the United Kingdom. Well, Senator, here are press clippings of just two weeks of the illicit opium traffic, heroin, hashish in the United Kingdom. I do not want these to go into the record, but according to the seizures made in the United Kingdom they have a larger opium traffic than we have in the United States. That is for smoking opium.

Senator Daniel. Yes; that is outside the Isles themselves?

Mr. Anslinger. No, no; that is in the Isles, in the United Kingdom; right in the British Isles. . . . And very likely this condition is due to very low sentences, although I notice they are going up.

Then a plug for Senator Butler's constituents:

Senator Daniel. They did have quite a problem in Maryland several years back did they not?

Mr. Anslinger. Oh, Maryland was one of the worst states here about 1950, 1951. You found teenagers dead from an overdose of heroin, in the gutter. You do not see that any more, not the way Maryland went right to work and whipped the problem.

And a final duet:

> *Senator Daniel.* Well, now, Commissioner, do you have any recommendation to make as to what is the best way for us to treat the addicts? We have 60,000 addicts estimated in the country. What do you think we ought to do about it? I would suppose that you would feel that they ought to be gotten off the streets.

> *Mr. Anslinger.* Yes, sir. The legalized—you have to get an addict under legal restraint. . . . We have got to have a system of compulsory hospitalization. That is my recommendation on how to treat the addicts. I do not think any other system—any other system is doomed to failure . . .

> *Senator Daniel.* You think compulsory commitment and treatment is the only solution?

> *Mr. Anslinger.* That is what I have felt, and I think you will find that the experts on the United Nations Narcotic Commission are in accord, that you must have hospitalization, compulsory hospitalization. That is the opinion of the Germans, the French; and nearly all the European countries feel that way.

Spokesmen for the American Medical Association told the Subcommittee that when the AMA position had been fixed by the famous resolution of 1924, the intent had been to condemn giving addicts large supplies of drugs for unsupervised self-administration rather than to oppose all administration of drugs to addicts not in confinement—referring thus to the confusion which had so long surrounded the word "ambulatory"—but they also advised that this AMA statement still stood, ambiguity and all, and that it had not been reviewed or clarified in the intervening thirty years.

Regarding the New York Academy of Medicine proposal, which had been referred to the AMA for action, they said that their House of Delegates had found that "additional information was necessary," and had accordingly referred the proposal to the AMA Council on Pharmacy and Chemistry, which had reported back in December 1954 that "clinics" had already been tried in the United States and were an absolute failure, and that such approaches tended to increase rather than diminish the problem. On the basis of this report "and additional pertinent material received from the National Research Council and the Federal Bureau of Narcotics," the AMA Board of Trustees had recommended that the resolution presented by Dr. Eggston (that is, giving AMA support for the Academy proposal) be not adopted.

So here crops up again the Anslinger-inspired resolution of the National Research Council already referred to, as well as, by open reference, the ubiquitous hand of the Bureau of Narcotics. And the role played by the report of the AMA's Council on Pharmacy and Chemistry makes necessary another slight diversion: the AMA Council had made no study and had done no appraising for itself when the matter was referred to it in 1954. Instead, it relied on a statement which had been prepared for it in 1952 by "the Committee on Drug Addiction and Narcotics of the National Research Council."

But preparation of the earlier NRC statement was acknowledged actually to have been the work of Dr. Harris Isbell, then Research Director at the Federal Narcotics Hospital at Lexington, a brilliant Public Health Service careerist who was nonetheless notably uncourageous—as were most government-employed scientists of that era—in challenging Narcotics Bureau dogma. The 1952 document (the one on which the 1954 AMA Council report relied) first appeared as a set of guidelines for physicians titled "What to Do with a Drug Addict," published as an article in the *Journal of the American Medical Association* and thereafter reprinted and widely distributed as an official release of the Department of Health, Education, and Welfare. And as a formal pronouncement of policy, thus expressly endorsed by both the private and official medical communities it is another timid retreat, scolding and threatening the profession. It opens with the Treasury directive which reproduces language from the *Webb* case—the very language the Supreme Court itself had vigorously repudiated in 1925:

> An order purporting to be a prescription issued to an addict or habitual user of narcotics not in the course of professional treatment, but for the purpose of providing the user with narcotics sufficient to keep him comfortable by maintaining his customary use, is not a prescription within the meaning and intent of the act; and the person filling such an order, as well as the person issuing it, may be charged with violation of the law.

Physicians and pharmacists are warned that they risk prosecution if they have anything to do with issuing or filling prescriptions "for the purpose of gratifying addiction," and are told that their good faith in the matter "will be established by the facts and circumstances of the case and the consensus of medical opinion with regard thereto, based upon the experience of the medical profession in cases of similar nature"—in a word, that they are likely to wind up as criminal defendants if they get near the line. Then follows this (and bear in mind that what I am about to quote began in a directive from a tax-enforcing police agency, was thereafter picked up and repeated as an authoritative statement by a government physician to the American Medical Association, was thereupon endorsed and published as gospel by the AMA, was redistributed broadside at public expense as an official publication of the Department of Health, Education, and Welfare, and is now turning up as an exposition of the reasons why the AMA played a part in scuttling the interesting and conservative proposal of one of its own affiliates, the New York Academy of Medicine):

> Mere addiction alone is not regarded or recognized as an incurable disease. It is well established that the ordinary case of addiction yields to proper treatment and that addicts can remain permanently cured when drug taking is stopped and they are otherwise physically restored to health and strengthened in will power. . . .
>
> In general, the physician will be acting in accordance with the consensus of medical opinion with regard to addiction and will be complying with the letter and spirit of the regulations if he follows two principles: (1) Ambulatory treatment of addiction should not be attempted as institutional treatment is always required; (2) Narcotic drugs should never be given to an addict for self-administration.

At the end Dr. Isbell set forth once more (still in the document prepared by him for the AMA Council on Pharmacy and Chemistry in 1952) the full wording of the 1924 AMA resolution as "the reason for establishing these principles."

Nonetheless, one of the AMA witnesses (and now we are back with the 1955 Daniel Subcommittee hearings in New York), Dr. Leo H. Bartemeier, a psychiatrist appearing as chairman of the AMA Council on Mental Health, told the Subcommittee that he personally took a much broader view; he thought that some kind of out-patient treatment should be tried at least on an experimental basis and that ambulatory treatment might be quite possible if the approach were different:

> Many patients who come to a psychiatrist's office for treatment who have been suffering for years from emotional disorders have been self-medicating themselves with large doses of barbiturates, bromides, or other sedative drugs for long periods of time.
>
> When a psychiatrist undertakes the psychotherapeutic treatment of such patients he would most certainly feel it inadvisable to immediately prohibit the emotional calming effects that these drugs produce. Such a move might not only interfere with his immediate

treatment of the patient but would in all likelihood bring about a situation wherein the patient would reject the therapist and refuse further treatment. In patients of this sort it is only after a long term of treatment during which time a feeling of confidence had been allowed to develop between the patient and his doctor and when much of the patient's anxiety and apprehension had been relieved that the patient would feel secure enough in the doctor's care to slowly cut down his need for such sedative drugs. Although this may not be an exact parallel to psychotherapeutic treatment of the drug addict, certainly there are strong elements in both types of patients that are the same and I would think, therefore, that it would be necessary for a psychiatrist or other doctor in the treatment of drug addicts on an ambulatory basis to continue to supply narcotics over at least part of the time that the patient is under his care.

■ SIXTEEN

The Narcotic Control
Act of 1956

■ EVEN TO THOSE who did not expect much of it, the way the Daniel Subcommittee wound up its work, after the marathon hearings, was remarkable. In January 1956 it produced a document of nine pages, submitted as its findings on the illicit narcotics traffic, and in April, a twenty-one-page report dealing with treatment and rehabilitation. The United States had more addicts than any other Western nation, the Subcommittee concluded, with an alarmingly large percentage under twenty-one. The problem was growing at a startling rate, with incalculable cost "in human lives shortened or destroyed."

Addiction was causing half the crimes committed in metropolitan areas, and a quarter of all reported in the entire nation. Drug use was found to be "contagious" and addicts at large were spreading the habit "with cancerous rapidity."

With only 20 per cent of the known addict population in custody, the Subcommittee found it inevitable that "this contagious problem" would grow unless all addicts were removed from society for compulsory treatment, and if they could not be cured, "placed in a quarantine type of confinement or isolation." International smuggling activities aimed at the United States were declared to be increasing by leaps and bounds, and subversion through drug addiction was found to be an established aim of Communist China, which was officially pushing the

142

exportation of Chinese-manufactured heroin to enslave Americans at home and U.S. servicemen elsewhere in the free world.

American addicts were entering and leaving the country brazenly ("emphasized in the sworn testimony of one female addict who told the Subcommittee that she hid $1,000 worth of heroin in her vagina and smuggled it across the border at Nuevo Laredo each week for nearly a year").

The Subcommittee accused the Supreme Court of permitting major dope traffickers to escape trial by its too-liberal interpretation of constitutional safeguards; it found the Narcotics Bureau could not fight the traffic effectively without being freed to tap telephones; the allowance of bail in narcotics cases was intensifying the flow of drugs into the country; and Bureau agents ought to have statutory authority to carry weapons. Existing *maximum* penalties (five, ten, and twenty years for succeeding offenses) were, according to the Subcommittee, too low—wherever penalties were increased, it was claimed, the incidence of drug addiction and offenses like smuggling dropped proportionately.

The treatment and rehabilitation report devoted ten of its twenty-one pages to a diatribe against so-called clinic proposals, which, according to the Subcommittee, contemplated setting up centers all over the country to hand out free drugs indiscriminately to addicts; the mere discussion of such a program, the report claimed, was stirring up controversies that seriously impeded existing law-enforcement efforts. Addicts could only be dealt with in "hospitalization or other confinement"; physicians agreed that any other treatment procedure would be "absolutely impractical"; and, according to a Public Health Service spokesman (this time the Subcommittee is doing the quoting in its report):

> Suppose we did try to set up a narcotic "bar" and run this service. Certainly, we are not going to give the addicts the drugs to take themselves, for they might sell them. We have to have the drugs and administer them, which means that one of these narcotic barrooms will have to be set up at spots around the large cities; they would have to be manned 24 hours a day, seven days a week. The addict requires drugs four or five times a day, otherwise he will become ill. Therefore, he is going to spend all of his time waiting in the so-called clinic lineup to get his drugs. In my opinion, it is an utterly unworkable thing.

To settle the question once and for all, the Subcommittee devoted one of its score of pages to this:

> One of the Nation's outstanding law-enforcement officers, Sheriff Owen W. Kilday, of Bexar County, Tex., testified that he, at one

time, had strongly approved of the clinics as a possible means of destroying the drug peddler's market and, ultimately, the illicit narcotics traffic. However, due to an investigation in San Antonio which showed that a peddler had systematically enticed 40 to 50 boys and girls of high-school age to begin using narcotics, he came to the conclusion that ". . . if you did away with the market, they would create another one and I am opposed to it all the way. I don't believe there ought to be any clinic whatsoever."

The report further concluded that no such approach to the problem could be undertaken because it would be unreasonable to expect employers to give jobs to addicts. Besides which, as another PHS doctor stated:

> It is important, particularly in people who are married, that one of the things wives tell us about the addicted man is that he is sexually impotent and that he, therefore loses his function as a male. Let us take the woman. If she is addicted and physically dependent, she becomes sterile and unable to have any children. This sometimes has great significance to the husband.

Even experimenting with drug therapy for addicts would, as the Subcommittee had learned from Commissioner Anslinger, oblige the United States to withdraw from all its treaty commitments, require major changes in the federal statutes, and conflict with the laws of all the states. The 1920 experience proved —according to the report—that drug clinics were all crime breeders and total failures; and finally, any such notion would be unthinkable because it would give a stamp of respectability to "the heinous habit" and because in the opinion of the Subcommittee "it would be absolutely immoral to give in to drug addiction and help perpetuate such pitiful conditions for the individual human being."

The Senate was urged to adopt resolutions pushing Commissioner Anslinger's pending international projects: urging recalcitrant nations to ratify the U.S.-sponsored protocol of 1953 limiting cultivation of the poppy plant; pressing the U.N. to move faster on the proposed Single Convention; pushing countries like Belgium, France, and Great Britain, whose medical professions still esteemed heroin, to follow the U.S. lead and outlaw it; and even urging that the U.N. Division of Narcotic Drugs, which had recently been moved to Geneva, be returned to the U.N. headquarters in New York, "where the full force of wide public opinion can be brought to bear in the fight against illicit narcotics traffic."

On the domestic scene, the Subcommittee called for sharp increases in maximum and minimum penalties for drug offenses, with captial punishment for smuggling and sales involving heroin, "the most deadly of all":

> Heroin smugglers and peddlers are selling murder, robbery, and rape, and should be dealt with accordingly. Their offense is human destruction as surely as that of the murderer. In truth and in fact, it is "murder on the installment plan," leading not only to the final loss of one life but to others who acquire this contagious infection through association with the original victim.

The Subcommittee proposed that ordinary limitations on the right of federal drug agents to search and seize be abrogated, and that Anslinger's men be authorized to tap telephones, carry firearms, and arrest without warrants. Persons accused of drug offenses should be held on higher bail than other defendants and convicted more swiftly by the courts lest they commit new offenses while awaiting trial. The Bureau's reporting system to list all addicts coming to the attention of any public authority should of course be made a mandatory requirement for all affected agencies. And the Bureau itself should be enlarged and given bigger appropriations.

The Subcommittee's final recommendation in the illicit-traffic report was that addicts and marijuana users, and anyone who had been convicted of any drug violation, *should be forbidden to travel outside the continental limits of the United States except under special procedures approved by the Secretary of State and the Bureau of Narcotics.*

Regarding treatment and rehabilitation, the Subcommittee recommended that no one be admitted to any drug program on a voluntary basis; that, instead, procedures be set up for "civil type commitment requiring a mandatory period of treatment." The report urged that federal facilities be made available to receive addicts committed under state laws provided the state court ordered mandatory incarceration. Once released after confinement, addicts should be kept under supervised probation for at least three years, with periodic examinations so that they could be immediately returned to custody in the event of a relapse. Any addict caught more than three times should be designated "habitual" and committed "to an indeterminate quarantine-type of confinement at a suitable narcotics farm."

Lest anyone mistake any of these latter proposals for tenderheartedness, the Subcommittee concluded:

It should be noted that these recommendations for treatment and rehabilitation are not intended as a substitute for criminal confinement of those addicts who are convicted of law violations. They should pay their debt to society the same as non-addicts, and proper law enforcement and confinement in such instances will do much toward minimizing the narcotics traffic and addiction in the United States.

While the Daniel Subcommittee was coming to these conclusions on the Senate side, Congressman Boggs, sponsor of the original mandatory-minimum penalties in 1951, moved into the play again in the House. He soon turned up as chairman of a Ways and Means Subcommittee on Narcotics, and his hearings were supposed to deal primarily with barbiturates and amphetamines (an eventual winner for the politicians, but not until a few years later). Boggs's loyalty to the Bureau continued, and he found ample opportunities to parrot the Anslinger call for stiffer penalties, curtailment of probation and parole, and more agents, more money, and more power for the T-men.

The Boggs Subcommittee even repeated some of the official line from which Anslinger himself had retreated in the interim:

> Recommendations were presented during the public hearings that an educational program be instituted in the schools to make students aware of the evils of narcotics. However, careful consideration by the Subcommittee of the efficacy of such an educational program has led to the conclusion that it would tend to arouse undue curiosity on the part of the impressionable youth of our Nation unless undertaken with extreme caution. Many young persons, once their curiosity is aroused, may ignore the warnings and experiment upon themselves with disastrous consequences. The Subcommittee is, therefore, opposed to direct routine education of our youths and we are supported in our view by the United Nations Commission on Narcotic Drugs and by Narcotics Commissioner Harry J. Anslinger, who recommend against any such education program.

So-called clinic operations also came in for more thrashing in Boggs's report:

> To permit a governmental institution to engage in the ghastly traffic in narcotics is to give the Government the authority to render unto its citizens certain death without due process of law. The most effective weapon against the spread of addiction and the elimination of existing addiction is severe punishment in the form of mandatory sentences which effectively deter traffickers. It is your Subcommittee's view, therefore, that trafficking in dope and

the murderous consequences that attend such trafficking should not be undertaken under Government auspices and that instead the Federal and State Governments should proceed in the opposite direction and make the illicit traffic an increasingly hazardous business.

Out of all this came the Narcotic Control Act of 1956, signed by President Eisenhower on July 18, 1956. In one package, rushed through Congress with virtually no questions or dissent, this Act brought into the law exaggerated new presumptions as to possession of marijuana (which the Supreme Court recently knocked out on constitutional grounds in Timothy Leary's case); increased the minimum and maximum penalties for *all* drug offenses to two-to-ten years, five-to-twenty years, and ten-to-forty years for succeeding convictions; increased the fine in all categories to $20,000; and imposed five-to-twenty years upon *first* conviction for any smuggling or sale violation, and ten-to-forty years thereafter, with a separate penalty of ten-to-forty years for any sale or distribution by a person over eighteen to a minor, and from ten years to life, or death when a jury so recommended, if the drug was heroin. All discretion to suspend sentences or grant probation, and all parole eligibility—generally available to anyone convicted under any other federal criminal law—were prohibited except for first offenders convicted of possession only.

Narcotic agents and, for good measure, customs officers were given authority to carry guns, to serve warrants, and to arrest without warrant. A new compounding offense was added to allow an extra charge and added sentence in prosecuting federal drug cases—making use of any interstate communication facility in connection with a drug violation, carrying a separate two-to-five-year term and $5,000 fine.

The extraordinary suggestion that no addict, drug user, or drug offender should be allowed to enter or leave the United States without registering at the border gave Congress no pause. (This Act was, incidentally, an early instance of the objectionable congressional practice, now standard in crime legislation, of throwing disparate provisions, good, bad, and fatuous alike, together under a press-agent title.) Not only anyone who had ever been convicted of any drug violation but *anyone who was currently an addict or user* was required to register and obtain a special certificate when leaving the United States, surrendering the same on his re-entry. The penalty for failure to comply with this ludicrous requirement was, however, no joking matter: upon conviction the offender was subject to *minimum* imprisonment of one year and as much as three years, plus a discretionary fine of $1,000.

The 1956 Act simultaneously amended the immigration laws to make narcotic offenses grounds for the exclusion or deportation of aliens, and to preclude courts from recommending against deportation in proceedings involving convicted narcotic offenders. At the outset Commissioner Anslinger even got most of his desired addict-reporting system to compel exposure of known addicts whenever they came to the attention of any federal, state, or local law enforcement agency; but since other powerful bureaucracies in Washington rebelled at being obliged thus to report to a minor Treasury unit, this was changed to a permissive provision.

Elsewhere in this narrative we shall have a more extensive look at heroin, which is only one among numerous opium derivatives and *not* possessed of any unique quality which sets it notably apart from, say, morphine, or synthetics like demerol and methadone. But its allegedly arch-evil nature has been played up by official propagandists for so many years that lawmakers stampede at the mere mention of it. In 1924 Congress outlawed all importation of opium for the manufacture of heroin, thus in effect making production illegal in the United States. Now, besides singling it out for the death-penalty provisions, the drafters of the 1956 Act wrote in another compounding heroin offense: anyone who had somehow contrived to keep a pre-1924 supply lawfully in his possession until 1956 was required to turn it in to the Secretary of the Treasury within 120 days, and thereafter any heroin possessed by anyone would automatically be contraband. Further, the drug could not thereafter be distributed for any purpose whatsoever except scientific research (that is, it could not be dispensed for medical use), and even then special approval had to be obtained from the Secretary of the Treasury and was, of course, never thereafter given.

To conclude this painful chapter, it must be recorded that the legislators who enacted the 1956 law, and the enforcers who campaigned so hard for it, soon had their first exemplary case. Within a year, an epileptic Mexican-American named Gilbert Zaragoza, with an IQ in the low seventies and a pathetic record of minor brushes with the law, was trapped, at the age of twenty-one, selling heroin to a seventeen-year-old addict-informer who worked for the Narcotics Bureau in Los Angeles. Both Zaragoza and the Bureau's "special employee" were addicts, and Zaragoza's selling activity was the easiest, and perhaps the only, way for him to obtain his own supply. It has been suggested that the Treasury agents were really trying to trap the peddler for whom Zaragoza worked, and that it was only on account of the ineptitude of the seventeen-year-old stool pigeon that near-moron Gilbert became enmeshed as principal instead of intermediary.

But in any event, he was charged and prosecuted under the new sale-to-minors section, and when the jury balked at recommending death he received a life term from a federal judge who told him that society was going to use his life "to set an example for others."

And that ominous comment was literally true. Other offenders —even the worst imaginable perpetrators of vicious crimes— who walked the prison compounds with Zaragoza could at least look forward to a chance of parole. Not he. According to the mandatory terms of the law and his sentence (which the judge steadfastly refused to reconsider) he became an inmate of the federal prison system, hopelessly and irrevocably, for the rest of his natural life.

Zaragoza and the stream of thirty-, forty-, and fifty-year inmates who followed him into the federal institutions, who were barred from parole and therefore had no incentive to take part in rehabilitative programs, played havoc with enlightened prison administration throughout the federal system. But in the eyes of lawmakers that was seemingly a trifling price for the political benefits that are always believed to flow from posturing as relentless warriors in the battle against dope. (It should be noted that in 1962 President Kennedy quietly used the pardon power to release several dozen of the most hapless victims of the 1956 Act.)

The final wry note is that constructive suggestions which had crept into the Daniel Subcommittee's proceedings got nowhere. For instance, it would have been a step forward for Congress to have thrown open the federal narcotics hospitals to addicts referred there for treatment by state authorities, even if only on a criminal-commitment basis. Authorization for such an arrangement was proposed separately, in joint resolutions, offered in both houses in the same Congress, but these died of neglect. Likewise, though the Bureau had receded from its adamant position against educational efforts concerning drugs, bills and resolutions proposing federal efforts in this direction were stifled in the committees where they landed. No attention was paid to providing supervision or follow-up assistance for addicts once discharged from prison, and the Subcommittee's specific call for expanded research on the causes of addiction and the rehabilitation of addicts evoked no responses on Capitol Hill.

Passage of the Narcotic Control Act of 1956—a result in part of the American Bar Association's optimistic resolution *asking* Congress to review the field—stands as the most abject surrender to police-mindedness in all the span between Mr. Harrison's law in 1914 and the efforts of Messrs. Nixon and Mitchell in 1970. Let the Daniel Subcommittee itself conclude this episode for us:

> It is to be hoped that the facts produced by our Subcommittee, together with the evidence adduced by a House Ways and Means Subcommittee . . . will result in the enactment of legislation and provide the basis for appropriations necessary to remove the illicit narcotics cancer from our society. If the Congress fails to act, it must accept a great part of the responsibility for the continuation and possible increase of the problem in the future. . . .
>
> If the Congress acts, partially as a result of this investigation, this experience will have been the most satisfying of our public service, because Congress will have performed a great service to humanity. If the illicit drug traffic of our country can be cut to the irreducible minimum, we will have saved many of our citizens of today and tomorrow from the worst type of moral and human degradation.

SEVENTEEN

Follow-the-Leader in State Capitols

■ BEFORE THE TURN of the century there was little public concern with drug abuse at any level of government, although an occasional warning was heard about possible dangers. Beginning with a San Francisco ordinance in 1875, a few local communities where opium smoking threatened to become widespread had enacted measures aimed narrowly at the nuisance of opium "dens," and in some jurisdictions the unregulated sale of opium and cocaine was also prohibited. Kansas and Tennessee passed the first prescription laws, in 1902, and a handful of other states followed. The American Pharmaceutical Association had taken note of the problem obliquely in relation to proprietary remedies as early as the 1870's, and began promoting uniform state legislation on patented nostrums in 1902. But for the most part these early provisions amounted merely to requiring pharmacists to keep some kind of register of drugs dispensed, as in the case of poisons.

It was the patented drug preparations that first stirred public and official interest. In 1904 a series of scandals was touched off by revelations about adulterated food and secret ingredients in drug preparations. Despite one of the most powerful propaganda agencies of its day, the Proprietary Association of America, which purportedly represented a $75-million-per-year industry, the nostrum promoters were battered by publicity about the true

alcohol and opium content of some of their most popular house-
hold remedies (Kaufman's Sulphur Bitters—40 proof; Kopp's
Baby Friend—morphine; Ayer's Cherry Pectoral—heroin), and
particularly by a disclosure that when some of these same proprietary items were exported to England they were required to
carry across their labels a conspicuous black legend, "POISON."

The American Medical Association soon became committed
to this fight, demonstrating how much power it *could* muster on
occasion, organizing flying squads of physicians to stir up community leaders and press for federal legislation and at the same
time trying to combat local abuses through its own membership
and such related groups as it could influence.

In 1905 President Theodore Roosevelt added his support, and
with a final push from Upton Sinclair's great *Jungle,* which
shocked the nation with its portrayal of conditions in the Chicago
stockyards, Congress was induced to pass the first federal Food
and Drug Law. Under its provisions, purveyors of drug compounds were merely enjoined to indicate the contents of their
preparations on their labels if they shipped in interstate commerce, but passage of the federal Act awakened new interest in
the subject and stimulated parallel action among the states.

By 1912 every state but one (Delaware) had enacted some
controls on prescribing or selling opiates and cocaine, although
the provisions were usually hortatory, either without sanctions or
backed only by nominal misdemeanor penalties. The most effective control of prescription practices remained the possibility of
censure, or even license revocation, through self-policing bodies
within the medical community.

However, the situation changed abruptly after passage of the
Harrison Act and the emergence of the Treasury Department as
a federal enforcement agency. Medical doctors were soon put on
the defensive even in the legitimate use of controlled drugs. Not
only would the T-men tolerate no ministrations to addicts with
respect to their addiction, but even in cases where analgesics
were medically indicated, such as painful terminal illnesses, the
agents showed little deference toward medical prerogatives. As
Commissioner Anslinger once told an investigating committee:

> There is complete cooperation and a feeling of confidence be-
> tween the enforcement officer—he does not act like a policeman,
> in other words. He is more in the nature of a fatherly advisor. And
> one thing about these professions: they lean on the enforcement
> officer a great deal for advice. . . .

Now and then you will find there is a weak link probably in a state. . . . We always catch up with him very quickly, and certainly he is brought to heel very quickly.

In the savage twenties, accordingly, little was done about controlling drug abuse at the state level; enforcement was so dominated by the federal men, and doctors and pharmacists handling drugs in legitimate channels were so intimidated, that there were virtually no borderline regulatory problems to be disposed of. A few states followed New York's Town-Boylan Act—Massachusetts, Rhode Island, and Pennsylvania had similar control laws by 1921—but the burden of enforcement was left to the national authorities.

However, shortly after the new Narcotics Bureau was established in 1930, the federal agency itself began to push for supplementing state laws. The Harrison Act grounded only on the federal tax power, so there was no question of pre-emption, and a wide range of overlapping state-law offenses could be created without raising problems of double jeopardy. In 1932 the National Conference of Commissioners on Uniform State Laws, the quasi-official body which prepares model legislation in areas where all the states have similar interests, promulgated a Uniform Narcotic Drug Act, patterned after the Harrison Act, which set up a strict system of licensing and controls tied directly to the federal procedures, and brought into play a full range of separate state criminal penalties.

The all-important exemption for medical prescribing was written into the state act in the federal language: "in good faith and in the course of his professional practice only." Restricted drugs could be possessed lawfully by an unregistered person only if they had been obtained by a valid prescription, and then only if they were still in the container in which they had been lawfully delivered. One innovation in the Uniform Act was aimed specifically at physicians, pharmacists, and other professional persons: upon conviction of a narcotic offense, the state judgment and sentence had to be filed with any professional licensing board or registry by whom the convicted defendant had been licensed or registered, and the court might, in its discretion, summarily suspend or revoke any such license or registration.

Evidence of the ubiquitous influence of the Narcotics Bureau appeared in another unusual provision, which made it the express duty of all state and local enforcement authorities "to cooperate with all agencies charged with the enforcement of the laws of the United States . . . relating to narcotic drugs."

As originally drafted, the Uniform Act contained optional language for bringing cannabis under state controls. But in 1942 amendments were promulgated by the commissioners to parallel the 1937 federal Marijuana Tax Act and bring the latter drug arbitrarily into the full pattern.

The Uniform Act was endorsed by the American Bar Association and other groups, and was quickly passed by a majority of the states. Even legislators in places where there was virtually no drug problem responded to the lure of a popular cause which had no articulate opposition and which affected no one who could hit back. By the end of the 1940's every state except Kansas, Massachusetts, New Hampshire, and Washington had adopted the Uniform Act, and these four had comparably repressive statutes of their own. Uniform acts are traditionally promulgated without recommendations as to penalties, and in the early days most state sanctions tended to be lighter than the federal, maximum terms of imprisonment running not infrequently to no more than six months or a year, and maximum fines from $500 to $1,000 (the usual top range for misdemeanor categories).

In 1937, in connection with the marijuana hullabaloo, Congress introduced increased penalties for second and subsequent drug offenses against federal laws, and these recidivist sanctions thereupon made their appearance in some of the state codes. But it was only after Congressman Boggs pushed through his extreme minimums and exaggerated punishments in 1951 that state lawmakers—again with vigorous pressure from the Narcotics Bureau —started to respond with enactment of what came to be known as "little Boggs acts." Ohio led off, with penalties for *possession* of from two to fifteen years for a first offense, five to twenty for a second, and ten to thirty for any subsequent conviction, with harsher mandatory punishments for sales, commencing at ten to twenty and jumping to thirty to life. New Jersey followed, with graduated general penalties of two to fifteen years, five to twenty-five, and ten to life, coupled with ingenious embroidery such as punishing any physician who learned of a case of addiction and failed to report it promptly to the authorities, anyone who induced any unlawful use of a drug, and anyone who merely *was* a drug addict (treated as a vagrant, $1,000 fine or one year or both). Nearly a dozen states followed the New Jersey line in one way or another, making the mere status of being a drug addict a separate offense, until the Supreme Court at last held all such provisions unconstitutional, in *Robinson* v. *California* (1963).

New Jersey also drew resounding praise from the Narcotics

Bureau for pioneering a statute which required, on pain of misdemeanor sanctions, any person who had ever been convicted of any crime involving narcotics and who planned to remain in the state of New Jersey longer than twenty-four hours to complete a long registration form with his name, aliases, arrest record, and prior places of residence—which, with a photograph and fingerprints, was then circulated to all state and local police agencies. (The moving force behind these Bureau-blessed innovations in the Garden State was William F. Tompkins, then U.S. Attorney for New Jersey, who subsequently turned up as Anslinger's coauthor on *The Traffic in Narcotics,* and then appeared in Washington as President Eisenhower's appointee to head the McCarthy-spawned Internal Security Division in the Department of Justice.)

State after state jumped into the ten-twenty-forty-year category, with severe mandatory minimums, and not a few added maximums of life imprisonment or even death for flagrant transgressions. The federal pattern was also frequently followed in wiping out eligibility for probation and parole among convicted drug offenders.

But since most states had neither the funds nor the personnel to enforce these laws vigorously, what often happened was that Treasury agents could decide, after they had made each case, whether it would be more hurtful to the defendant to prosecute him in a federal court under the federal law, or to turn him over to the state for prosecution (while often retaining actual control) under some suitably harsh state statute. The option was particularly useful to the T-men where safeguards as to confessions, entrapment, search and seizure, and the right to counsel were weaker in state criminal practice than under the federal Constitution as applied in federal courts. (It was in ending such disparities, by expanding federal standards to cover state practices, that the Warren Court stirred anguished protests from the law-enforcement community. A disproportionate number of the worst constitutional abuses have always arisen in narcotics cases, and the Anslinger forces were always prominent among the protesters.)

A few states have long included drug addicts in civil-commitment procedures allowing the incarceration of inebriates and insane persons, and in the 1950's, besides the new measures making addiction per se an offense punishable by imprisonment, much attention was given to methods by which the addict might be removed from society involuntarily through such civil procedures. Nearly a score of state legislatures passed laws under which persons found to be addicts might be turned over to probation officers or public-health authorities for "treatment," either for a maximum term or for an indefinite period until they were "cured." The difficulty was that with the exception of three jurisdictions—California, New York, and, for a while, Illinois— the legislators contented themselves with passing tough-sounding new measures and exchanging accolades with one another without making any corresponding appropriations or provisions for suitable treatment facilities.

The net effect was that these civil-commitment laws often gave local prosecutors a second line of attack: if they could not convict an addict for such criminal offenses as possessing either drugs or paraphernalia (a number of states had made unauthorized possession of hypodermic needles unlawful), they could institute proceedings for involuntary commitment on a noncriminal basis. And the addict would wind up imprisoned just the same, often in the same penal institution. Some of the least-affected jurisdictions blossomed forth with most elaborate civil statutes; Colorado, Florida, Iowa, and Mississippi, for example, all have statutory machinery for committing and confining addicts until cured, and then following them indefinitely with probation supervision.

Apart from these inadequate and misdirected commitment laws, and the three states mentioned above, no programs of significance were developed in any local quarter to provide care for addicts. The Bureau forbade any facility that might remotely suggest revival of the so-called clinics. And although they gave lip-service to the distinction between mere users and peddlers, Anslinger's men consistently waged their enforcement war indiscriminately against both, so that an overwhelming majority of persons convicted for drug offenses continued to be addict-victims of the traffic.

In responding to the problems this caused in administering the federal prison system, Congress had been induced in 1929 (over the bitter opposition of the then Surgeon General) to authorize the establishment of two special facilities, first called "narcotic farms" and later renamed "hospitals," to be administered by the Public Health Service. The first of these opened in 1935 at Lexington, Kentucky (headed by Dr. Kolb, as we have noted), although a limited drug-research program had been initiated several years before in clinical facilities at Leavenworth Penitentiary. The second, at Ft. Worth, Texas, was opened in 1938.

Under the 1929 federal law, addicted persons convicted of crimes in a federal court could be sent to the Public Health Service hospitals by the sentencing judge in lieu of being committed to ordinary imprisonment, and this became the principal function of the hospitals, which were, in fact, run like medium-security penal institutions. But the law also permitted the hospitals to accept voluntary addict-patients who applied for admission. It soon became apparent that most of these voluntary applicants, who were under no compulsion to stay for any fixed period, would leave as soon as physical withdrawal had been accomplished and they began to feel the first symptoms of genuine relief. It even appeared, sometimes, that the addict's primary purpose in committing himself was to reduce his tolerance to a manageable level so that he could resume drug dependence with a smaller daily intake.

The hospital authorities had determined that the minimum therapy regime which gave any promise of success was about six months, so a makeshift arrangement was worked out with local courts in Lexington. Under a Kentucky statute making drug addiction a one-year misdemeanor, voluntary applicants were processed by what came to be known as "blue-grassing"—being required to plead guilty to addiction before a Lexington judge and to accept a previously agreed upon one-year sentence, which the judge would then suspend on condition that the addict submit himself to hospitalization. This system, raising grave constitutional questions, was only partially successful, however, and was eventually abandoned (and simultaneously held to be invalid by a federal court anyway). Thereafter the hospitals screened their voluntary applicants severely and cut back on the number of noncommitted admissions they would take.

Even though the Daniel Subcommittee had called for permanent "quarantine" of addicts and a bill to permit federal hospitals to accept patients referred by the states had been introduced in 1956, nothing was done along this line, as Congress saw fit only to toughen the criminal sanctions. But these federal recommendations gave new impetus to programs in California and New York, where the addict population had begun to concentrate after World War II. In California, an elaborate measure specified that no physician could treat narcotic addiction by administering drugs even in reduced amounts except when the patient was in confinement in an approved private institution or a jail or public hospital, and that each such treatment had to be reported to the authorities by the physician; the law even prescribed limits on permissible dosages. Persons addicted to narcotic drugs—or to any other habit-forming substance "so far . . . as to have lost the power of self-control"—could be committed for a period of up to two years to the California Department of Mental Hygiene. The Department soon developed extensive treatment facilities, also working out a genuine follow-up system for keeping track of addicts when they returned to the community.

New York, which has long spent more on the rehabilitation of addicts than the entire federal budget for the same purpose, also initiated a hospital-commitment program at this time, making use of the state's general mental-health facilities. Simultaneously the state, with New York City, opened the Riverside Hospital project, where addicted persons under twenty-one years of age could be treated and then carried on an outpatient basis for a maximum of up to three years.

Each time a new problem is faced in the District of Columbia, it is asserted with boring monotony that since the District is a federal jurisdiction it should become a trail-blazing model and set standards to inspire all the states. That was the cry in 1953 when Congress, in a flurry of ringing pronouncements about how Washington's drug problems were going to be solved once and for all, passed an act setting up involuntary civil commitment for District addicts so that they could be sent to the Public Health Service Hospital at Lexington. However, no one in the entire enacting process bothered to note that there was nothing in the U.S. Code which could be stretched to authorize Lexington to accept patients so committed, and the D.C. statute commenced as a dead letter. By the time the Lexington authority was properly adjusted two years later, Washington's program had lost momentum and never amounted to anything more than a token facility loosely combined with the inadequate bedspace provided for the treatment of alcoholics.

In wartime research during the 1940's a new series of alkaloids was discovered to have acute antagonizing effects on the symptoms of morphine poisoning. These substances, the best-known of which is N-allynormorphine, manufactured under the trade name Nalline, precipitate the withdrawal syndrome when administered to an addict who is on an opiate. California authorities, followed by probation officials in a few other jurisdictions, seized upon this drug as a way to keep track of purportedly cured addicts when they returned to society. As a condition of release from prison or civil commitment, the addict was required to present himself periodically for injections of Nalline, which generally produced no effects unless he had resumed the use of a narcotic.

In some quarters there was always strenuous opposition to the use of this control, at least on a *compulsory* basis, not only because Nalline, if inexpertly administered, is dangerous and capable of producing side effects, including death, but because of the inherent repulsiveness of coercing people with drugs, and especially of compelling abstinent addicts to submit to a procedure involving injections. As Dr. Kenneth Chapman has stated:

> Nalline has certain possibilities to be used as what we would call—and I use a psychiatric term here—a chemical super ego. I am personally and unequivocally against using any drug to coerce anybody to do anything, any time, anywhere. This is one of my personal, moral and ethical convictions. . . .
> I think there is a great danger, in addition, that this will become a short circuit, a substitute for community rehabilitation. This is what we have seen all along in the whole field of treatment of narcotic addiction. We build big hospitals, more institutions, a lot more people keep talking about length of time intramurally, but we don't do one thing about treating the persons in the community except to try to set up some quick, short circuit substitute for keeping him off drugs.

The California authorities subsequently found that small dosages of Nalline usually produced characteristic pupillary reactions in drug-intoxicated addicts, without the more violent symptoms and high risk of adverse side effects. But this procedure was not very accurate, giving false negatives and positives in possibly 15 per cent of the subjects tested.

The latest "chemical super ego" is urine testing by thin-layer chromatography and gas chromatography, which can be performed on very small samples, is more accurate than Nalline, and is free of danger. Although these tests require some expertise and laboratory equipment, they have dropped steadily in cost from $20 to $30 to less than $3 per test. New York, California, and the District of Columbia now make extensive use of the thin-layer procedure to supervise released addicts and parolees. New York, Illinois, Maryland, California, and a few other states are also experimenting with more or less voluntary testing of some school groups in high-addiction areas.

In 1970 local District of Columbia courts handling run-of-the-mill criminal offenders began requiring anyone charged with a drug offense, who had a record of addiction, or who looked like an addict, to have a urine test at the time of his arrest (with the implied threat of denial of bail for those who refused), and ordered urine-test supervision for halfway house inmates and probationers and parolees as a condition of release in these categories. It was soon found that elaborate precautions were necessary to prevent skullduggery with samples; each donor was color-photographed for identification and observed in each offertorial act; and still the processing of hundreds of tests daily remains somewhat hit or miss.

The District of Columbia court program provided specifically that no test results could under any circumstances be used as evidence or to incriminate the subject in any other way. But notwithstanding this concession (probably required by the Constitution anyway), the program has been frankly aimed at' coercing abstinence. The same testing procedures can be effective, if elaborated, in disclosing the presence of nonaddicting drugs like amphetamines and even cannabis. They will not differentiate heroin from morphine, however, since the former, despite all the claims as to its danger, metabolizes exactly'like the latter, and the procedures are so sensitive to nicotine and alcohol that great care must be taken to avoid false positives from boozers and chain-smokers.

Urine testing will certainly play a useful role as an adjunct of genuine therapy, and is already being used with good effect in some of the methadone programs, as we shall see. But it is also, alas, stirring the interest of many enforcement-minded lawmakers. Compulsory test measures to be administered by police authorities have already been introduced in a number of state legislative sessions. So it is likely—indeed certain—that our drug-cops are soon going to be set prowling among us with sample bottles, and that to the full extent allowed by the courts at least some jurisdictions will try coupling mass testing with civil commitment and conditional release. Messrs. Anslinger, Daniel, and Boggs could scarcely have foreseen anything more to their liking.

EIGHTEEN

ABA-AMA, No Match
for HJA

■ AT THE SAME TIME (February 1955) that the American Bar Association addressed Congress, asking for a review of the federal drug program, ABA spokesmen also approached the American Medical Association and proposed that the two sister groups undertake a joint study. Obviously the subject concerned the legal and medical professions equally, and the sponsors of this project had great hopes for it. A forceful stand taken in that period, backed by the authority of these two professional bodies, might have sufficed to bring enforcement of the Harrison Act back into perspective by forcing federal officials to acknowledge that the law meant what the Supreme Court had said it meant in the *Linder* case. Furthermore, such an authoritative joint study might have breached the secrecy which had so long enabled Commissioner Anslinger to exploit public ignorance and play on exaggerated fears.

If nothing else, the lawyers believed that once the good doctors realized how the medical profession had been so long pushed around by mere tax collectors they would be stirred to anger and action. If a substantial group within the medical fraternity ever set out to reclaim its prerogatives from the drug police, at least a jolly scrap would ensue, in which the bar might be able to tip the scale toward victory for its sister professionals.

It would probably be stretching to suggest that the haste with which Senator Daniel and Congressman Boggs moved into their respective investigations, immediately after the ABA action, was induced by apprehension as to what might come of this joint ABA-AMA study, although it may be noted that the Narcotics Bureau pushed both congressional ventures from the very day of the ABA resolutions. But in any event, Senator Daniel rushed precipitously to his conclusions, as we have seen, while the Joint ABA-AMA Committee moved slowly. It was still in the processes of organizing and funding when Congress passed the Bureau-dictated Narcotic Control Act of 1956. And it encountered delays and obstacles at every turn.

It will be remembered that the American Medical Association had just taken a submissive position—as described by its spokesmen before the Daniel Subcommittee in the New York hearings—based on the report of its Council on Pharmacy and Chemistry, which rejected the New York Academy proposal out of hand. But the Academy proposal had also been referred to the AMA Council on Mental Health, and whereas the former had leapt to its conclusions without independent study, the latter still had under way a careful review, with a much more liberal orientation. (Recall Dr. Bartemeier's partial dissociation from the AMA position at the Daniel hearings.) The joint ABA-AMA project nearly foundered at the outset because the AMA hierarchy first said the Association's position had been fixed by the Council on Pharmacy conclusions, and then questioned the need for any further study because of the forthcoming report of its second Council. But this difficulty was overcome by appointing as one of the AMA members of the Joint Committee Dr. Robert H. Felix, who was also chairman of the Council on Mental Health, and when the latter Council finished its work, which included a thorough survey of medical and pharmacological material on addiction, its report became a starting point for the Joint Committee.

Then there was delay because of fears among bar leaders that the Joint Committee might stray away from narrow legal consideration and involve the Association in "sociological controversies." The ABA Board of Governors ruled that despite the joint nature of the venture, working funds could only be sought through an ultraconservative ABA subsidiary, the American Bar Foundation. The Foundation announced its unwillingness to aid a project so far from the traditional aspects of legal practices, and it was further ordained that if funds were independently obtained, administration of the project would have to be controlled exclusively by the ABF, including even the selection of participants and the direction of research.

The AMA delegation flatly refused such bridling conditions, and after a period in which the whole undertaking came close to foundering again, the impasse was resolved by obtaining help in the form of a small grant from the Russell Sage Foundation, one of the few funding bodies with its own operating staff.

Once under way—the foundation grant was obtained in October 1956, twenty months after the initial ABA resolution and three months after President Eisenhower had signed the Narcotic Control Act—the Joint Committee commissioned a survey of existing data to provide a basis for recommending research projects, or, if it proved possible, to support conclusions drawn from existing source material. Simultaneously a review of drug laws and policies elsewhere in the world was undertaken.

Another year elapsed. In November 1957, in the light of studies completed to that date, the Joint Committee agreed on five specific projects: a small-scale, carefully controlled outpatient facility or "clinic" where addicts could be treated experimentally, which the Committee felt could most appropriately be set up in Washington, D.C.; research aimed at learning more about relapse and causative factors in addiction; an evaluation of educational campaigns and other preventative techniques; legal research to clear up confusion in existing federal and state laws; and a detailed study of the way in which existing laws and policies were currently being administered.

Accompanying these recommendations was a seventy-page analysis, prepared by Judge Morris Ploscowe, summarizing developments after the 1914 Harrison Act and gently suggesting that severity of punishment might not be the only or even the best way to deter addiction, that nobody could be sure of the number of addicts, though the problem had remained a vexing one for forty years, and that criminality associated with addiction might spring more from the need to get money to pay the peddlers' prices than from inherent evil in the affliction itself. Analyzing the nature of addiction (with a copious sampling of authorities), Judge Ploscowe concluded that addicts should be regarded primarily as sick persons, sometimes drawn to drugs by underlying personality disorders rather than by lack of character or criminal inclination, and that the spread of drug abuse was due to complex sociological factors rather than solely to the malevolent "contagious" nature of the addict.

In a review of the *Linder* case and subsequent court decisions, the Ploscowe study concluded that notwithstanding the contrary position of the Narcotics Bureau, physicians could legally treat addicts, including the prescribing of narcotic drugs, so long as the treatment was in good faith and according to proper medical standards. Finally, it was suggested that throwing addicts into prison was not a good solution, that the New York Academy proposal deserved further consideration, and that experimenting with outpatient treatment for addicts should be encouraged.

If the foregoing recitation sounds bland and the research proposals less than ultimata, that is what it was and they were not. The Committee had used most of its grant, so as an economy the Ploscowe review was combined with a survey of drug policies in other countries and a brief interim report addressed to the parent Houses of Delegates, and the whole was printed in temporary form as an unbound document which looked more like proofs than a finished tome. Only enough of these were printed for the two Associations, with a small overrun for distribution to interested persons. Out of excess caution, because the report was not being submitted for final action, this makeshift version even bore a legend marking it confidential and not for general distribution.

On every occasion, from its first organizational meeting, the Joint Committee had extended invitations to Commissioner Anslinger to attend and participate or to send a nominee, but these invitations were consistently declined. When Judge Ploscowe's study and the Joint Committee's proposed recommendations were still in draft form, they were sent to the Commissioner with an invitation to comment, or to meet for a discussion. Anslinger replied:

Dear Judge Ploscowe:

For your kindness in sending me, with your letter of February 24 [1958], the interim report of the Joint Committee of the American Bar Association and the American Medical Association on Narcotic Drugs and asking for my comments and suggestions, I am grateful. As for my comment, after reading this report I find it incredible that so many glaring inaccuracies, manifest inconsistencies, apparent ambiguities, important omissions and even false statements could be found in one report on the narcotic problem.

My suggestion is that the person (unquestionably prejudiced) who prepared this report should sit down with our people to make necessary corrections. We do not wish to censor the report. Our concern is to have you submit for consideration a factual document, regardless of policy, whether it be narcotic law enforce-

ment, clinics, the British System, hospitalization or penal provisions. It would then be possible for those who are to recommend appropriate action to have the facts at their disposal.

Sincerely yours,

H. J. Anslinger,
Commissioner of Narcotics

The Bureau nonetheless requested a large number of copies
of the printed version from the Joint Committee's sparse supply,
and the Committee promptly furnished them. Thereafter, instead
of addressing himself further to Judge Ploscowe, Anslinger purported to set up his own Advisory Committee "composed of
distinguished experts"—"purported" because this body never
actually convened as such, and turned out to be merely a list
of names, headed by Senator Daniel (who had meanwhile become Governor of Texas) and including Hale Boggs and a motley
assortment of nearly everyone who had ever spoken out in favor
of the Narcotics Bureau's "official line" in years past. Allegedly
the Joint Committee's document was distributed to this group.
But with only a handful of comments written for the occasion,
Anslinger then combined old snatches and excerpts from all
directions and put together in paste-and-shears fashion a 186-
page booklet entitled "Comments" on the ABA-AMA Interim
Report.

We shall turn in a moment to the physical form in which this
melange came to be published and circulated, as an official document of the United States Treasury Department, by the Government Printing Office, with public funds (after Anslinger had in
all seriousness demanded money for its dissemination from the
Russell Sage Foundation and the Bar and Medical Associations).
But first consider some samplings of its flavor. On the opening
page appears an introductory "Memorandum for the Advisory
Committee," consisting in its entirety of the following:

> When one examines the composition of the Joint Committee of
> the American Bar Association and the American Medical Asso-
> ciation, one finds that the members are, almost without exception,
> individuals who have identified themselves with one panacea.
> These single minded individuals then emerged under what ap-
> peared to be the sponsorship of the ABA and the AMA. The
> public is conditioned to expect that ABA and AMA committees
> are oriented toward impartial deliberation, rather than propaganda.
> In this instance it would appear that the conclusions of the com-
> mittee were determined by the composition of its membership,

and for all practical purposes, their conclusions preceded the formation of the Committee. This should be called to the attention of whosoever may be interested in the report.

The issue crystallized by the committee tends to obscure many important areas for research in the field of narcotics addiction.

H. J. Anslinger
Commissioner of Narcotics

The "comments" first featured, by excerpts, the statements Anslinger himself had pushed through the National Academy of Sciences and National Research Council, rejecting maintenance therapy, ambulatory treatment, and all "clinic" proposals, and the United National Economic and Social Council declaration of 1956, rejecting "ambulatory" and "clinic" again. Then Malachi L. Harney, who had just retired from a lifelong career as Anslinger's closest associate in the Bureau, contributed a rambling diatribe against the "English System," insisting that in the United Kingdom there is more drug addiction than in the United States (a statistical result achieved by adding to the British figures estimates of the traffic in Hong Kong and Singapore), and that the Joint Committee used techniques "reminiscent of the Hitler 'Big-lie!' "

A Deputy Chief of Police from Los Angeles contributed the opinion that "the negligence of the Committee in failing to analyze the differences of the peoples of England and the United States is regrettable" (referring to the fact that there are more "noncausasians" in America), and that the Committee "should have been frightened into a sober consideration of the evidence," it being "almost inconceivable that the committee neglected to evaluate this reality." Starting from the fact that in the United Kingdom almost 100 individuals connected with the medical profession—doctors, nurses, and hospital staff members—were currently known to be addicted, in an estimated total of 382,000 such persons, this commentator makes his point by some remarkable figuring: since the number of known nonmedical addicts *not* connected with the medical profession in Britain was currently 233 (in a population of about 55 million), he manipulates the two ratios to reach the following conclusion, presented thus:

To summarize: In Britain, THOSE WHO CAN OBTAIN THE DRUG WITH EASE HAVE AN ADDICTION RATE THAT IS 5,500 PERCENT GREATER THAN DO THOSE WHO DO NOT HAVE THE DRUG READILY AVAILABLE TO THEM. An impartial investigator needs no further evidence to reasonably conclude that the easier or more readily available opiates are to the

English people, the greater is the possibility of their becoming drug addicts.

Some paragraphs labled "Conclusions" are offered as a consensus of Anslinger's entire group—which, it will be recalled, never really existed as a committee:

> The Advisory Committee is utterly amazed that the ABA-AMA group recommends measures similar to the British system as a panacea for the problem in the United States. This shows a complete lack of penetrating analysis. . . .
> We unanimously reject these recommendations. The proponents of the British system conceal their ignorance by ostentation of seeming wisdom.

And so on, page after page. A doctor named Quinn was listed on the Advisory Committee to enable reproduction of the following item which had previously been published in the *Los Angeles County Medical Association Bulletin*:

> The doctor who is committed to an institution soon discovers that he can think things out for himself; he soon realizes and finally admits to himself that he can break the habit only if he is locked up where he has no access to narcotics. . . .
> The idea of establishing clinics for narcotic addicts where the addict can be furnished narcotics cheaply intrigues many people. Proponents of the idea naively assume that the person is quite normal as long as he can obtain narcotics. They should talk to doctor addicts who point out how their whole lives are meaningless except for one thing—and that is getting a shot 4 hours from now. Family, children, friends, and patients mean nothing to them. For example, in delivering a baby they will nonchalantly cut through into the rectum with no sense of remorse whatsoever, since in their state of mild euphoria nothing else is particularly important anyway.

Another Californian, Anslinger's perennial apologist, Dr. Bloomquist, then a faculty member at the Los Angeles College of Medical Evangelists and billed as a "narcotic expert," contributed a polemic against overpermissiveness in raising children: "We see the result of this pathetic psychology today in a significantly large collection of youthful vipers whose disrespect for authority, parental, religious, governmental or otherwise, is responsible for a wave of juvenile delinquency unparalleled in the history of our Nation." Referring directly to the Joint Committee, Dr. Bloomquist urged his colleagues to "have no part in permitting a handful of emotionally disturbed individuals and their well-

meaning but unwise supporters to force upon the majority of
Americans a habit so foul that its propagation can result in
nothing but destruction of our nation." Likening the Joint Committee's work to "promoting a fifth column," he continues:

> There are many points mentioned in this report which make it
> difficult to believe it is sponsored by men of the integrity of those
> on the committees involved in its preparation. The very fact that
> such men have closed their eyes to the danger of the program pro-
> posed should fill those charged with the responsibility of con-
> trolling the narcotic problem in America with energy sufficient to
> counteract the dangerous attitude which general release of this re-
> port could bring to Americans.

Another doctor raised a point, albeit more temperately, truly
calculated to shake his colleagues:

> The experience with these patients indicates, however, that the
> physician in private practice is not likely to find that his income
> will be augmented by treating persons who correspond to the
> various psychiatric categories which are characteristic of addicts
> in the United States. . . . It should be pointed out that in En-
> gland medicine is socialized, and the physician's income is not
> dependent on fees for service. The British physician is not con-
> cerned with the ability of the individual patient to pay.

Still another sounds as if Anslinger's men were twisting both
his arms:

> True, there have been minor leniencies extended by the Federal
> Bureau of Narcotics for the convenience of the ethical physician
> in his administration to his patients (e.g., exempt preparations; cer-
> tain humane considerations, such as the permission to administer
> to the incurable patient such amounts of narcotics left entirely to
> the attending physician's discretion as may be calculated to relieve
> or benefit said patient; the provisions set forth in the Harrison
> Act, to allow the physician in the course of his legitimate practice
> to administer narcotics to the aged and infirm addict in those cases
> where deprivation of such drugs would endanger said patient's
> life). All of the above, of course with the exception of the dis-
> pensing of exempt preparations, are contingent upon the physician
> in question contacting the Bureau and presenting the *bona fide*
> details of the medical problem confronting him in such type of
> patients. All of the above is merely expounding the obvious; how-
> ever, it illustrates the fact that the Federal Bureau of Narcotics
> has through the years been most *reasonable* in their position as
> regards the physician, the addict, and their interpretation and en-
> forcement of the act.

Et cetera. A California judge wrote, "The ABA-AMA Interim Report is so utterly confusing and bereft of basic principles of logic, that I have spent many days in what seems to be a futile effort to piece together its several segments." With the Bureau as the source, someone relates a 1937 story of a youthful addict "who had murdered his entire family, father, mother, two brothers, and a sister." The weapon was the family ax; the cause of the multiple crime was marijuana. "Marijuana is a lethal weapon, a killer weed." Marijuana is "the worst of all narcotics— far worse than the use of morphine or cocaine."

How did Japan conquer the Orient? By fostering drug addiction:

> Has the Joint Committee given consideration to the ash heaps that lay in the cities of Harbin, Mukden, and Tientsin, during the Japanese invasion of China, bearing mute evidence of the toll of drug addiction—the deaths of thousands of drug addicts, who were the victims of Japanese narcotics clinics ON A WHOLE-SALE BASIS? . . .
>
> In its survey of existing sources of material available that could be relied upon, did the joint committee give consideration to the Press Release of January 26, 1942, issued by the U.S. Treasury Department, wherein it is stated: "Press reports have stated that, in 1935, in the principal cities of Manchuria, nearly 6,000 persons died of narcotic addiction." This statement is supported by the minutes of the Opium Advisory Committee of the old League of Nations.

Who would take greatest comfort from the ABA-AMA report? The nation's communist enemies, thus aided incalculably in their efforts to destroy the United States.

Joint Committee members were subjected to personal abuse ("rendering a distinct disservice to the avowed policy of law and order found in the canons of the American Bar Association of which he is a member" . . . "frightening ignorance or callous disregard" . . . "one so biased and uninformed" . . . "does not appear to be quite honest"). And there were large servings of jibberish:

> Students of Modesto (California) High School, according to newspaper dispatches published December 12, 1951, ". . . called on the California Legislature to prescribe the death penalty for persons convicted of selling narcotics to minors. . . . the request is contained in a petition already signed by more than 2,200 students." Here is an example of youth being aroused to the death-dealing properties of contraband narcotics, but the ABA-AMA

Joint Committee will not go along with them. Contrast this youth movement with the sentence imposed upon George Yokoyama by a California judge who placed the defendant on probation for two years, fined him $150, and ". . . to be paid in installments," following his conviction of having approximately *900 pounds of growing marijuana*—enough of the killer-weed to send hundreds of juveniles reeling into a world of moronic behavior, crime and near-insanity.

We shall return briefly to the text of this singular Treasury document, because in the end the zeal of some of Commissioner Anslinger's commentators backfired and compelled him to retract. But first let us note its publication history and some related matters. As has been indicated, the Joint Committee's Interim Report was only published in a limited number of unbound copies, bearing the legend "Confidential." It was expected that when the ABA and AMA Houses of Delegates voted approval, as both did early in 1958, a large printing would be made in permanent form with additional funds tacitly promised by the Russell Sage Foundation. But that was not to be. Directly and indirectly Russell Sage trustees were approached from the Treasury Department—the same Treasury Department which of course holds life-and-death power over all foundations through its discretion in granting tax exemptions—and given to understand that they were sponsoring a "controversial" study, that the ABA and AMA spokesmen were irresponsible if nothing worse, and, in short, that it would be discreet to drop the project. And that is what the trustees did; nor are they censurable for it, since their foundation had other important works underway and the serious disfavor of Treasury could have jeopardized everything. But soon the supply of the Joint Committee's printed report gave out. And then came the most below-the-belt blow of all. The half-finished, unbound copies had been encased in a blue backing that folded over to make a simulated cover, on which was printed in black ink and bold type the title reproduced on page 172. Official U.S. Government publications are usually covered with white stock, or a standard gray or buff. Commissioner Anslinger's "Comments" came out in a shade of blue that closely approximated the paper used by the Joint Committee. And the size, title and type (page 173) were calculated deception.

Remember that the only copies of the Joint Committee's work were the limited number prepared for submission to the ABA and AMA Houses, all bearing the restriction "Confidential," that the supply was gone, and that Anslinger had succeeded in cutting off funds for a further printing as well as any funds to carry on additional projects contemplated by the Joint Committee. In this state of affairs, the Treasury "Comments," in their deceptive cover, were scattered broadside. At every important meeting of a local medical or bar association a carton of the Treasury polemic was likely to turn up for distribution. Library orders were confused, and at one point the American Bar Association itself began, in a bureaucratic muddle, to refer requests for the Joint Committee's Interim Report to the Treasury Department.

For what satisfaction it may have given the abused Joint Committee members, the exuberance of these Treasury "Comments" finally caused them to receive a setback. One of the police spokesmen had folded into his mix an attack on the U.S. Supreme Court consisting in part of the following:

> This Nation is becoming increasingly aroused as more and more obstacles are erected by the courts to hinder law enforcement and to assist the narcotic peddler and other law violators to escape punishment. This awakening was magnificently stated recently. . . . "In the struggle between the forces of law and order and those of crime and treason, on which side are the men who are the judges of the Supreme Court of the United States? These nine men have opened the secret files of the FBI to the criminal; they have struck down the criminal laws of the States; . . . in countless other decisions, they have gladdened the hearts and built up the power of criminals and subversives. I ask you—on whose side do you think they are?"

And Anslinger's own Mr. Harney had reached crescendo thus: "We are presently the victims of a Supreme Court majority which to me seems almost hysterical in its desire to suppress any freedom of action of law enforcement officers."

This proved too much. The press ultimately focused on the spectacle of an official agency of the executive branch, and the prestigious Treasury at that, using public funds to circulate an unseemly attack on the High Court. Embarrassed, Anslinger publicly withdrew the publication. But for several years thereafter anyone who requested a copy would receive it, with the offensive allusions to the Court merely penciled out. And the Commissioner himself never relented in his attacks. In speeches and network appearances he continued assaulting the ABA and AMA spokesmen as do-gooders, "bleeding hearts," and incompetent interpreters of what the narcotics laws really meant.

Deprived of funds (other foundations proved to be as jittery

NARCOTIC DRUGS

INTERIM REPORT

of

THE JOINT COMMITTEE OF THE AMERICAN BAR ASSOCIATION AND THE AMERICAN MEDICAL ASSOCIATION ON NARCOTIC DRUGS

AMERICAN BAR ASSOCIATION

RUFUS KING, ESQ., *Chairman*

JUDGE EDWARD J. DIMOCK

ABE FORTAS, ESQ.

AMERICAN MEDICAL ASSOCIATION

DR. ROBERT H. FELIX

DR. ISAAC STARR

C. JOSEPH STETLER, ESQ.

MORRIS PLOSCOWE

Director Narcotics Control Study

NEW YORK   1958

Comments on

NARCOTIC DRUGS

INTERIM REPORT OF THE JOINT COMMITTEE

OF THE

AMERICAN BAR ASSOCIATION

AND THE

AMERICAN MEDICAL ASSOCIATION

ON

NARCOTIC DRUGS

BY

Advisory Committee to the Federal Bureau of Narcotics

U. S. TREASURY DEPARTMENT
BUREAU OF NARCOTICS
WASHINGTON, D. C

as Russell Sage) and subjected to this remarkable attack, the Joint Committee summarized its conclusions in a Final Report the following year and disbanded, recommending that at least the experimental and research efforts it had outlined be carried forward through the established facilities of its parent groups.

For a time it looked as if the Joint Committee's work might not only be lost for want of permanent publication, but might be perennially confused with the shabby Treasury "Comments." Finally, however, in 1961, through the good offices of Lindesmith (and in spite of additional blocking efforts by the Bureau), the Interim and Final Reports, together with their appended studies, were published by the University of Indiana.

As for the Joint Committee's recommendations, a few years after it had disbanded, the American Bar Foundation commissioned a staff member to evaluate what it had done—and this resulted in an ABF study which gave the Joint Committee yet another polite buffeting. The staff reviewer found it "not readily apparent" what Judge Ploscowe had been talking about when he referred to an experimental clinic, and found it "difficult to determine" what the Joint Committee intended. He concluded that because any experimental drug program would involve "complex medical-legal questions," might raise ethical problems, and—Judge Ploscowe to the contrary notwithstanding—would conflict with present laws and treaty obligations, the suggestion ought to be shelved until the way was better paved by research and educational efforts.

The Joint Committee's views about the value of educational and preventive measures fared slightly better in this appraisal, being tentatively accepted, although the report noted that Judge Ploscowe should have been more specific and predicted that not much would really be accomplished along such lines. In the matter of legal research, the ABF evaluation concluded that Judge Ploscowe and the Joint Committee had not understood one another, and that although some of the problems were "discussed fully and competently by Judge Ploscowe," tackling them would require large expenditures of time and money and would probably not produce meaningful results.

Finally the Joint Committee's dissatisfaction with too-severe criminal penalties was dismissed as starting from "an unproved assumption," and it was concluded that "evidence has not been marshalled to demonstrate that severe penalties are or are not the answer to the narcotics problem of the United States." From this it followed that further studies would be "both presumptive and unpropitious," and so the Joint Committee's discussions in this area were put aside with a near-scolding: "Any proposal for sweeping revision of legislation in this field should reflect the most careful consideration of all possible factors and be supported by the most complete evidence of the need for change."

■ NINETEEN

The National Institutes Symposium

■ AT THE HEIGHT of its activities the ABA-AMA Joint Committee received support briefly from a strong ally positioned directly on the Bureau's flank. Because of intense public interest in science and, above all, in highly promoted "wars" on disease, the National Institutes of Health had become so popular with Congress that NIH spokesmen sometimes had to go to Capitol Hill and beg the lawmakers not to appropriate any more money for their research budgets. And occasionally even this unusual plea had no effect, for every constituency in the nation could be counted on to react enthusiastically when its elected spokesmen sent word of how diligently they had fought for more money to cure cancer, more support for Dr. Salk, or increased efforts to put an end to other human ailments. In 1958, led by three courageous doctors from career positions in the National Institute of Mental Health, the Institutes moved boldly into the drug-addiction field.

Supported by their chief, Dr. Robert Felix, who was one of the AMA members of the Joint Committee, Dr. Kenneth Chapman and Dr. Robert B. Livingston, with cooperation from more conservative Dr. Harris Isbell (who had prepared the 1952 Council on Pharmacy and Chemistry report mentioned a few chapters back), organized a symposium on drug-addiction problems, under official sponsorship of the Department of Health,

176

Education, and Welfare, which brought together, at Bethesda in March 1958, the most fairly balanced group of discussants ever assembled to consider this subject. Even Commissioner Anslinger participated in the initial arrangements, although he declined to attend the symposium itself when it became apparent that among the participants there would be outspoken critics of his Bureau.

Nonetheless, tough penalists like Assistant Attorney General William F. Tompkins, co-author with Anslinger of the 1953 Bureau credo "The Traffic in Narcotics," and M. L. Harney, whose eloquence we have already sampled, did participate. In the same discussions, joining an assemblage of expert and moderate younger doctors from the Public Health Service, seniors like Dr. Lawrence Kolb and Dr. Walter Treadway, retired Assistant Surgeons General who had devoted their entire professional lives to the subject, made uninhibited contributions. The federal judiciary was represented by Judge Dimock, another member of the ABA-AMA Joint Committee. Related disciplines from chemistry through sociology had their spokesmen. In addition to Tompkins, the Department of Justice also sent James V. Bennett, long-time Director of the federal Bureau of Prisons and one of the world's most eminent and humane penologists.

Since I have perhaps been less than charitable in portraying law-enforcement exponents and their roles in this story, let us pick from this symposium some moderate statements of the law-enforcement arguments. For it is not open to question that there is a significant place in drug-law enforcement for the policeman and, moreover, that through the years repressive efforts have indisputably had *some* beneficial effects in the United States. No doubt an undeterminable number of addicted persons simply cured themselves and gave up the use of drugs, just as many drinkers doubtless abandoned alcohol, when prohibition efforts against both were first launched in the twenties. It seems certain also that many potential drug abusers have been deterred—simply scared off—by our severe laws in the ensuing decades.

Rigorous control of manufacture and distribution through legitimate channels must be credited, in the case of opiates and cocaine at least, with almost total elimination of diversions from such sources into the black market. And putting aside the question of how they got onto the scene in the first place, so long as the nonaddicted, profit-motivated smugglers and peddlers continue to function, no one denies that they ought to be fought with all the repressive energy we can muster against them.

Thus Dr. Treadway mildly acknowledged the economic truth behind one of Commissioner Anslinger's points (addicts are "infectious" and "lepers"):

> It is known that addicted individuals, having acquired a supply, are very apt to dispose of part of it for a consideration, thus assuring their own future purchases. It is known also that these addicted peddlers, or addicted pushers as they are called, may assiduously endeavor to recruit new addicts, often for the same reasons. This kind of peddler is a very great hazard and danger to the community because of serving to create new addicts.

Dr. Kolb admitted that partial responsibility for the way the enforcement pattern emerged in its early days lay on his own profession:

> Although the first steps towards the indictment of physicians were started by law-enforcement officers, some physicians in strategic positions to influence public opinion gave powerful support to the law officers. It is possible that without this early and ill-considered action, the United States would have developed a sane policy which recognizes that addiction is primarily a medical problem, but also one which requires some police action to insure adequate control.

In presenting the case for repression, Assistant Attorney General Tompkins told the symposium, referring first to the Harrison Act:

> Throughout the years, the vigorous enforcement of this statute has markedly curbed illicit narcotic traffic and its application has met with the outspoken approval of a number of U.S. District Court judges. . . . I have noticed in my travels around the country and in my conversations with Federal judges that the overwhelming majority of them feel very strongly on this problem of peddling dope.
>
> Although it is still definitely too early to determine what effect the Narcotic Control Act of 1956 will have on the traffic, there are indications that, where severe sentences are consistently imposed, many of the persistent traffickers have dropped out, or have been sent away to long prison terms and probably will not show up in the traffic again. . . . It is fair to say that the illicit narcotic traffic in the continental United States is approaching somewhat that condition in Hawaii in 1955 which was described in a letter from Judge McLaughlin. "Things are tough hereabouts for addicts these days as a result of Judge Wigg and I seeing eye to eye regarding narcotic peddlers. After a few 10-year sentences, the boys folded up." . . .

When you consider that the illicit narcotics traffic is one of the pillars of organized crime in America, good enforcement, vigorous prosecution, and stern justice are an integral part of the solution. I feel certain that there is general agreement on these principles and I also feel very certain of this: That the American people want these principles observed and that they are certainly entitled to no less.

Even ebullient Mr. Harney came through with some good points, and not ungracefully. Referring to instances related by Dr. Kolb in which overzealous narcotics agents had interfered with the treatment of patients genuinely ill with such painful ailments as cancer, Mr. Harney said:

With one of the individuals particularly it's a matter of great distress that I should have to disagree with him in any respect, and that is with the venerated Dr. Kolb from whom I learned some of the first and best things that I have ever learned about the drug addiction problem. However, I know that some of my colleagues in the police profession here were greatly distressed at some of Dr. Kolb's observations. Those which Dr. Kolb mentioned from his personal knowledge illustrate one point that I ought to make with my colleagues in the law enforcement profession. That is, when you get into the business of enforcing the law in this area, you must proceed with great circumspection. One thing we all know, in law enforcement, as in medicine, when you make mistakes, the consequences are likely to be tragic.

The question as to whether or not narcotic addiction is a sin is something perhaps for the Pope to pass on for some of us. The question of whether or not situations connected with narcotic traffic or narcotic control are legal or illegal are for the legislatures, expressing the wisdom of the people, to decide. Some of us can have our personal exceptions, but when a program is laid down, we ought to carry it out in the best conscience, and see that it is carried out. Anything verging on the side of foot-dragging should probably be designated by a worse name.

You can call this a habit or what you want, or differentiate it from or compare it to alcohol and so on, but I will still say as a simple policeman who has walked the streets with these addicts that this stuff is a poison, and that people who sell it sell poison. . . . And I think some of the medical people here who have tried to revive some of those fellows that got an overdose—who accidentally got some good heroin in those days of scarcities that law enforcement brings about—perhaps they recognize that they were dealing with a case of acute heroin poisoning.

Then came a spirited exchange between Harney and Kolb. Harney had referred to the London murder trial of Dr. John

Bodkin Adams (which resulted in an acquittal) and to newspaper accounts that Adams had administered heroin to hundreds
of people in such a way as to cause their deaths. Kolb challenged
him:

> I would like to know where his information about Dr. Adams
> comes from. Two distinguished enforcement people in the United
> States said that Adams killed 400 old people in Eastbourne by
> making addicts of them, and then giving them heroin until they
> died. That seems to me to be just fantastic. Knowing that it is
> almost impossible to kill an opiate addict by giving him more of
> the drug, and that is what was implied in the statement, I wrote
> to the British Ministry of Health for information about the Adams
> case.
> This is the response which I received. . . . "So far as the Adams
> case is concerned, there is no evidence whatever that he created
> 400 addicts or killed 400 people. Perhaps all this can be best
> covered by saying that no credence should be given to this sensa-
> tional report . . . and, indeed, no writer in this country would
> be likely to venture to repeat these libels even for the purpose of
> refuting them. Nor is there any truth in the statement that the
> authorities were attracted to the situation by the high death rate at
> Eastbourne." . . . I have not been able to find in any official
> reports or scientific articles anything to substantiate the statements
> that Mr. Harney and my other two friends have made about the
> Adams case.

Harney replied that his knowledge of the Adams situation was
largely confined to what had appeared in the American press, and
then the following dialogue took place:

> *Kolb:* My second question is: Does Mr. Harney believe that being
> a drug addict or the selling by a pusher to a drug addict is as
> serious a crime as murder, kidnapping or rape? That is what
> has been told to our Congress, and on that basis our Congress
> has passed one of the most tragic laws that ever got on any
> legal document anywhere.
>
> *Harney:* There are a lot of murderers for whom I have more
> respect than dope peddlers. There are many people doing time
> for murder who are creatures of one horrible impulse to which
> they succumbed and for which they must live the rest of their
> life in remorse. For these people I have the greatest sympathy.
> As for the man who deliberately sets out to engage in narcotic
> traffic, you and I see a little different type, of course, doctor.
> He is all cleaned up and slick, and he minds papa when you
> have him in the hospital corridor. But the fellow who goes
> around, up and down the streets with our undercover boys, he is

a pretty sad fellow. That is a situation I wouldn't put any human being into. And a person who for money, for blood money, puts a fellow human being in that position, he is worse than a great many murderers.

Kolb: In reference to this I want to point out again that there is only one reason to regulate heroin and other opiates. The reason is the physical dependence, because of which habitual users have severe withdrawal symptoms when the drugs are withheld. This is an important thing to protect people from, *but the assumption that these drugs cause deterioration and crime is utterly unfounded.* [Italics in original.] To send persons to the penitentiary for 10 or 15 years for possessing one heroin tablet, as some of the "educated judges" that Mr. Harney has talked about have done, is a tragic thing that must eventually end just as witch burning eventually ended. The witches are now treated in mental hospitals, but we needed laws for this just as we need laws to regulate addiction. Sickness is the paramount thing in both cases. . . .

We need sane narcotic laws, administered by people who know that their function is to enforce the laws and not to dictate what the laws should be. What is there about drug addiction that it should be made the worst possible crime in the United States? I think that any informed person who gives the matter any thought at all will find that any such assumption is unwarranted. I know that drug addiction has decreased through law enforcement, but I think it would have decreased to the same extent if we had the same sort of enforcement as they have in England and some of the other European countries. . . .

The story of the 1920's and the breach between the medical profession and federal agents was summarized by Dr. Kolb much as I have tried to unfold it in the preceding pages:

In point of fact, the slavery so easily acquired or imposed by a continued daily use of opiates is such a fearful thing that it does demand control measures beyond those needed for all other potentially harmful drugs. But what has happened in this country is the almost total failure to provide for the necessary and proper measures. On the basis of a very evident need to prevent and cure the slavery to opiates, there has built up in this country an enormous mass of misinformation about their physical and moral effects. The collectors and disseminators of this misinformation have included sincere laymen and law enforcement officers aided to a considerable extent by otherwise competent physicians. For the most part, these people have exhibited the capacity to generate enthusiasm and zeal for the suppression of vice rather than the desire to obtain and spread proper knowledge of drug addiction.

The proposition that Communist China was intentionally fostering drug addiction in the United States drew this comment:

> A Western power fought two wars against China to force her not
> to interfere with the opium trade. The Chinese have in the past
> and probably still are smuggling opium into other countries. In all
> of these cases, the motive has been money. It is a very recent
> American invention that opium is being used to weaken countries
> for the kill. It is well known that neither opium nor any of its
> derivatives, including morphine and heroin, have any such sinister,
> magical properties. Only in an atmosphere already clouded by
> propaganda and permeated with fear could the contrary and un-
> tenable idea take root and grow. The erroneous idea has flourished
> in this country and has helped to bring about the enactment of
> drastic, tragedy-producing narcotic legislation.

And on marijuana:

> Marijuana is undoubtedly a potentially harmful intoxicant, but
> there is no sense in sending a person to the penitentiary for ten
> years for having one marijuana cigarette in his pocket, a cigarette
> that would surely have no more effect on him than one drink of
> whiskey. Such treatment is ridiculous, fantastic, and a disgrace to
> our civilization.

Dr. Chapman quoted guiding principles in the treatment of
drug addiction from the World Health Organization as follows:

> It should be very clearly understood that the maintenance of drug
> addiction is not treatment. Nevertheless, under certain circum-
> stances complete withdrawal of the drug of addiction might be
> deferred. There are well-recognized, obvious medical conditions
> such as severe chronic or terminal illnesses, where continued ad-
> ministration of drugs is indicated. In addition, experience with the
> problems of addiction in several countries and newer knowledge of
> the psychology of addiction leads the medical profession to believe
> that in exceptional cases it is within the limits of good medical
> practice to administer drugs over continuing periods of time.

Although expressing reservations about reviving "clinic" facilities
on any large scale, Dr. Chapman concluded for himself and his
colleagues:

> We question the attitude of those few physicians who deny the
> addict benefit of current knowledge, and others not trained in
> medicine who aid and abet such physicians. Their attitude betrays
> a lack of understanding of the physiology and psychology of addic-
> tion. These individuals would not withhold or condone withhold-
> ing antibiotics from anyone who has pneumonia. The excuse of

these physicians is anachronistic and includes such statements as, "We do not want to coddle the addict; it will teach him a lesson."

Judge Ploscowe tried to wave the olive branch:

> One of the problems is whether we must accept either point of view as completely accounting for reality. I think part of the trouble here has been an attempt to say either/or. Nobody in his right mind would cut out law enforcement. The problem is where lies the domain of medicine? Apparently there is some desire to eliminate medicine altogether and turn the thing over completely to law enforcement, or vice versa. Here is the basic issue: where are the respective domains of medicine and of law enforcement?

Then followed Dr. Isbell, sounding a cautionary note:

> The clinical field of addiction has always been plagued by extravagant claims made for new withdrawal treatments. Every potent new type of central nervous system drug, each new hormone and each new vitamin is certain to be reported to be a "cure" for addiction. The fixation on withdrawal treatments is due to the failure of many physicians who, unmindful of the psychiatric components of addiction, mistakenly believe that the addict will be "cured" only if he can be relieved of his drug. . . . Himmelsbach found that small amounts of opiates were the best treatment of the withdrawal symptoms.

The Himmelsbach referred to is Dr. Clifton K., another Public Health Service colleague and another "great" in the field of addiction research; and it would be amiss to acknowledge the eminence of these men without also mentioning Dr. Nathan B. Eddy, who told the symposium, among other things:

> Dilaudid was introduced with the claim that it was relatively nonaddicting. An outstanding physician was quoted in the popular press as saying that it was more powerful than morphine and as harmless as water. . . . Dr. Isbell, I believe, rates Dilaudid as approximately on a par with heroin in addiction potential. Both heroin and Dilaudid are undoubtedly valuable drugs medicinally. They could be used in place of morphine. But I think we can stand the ban on heroin if it will in any manner help the situation with respect to illicit traffic.
> I started my first experiment on morphine tolerance 36 years ago. I'm getting near the end of the road. We haven't reached the goal that has been before us for so many years and very probably I'm not going to reach that goal. But I'm not willing to admit that the goal can't be reached. I think there ought to be a safer analgesic than any we now have, and I believe that one day we are going to find it.

Dr. Himmelsbach himself thereupon entered the discussion:

> We were all very young officers in the Service and very young in this field. . . . We had plenty of patients who were rather heavily addicted. They came to us with a quite strong physical dependence and very little else wrong with them. . . . In those days physicians paid almost exclusive attention to the treatment of withdrawal. When they spoke of treating drug addiction, that is what they had in mind and were concerned about. This accounts for the amount of time we had to spend in working on withdrawal treatments and trying to learn whether or not they had any value. The surprising thing to us was to discover that the doctor had at his command the best available medicine. It was found that the morphine abstinent syndrome could be substantially mitigated by the careful use of morphine itself. Following Dr. Kolb's suggestion, it was easy to develop a fairly satisfactory means of gradually separating the man from the drug. We found no one whom we couldn't take off under the methods that were developed in those days, and most patients seemed to us healthier at the end of withdrawal from even heroic levels of drug use.

Some of Judge Dimock's observations are:

> Sometimes I try to find out how these people got started on the drug. Here again they always tell me what they think I would like to hear. In fact, one of our probation officers told me that when she asked some young girl addict how she got started that the answer depended upon what story had been in the daily news the day before. *I find no evidence that the use of narcotics leads to the commission of crimes of violence.* [Italics in original.] . . .
>
> Whether the mandatory prison sentences do any good, I don't know. Of course, no judge likes to have his discretion interfered with; and yet I don't think that I am entirely unreasonable in objecting to the necessity of having to send a hare-brained saxophone player away for 10 years for having a pack of marijuana cigarettes in his pocket.

Statistics came in for a drubbing from an eminent sociologist, Professor Isidor Chein:

> The great bulk of available data is based on arrests. Unfortunately, the number of arrests is far from a simple function of the number of users. It depends on the amount of police activity. It depends on the adaptability of possessors to the existing possibilities of detection, and the rate at which law enforcement officials can accommodate themselves to current skills and techniques of evading detection. It depends on the kind of police activity. Thus, if the police are concentrating on the primary sources of distribution, we may expect that the relative number of arrests will go down—

simply because it is a more complex and difficult job to get at the primary sources and takes more man-hours of police energy. Contrariwise, if the police are concentrating on the consumer end of the business, the number of arrests will go up. The easiest way to produce a large number of arrests is to concentrate on the known addicts at large in the community. Statistics don't lie; but the people who take seriously estimates of incidents on the basis of presently available statistics are surely not statisticians.

Prison Director Bennett avowed that for thirty years he had been convinced "that the way to make our prisons more effective as crime deterrents was to get the narcotic addicts out of these largely punitive institutions," and continued:

The Bureau of Narcotics currently estimates that there are approximately 43,000 persons addicted to opium, morphine, marijuana and the synthetic drugs or 1 in 4,000 of the general population. To put this estimate in perspective we can compare it with the number of chronic alcoholics which is generally agreed to be approximately 5 million. . . .

The case of the "average" Federal narcotics law violator can be illustrated by the following case history—selected almost at random from our case files: R. G. is a 30-year-old Negro who is serving five years for sale of a few grains of heroin to an informer. He comes from a large Eastern city, was reared by a father who had frequent psychotic breaks and a stepmother who rejected him. He completed two years of high school and is the father of an illegitimate 7-year-old child. He began to experiment with the use of marijuana during his late teens. At 19 he began to use heroin, and shortly thereafter was placed on probation for three years for forging a narcotics prescription. After one year he violated probation by returning to the use of drugs. He was committed to Lexington on a 4-year commitment, was granted parole after serving more than two years and was returned after a few months as a violator. He had again relapsed into the use of drugs. While in the hospital he was a volunteer in research projects dealing with problems of addiction.

He was again committed to Lexington on his current commitment and again he was described as cooperative, pleasant and dependable. Three months after his conditional release in the summer of 1957, he was again using drugs and a few weeks later was returned to custody as a violator. In addition to the charges involving narcotics he has a history of several arrests and convictions for petty offenses. This man is a typical example of the current crop of narcotic violators. Change his name and modify the descriptive data only slightly and the circumstances will fit hundreds of commitments received in Federal institutions during the past ten years. . . .

In quite recent years the role of the hospitals, insofar as the treatment of prisoner-patients is concerned, has of necessity become a more limited one because so large a proportion of the convicted addicts have been committed for such long terms as to make them unresponsive to treatment. They are so discouraged, defeated and embittered by the long sentences they will not co-operate in self-improvement. Thus, in the space of a quarter of a century we have apparently made a full circle in our approach to the needs of the convicted addict. The problem seems well on its way once again to becoming a "prison" problem. I confess we face this prospect with a feeling of discouragement and a sense of futility.

Another important consideration to be taken into account in determining penalties and prosecution policies is how much of a menace the addict may be to others than himself and his own kind. It has been pretty well established that the drug user does not commit serious crimes of violence—aggravated assault, bank robbery, kidnapping and major crimes of that type. I know from my own experience that the "junkie" is not considered reliable by other prisoners. They shy away from him, do not take him in on any criminal plans for fear that he will "squeal" when deprived of narcotics. They look upon him as a "chicken," who has only enough courage to snatch pocketbooks, forge a small check, act as a pimp or a prostitute. There are no real desperados who use drugs or will team up with anyone who does.

Prisons, both state and Federal, in the years immediately ahead will be faced inevitably with the problems of narcotic offenders, addict and nonaddict alike, who are weighed down by the hope-lessness and the bitter futility of sentences which seemingly stretch into infinity. What can the institution offer the man serving 30, 50, or 80 years with no prospect for parole or hope of mitigation of his sentence? Now, I am not saying, mind you, that severe penal-ties are not necessary for certain types of these cases. I believe they are. But like Judge Dimock, I think that each case has got to be considered on its individual merits and the person committed according to the character and quality of his offense.

As institutional officials confront the dangers of escape, contra-band, and other hazards which are present as the result of a new concentration of narcotic law violators with long sentences in in-stitutions housing other offense groups, there will be a natural tendency for many institutional programs to become more restric-tive in character. Some of the benefits of a more relaxed insti-tutional climate which has been developed over the past decade may well be lost in the process. The hopeful prisoner will naturally suffer as a result, custodial costs will mount, and other rehabili-tative activities will be handicapped.

Still another real concern is the costs which accrue from the requirement that long-term institutional care be provided for the narcotic violator. . . . Assuming no increase in costs and only the anticipated increases in population which result from the longer terms of imprisonment imposed, the bill to the taxpayer five years from now may well be at the seven million dollar mark. This is obviously a heavy price to pay for a program which cannot hope to provide much more than custodial care. We must therefore face up to the question as to whether funds would be better spent on some form of community supervision and care of addicts. In this connection it must be remembered that the addict released from prison is doubly stigmatized. He must face not only the hostility and the suspicion which the community reserves for the "ex-con," but he is also an "untouchable" because he has used drugs.

Mr. Bennett concluded his observations as follows:

My own view is that the problem of narcotic addiction must ultimately and properly be defined as a health problem not as a problem of morals, or a problem of crime. The past twenty-five years have, I feel, demonstrated amply that neither the punitive approach nor hospitalization alone provides the answer. . . . A practical solution to this most difficult problem cannot be found in actions based upon fear or motivated by vengeance. It is to be hoped that the day is not too far distant when reasonable men who share in the responsibilities for finding solutions, whether they come from the field of law enforcement, administration of justice, or public health, may take the opportunity to reevaluate our present methods in the light of objective facts and chart new patterns for the future.

Then the symposium heard an articulate psychiatrist, Professor S. Bernard Wortis:

I am sure all of you realize that addiction is the only disease—the *only* disease—with proven physiological and mental disturbances in which the physician in the United States of America is restrained by the threat of law from furnishing the patient sufficient comfort that he may engage in a useful profession or occupation. This restraint is lacking in many other countries, with no apparent serious public harm. Now medicine and physicians see drug addiction in one perspective. The law and some law enforcing agencies see it in a different perspective and with their special prejudices. And the public is periodically fed exaggerated, fearful perspectives of the drug addict as a heinous, aggressive criminal.

The public has been led to believe by many dramatic headlines and lurid news stories, that opiates, by themselves, apart from the physiological phenomenon of physical dependence, directly incite the drug user to violent, aggressive assaultive criminal acts and sexual crimes. Nothing could be farther from the facts; for opiates calm the user, create a pleasant dreamy state, and depress sexual drive. . . . The most impartial students of this facet of drug addiction have clear evidence that no significant percentage of addicts commit violent crimes while under the influence of drugs.

As has been said here before, alcoholism, and certainly driving under the effects of alcohol, is a much more serious public health matter. For example, at Bellevue Hospital, we see approximately 10,000 alcoholics a year and many with delirium tremens which is a serious complication. Many of them die. You all know from studies of driving accidents in many States that the alcoholic who is behind the wheel is a serious killer. Yet our press does not crucify the sick alcoholic as it does the sick addict. All of this, of course, must quite naturally raise the question of whether the confirmed drug addict should have a means of obtaining his drug legally so that he will not have to engage in criminal acts to raise the money needed for the drug, needed to avert the pain of withdrawal.

I have once again taken my readers through a long course of quoted material for two important reasons. First, this good-natured and for the most part high-minded exchange of views, which took place in the spring of 1958, was the nearest thing to an honest confrontation between Commissioner Anslinger's law-enforcement forces and their critics that has ever taken place. I reproduced these excerpts for their content. They give authority to many of my own arguments, and I submit that the forces of reason fairly swept the field.

But a second purpose was to provide a full insight into the not-so-funny remainder of the story. When the participants took leave of one another, many felt, with satisfaction, that their deliberations had indeed illuminated the subject, and that the proceedings, which were to be published forthwith by the National Institutes of Health, would become a useful reference and might eventually contribute to a revamping of attitudes and policies.

But they reckoned without Mr. Anslinger. Remember that the sponsors and many of the participants were federal employees —Public Health Service doctors answerable to the Surgeon General and above him to the Secretary of Health, Education, and Welfare, Prison Bureau officials answerable to the Attorney General, and Anslinger's own Treasury men. *And every one of the federal government participants who had expressed views out of line with the Narcotics Bureau position found himself under some kind of pressure and attack.* Men at the top like the Surgeon General, Dr. Felix, and Mr. Bennett were chastised indirectly—a word dropped at Cabinet meetings or excoriating remarks from members of the Anslinger claque in Congress. Even Judge Dimock, invulnerable as a life-appointed federal judge and ordinarily accorded the respect due his office, found himself being rudely criticized. And for some of the less secure participants the blows that fell were meaner and more telling— letters of censure for their presumption in daring to question policies of the Bureau, calculated to land in their personnel dossiers and which in the arcane workings of such things may well have damaged their careers.

Nor was that all. The NIH doctors who had organized the symposium and were preparing its papers and discussions for publication ran into a bulldozing campaign to suppress it. For *five years,* under three HEW secretaries, the edited transcript remained locked up by an informal "secret" classification. When it finally went to the printer in May 1963, other events which we have yet to recount had greatly altered the picture—among them the resignation gently extracted from Commissioner Anslinger himself by President Kennedy and his Attorney General brother.

■ TWENTY

The British and
Other "Systems"

■ TROUBLING CHAPTERS in the American story still lie ahead. The nation has scarcely fared better in the decade since Commissioner Anslinger relinquished the reins than during his overbearing incumbency. But at this point let us clear up the mysteries allegedly surrounding the "British System," and then look briefly at policies and problems in the rest of the world.

Obscuring the British experience has long been a major objective of drug-law enforcement forces in the United States, yet nowhere is it easier for American observers, approaching from common antecedents and with no language barrier, to get at the truth. And the truth in this instance is singularly enlightening. For the British story makes much of America's half-century preoccupation with "dope" laughable.

Understandably, the calm prevailing on the drug scene across the Atlantic all these years has been a whole bush of thorns in the sides of Anslinger and his successors. That they have so long succeeded in misleading the American public, and with such crude distortions and deceptions, may have implications about the way the country is governed that go far beyond the compass of this work. (Right now, in the early seventies, conservative drug-maintenance proposals in Washington and New York still

190

evoke such official comments as "a phony experiment modeled on the British plan that has become a disaster" or "the entering wedge to get into . . . the plan that failed in England.")

Commencing with their joint promotion of the opium traffic in China, through most of the nineteenth century and, generally, until after the Hague Opium Convention of 1912, England and the United States followed closely parallel courses. Both nations gradually reacted to the spectacle of their citizens growing rich in the exploitation of addiction in the Far East. Both accepted opium smoking in their own societies as an exotic but unimportant fad confined to immigrant Orientals and a few avant-garde figures like Coleridge, DeQuincy, Wilde, and Poe.

There was a slight parting of ways in the response to drug-laden patent medicines: as we have already noted, the British early clapped many such nostrums under controls developed for "poisons," while Yankee lawmakers did virtually nothing about them until well into the twentieth century. Also, controls over pharmacists were imposed earlier and observed more carefully in England than in the United States. The first British Pharmacies Act was passed in 1852.

Great Britain had been a moving force, along with the United States, in promulgation of the 1912 Hague Convention, and the British Dangerous Drugs Act, passed by Parliament in 1920 to carry out Convention obligations with respect to controlling domestic traffic, was strikingly like the U.S. Harrison Act. Raw opium and opium prepared for smoking were banned: everyone in England handling "dangerous drugs" (heroin, morphine, cocaine, etc.) was required to register, obtain a license, and keep accurate records; pharmacists dispensing such drugs were obliged to keep special prescription files and sales records and to make them available for inspection by the regulatory authorities; physicians were also required to keep detailed records, although this requirement was never vigorously enforced.

The Secretary of State for Home Affairs was given authority to make regulations governing administration of the Act, and it is noteworthy that the regulations he prescribed left open the very ambiguity concerning the rights of physicians which caused so much trouble with the Harrison Act in America. The British regulations exempted from control any person who, being a duly qualified medical practitioner, "shall be authorized, so far as may 'be necessary for the practice or exercise of his said profession, function or employment, and in his capacity as a member of his said class, to be in possession of and to supply drugs."

Moreover, the Home Office thereupon put out an interpretative ruling which sounded like a strict interpretation indeed:

> The authority granted to a doctor or dentist to possess and supply dangerous drugs is limited by the words *so far as may be necessary for the practice or exercise of his profession.* [Italics in original.] In no circumstances may dangerous drugs be used for any other purpose than that of ministering to the strictly medical or dental needs of his patients. The continued supply of dangerous drugs to a patient solely for the gratification of addiction is not regarded as "medical need."

But here the parallel ends. In the United States the Treasury Department took matters into its own hands and in 1922 won the tricky *Behrman* mandate from the Supreme Court, thus enabling enforcement agents to tell the medical profession what its rights were. In Britain the solution was entirely different. At the instigation of the government, the Royal Medical Society appointed a committee of eminent doctors, under the chairmanship of Sir Humphrey Rolleston, and in 1924 this committee undertook a careful study of the role of the medical profession and the prerogatives of the medical practitioner with respect to the narcotics addict. Two years later the committee reported its findings to the Home Office, in part as follows:

> *Precautions to be Observed in the Administration of Morphine or Heroin.* The position of a practitioner when using morphine or heroin in the treatment of persons who suffer from addiction to either of these drugs obviously differs in several important respects from that in which he is placed when using the drug in the ordinary course of his medical practice for the treatment of persons not so affected. Not only will the objects of treatment usually differ, but also the dangers to be avoided and the precautions that are therefore necessary. . . .
>
> Morphine or heroin may properly be administered to addicts in the following circumstances, namely, (a) where patients are under treatment by the gradual withdrawal method with a view to cure, (b) where it has been demonstrated, after a prolonged attempt at cure, that the use of the drug cannot be safely discontinued entirely, on account of the severity of the withdrawal symptoms produced, and (c) where it has been similarly demonstrated that the patient, while capable of leading a useful and relatively normal life when a certain minimum dose is regularly administered, becomes incapable of this when the drug is entirely discontinued.

The Rolleston report then set forth medical precautions to be observed in treating addicts. The doctor was urged to seek a second confirming medical opinion before beginning a narcotics regime. It was suggested that he keep in touch with the Home Office as to the basis on which the patient was being treated, and if he found he had lost control he should bring pressure to induce the patient to enter an institution. With respect to the handling of incurable addicts, the report directed:

> *Precaution in Treatment of Apparently Incurable Cases.* These will include both the cases in which the severity of withdrawal symptoms, observed on complete discontinuance after prolonged attempted cure, and the cases in which the inability of the patient to lead, without a minimum dose, a relatively normal life appear to justify continuous administration of the drug indefinitely. They may be either cases of persons whom the practitioner has himself already treated with a view to cure, or cases of persons as to whom he is satisfied, by information received from those by whom they have been previously treated, that they must be regarded as incurable. In all such cases the main object must be to keep the supply of the drug within the limit of what is strictly necessary. The practitioner must, therefore, see the patient sufficiently often to maintain such observation of his condition as is necessary for justifying the treatment.

If an incurable patient was going to be out of touch with the doctor for some period, as on a trip or during the doctor's own holiday, it was urged that only a minimum supply be made available to him and that if possible the patient be temporarily referred to another doctor for continuing care.

For forty years these so-called Rolleston Rules, with the relaxed illogicality that makes British law enforcement the most reasonable and efficient in the world, were, though they lacked official force, directly appended to and printed with the Home Office Regulations (which say a doctor may not prescribe solely to gratify an addict's habit), so that even though the law and governing regulations remained menacingly narrow, safe limits of good medical practice were expressly spelled out for doctors in England.

British enforcement efforts have always been aimed at reinforcing control by medical practitioners instead of menacing the doctors themselves, as is illustrated in another Dangerous Drug Regulation regarding possession:

> . . . a person supplied with a drug or preparation by, or upon a prescription given by, a medical practitioner shall not be deemed to be a person generally authorized to be in possession of the drug or preparation if he was then being supplied with a drug or

preparation by, or on a prescription given by, another medical
practitioner in the course of treatment, and did not disclose the
fact to the first-mentioned medical practitioner before the supply
by him or on his prescription.

Thus there was created an offense which could only be committed by the addicted person and, in effect, only against the
doctor: the offense of defrauding the latter by applying to him
as a patient when in fact the patient is already receiving drugs
from another doctor. And it is noteworthy that over the years
this offense often accounted for as many as half the prosecutions
instituted in Great Britain for violations involving manufactured
drugs (heroin, morphine, cocaine, and the synthetics).

There has never been anything in the United Kingdom remotely resembling the army of enforcement agents maintained
to cope with the drug traffic in the United States. A few police
officers are assigned to inspection and enforcement duties under
the dangerous drug laws, a score at Scotland Yard covering
Metropolitan London, a half dozen in each of England's other
large cities like Manchester and Liverpool, and one or two in
smaller centers. These officers examine pharmacy records and
investigate any reports of shortages, pilferage, or theft involving
drugs. By watching prescriptions, they quickly see if a doctor
begins providing unusual amounts or if one patient appears to be
receiving unreasonable dosages. When this happens, they do not
take any prosecutive steps, but merely report to the Dangerous
Drug Branch in the Home Office.

The Home Office is not an enforcement agency, but its Dangerous Drugs Branch, with half a dozen inspectors under a
chief, is charged with receiving reports from the police and
keeping central records. This unit also receives and maintains
reports by medical practitioners of addicts under their care,
formerly furnished on a voluntary basis but now required, by a
recent change in the law and the regulations, for each individual
under treatment.

In England, as elsewhere throughout the world, there is a
relatively high incidence of addiction among medical practitioners themselves and in the ranks of other persons whose voca-
tions give them ready access to drugs. But even in these cases,
as well as when a doctor is found to be abusing his prerogatives
by too large a volume of prescriptions, the enforcement authorities traditionally would not dream of prosecuting, nor even of
addressing the doctor directly with respect to his alleged abuse
or offense. Instead, the Dangerous Drugs Branch would refer the

matter to the Ministry of Health, which would direct a regional health inspector or a member of a local medical board to call on the doctor and discuss whatever the problem seemed to be.

Criminal actions against doctors have been rare; if the implied warning and reprimand of a visit from a health inspector did not suffice, the ultimate sanction was usually a temporary suspension of authority to prescribe drugs. A doctor who is himself addicted need only place himself under the care of a fellow physician to avoid further difficulties and carry on with his practice while undergoing an attempted cure—or ultimately, if necessary, while he is maintained on a stabilizing regime of drugs.

It is not open to question that with police supervision which has always been excellent though limited, with the vigilance of medical practitioners themselves, and with the supervisory activities of the Home Office inspectors and the Dangerous Drugs Branch, there has never been any very large undetected body of drug addicts, or "invisible" problem, in Great Britain. The British authorities think there may be a few people with ample means who supply themselves privately with drugs from abroad, but not a significant number. They are confident that except under very unusual circumstances every new addict comes to their attention through one or another of their supervisory activities within a matter of months. So the statistical picture has always been in pretty good focus—doubtless clearer than comparable statistics for countries like the United States and Canada where the entire problem has been so long submerged in the underworld.

And what are the statistics? In the 1920's the nonmedical addict population in the United Kingdom is believed to have fluctuated in the low thousands (as the combined U.K. census for England, Northern Ireland, Scotland, and Wales approached the 45 million mark). By 1935 the addict count was reduced to 700, and 120 of those were to be found in the medical profession. During the 1950–60 decade it dipped to the range of 300 to 400 (1960 U.K. population: 52 million). In 1954, for example, the number was 317, of whom 148 were male and 169 female, and among whom there were seventy-two doctors, sixty-nine dentists, two pharmacists, and one nurse. In 1959 the number had increased to 454 (196 men and 258 women), and there were *none* known to be under the age of twenty, fifty in the twenty to thirty-four age range, ninety-two between thirty-five and forty-nine, and 278 over fifty (plus thirty-four for whom age data were not available).

The slight upward trend noted in 1959 continued, to 470 in 1961, 532 in 1962, and 635 in 1963—and for this the explanation, in part at least, is interesting. In 1957 Lady Frankau, a London physician world-renowned for her work with alcoholics and drug addicts, began treating a few Canadian and American addicts who turned up in London as refugees from persecution at home. This started a small migration, and a few other London doctors began to take on such patients. The number of these addict emigrés who could afford to seek help by self-imposed banishment was pathetically small, but by the middle sixties the total number included in the British rolls was several hundred, with a cumulative total of about a thousand who had come for treatment, been withdrawn from drug use, and dropped out of the program to be replaced by others. In 1964 the addict population, more than half of it centered in London, was 753, and by 1967 the figure had jumped to 1,729, which will be the subject of further discussion in a moment.

Some idea of British enforcement policies, so different on every count from the hounding, dragnets, and savage sentences with which Americans are familiar, can be obtained by looking at prosecution records. Sanctions available to enforce the Dangerous Drugs Acts have always been substantial. Initially, the maximum fixed by Parliament was two years' imprisonment; then by an amendment in 1951, doubtless in response to the contemporaneous furor in the United States (total U.K. offenses in all drug categories in 1951: 243), maximums were increased to ten years' imprisonment and a £1,000 fine—but in practice such penalties have virtually never been meted out in drug cases by British courts. The prosecution option of "summary conviction"—another sensibly informal British institution—reduced maximums in such proceedings to twelve months and £250 (and the statutes also limited punishment for violations blamed solely on inadvertence to a £50 fine). Prison sentences imposed on *addicts* for any reason were rare. In the 1950's no more than a dozen addicts per year turned up in the entire British prison system, including those who were committed for all types of offenses and not merely for drug violations. The number is believed to have increased severalfold in the sixties, which still left it at less than 100 new addict-inmates per year.

In 1956, to analyze another sample (this was the year the U.S. Congress passed the Narcotics Control Act, with its life-and-death punishments), there were only 144 prosecutions for violations of the British Dangerous Drugs Act in all the U.K.

court systems. Of these, 103 related to marijuana and drew only a handful of sentences, ranging from six weeks' to five years' imprisonment (the latter for large-scale smuggling), and fines from £2 to £250. Twelve prosecutions were for opium offenses, with sentences ranging from two to six months' imprisonment and fines from £5 to £100, and twenty-nine were for violations pertaining to manufactured drugs, over half of them prescription forgeries or the offense of seeking a supply from a second doctor when the patient was already under the care of one practitioner. Eight of the manufactured-drug cases involved failure by dispensing persons to keep drugs in locked receptacles, or similar technical violations of the regulations, and in all twenty-nine cases the sentences ranged from one day to six months, with fines from ten shillings to £100.

By 1966 the prosecution pattern had altered somewhat, chiefly because of the addition of a penalty for unauthorized possession, coupled with a large increase in the number of marijuana charges. Thus in the United Kingdom there were 1,513 drug cases in 1966, with 1,119 convictions for marijuana, including in turn 1,083 for unauthorized possession, ten for smuggling, and seventeen for another new offense—permitting premises to be used for smoking or dealing in cannabis. Fines imposed in these marijuana cases ranged from £1 to £1,000, and prison sentences from one day to five years. The British authorities were also plagued by another new marijuana problem: four cases of domestic cannabis growing were discovered, "involving a few plants grown in gardens." The 1966 convictions in all United Kingdom courts for opium offenses numbered thirty-six, with fines ranging from £2 to £100 and prison sentences from three to twelve months, while in the morphine-heroin-cocaine category there were 242 convictions, of which 155 were for unlawful possession, thirty-three for unlawful procuring, fourteen for unlawful supplying, and thirty-two for obtaining drugs by larceny or fraud. Fines imposed in connection with the latter (manufactured-drug) offenses ranged from £2 to £100, and prison sentences from one day to four years.

In the blackout of all nonofficial information about drug policies maintained in the United States by the Treasury Department after 1920, there were astonishingly few references to what was happening in England until Professor Lindesmith began making himself heard in the late 1940's. And from the outset the Narcotics Bureau responded with manic outbursts of denial and denunciation. This was regrettable because there are, in truth, some reasonable considerations which suggest that British attitudes and policies are *not* a perfect yardstick by which to measure the U.S. problem. Although addiction was commonplace and reportedly on the increase in the United Kingdom at the end of World War I, there had been nothing resembling the hysteria that gripped America in that period, and the addiction problem itself was doubtless much smaller because of Britain's better handling of nostrums plus her longer and more complete involvement in the war. Population elements in the two countries are notably different, and it is true that the British, more homogenous and more rigidly stratified, are also generally more law-abiding. Besides which, England had had nothing to launch her on the wrong foot which could be compared to America's off-balance start while simultaneously coping with national prohibition.

But these reasonable distinctions were obliterated by the intemperance with which Anslinger and his echoers felt obliged to express themselves on the subject. A few typical pronouncements have already been noted, because the "British System" was necessarily a controversial element in the Daniel Committee hearings, in the work of the Joint ABA-AMA Committee, and at the NIH Symposium. But the Bureau's counterattacks antedated and continued after those exchanges.

Even elementary regard for consistency seldom operated as an inhibitory factor in the law-enforcement camp. On the one hand, British practices were equated with the other Bureau anathema, the so-called "clinic" experiments of the 1920's, and it was asserted that following the British example would mean handing out drugs without controls and at little or no cost to anyone who was—or wanted to become—an addict. On the other, it was vigorously insisted that the problem in England and the way the British dealt with it were essentially identical with the American experience. In 1953 Commissioner Anslinger wrote:

> Under this plan anyone who is now or who later becomes a drug addict would apply to the clinic and receive the amount of narcotic drug sufficient to maintain his customary use. . . . No Government in the world conducts such clinics, no matter what is said about England. What about all the seizures there? What about the trouble doctors are having keeping their bags from being stolen?

With respect to such rhetorical questions what were the facts? They were that British seizures of smuggled drugs throughout this period never amounted to more than a few kilograms per year, and that sometimes a full annual reporting period would pass without a single drug theft or attempted theft.

Referring unblushingly to "the present wave of drug addiction" in the British Isles, Anslinger continued this same 1953 argument:

> In England, the British Government reports annually only 350 drug addicts known to the authorities—mostly doctors and nurses. When we asked them about the statistics on seizures of opium and hashish (marijuana), they say: Negroes, Indians, and Chinese are involved. In this country, we don't distinguish; we take the situation as a whole. England, during the past year, has had a surge of hashish addiction among young people. A year ago they were looking at the United States with an "it can't happen here" attitude. Suddenly hashish addiction hit the young people. Ordinarily hashish is only something for the Egyptian, the Indian. Now the British press is filled with accounts of cases of addiction of young people.

Hashish, of course, is not identical with marijuana, and there is no such thing as "hashish addiction." But in any event, for the years to which the Commissioner referred, the total number of prosecutions for *all* categories of marijuana offense ranged between 100 and 150.

In 1954 the Bureau, following its customary practice of using official Treasury Department channels and U.S. taxpayers' money to disseminate its views, put out a document entitled "British Narcotic System," aimed specifically at Lindesmith:

> Several years ago a professor of sociology at an American university . . . wrote an article in which he advocated that the United States adopt the British system of handling drug addicts by having doctors write prescriptions for addicts. He reported that this system had abolished the black market in narcotics and that consequently there were only 326 drug addicts in the United Kingdom. . . .
>
> Nothing could be further from the truth. The British system is the same as the United States system. The following is an excerpt of a letter dated July 18, 1953, from the British Home Office, concerning the prescribing of narcotic drugs by the medical profession: "A doctor may not have or use the drugs for any other purpose than that of ministering to the strictly medical needs of his patients. The continued supply of drugs to a patient either direct or by prescription, solely for the gratification of addiction is not regarded as a medical need." The British Government is a party to all of the international narcotic conventions to which the United States is a party. They enforce treaties in the same manner as the United States. The British and United States systems for enforcing narcotic laws are exactly the same.

The excerpt from the Home Office letter thus officially reproduced is, of course, a perfectly accurate paraphrase of the regulation quoted earlier, and accurate also in the sense that "solely
for the gratification of addiction" is a law-enforcement term, not
descriptive of medical administration in the United Kingdom or
anywhere else.

Commissioner Anslinger, as the U.S. spokesman at the U.N.
and with the full prestige of the United States government behind
him, could extract statements like the Home Office letter from
his official confreres almost at pleasure, and from time to time
the Bureau circulated other similarly misrepresentative observations. On one occasion the United Kingdom representative on the
U.N. Narcotic Commission provided him with the following:

> Dangerous drugs are subjected in the United Kingdom to a wide
> degree of control and the exacting standard demanded by the inter-
> national agreements to which the United Kingdom is a party. The
> indiscriminate administration of narcotics to addicts would be in-
> compatible with those obligations and is not now, and never has
> been, a feature of United Kingdom policy.

Indiscriminate administration in Great Britain? Of course not.
But this was trumpeted as a crushing put-down for American
reporters of the English experience.

In 1958, after Mr. Harney had contributed his statement about
the Hitlerian "Big Lie" technique, the Bureau circulated what
purported to be another letter from an unidentified official in the
British Home Office containing the following:

> As regards the visits of Americans to this country we are in this
> difficulty; that it is not possible for us to refuse to have a talk with
> visiting Americans who asked to be allowed to visit the Home
> Office to discuss the so-called "British system." However, when
> we do see these visitors any remarks which we make are rather on
> the lines of what Mr. Harney has said, and we make it clear that
> there is not in fact any such thing as a "British system" which is
> an invention of certain Americans who wish to prove a particular
> point of view. . . .
> The higher consumption of narcotic drugs in the United King-
> dom as compared with the United States is in my view mainly a
> reflection of the fact that we have a free National Health Service.

Higher consumption of drugs in England? Somehow relevant
in a discussion of the illicit traffic? Not at all, because what the
last statement refers to is simply the fact that British medical
practitioners use more morphine (and heroin when it is indicated)

as analgesics in connection with their general practice than their intimidated American fellows.

In 1959 Mr. Anslinger came up with a trio of American doctors who seemed eager to chorus his line. Their role in the controversy may be explained by the fact that two of them were public employees of the State of New York (where Attorney General Javits was then propelling himself toward the Senate with a tough-on-dope campaign), while the third was a professor at the state-owned University of Illinois (where Mr. Harney had just been named head of a new Illinois State Bureau of Narcotics). The New York doctors—Larimore and Brill—came back after a month in England to report that there really was no such thing as a British "system," that doctors there had no more freedom to prescribe drugs than in the United States, and that "the opinion prevalent in some quarters that . . . the British system is better than ours" is largely accounted for by misunderstanding. They noted, curiously, that nearly all the British experts with whom they conferred told them that no one else from the United States had ever before been in touch with them (the experts), and that the British were somewhat huffy about any references to a "system," which they thought was an invention by Americans.

The Larimore-Brill team drew large conclusions from small figures: for example, an increase between 1949 and 1956 of from thirty-three to fifty-four drug addicts annually admitted into mental hospitals was characterized by them as "a definite increase"; on the basis of twenty-four addict-inmates among the then total British prison population of 40,000 (three of whom were only marijuana users), they concluded that the British drug addict is a low-level criminal, below the meanest pimp, and that "other criminals will have nothing to do with the addict, not only because they don't trust his judgment, but also because they despise him"; and on the authority of a casual reference by one commentator to Notting Hill, the scene of summer riots in London, they alluded to "what appeared to us to be a potentially serious situation from a narcotics standpoint in the Notting Hill section"—where, to their astonishment, no "practical preventive measures" have been employed "to forestall the development of widespread addiction in that area."

Their overall conclusions in 1959 were that the British and U.S. problems were the same and were being approached in the same way and—simultaneously—that the absence of *any* significant problem in Great Britain was due not to the way controls had been handled, but to the fact that the English "have a

definite abhorrence of narcotic drugs." These good doctors
revived once more the analogy between drug addiction and
infection, this time likening the addict to a typhoid bacillus and
characterizing the environment in which he operates as "one
contaminated by human wastes to promote the spread of the
agent and its introduction into the host."

The Illinois doctor, Ausubel, must have pleased even Mr.
Harney. Said he of letting policemen dictate to his medical confreres: "The potentially ruinous consequences of large-scale addiction are so great that control of narcotic drugs cannot simply
be left to the discretion of the medical profession." Coming to
the British experience by way of the New York Academy proposal, which he termed merely a "clinic" plan, Dr. Ausubel
scorned the latter as "excellent Marxism" and "incredibly naïve,"
and said it was based on a mere fifteen "identifiable logical
fallacies and errors of fact." *His* analogy was to malaria instead
of typhoid, with the additional fillip that treating addicts through
medical facilities would be like establishing "clinics to dispense
jewels free of charge to known jewel thieves." Having thus
gathered momentum, Dr. Ausubel sailed head-on into the British:

> As if these issues were not already sufficiently complicated, the
> proponents of legalization and ambulatory treatment have muddied
> the waters further by injecting the far-fetched analogy of the
> British system into their arguments. Legally the British system
> is very similar to our own. . . . The British system, however, has
> an interpretive joker in it which in practice legalizes lifelong addic-
> tion for addicts without appearing to do so in a statutory sentence.
> . . . The deliberate ambiguity of this legalistic dodge kills many
> birds with a single stone. . . . Although this practice is the epi-
> tome of amoral expediency, it apparently has not led to wide-
> spread addiction even though the figure of only 359 addicts in the
> entire British Isles is too small to be credible. . . .
>
> The principal logical fallacy committed by those who advocate
> the exportation of the British system to the United States is to
> impute a causal connection between the method of control cur-
> rently employed and the relatively low rate of addiction. Actually,
> no such connection exists. . . . Only 0.2 percent of the population
> in the United Kingdom is of non-Caucasian stock, as compared to
> 16 percent of the American population. The significance of this
> difference lies in the fact that two-thirds of the addict population
> of the United States is recruited from the latter 16 percent.
>
> Because of the much greater number of active and potential
> addicts in the United States, however, the adoption of the British
> system would soon create a half million new addicts without
> eradicating the illicit market.

In 1965, six years after their first report, Larimore and Brill were sent on another junket to England for the purpose of making a second report to Governor Rockefeller "because of the continued interest and misunderstanding in some quarters here concerning the 'British System.'" They noted—accurately—that the British addiction problem had *doubled* (from roughly 350 to 700 addicts) and reported a shocking increase in heroin victims, "mostly young males with a smaller admixture of young women, largely prostitutes." They observed that "the addict now plays an active role in the spread of the habit," and that the British were following the U.S. lead in their increasing concern about non-narcotic stimulants and sedatives, although they reported that there had been no increase in the number of addicts in British prisons and that marijuana was not yet thought to constitute a problem of much significance.

Prowling Piccadilly at night, Larimore and Brill observed "youthful vagabondage" characterized by "beatnik" types who were unwilling to work, often quite unkempt in appearance, untrustworthy, unreliable, amoral, manipulative, and difficult. They concluded, in short, that the British approach to the drug problem was now proving to be a total failure—with a few additional irrelevancies, such as a notation that the British were "aware of the catastrophic outcome of the recent attempt at a clinic plan in Israel" and a paragraph about how England had tried "clinics" for the administration of drugs unsuccessfully in Asia and Africa prior to World War II (thus chiming in on another Bureau theme, that the success of drug controls in the British Isles ought really to be measured by conditions prevailing under the Union Jack in Singapore and Hong Kong).

The most regrettable thing about this second Larimore-Brill report, distributed all over America with official sponsorship by Anslinger's successor, Henry Giordano, was that there actually *had* been changes in the British situation which merited consideration. In 1958 the Minister of Health appointed a Review Committee to consider whether modifications should be made in the standards set forth by the 1926 Rolleston Report. The chairman was Sir Russell Brain, from whom the Committee took its name. In November 1960, after extensive study and hearings, the Brain Committee made its report, concluding that no noteworthy difficulties had arisen from the policy of permitting doctors to provide drugs to known addicts, that the few irregularities which had come to light over the years did not warrant regulatory changes to correct them, that the problem of addiction was still "a small one," and that although there had been an increase in the use of cannabis it could not be classified as an addicting drug and required no special administrative measures as of that time. The Brain Committee's principal suggestion was that the Home Office Memorandum which contained the Rolleston Rules "could be presented in a more readable form."

But this first Brain Report came just when the influx of addicts from Canada and the United States was beginning to hit London, and soon thereafter the hippie movement started to grow in England, especially in London, where it seemed to have more vitality than parallel trends in the United States. And though not justifying the exultant cries raised by hard-line U.S. narcotic authorities, there is no question that some new problems *did* appear to plague the British. Three or four London doctors, possibly as many as half a dozen, began to prescribe heroin in large amounts, defying the gentle sanctions which had theretofore sufficed to hold the medical profession in line. Marijuana smoking jumped alarmingly. Abuse of the amphetamines and barbiturates became more widespread, and the British press, doubtless once more reflecting somewhat the American excitement over the same subject (a story which awaits us in a future chapter), began giving these substances increased attention.

Some observers say Parliament is more sensitive to its electorate than the American Congress. Be that as it may, in 1964 the British lawmakers responded with two new Acts: a new Dangerous Drugs Act, expanding the list of controlled substances, renaming "Indian hemp" cannabis, and creating the new offenses of growing cannabis or permitting it to be smoked in one's premises; and the Drugs (Prevention of Misuse) Act, establishing for the first time a statutory penalty—up to two years—for unlawful possession of abusable substances (in narrow categories covering, at the outset, only some of the amphetamines), setting up a tighter import-license system, and broadening the search-and-seizure powers of drug-law enforcers. These 1964 measures, and particularly the cannabis offenses and possession penalties, account for the jump in numbers of prosecutions which we have already noted.

Simultaneously, the Minister of Health reconvened the Brain Committee, requesting its members to "consider whether, in the light of recent experience, the advice they gave in 1960 in relation to the prescribing of addictive drugs by doctors needs revising and, if so, to make recommendations." The Committee reported a second time in July 1965, acknowledging a "disturbing rise in the incidence of addiction to heroin and cocaine, especially among young people," and observing that the main source of supply had been reckless prescribing by a small number of doctors. The Committee's report urged, accordingly, that restrictions be imposed on the powers of doctors to prescribe heroin and cocaine and that the system of reporting addicts to the Home Office, which had theretofore been voluntary, be made mandatory by statute. Moreover, the Committee suggested the establishment of a number of "special treatment centres," particularly in the London area, and compulsory detention of addicts, when necessary, in these centers.

In the Dangerous Drugs Act of 1965, Parliament consolidated the 1964 law with earlier measures and further tightened controls on imports. Two years later, in the Dangerous Drugs Act of 1967, the British lawmakers further responded to the Brain recommendations by authorizing the Secretary of State for Home Affairs to limit the power of doctors to prescribe drugs and by setting up procedures to refer disciplinary cases to a special tribunal established by the Act for that purpose.

Under these powers, the Home Office and the Ministry of Health promulgated regulations restricting the authority to prescribe heroin and cocaine to doctors holding special licenses, and have subsequently used this licensing power to channel the prescribing and dispensing of these drugs through hospital centers (there are currently fifteen in the London area, one in Portsmouth, and one in Birmingham) and through a small number of specially licensed practitioners in other parts of the United Kingdom. As the new control patterns took effect, more and more addicts appeared at the centers, and it is not unlikely that the total number of users of heroin (morphine and synthetics were not similarly controlled) might have passed the 3,000 mark at its peak in 1969–70. It is also true, indisputably, that many of these new addicts were young people seduced by Britain's first real drug subculture. Abuse of amphetamines, including "mainlining" of methedrine, became popular enough to attract notice and led to a voluntary agreement among doctors, pharmacists, and hospitals not to give out these drugs in injectable form.

There is general agreement, nonetheless, that true addiction (including a swing from heroin to morphine and methadone), serious abuse (heavy use of cocaine, amphetamines, and barbiturates), and the widespread practice of mixing drugs in large doses leveled off in the United Kingdom in 1970, if it did not actually start declining. Pot smokers apart, the drug-involved element seemed to stablize in the range of no more than a few thousand; there was a decline in new applicants for treatment at the centers, and by early 1971 medical authorities began to feel that they had brought the situation under control.

But the momentum of press-generated excitement and political byplays could not be wound down so easily. The Advisory Committee on Drug Dependence, led by Sir Edward Wayne after Lord Brain's demise, carried on with more studies and recommendations, though generally counseling restraint:

> Behind some criticisms that we heard of the law we sensed resentment that users of cannabis should be subject to the same criminal procedures as other drug-users, and a wider doubt as to whether in order to check some forms of drug misuse a sledge hammer had been employed to crack a nut. The balance here between law and liberty is not easy to get right. . . .
>
> The problem presented to society by the misuse of drugs is a serious one. But it is not so serious as to justify what is, for practical purposes, the removal of all rights for the protection of individual privacy from a substantial section of the population.

In 1970 the Labor government proposed a new, comprehensive measure which died in Parliament when the Conservatives took over following the June general elections. The Conservatives thereupon picked up most of the same features, however, and in May 1971 their Misuse of Drugs Act, replacing all anti-drug legislation that had preceded it, became law. The penalty for trafficking offenses is now a maximum of fourteen years, plus an innovation that currently fascinates lawmakers on both sides of the Atlantic: an *unlimited* fine. Three classifications of drugs, subject to reclassing by the Home Secretary, determine the gradation of penalties for *possession:* for Class A, including all the major addicting and abused substances, seven years; for Class B, where cannabis is placed with substances like codeine, five years; and for Class C, borderline drugs and compounds, two years—with, in all cases, the unlimited monetary punishment as well. The summary-conviction option is also retained, however, providing alternatives of twelve months/£400, six months/£400, and six months/£200 for classes A, B, and C, respectively.

In announcing the new law, the government was self-laudatory for its leniency in cutting the marijuana penalty in half—from the prior ten years and £1,000 to five years and a fine without limit.

The long-standing statutory protection for doctors and other prescribers acting in good faith in the practice of their professions was virtually wiped out by this Act. The Home Secretary may now specify what are approved prescribing and dispensing practices by regulation. He may also impose special restrictions on particular drugs, like the present heroin and cocaine licensing requirements. Provision is made for a permanent Advisory Council and an Expert Committee to advise the Secretary, and new disciplinary procedures for errant physicians are spelled out. The stringent search, seizure, and arrest provisions of prior Acts are retained and made applicable to all drug-law enforcement. Noting that the British Medical Association appeared to approve every one of these police-oriented encroachments on its prerogatives, an articulate actor on the scene (Hon. William Deedes, M.P.) was constrained to write: "How fortunate are the shepherds of such a docile flock."

And that brings the British story up to date, except for a look at what—after all this, in 1971—Attorney General Mitchell has to say on the subject:

> Some have said, "Let's legalize the possession of drugs and provide them free under a doctor's care." According to this argument the addicts won't have to steal to get money for dope. And by taking the profit out of the illicit traffic the pushers would go out of business.
>
> This is the approach taken in Great Britain, and in the opinion of our observers it is proving to be wrong. The dope pushers have moved into Britain in a big way, and are providing narcotics to the addict over and above what he receives through medical care. And there is a tendency of pushers and addicts alike to spread the disease. So what I would call the "surrender" approach hasn't proved itself.

The official response to this in London, where it caused a mild furor, was that Mitchell was making "a 'political' speech strictly for domestic consumption." The less official characterization from medical and legal commentators was reduced by the London *Times* to a single word: "Rubbish!"

It is too early to assess the effects of the 1971 Misuse of Drugs Act. The British do not lose their perspective easily. But if the situation *does* worsen in their new drift toward tougher laws, more aggressive regulation, busier police, and meeker doctors, it must not be overlooked that what is really happening is that they are at long last toying with features characteristic of what could be called the "American system."

■ TWENTY-ONE

Proselytizing the World

■ HALF THE STORY of American aspirations to wipe out drug trafficking by international cooperation can be revealed in a single observation—that there is only one parallel in the history of modern nations, and that is the contemporaneous effort to put an end to wars by disarmament. This analogy was actually noted, somewhat ruefully perhaps, in a League of Nations study in 1933; and indeed the *theory* is impeccable in both cases: if all nations agreed to lay aside their weapons—or to devote major efforts to hunting out poppy fields—mankind would assuredly be greatly benefitted.

But even as it might be said that in recent years most of the world has been concerned chiefly with disarming only the United States (and now a few other nuclear giants), so the reverse has been true with respect to drugs: only the United States, sometimes virtually alone, has been trying seriously to induce the rest of the world to restrict drug crops and repress drug production for international markets. This is more easily understandable when one recalls what has been stressed several times already: *for the past half century there has really been only one important illicit market for drugs in the world, and that is the one the United States maintains at such great cost to all concerned in North America.*

As if to advertise this state of affairs, the U.S.-dominated U.N. Commission on Narcotic Drugs sometimes publishes the price ranges of drugs in illicit markets, noting in 1968, for example, that representative spreads for black-market heroin were as follows: in Thailand, $384 to $576 per kilogram refined, and $211 to $288 unrefined (adulterated); in Iran, $2,400 to $2,900 per kilogram wholesale and $7 per gram retail; in Greece, $3,900 per kilogram wholesale and $10,800 to $13,800 retail; in Turkey, $5,555 to $6,666 per kilogram; in the United States, $25,000 to $35,000 per kilogram refined, $18,000 to $25,000 unrefined, and on the streets of U.S. cities $1 to $50 per capsule or packet, depending on the range of purity (1 to 25 per cent; from a trace to a grain or two). At $10 per "cap," one kilogram of refined "H" thus brings a return in Yankee dollars reaching well into six figures, less, of course, the cost of a little milk sugar or similar cutting substance and some gelatin or glassine packaging. The Canadian street price was reported to average $13 per capsule.

It will be recalled that even the beginnings of the international story, which Commissioner Anslinger always characterized as a dramatic instance of world collaboration, came about because of special problems encountered by the United States in the Philippines following the Spanish-American War. At least this was a major factor, along with President Roosevelt's humanitarian concern over the continuing exploitation of the China traffic, in causing the United States to initiate the Shanghai Conference of 1909, from which came a barrage of hortatory resolutions calling on all governments to suppress opium, control the production of morphine by "drastic" measures in their own territories, and prevent exportation from their ports to countries which had banned or restricted inbound shipments. The latter was a novel concept—that we could call upon the world to choke off at the source substances we wanted to keep from flowing inward across our boundaries.

The United States was likewise the moving force behind the 1912 Hague Conference, convened to implement the Shanghai principles. Here we elaborated the arguments for stringent international controls: drug traffickers could not be counted on to respect national frontiers; since most countries did not raise drug crops they were dependent on international trade for their supplies; drug smuggling is easy because of the small bulk of the substances involved; and since drug addicts imperatively demand their drugs and will pay any price, the traffic would attract unscrupulous persons and criminals, and lead to the development of international gangs. Accordingly, it was urged, even countries having no drug problems within their own borders would have to start policing manufacture, export, and transshipments or they would provide bases for smuggling operations into countries which *did* have black markets.

Thirteen governments were represented at the Hague. The Convention was to take effect upon ratification and the signing of a special protocol by the thirteen, but when the delegates took it home to their respective foreign ministries nothing happened. Special conferences were convened again, later in 1913 and in 1914, to push for action as the clouds of World War I gathered, but it was not until February 1915 that the United States persuaded two other powers—China and the Netherlands—to sign so that the Convention could be launched as more than a simple bilateral agreement. (This episode and the last-mentioned date are of particular interest when it is recalled that the Harrison Act, passed by Congress with so much eclat in 1914, was justified by its proponents in large part as necessary fulfillment of an *international* obligation.)

Quite possibly the whole story of world cooperation in the drug field might have ended here had not the United States, in its dominant position at the Paris Peace Conference, sponsored a provision in the Peace Treaties to the effect that ratification of the latter should be deemed automatically to be ratification of and adherence to the Hague Convention. Since the Paris treaties carried all the benefits and privileges of League of Nations membership, most sovereign states signed up in ensuing decades. But a few more were driven in, again by the United States, as late as World War II. This came about because Congress had provided in the American Narcotic Drugs Import and Export Act that the United States would only export controlled drugs to countries which were parties to the Hague Convention; so when war disrupted ordinary channels through which nations obtained their legitimate supplies, a number of nonsignatory powers had to turn to U.S. sources. Such countries as Afghanistan, Egypt, Paraguay, and Saudi Arabia joined the fold this way. By the end of 1945, the only holdouts were Lithuania, Iran, San Marino, Sudan, the U.S.S.R., and Ethiopia.

In 1920 the League General Assembly had created a special Advisory Committee on the Traffic in Opium and Other Dangerous Drugs. Members of this Committee were appointed by the League Council in 1921, and although the United States was already dissociated from League affairs, it received an invitation to participate, through an observer, as a "specially concerned" nonmember. And from this position, commencing in 1923, the United States made its views felt with an increasingly heavy hand.

The Second International Opium Conference, called by the

League, met in Geneva in 1924 and was attended by delegates from thirty-six nations. The U.S. representatives, after being rebuffed in their proposal for a world ban on heroin and trying unsuccessfully to persuade the Conference to outlaw all drug production for nonmedical purposes, withdrew from the deliberations, taking the Chinese along. The work product of this Conference, the Geneva Convention of 1925 (which came into force in September 1928), was substantial nonetheless, setting up an obligatory import-export licensing system, rephrasing and tightening the exhortations of the Hague document, and creating a new control agency, the Permanent Central Board, entrusted with the collection of statistics and a watchdog-and-warning supervision over the accumulation of stocks of drugs and international trafficking. And again, even though the United States never ratified the Convention, from the outset a U.S. representative was given a special place on the Permanent Board.

Commissioner Anslinger appeared on the scene in 1930, with, as has been noted, a background in diplomacy; the official U.S. position on all matters pertaining to drugs thereafter coincided with his personal views; and significant developments on the world front have in turn almost always coincided, sooner or later, with the positions pressed by his U.S. delegation.

First the struggle for production controls, which had been unsuccessful in 1925, was renewed and bore fruit in a new Limitation Conference convened in Geneva in 1931. The Americans had been pushing, through the Opium Advisory Committee, for a treaty to establish iron-bound manufacturing quotas, and this caused a number of countries to increase their output or open new manufacturing facilities so that they would not be slighted in what threatened to be a monopolistic freeze of the status quo. But the 1931 document provided flexible controls, to be administered by a newly created Supervisory Body, limiting the manufacture of drugs to the legitimate demand which could be demonstrated in each case by a manufacturing country. Every participating government was bound to submit to the Supervisory Body an annual estimate of its legitimate needs, and the Body then prepared from these a Statement of Estimated World Requirements. Countries exceeding their estimates or otherwise getting out of line were supposed to file explanatory statements with the Central Board.

In 1931 the Americans again pushed hard for a total ban on heroin (which actually differs from morphine and synthetic opiates in its effects on addicts not much more than martinis differ from bourbon and branch water for the confirmed five-o'clocker, and which has unique therapeutic value in treating certain pulmonary disorders), but other delegations resisted once more, expressing strong doubts whether the value of this opium derivative did not outweigh its dangers. The upshot was a compromise action:

> The Conference:
> Recognizing the highly dangerous character of diacetylmorphine as a drug of addiction and the possibility in most, if not all, cases of replacing it by other drugs of a less dangerous character;
> Recommends that each Government should examine in conjunction with the medical profession the possibility of abolishing or restricting its use, and communicate the results of such examinations to the Secretary-General of the League of Nations.

The fruits of this, tallied and reported by the Opium Advisory Committee in 1938, were that nine countries agreed to total abolition, seven reported that they had already imposed severe controls, twelve favored moderate restrictions, and fourteen explained why they were not willing to consider *any* abolition or restriction.

And since we have thus jumped ahead on the heroin story, let us follow it a little further, to an illuminating collision between Anslinger and the British Medical Association, in bygone days when the BMA was at its doughty best. United Kingdom spokesmen were vigorous among those opposing restrictions on the drug after the British profession had been consulted through the Ministry of Health and the BMA. But Anslinger was persistent. Year after year his reports as U.S. delegate to the Opium Commission kept worrying the point. For example, in his 1951 account (doubling as the official U.S. Report to the United Nations and the annual U.S. Treasury Report to Congress) he inserted:

> During the sixth session Commissioner Anslinger, the United States Representative on the United Nations Commission on Narcotic Drugs, gave a statement on the illicit traffic in diacetylmorphine (heroin) which is reproduced below:
> . . . There apparently exists heroin stocks in Italy in the hands of dealers of over 200 kilos of heroin, or equal to about a 10-year supply. These stocks constitute a great danger to the illicit traffic in various countries, particularly the United States where large quantities have been smuggled from Italy. The Italian Government should take immediate steps to safeguard these stocks, and to cease manufacture of heroin for 10 years or until the stocks are exhausted.

I ask that the Secretary General send a letter to the Italian Government suggesting that such steps be taken. . . .

It is with considerable concern that one views the reported flow of heroin from Tientsin and points in Manchuria into Japan via Hong Kong. . . . I have a photograph of the packages bearing the Tientsin label. . . . This traffic should be suppressed by the Communist authorities in China. It is apparent that the crest of teenage addiction has been reached and will continue to decline if the governments mentioned continue to tighten up their controls and if all governments provide heavier penalties in the way of mandatory sentences and if Communist China closes the heroin factories in its territory.

And again in 1956:

The Commission on Narcotic Drugs reemphasized its previous recommendation that the manufacture, import, export, and use of heroin be prohibited. Most governments have taken measures for the prohibition of heroin. Egypt has prohibited the manufacture and import of this drug, and has stopped its use for medical purposes. In March, 1956, Italy prohibited the manufacture, import, and export of heroin, and has strictly controlled its distribution. The United Kingdom has banned importation and exportation of heroin, but a legal obstacle prevents prohibition of its manufacture.

The "legal obstacle" referred to was not legal at all—it was the angry and vociferous British doctors. Responding to pressure openly characterized as being applied by the United Nations and U.S. Delegate Anslinger, the Secretary of State for Home Affairs had announced in the House of Commons a proposed total ban on the manufacture of heroin. The *British Medical Journal* challenged the move, and the Association formally objected by resolution to the fact that medical opinion had not been sought. The controversy blossomed into Parliamentary questions and brisk exchanges of letters in the London *Times,* which was itself inspired to editorialize:

Heroin addiction is undoubtedly a serious problem in many countries, but is this a valid reason for depriving patients in this country of an essential drug, provided always that export of the drug is barred? . . . The National Health Service exists for the benefit of the sick and suffering citizen, and from time immemorial the alleviation of pain has been one of the first claims upon the physician. The Minister of Health is taking upon himself a serious, and unjustifiable, responsibility in agreeing to the deprivation of so many patients of their one source of relief from what is so often excruciating pain. After the arguments of the deputation from the

British Medical Association have been heard, the Government should have better, and second, thoughts.

Under these pressures the Home Secretary receded, the manufacture of heroin for home consumption in England was continued, and further consideration of domestic restrictions was postponed indefinitely. British practitioners are still indignant, nonetheless, about one distortion that has continued: at the height of the controversy heroin was withdrawn from the British Pharmacopeia, and solely on this basis American authorities have been asserting ever since that Great Britain fell into line and "banned" the drug.

Returning to the international scene in 1931, the Limitation Convention went further, despite the American setback on heroin, than any comparable agreement had ever gone in limiting sovereign control of a domestic activity by delegating authority to an international body. Under procedures worked out by the League Secretariat in following years, and as more nations adhered, it achieved much of its desired effect, exposing to view and control the *legitimate* production of regulated drugs (opiates, cocaine, and cannabis) throughout most of the world community. Even nations not adhering to the Convention could be affected by it, for the Supervisory Body was empowered to make estimates for nonparty states as well as for adherents, and if a nonparty permitted production grossly exceeding its estimated needs it could be penalized by an embargo against further shipments of drug supplies to it by party-states.

The next Convention, drafted in 1936, was also launched by the United States as an initiating party—and then the U.S. delegation again withdrew when it could not obtain the strict terms Anslinger wanted. The subject matter this time was particularly favored by him: the strengthening of criminal penalties imposed for narcotic offenses, and facilitating extradition of drug traffickers wherever they might take refuge. Each signatory was also required to set up a central national police agency to coordinate its drug-law enforcement efforts.

The United States walked out, and refused to sign, because the Convention covered only manufactured drugs, excluding raw materials and smoking-opium. This was unacceptable since, as Anslinger himself ingenuously confided, it afforded no constitutional ground (or, more truthfully, no way around the U.S. Constitution) for federal repression of cannabis and the opium poppy at home. The 1936 Convention nonetheless became effective in

1939, just after the outbreak of World War II, with ratifications by ten countries; by 1945 it had a total of thirteen adherents.

Early in 1941, before the United States became embroiled in the war, Anslinger protected his domain by inviting all the narcotics officials in the League Secretariat, the Supervisory Body, and the Permanent Central Board to move their operations from Geneva to branch offices in Washington. Thus while most League agencies vanished in the holocaust, the machinery for international drug controls survived intact, more beholden to the U.S. delegate than ever.

An American propaganda line after Pearl Harbor was that the Japanese had spread drug addiction as a prelude to military subjugation—"opium pellets were sent as a vanguard of the military attack"—in their sweep westward into Manchuria, Korea, and mainland China. This gave Commissioner Anslinger the kind of chance he never failed to seize. Even before the Pacific war began to turn in the Allies' favor, the U.S. Bureau began sowing fears around official Washington about what would happen when American troops were deployed in areas where they might be exposed to opium dens. The Commissioner pointed out that drug addiction is caused by association, so all opium smokers in liberated countries would have to be regarded as sources of infection. He also pointed out that the Filipinos who stood bravely with U.S. troops at Corregidor would surely have collapsed much sooner had America not had the foresight to suppress the sale of opium in their islands.

In January 1943, representatives of Great Britain, Canada, Australia, New Zealand, the Netherlands, and China were summoned to the Treasury Department to discuss what was going to happen when some island or territory where they had formerly permitted opium smoking came to be recaptured. Anslinger pointed out to these errant allies that opium monopolies did not reduce the number of smokers, that only full international cooperation by all concerned could provide a solution, and that the production of poppy crops would thereafter have to be strictly controlled. Doubtless to their discomfiture—remembering the posture of the war in early 1943—he also told them that American public opinion was so crystallized against drugs that if the American navy liberated former colonies like Hong Kong, the Americans could not shift command back to the British if the British said opium was "in" while U.S. authorities were obliged to insist that it was "out." The upshot was that in September 1943 the U.S. government took the unusual step of addressing an official communication on the subject to each nation concerned, and before the year was out all had capitulated and promised to put an end to "the troublesome opium-smoking problem."

When the war ended, U.S. occupying forces actually took control in much of the Far East and thus American attitudes were widely imposed. In Japan itself, for example, General McArthur caused the enactment of a Japanese Harrison Act, complete with top-to-bottom registration requirements, an army of drug inspectors, and five-year prison sentences (the maximum sentence for any drug offense under Japanese law had previously been three months). In 1946 the Permanent Central Opium Board bestowed a glowing "well-done" for what was happening in Asia:

> It is evident that the American occupying authorities have taken great interest in the control of narcotics and have taken especial care to establish a strict centralized supervision. The Board desires to express its appreciation to the military authorities responsible at Pacific Headquarters for their work, to the Department of State, and to the Commissioner of Narcotics of the United States, who have also been directly concerned in bringing about this desirable result.

Nor was Germany neglected. All uses of heroin were prohibited forthwith, and all drug transactions were strictly regulated in the U.S. Occupation Zone, as soon as the Americans had established themselves. Anslinger found conditions elsewhere in Germany "unsatisfactory," however, and U.S. spokesmen accordingly pressed for a joint Narcotics Control Working Party to revise German laws on behalf of all four of the occupying authorities.

Simultaneously, Delegate Anslinger sponsored a formal request from the U.N. Commission:

> The Commission:
> *Requests* the Economic and Social Council to urge the Governments of France, the United Kingdom, the Union of Soviet Socialist Republics, and the United States to recommend to the Allied Control Authority to take the necessary measures, at the earliest possible moment, for the establishment of an effective control of narcotics for all Germany.

Yet even this was not enough, and the German situation remained unsatisfactory, because although in ensuing years the Americans drafted a Harrison type law for Germany, and a Working Party was set up to apply it, the other occupying powers soon lost their enthusiasm for the effort, eventually concluding that Germany's old Narcotics Law of 1929 was adequate.

Some other U.S. projects in the postwar period were similarly rebuffed. Harping further on the theme that Japan had deliberately used opium as an instrument of aggression, Anslinger tried to have official promotion of drug addiction classified as genocide, without success. His subsequent efforts to obtain formal censure against the government of Red China for deliberately fostering drug abuse among its political adversaries likewise came to nothing in the international forum (though as we have seen, he made good use of his own U.N. statements as scare material for home consumption in the United States).

Efforts led by the United States to induce world opium producers to outlaw the poppy continued despite the setback already noted, when the subject was excluded from the 1936 Convention. By 1939 a poppy-limitation draft, sponsored by the League Opium Advisory Committee, was being circulated in preparation for another convention. In 1944, while the war still raged, the U.S. Congress passed an elaborate resolution requesting President Roosevelt

> . . . to approach the Governments of all opium-producing countries throughout the world, urging upon them, in the interests of protecting American citizens and those of our Allies and of freeing the world of an age-old evil, that they take immediate steps to limit and control the growth of the opium poppy and the production of opium and its derivatives to the amount actually required for strictly medicinal and scientific purposes.

As a result, American spokesmen began directly urging friends and allies to agree on eighteen points, closely resembling the substance of the 1939 draft protocol and calling for an international monopoly, with quotas, an inspection system, and enforcement sanctions. This evoked a number of polite responses but only two actions: Afghanistan announced it was outlawing poppy growing as of March 1945, and Iran made a similar announcement in 1946.

In the United Nations structure, a new Commission on Narcotic Drugs was established under the Economic and Social Council, replacing the Opium Advisory Committee, and a new Narcotics Division was created at Lake Success. Once again, the U.S. spokesman on the new Commission was Harry Anslinger, and the Director of the Narcotics Division was an American nominee who had been a League staff member assigned to Washington by the old Dangerous Drugs Section. The Permanent Board and the Supervisory Body were re-established in Geneva, where the World Health Organization, with its Expert Committee on Drugs Liable to Produce Addiction, also made its headquarters.

Pressures for controls on raw opium continued after the war, complicated by the development of methods for extracting morphine base from the whole poppy plant ("poppy straw") as well as from the juice of scored pods in the traditional harvesting. Although agreement in principle was sometimes reached in international discussions, the proposals kept breaking down when it came to implementation. In 1953, as a result of a French suggestion to get away from the American monopoly plan, a mild protocol on production and stocks—principally exhorting affected governments to do something about the problem themselves, and with exceptions for countries which still permitted opium smoking—was actually drafted and agreed upon in New York; but this then lay about for ten more years before coming into force upon ratification by a sufficient number of adherents.

In 1948 another protocol was negotiated at Paris to create machinery for bringing new synthetic substances under the controls imposed by the 1931 Convention. Determination of the addiction-producing properties of such substances was to be made by the Expert Committee of the World Health Organization, but the U.N. Commission could place any substance under international controls forthwith on an emergency basis.

On a different front, when the government of Peru requested a U.N. study of the effects of chewing coca leaves in 1947, U.S. spokesmen used the request as a basis for urging repressive international controls of the coca bush along lines paralleling those pressed with respect to poppies. But the special protocol proposed for this purpose never got beyond the discussion stage.

In any event, all these lesser ups and downs at the U.N. were insignificant beside Commissioner Anslinger's grand project, dreamed of in the old League of Nations days and launched in the U.N. Commission by the U.S. delegation in 1948, the drafting of a comprehensive Single Convention to consolidate provisions of all existing treaties, to centralize the functions of all international control bodies and agencies—and to give the United States another way to push endeavors wherein it had previously failed, such as banning heroin, tightening restrictions on cannabis, limiting opium crops, and choking off sources of the coca leaf. At its May 1948 meeting at Lake Success, the U.N. Commission on Narcotic Drugs adopted a U.S.-drafted and U.S.-sponsored resolution addressed to its parent body, the Economic and

Social Council, requesting the Secretary-General to commence work on such a Single Convention.

Preparation of three drafts took ten years. At the outset, some provisions sounded as authoritarian as the language Congress employs in domestic U.S. drug acts. But it soon became apparent that other nations were not going to compromise their sovereignty by submitting to a supranational Bureau of Narcotics, and gradually the drafts were toned down, so that some terms of the Single Convention as finally approved in 1961 are milder than the old provisions which they supplant.

Yet those who were pushing repressive features also gained some ground. The preamble recites that drug addiction "constitutes a serious evil for the individual and is fraught with social and economic danger to mankind." A new central authority, the International Narcotics Control Board, is vested with the powers of all its predecessors, and functions with a good deal of independence and authority. Although its members are elected by national representatives, it has power to adopt policies affecting nations which have neither ratified the Convention nor even joined the United Nations, so that in this capacity it truly acts in the name of the entire international community.

New substances can be added by streamlined procedures based on the 1948 protocol; reporting requirements are simplified and extended, and each contracting party must submit estimates of its legitimate requirements which thereupon form a basis for production quotas. Manufacture of drugs is limited and controlled by the embargo sanction; and the Convention lumps the opium poppy, the coca bush, and the cannabis plant indiscriminately together as raw crops subject to control.

Any party in whose country the production of drug crops is permitted must set up a control agency, a licensing system, and a purchasing monopoly; and with respect to the coca bush (though, curiously, not as to marijuana), each party adhering to the treaty must see to it that wild bushes are uprooted and illegally cultivated plants destroyed. Some of the requirements are specific indeed (inner wrappings of drug packages shall bear a clearly visible double red band, which must not be placed on the outer wrapping; medical prescriptions must be made in counterfoil books; books and counterfoils must be kept for a period of not less than two years, etc.). And some are sweeping, with a familiar ring—for example, all possession of drugs except under legal authority must be outlawed; each party must create a central enforcement authority to coordinate repressive action against the illicit traffic; and every conceivable offense (eighteen are enumerated, plus "any other action which in the opinion of such Party may be contrary to the provisions of this Convention") shall be punished adequately—"particularly by imprisonment or other penalties of deprivation of liberty."

The Single Convention came into force with forty ratifications in December 1964. The United States adhered in 1967, and at present some eighty nations have become parties. The new eleven-seat International Narcotic Control Board, on which the United States is represented by one spokesman and several echoers, has commenced functioning. So for better or for worse, the remarkable phenomenon of direct international manipulation in this domestic field, and manipulation significantly dominated by the United States besides, is apparently going to remain with us. And the practice we have already noted, using home-front policies and pronouncements to lever the international community while at the same time using the international agencies to pressure lawmakers and public opinion at home, will likewise doubtless go forward.

Although Commissioner Anslinger retired from the Bureau in 1962, he continued in his U.N. post until early 1970, and there the same themes were pounded relentlessly: China still produces opium and heroin in sizable quantities "intended for smuggling to the United States"; Burma must substitute some other agricultural crops for her production of opium, and should rehabilitate her addicts forthwith; heroin is still a growing threat (having grown fairly steadily over the span of five decades); and Latin American nations should do more than they have done about coca. Cannabis misuse (hashish, bhang, marijuana) is a menace in most parts of the world, and more efforts should be made to educate Africans about problems of drug abuse which do not yet seem to alarm them sufficiently.

In 1966 the U.S. Bureau reported modestly to Congress that its cooperation with foreign governments had "grown into a policy of assisting all countries in the control of illicit narcotic traffic whenever such help is requested" and that "U.S. interest and cooperation with other countries has placed the Bureau of Narcotics in its position of leadership in international narcotic enforcement." Also in 1966—and doubtless looking apprehensively at its own impending demise, to be related in a subsequent chapter—the Bureau added a reverse twist, citing the Permanent Central Narcotics Board as authority for the proposition that drug-addiction problems in the world generally and in the United States in particular were really well under control:

However, the report [of the Board] compared present conditions with those existing before international control and concluded the present picture represents a striking measure of progress. The Board pointed out that the relative incidence of addiction to manufactured drugs has appreciably diminished, the number of persons misusing opium has been greatly reduced, and there is no significant diversion of manufactured drugs from the legal trade into illicit channels. The United States was recognized by the Board as a prime example of the decline of the addict population.

Mirroring sudden U.S. concern about hallucinogens and other new drugs (also the subject of succeeding chapters) the Bureau related the following of the U.N. Commission:

The Commission unanimously decided to recommend that the Economic and Social Council adopt a resolution on LSD. The resolution recommends that immediate action be taken by governments to strictly control the import, export, and production of LSD and similar substances and to place their distribution "under the supervision of competent authorities." The Commission further recommended that the use of LSD "and substances producing similar ill-effects either immediately or readily by conversion" be restricted to scientific research and medical purposes and their administration be only under very close and continuous medical supervision. The Commission condemned all other usages of such substances and urged governments to take all steps to prevent it.

(An elaborate Convention on Psychotropic Substances, imposing international controls like those specified by the Single Convention, subsequently went through several drafts and was adopted by a U.N. conference in Vienna in February 1971, to take effect when ratified by forty states. It covers such a grab-bag of natural and manufactured items that at every stage of its consideration its proponents felt obliged to stress anew that it would not affect alcohol or tobacco abuse.)

In 1967 the U.S. Bureau report to Congress featured the following resolution by the U.N. Commission on Narcotic Drugs on the subject of cannabis. It should be borne in mind that at this time U.S. enforcement authorities had come under attack from all quarters on the Marijuana Tax Act and the official attitudes they have so long fostered toward marijuana, and that resolutions adopted by the U.N. Commission are only recommendations to the Economic and Social Council, which in turn can only convey them for final approval to the General Assembly. So this, like most of the actions similarly reported in this country to serve the Treasury Bureau's purposes in the past, was no more than a crude U.S. plant, without scientific validity and lacking any real force in the international body:

> The Commission:
> *Recalling* that the Single Convention on Narcotic Drugs, 1961, obliges Parties to place cannabis under strict controls to prevent its abuse;
> *Considering* that the problem of the traffic and abuse of cannabis remains serious in many areas where it has long been encountered;
> *Observing* that the traffic and abuse of cannabis appears to be spreading to areas where it has not heretofore been encountered;
> *Noting* that considerable publicity has been given to unauthoritative statements minimizing the harmful effects of cannabis and advocating that its use be permitted for nonmedical purposes;
> *Recognizing* that cannabis is known inter alia to distort perception of time and space, modify mood and impair judgment, this may result in unpredictable behavior, violence and adverse effects on health, and that it may be associated with the abuse of other drugs such as LSD, stimulants and heroin;
> *Convinced* that inefficient controls over, apathy towards and lack of public awareness of the dangers of cannabis and its continued abuse contribute to drug dependence, create law enforcement problems and injure national health, safety and welfare;
> 1. *Recommends* that all countries concerned increase their efforts to eradicate the abuse and illicit traffic in cannabis;
> 2. *Further recommends* that governments should promote research and advance additional medical and sociological information regarding cannabis, and effectively deal with publicity which advocates legalization or tolerance of the non-medical use of cannabis as a harmless drug.

In 1970 the International Narcotics Control Board was still echoing U.S. themes about cannabis: "While progression from cannabis to heroin is not inevitable, there is evidence that numbers of heroin consumers in certain countries have begun with cannabis." And on the general drug situation the U.N. body reported as if it were looking at the American scene through the eyes of U.S. enforcement officials—and nowhere else:

> A further significant change is that drug abuse is no longer confined to maladjusted personalities, to minority groups, or to persons subject to economic stress. On the contrary it is now geographically more widespread, it includes much larger numbers, and in the

countries affected it has invaded all levels of society. A particularly disturbing feature is its extension in some closely populated areas to young children, some of whom have become addicted to heroin.

The American notion that drug abuse within the United States can be curbed by production restrictions throughout the rest of the world has flowered into a grand design, and the U.N. agencies have played along. In September 1970 the U.N. Commission recommended creation of a special fund to be used by the Secretary-General to reduce raw-material production and fight trafficking—to which the United States alone promptly committed $2 million. (Incredibly, we have also given several million outright to Turkey, by no means a friendly state, to be used to induce some 70,000 peasant poppy growers, and reportedly Turkish leaders who have part of the action as well, to give up profitable opium crops for sisal, sugar beets, sunflowers, and soy.) Says the U.N. Control Board:

> Stated in the briefest terms, what is involved is a series of radical changes in the economic and social way of life of large numbers of people, including the development of roads and other communications and assistance to the governments in providing themselves with the means of administrative control.

The same U.N. report notes that such other producers as China and Korea have no connection with any control schemes, while Afghanistan, Burma, Laos, and Thailand produce in areas that are hardly amenable to control by their own governments for *any* purpose. Illicit growing in the latter areas is often the only cash crop and yields in the aggregate at least five times as much opium as is attributed to Turkish sources. In one of its own summaries, the Board estimates that no less than 1,200 *metric tons* of opium are still being dumped annually into world markets for illicit use, enough raw material to produce 120 tons of morphine (which in turn would make 12 billion standard injections—or twice that number of heroin shots).

As for American efforts to push U.S. attitudes and fixations onto other nations individually, Canada is the only state which has been induced to go along most of the way. The first Canadian narcotics law was passed by her Parliament in 1908. The present basic Narcotic Control Act dates from 1929. It closely resembles the Harrison Act, with rigid controls and record-keeping requirements at all stages in legitimate dispensing, and severe criminal prohibitions aimed at illicit trafficking.

Canadians upped their penalties following the lead of the U.S.

Boggs Act, making illegal possession punishable by a minimum
mandatory sentence of six months, with no probation or parole,
while trafficking offenses range to a maximum of fourteen years
—and prisoners are not "coddled" in the Canadian penal system.

In the nineteenth century, Canada had her share of problems
with opium smoking, introduced by Chinese and Indian immigrants to her west coast. But she missed the hysteria of the U.S.
Prohibition experiment, and the Canadian addict population,
though comparatively larger than others in the Western world,
has remained relatively smaller than that in the United States.
In the 1950's, addicts numbered perhaps 5,000 in a total population of 14 million; currently the number is believed to have
doubled, with the population now standing at slightly over 20
million. When American authorities opposed education to inform
the public about drugs, Canada followed. When the Americans
banned heroin, the Canadians did the same, except that they
outlawed only importation, leaving Canadian doctors free to prescribe from what remained of existing stocks.

In Canada, as in the United States, federal authorities early
assumed responsibility for repressing drug use, and the famous
Royal Canadian Mounted Police has been nearly as autocratic
as its American counterparts. Canadian doctors have endured
their share of harassment. Her officials sing louder than anyone
else in American choruses denouncing British drug practices,
while official Canadian pronouncements are cited for such extreme propositions as that 93 per cent of her drug addicts were
criminals before they took up drugs and that addiction is usually
caused by "criminal association." The following position statement, prepared by an RCMP superintendent and issued by the
Canadian Narcotic Service, is a fair sampling:

> The solution to the narcotic problem does not lie in the creation
> of Government clinics where narcotic injections are given to addicts
> at cost price. This amounts to nothing more than officially condon-
> ing drug addiction and placing the stamp of public approval upon
> a vicious and soul-destroying habit. . . .
> However, of far greater importance is the fact that we should
> remember that we are not treating with ordinary every-day sick
> people when we are dealing with drug addicts. . . . The cause of
> development of the habit is inherent in the individual. The drug
> addict is a psychopath before he acquires the habit. . . . Habitual
> criminals are psychopaths, and psychopaths are abnormal individ-
> uals who, because of their abnormality, are especially liable to be-
> come addicts. To such persons drug addiction is merely an incident
> in their delinquent careers, and the crimes they commit, even

though they be to obtain money with which to buy narcotics, are not directly attributable to the fact that they are drug addicts.

It is the opinion of the writer that the Opium and Narcotic Drug Act should be amended to provide that a drug addict, after certification as such by three physicians, must be committed for a period of not less than 10 years to a narcotic hospital operated by the Federal Government. After the expiration of one year in the hospital, the patient would be released, but only on parole and to outside employment.

In the 1950's Commissioner Anslinger's opposite number from Canada on the U.N. Narcotics Commission, Colonel C. H. L. Sharman, kept reporting periodically on Canadian successes with revival of the whipping post for sellers of drugs, urging other nations to follow the Canadian lead in this innovation.

Italy has long been the European country most pressured by the United States with respect to its drug policies. Addiction was never much of a problem for the Italians themselves, but in the aftermath of World War II she became a haven for such deported Americans gangsters as Lucky Luciano and was also allegedly the main transit stop and processing stage in the flow of opiates from the Middle East to the U.S. illicit market. In 1950 Anslinger's Bureau began assigning agents to work abroad, establishing headquarters in Rome under Charles Siragusa, who later wrote:

> At both the 1950 and 1951 meetings of the 15-nation Commission of Narcotic Drugs of the United Nations, Commissioner Anslinger sought to bring pressure on the Italians to outlaw the legal manufacture of heroin. He made his plea on the grounds that the drug was flooding the United States underworld market. Although Italy was not a member of the Commission, its representatives attended as observers. Anslinger didn't know it at the time, but his eloquent addresses in the United Nations and our work overseas were gradually bringing the kind of pressure needed to shut off the Mafia's heroin sources on the Italian peninsula.
>
> The police overseas almost always worked willingly with us. It was their superiors in the Government who were sometimes unhappy that we had entered their countries. Most of the time though, I found that a casual mention of the possibility of shutting off our foreign-aid programs, dropped in the proper quarters, brought grudging permission for our operations almost immediately.

Italy followed the U.S. lead by altering her own domestic policies for a time, increasing her penalties for drug offenses, tightening controls on manufacture and distribution, and acquiring for her efforts a small domestic black market. But despite these formal nods toward the American viewpoint (and one

great scandal involving diversions to the U.S. through a prominent Italian drug house), Italian authorities have left handling
of the problem largely to medical practitioners, supervised
through provincial health officers. The Italian Central Narcotics
Bureau has functioned rather like the British Home Office, supporting medical control of addicts instead of persecuting doctors
and pharmacists.

More recently the flow of illicit drugs through Italy toward
America is supposed to have been diverted to other channels,
much of it now claimed to be coming through southern France.
U.S. interest in how the Italians handle their own problems has
waned, and as a result addiction there again seems to be minimal.
In 1968, the Italian government officially reported an estimated
total of 300 addicts in the country. In 1970, a study of addiction
concluded: "A glance at the verifiable figures, however, . . . con-
firms that in Italy the number of 'classical' drug addicts is small
—so small, in fact, as (in this case) to completely upset the com-
monly-held view that opiates such as morphine and cocaine still
constitute a social danger."

In France, addiction is characterized as "rare." In West Germany, although the situation was aggravated in the chaotic years
immediately following World War II by a black market in surplus synthetics dumped by the occupying forces (and by U.S.
pressures already described), addiction is now again regarded
as a minor problem. The Scandinavian countries count their addicts in dozens and hundreds, and even the U.S.S.R. spokesman
reports to the U.N. year after year that "drug addiction does not
constitute a significant social or public health problem" in his
country. Known Russian addicts numbered 1,361 in 1968, nearly
all medically induced cases, 97 per cent being treated or maintained without institutionalization. There is reportedly no black
market in drugs in Russia. Switzerland, though watching overuse
of hypnotics and stimulants, does not acknowledge drug addiction as worthy of official attention. Yugoslavia reports "no problem," and in Hungary nonmedical drug addiction is "unknown."

Nonetheless, virtually all of the countries in this enumeration
(excepting Russia and her satellites) are now experiencing increases in the use of cannabis for smoking, associated primarily
with restless and rebellious youth, while in Sweden there is deep
concern over abuse of the amphetamines, administered by injection and producing very bad side effects in a growing number
of Swedish "speed" users. The French put LSD under special
controls in June 1966 and added the amphetamines in October

1967. Spain (with 1,176 addicts, 981 of them medically induced and most of them older women) noted the use of LSD among students and youths, and proscribed it in 1967.

Along with the almost-certainly false claim that most (80 per cent) of the heroin smuggled into the U.S. comes from Turkish opium (since only a trifling amount is being intercepted and is, further, untraceable as to source in its processed form), American authorities have publicized another dubious revelation: that the processing of morphine base into heroin (a smelly operation comparable to running an illicit still) is virtually a monopoly of a few laboratories in Marseilles. While French public reaction swung between amusement and annoyance, American drug agents (now permanently stationed in a dozen European cities) swarmed into southern France and participated in several arrests and seizures; Attorney General Mitchell and other U.S. officials made excited speeches; French Corsicans were portrayed as a sort of junior Mafia; President Nixon reportedly interceded directly with President Pompidou; and finally, on February 26, 1971, a formal Franco-American police cooperation treaty was signed. At the signing, Attorney General Mitchell told Interior Minister Marcellin:

> Our action today in signing this agreement is another noble chapter in the history of comradeship between our two countries. Nearly two hundred years ago, we first fought together to achieve liberty on the other side of the Atlantic Ocean. In this century we have twice been comrades in arms to preserve liberty on this side of the Atlantic, and throughout the world. Today our two nations are, in a sense, striking another blow for liberty. The enemy we face destroys men's liberty and makes them slaves of a drug habit. Frenchmen and Americans have conquered tyrants together, and together we can put an end to this growing tyranny of drugs.

In the Orient, authorities still struggling with the opium problem Westerners helped nurture so long ago have sometimes outdone Mr. Anslinger. In the 1950's Chiang Kai-shek, for example, promulgated decrees calling simply for a prompt ending of all drug addiction in his Republic of China, with death penalties for addicts who failed to cure themselves, as well as for traffickers and for any public official who condoned poppy growing, drug selling, or drug use. Although not many Formosan heads have rolled, these Draconian laws are still in effect, and the practical result seems to be that the Chinese authorities tend to blink the problem, reporting diminishing numbers of addicts each year.

Cannabis and LSD are unkown in Formosa. What is happening in Red China is a subject of much speculation; opponents of the communist regime allege that the country is saturated with drugs, while those who look with favor on Mao's rule credit him with having virtually freed his people of addiction.

The Japanese (who were also saturated with dumped drug surpluses in 1945 and given repressive laws during the occupation), now claim to have virtually no problem, although they have adopted the American pattern to the extent that addicts must be reported and are technically subject to compulsory treatment in isolated hospital quarters. India acknowledges an aggregate of some 100,000 addicts in her population of 500 million, and still supports a registry of approximately 1,500 diehard opium smokers.

Addiction to the opiates is unkown in most of Africa, although Egypt and some of the new African nations are very concerned about cannabis (hashish and kif). Likewise in Latin America the opiates have never taken much hold, and local authorities are simple unaware of drug abuse as a problem. Coca-leaf chewing, long practiced by native populations in the Andes of Colombia, Bolivia, Peru, and Chile, seems to attract more scolding attention from U.S. spokesmen and the U.N. Commission than from the governments of those countries where it is still a tradition.

TWENTY-TWO

The White House
Conference, 1962–63

■ RETURNING to the U.S. scene at the beginning of the 1960's brings us to interesting "ifs." The Narcotics Bureau had silenced most of its critics. Questions raised by the Joint ABA-AMA Committee had been drowned out by the Treasury response; there was not even much likelihood that its work would be published. Participants in the 1958 NIH Symposium had been intimidated, and it seemed unlikely that that proceeding would ever blossom into a printed record either. The AMA had softened its stand so much it almost seemed to be parroting the Bureau. And nothing of significance was happening in Congress to challenge Mr. Anslinger's supremacy or question his cherished views.

So *if* John Kennedy had not won in 1960—and more narrowly, *if* Governor Brown of California had not given him crucial support in the California primary, the Democratic convention, and the ensuing campaign in Mr. Nixon's own home state—there might have been little to add to the story we have unfolded to this point. Anslinger was virtually without problems as the Eisenhower regime ended, and by all auguries he should have remained in control of his quiet tyranny for at least the best part of another decade. Instead he was unthroned somewhat brusquely in 1962, and his Bureau itself survived only a few more years. Ironically, his nemesis was the very phenomenon which had made him so powerful for so many years—the irresistible attractiveness of drug issues to politicians when they find themselves shy of better things to talk about.

In this instance the shy politician was former Senator William Knowland, who had returned to California in 1958 to run against Pat Brown for governor. Brown had served as Attorney General for the preceding eight years, during which period California had made some enlightened reforms, including re-evaluation of her narcotic-drug policies, liberalization of her handling of youthful offenders, development of treatment programs, and extension of the use of parole to avoid merely incarcerating addict-offenders for long terms of "straight" time. So Knowland took out after Brown with the charge that he had been "soft" on drug offenders and wanted to "coddle" dope fiends. A California legislative committee got into the act with hearings on the desirability of higher penalties and tougher enforcement policies, and Brown's running mate for the post of Attorney General, Judge Stanley Mosk, opened a crossfire at Knowland by characterizing narcotics as only one root of a great California crime wave and urging an investigation of the whole crime pattern in the state.

The Brown-Mosk ticket won, but the campaign had aroused the local citizenry. California Elks canvassed for two million signatures on petitions calling for *minimum* sentences of thirty years for all drug offenses, with no parole or probation. It was discovered, as usual, that drug addiction had suddenly started making great inroads into the ranks of schoolchildren, and lawmakers in Sacramento stumbled over one another in the rush to announce harsh proposals. In 1959 Governor Brown sought to calm the situation by ordering a factual study by the California Board of Corrections, which reported moderately that the problem was growing in a steady and "disquieting" way, stressed that drug abuse was too complex to be solved merely by further increases in criminal penalties, and recommended most strongly that marijuana be differentiated from true narcotics and that marijuana offenses be dropped to the misdemeanor level.

The Board found, moreover, that—excluding Los Angeles County—there had been no significant changes either up or down in drug-arrest rates over the preceding decade for the rest of the state, and it noted that there were virtually no "major perpetrators of the narcotics traffic" among all the thousands of inmates serving time in California prisons for drug offenses (muffling the implications of the last point slightly by suggesting that doubtless the federal government had mopped up all the big-time smugglers and peddlers, so one would have to look for them in federal institutions).

But though the Board's study thus illuminated some of the realities in the situation, even it touched off new controversies and helped keep the drug issue in public view on the West Coast. In the 1960 elections, California campaign oratory again rang with challenges, promises, and high-pitched alarms. Attorney General Mosk called for a sweeping new investigation of narcotic drugs on a national scale, and this was picked up by the California delegation in Congress, where several resolutions were introduced calling for the convocation of a White House Conference on the subject. These proposals were in turn played up in home constituencies when their congressional sponsors went out campaigning. Governor Brown was not himself a candidate in 1960 but, as already noted, he played such a key role in helping the Kennedys capture the nomination, and then in almost winning the state away from Nixon, that he had unusually strong claims on the victor. He was offered a major administration post, but turned it down.

The Governor and other Californians reportedly had sought to commit Kennedy to the proposed White House Conference during his campaign, but had been met with indifference on the ground that drug addiction was not then a matter of great national interest. Even after the new regime was installed in Washington, both the President and his brother at the Justice Department remained notably cool toward the suggestion. One reason was certainly that Commissioner Anslinger, and hence his strong band of supporters in Congress, violently opposed it; Anslinger was content—and wisely so, as hindsight indicates—to ride along quietly with a minimum of attention from the New Frontiersmen. Another reason was that Kennedy family strategists were concentrating on building the image of the Attorney General as a fearless crime fighter, basing, of course, in the Justice Department, and it would have been inconsistent with this aim to use the White House to give any big play to the Narcotics Bureau in Treasury. Administration spokesmen openly registered their opposition to the various White House Conference proposals pending in Congress.

Governor Brown, however, was under no disability with regard to keeping things stirred up in his own state, and this he did by announcing that 1961 was going to be "Fight Narcotics Year" for his administration in Sacramento. Furthermore, at this point the Brown forces sounded a tiny new note that was soon to become a roar: the Governor announced his support for a new drive to curb abuses of amphetamines and other "dangerous drugs" outside the traditional narcotics categories. The phrase "dangerous drugs" had been in use for decades, in the British Act, at the Food and Drug Administration to refer to any substance requiring protective controls, and at the Narcotics Bureau to designate all drugs capable of injurious abuse. It was probably Commissioner Larrick of FDA who first began to get serious attention from the popular press by talking about the menace of amphetamines when used by truck drivers to keep themselves awake on long hauls.

Even so, it is a virtual certainty that the White House Conference proposals would still have died of neglect had it not been for another political happenstance, namely, that President Kennedy's arch-rival, Richard Nixon, challenged the President's great friend Pat Brown in the 1962 California gubernatorial race. Moreover, Nixon chose to reopen the old lines of attack on Governor Brown as being soft-hearted in meting out retribution against dope peddlers (who were, of course, undermining California in particular and America in general, and who were, not unexpectedly, discovered once again to be decimating the ranks of youth). The Kennedys' response was all-out. The President endorsed Brown's candidacy and made several appearances on his behalf. And the Attorney General let it be known, in response to trial balloons floated by non-Californians like Mayor Wagner of New York, that the administration might now look with more favor on a White House Conference.

The White House began issuing messages acknowledging the new menace of "dangerous drugs," and in May 1962 the President himself revealed, in connection with a glowing tribute to Governor Brown for progressive leadership in dealing with addicts, that he now leaned toward the idea of a national convocation, and that he had the matter under active study. In September, the calling of a White House Conference was formally announced.

Simultaneously the President released a document entitled "Progress Report" which had been produced by eight doctors (three M.D.'s, four Ph.D.'s, and one who held both degrees) designated as an Ad Hoc Panel on Drug Abuse to confer with the White House Science Advisor and give advice on what should be done. The members of this panel could not be faulted for their collective eminence, but none of them had theretofore been closely identified with drug-abuse problems, so their findings were developed from what might be termed a slightly fresh viewpoint. They started from the hypothesis that nearly all compulsive drug abusers could be rehabilitated, by which they meant withdrawn from drugs and re-established in society, since they found drug abuse was inevitably a manifestation of some underlying psychological or physiological disorder:

> Compulsive abuse of drugs is not an illness to which any member of society can succumb. Instead, it is limited to those susceptible persons with prerequisite disorders; individuals who would not otherwise be normal members of society but whose inadequacies would in all likelihood manifest themselves in some other way.

Accordingly they rejected proposals for imposing long prison sentences on drug offenders, on the one hand, and for placing addicts on any kind of maintenance regime, on the other. Instead they urged lengthy and extensive parole supervision in all cases, following the pattern that had been developed (not surprisingly) in California.

This panel (which adopted the figure of 45,000 for the total number of drug *users* in the United States as of mid-1962) also slapped down some of the Narcotics Bureau's most sacred dogma: heroin, they said, has no effects significantly different from those of morphine; drug addiction is almost never induced by drug peddlers "with economic motive in mind"; it is not realistic to distinguish sharply between users and peddlers, since most of the traffic is carried on by addicts who peddle to support their own habits; and doctors have a clear right under existing laws to treat addicts, so the medical profession ought to take matters into its own hands and set its own standards of good medical practice in the field. Regarding education about drugs, the panel observed: "The general public has not been informed of most of the important facts related to drug abuse and, therefore, has many misconceptions which are frightening and destructive." On marijuana:

> Though this drug has long held the reputation of inciting individuals to commit sexual offenses and other antisocial acts, the evidence for this is limited. . . . It is the opinion of the Panel that the hazards of marijuana use have been exaggerated and that long criminal sentences imposed on an occasional user or possessor of the drug are in poor social perspective.

And regarding drug abuse and youth, the report concluded:

> The claims of an increase of juvenile narcotic addiction may have been correct in the immediate post World War II era, but the available statistics do not indicate such an incidence now. . . .

The most frequent narcotic drug abuse appears to be centered in the 20–35 year age group, with a peak occuring in the middle years.

Noting indications that drugs in the barbiturate and amphetamine categories were beginning to be abused, the panel recommended that the medical profession (not lawmakers, but doctors) "should adopt guidelines concerning their proper use." The panelists thought it possible that these latter drugs might come to be more widely abused, and possibly by more juveniles, because they were so cheap, so easy to handle, and so readily obtainable, but they dismissed LSD and related hallucinogenic compounds as "of minor importance in the general picture of drug abuse." Their overall conclusion was this:

> Important as is the drug problem it is often grossly exaggerated in the daily press, and hysteria replaces sober judgment in many discussions and decisions. The exploitation of this tragic waste of human talent must cease to function as a promotion for mass media sales.

The Ad Hoc Panel bore down heavily on one new concept which somehow never took hold, but which suggests interesting speculations about other lines that *might* have been developed at the ensuing conference had the direction been a little different: the panelists were impressed by recent research indicating that the abuse of all drugs, including even the most addicting opiates, was widely engaged in on a casual or "spree" basis, in patterns similar to that of the nonalcoholic who occasionally takes on a good Saturday night load. Rejecting statistical measurements of the extent of true addiction, the panel thus implied that part of the clandestine drug traffic might not be related to serious addiction and abuse problems but to supporting use on a "spree" basis without significantly damaging social consequences. However, this theme has not attracted much attention since, even though the evidence as to "spree" use is substantial.

Commissioner Anslinger's resignation was announced in August 1962, just before the Ad Hoc Panel released its final report, and it came as a surprise even to his nonadulating watchers. He continued to serve in his post at the U.N. Commission, but seemed to withdraw from the national scene. The naming of his successor also stirred surprise and puzzlement, at least among those who had been led to hope for changes in policy. Instead of a doctor (as was rumored), or at least a fresh-minded outsider (as was expected), the President chose career Bureau official

Henry L. Giordano, who had served Anslinger faithfully ever since joining up as a field agent in 1941 (and who happened, coincidentally, to be a Californian).

The White House Conference had been announced in a brief statement in which the President named his brother, the Attorney General, to serve as general chairman, and said that in deciding to call the conference he had discussed the matter with Governor Brown of California, who had agreed that such a gathering would be helpful.

We shall have more to say about so-called dangerous drugs in later chapters. But the events of 1962–63 being considered here had a great deal to do with America's commitment to her present campaign against them, a campaign which may yet prove less wise and more hurtful than even the great 18th Amendment aberration. In the interim between President Kennedy's reluctant commitment to sponsor the conference and its actual convocation, pressure was generated within the administration to come up with something different, preferably a fresh theme dissociated from the shopworn Harrison Act, and outside the Treasury Department's field so it could be developed as a vehicle for promoting the image of the Attorney General. That was what the Ad Hoc Committee's survey was really supposed to turn up. And what it led to was the new concept—or, more accurately, new bird-call phrase—"drug abuse," which could embrace "dangerous" drugs.

Accordingly, what had been described in May as a White House Conference on "Narcotics" was rechristened "Conference on Narcotic and Drug Abuse," and President Kennedy himself opened the proceedings on September 27, 1962, with a plug for the new theme:

> One area of inquiry meriting special attention deals with the growing abuse of nonnarcotic drugs, including barbiturates and amphetamines. Society's gains will be illusory if we reduce the incidence of one kind of drug dependence, only to have new kinds of drugs substituted. The use of these drugs is increasing problems of abnormal and antisocial behavior, highway accidents, juvenile delinquency, and broken homes. An especially disturbing aspect of the alarming increase in the illegal traffic in these drugs is their particular attraction to juveniles because of the ease with which they can be obtained and their extremely low cost in comparison with narcotic drugs.

Attorney General Kennedy's message left himself a very clear field indeed:

As you know, this Conference was not called to provide a forum for certain theories nor to reach what might at best be arbitrary solutions. This Conference is designed—as the preceding panels have demonstrated—to help us recognize what we know about the problem and, perhaps more important, how much we don't know. Our major aim is to reemphasize that we do, indeed, need answers and to determine how we can best find them on a rational and national basis. . . .

Above all else, sound information must form the basis of future legislation—legislation which is broadly directed toward the general problem of compulsive drug abuse, so that it will be both appropriate to the situation at hand and flexible to meet new and changing manifestations of this unresolved disorder. . . .

I hope, however, that we can point the way to more than information. I hope we can also chart directions for action.

More than 400 people turned out for the conference, and their number included virtually everyone who had been prominently connected with any aspect of the drug problem in recent years. But for the most part the long-time experts and the old-timers were in the audience rather than among the speakers or panelists, and the format of the conference excluded symposium discussion. Californians were much in evidence. Governor Brown, the only governor, shared the program on the first day with the President, three Cabinet members, and Mayor Wagner, the only mayor, while a dozen other Californians, led by Attorney General Mosk, made their appearance as panelists during the two days of the proceedngs.

Since its mandate was merely to exchange views, not to arrive at solutions, the conference provided little more than a publicity medium for favorite spokesmen. Secretary Dillon of Treasury restated the traditional position of the Narcotics Bureau—severe penalties, no drugs to addicts under any circumstances, but due regard withal for human and social problems: "Narcotics addiction is neither a normal, nor a socially acceptable practice. . . . Whatever its cause, treatment and cure must be sought." HEW Secretary Celebrezze said the conference marked the beginning of a new era and that everyone should put aside his old superstitions and fears, but at the same time we should not lose sight of the importance of a continuing drive against the criminal traffic in addicting drugs. He then added a pitch for the new category:

We badly need stricter controls over the manufacture and distribution of the addicting nonnarcotic drugs, which today constitute a major problem in enforcement. These drugs enter illicit channels in ever-increasing quantity, and our young people, particularly, are led into addiction under the mistaken belief that these drugs are relatively harmless.

Governor Brown sounded uncharacteristically tough, talking about his "grim war on narcotics," but he himself explained that he had only a few days left in his campaign against Nixon: "I'm in the position of a rancher who rides away from his range in the middle of the night when he knows there is a rustler in the area." He reported that California had definitely "turned the tide," that in the preceding year state officials had "quarantined 1,000 addicts for intensive treatment under tight control and strict discipline," and that there were more than 5,000 drug offenders serving time in California prisons. The Governor related with pride how hard he had worked for stiffer criminal penalties, and said that drug addicts suffered from a contagious disease and must be isolated; they were, he said, like typhoid sufferers who must be forcibly kept away from poisoned wells. He told of a new California law which permitted incarceration of addicts for periods of up to five years, and announced that his state was building a rehabilitation center for the treatment of addicts in custody. Then he too chimed the new note:

> In California, our vigorous narcotics enforcement program is causing the sale of marijuana and heroin to level off. . . .
> But the decline in heroin sales has been accompanied by a sharp increase in the use of dangerous drugs such as phenobarbital, seconal, nembutal, and benzedrine. In short, the peddlers are turning to a new line of merchandise which is less dangerous for them but every bit as deadly for their old customers. This is an escape hatch which I intend to close as quickly as possible. I believe we must be as severe on those who spread misery through dangerous drugs as we now are with those who sell heroin.

Mayor Wagner of New York said the conference was "the dawning of a new day," and that everyone ought to address the subject "seriously rather than sensationally." Then, after repeating how little anyone really knew about the problem, he took some wide swings at his city's addicts:

> In many if not most cases—and we have, of course, no facts on this—the addict becomes not only a social outcast but an enemy of society, an enemy of law and order.
> It can scarcely be contradicted that the present crime situation in New York City is traceable to a major extent to the insatiable driving need of narcotic addicts for the money to satisfy their

habits, regardless of the most heroic police measures to control the thief and the mugger.

Even Mr. Anslinger made a subdued appearance, speaking about international controls and his work at the U.N., and ending with an appeal (which must have stuck in his throat) from the U.N. Commission to national governments to "take appropriate measures" to place the production, distribution, and use of the barbiturates and other nonnarcotic drugs—whose repression he had always vigorously opposed—under strict national limitations.

Other speakers hammered the same theme. Commissioner Larrick of the Food and Drug Administration reported the struggles of his agency to stem the rising tide:

> This audience does not need a recitation of the deplorable and, in many cases pathetic, situations which were reported to us. People of all levels of society are involved. We followed through on reports on the sale of these drugs without prescriptions, as well as the repeated illegal refills of prescriptions without the authority of the prescriber. We engaged in undercover work to break up the sale of amphetamines to truck drivers.

California Attorney General Mosk pulled all stops:

> When we talk about addiction in California, we are not talking only about heroin and other opium derivatives; we are talking about the dangerous drugs, to which considerable reference has already been made. We have seen a dramatic rise in the misuse of these drugs during the past 18 months. Our State bureau of criminal statistics which is an arm of my office, pinpoints the 1961 increase over 1960 in the illegal use of these drugs at 31 per cent. Among our juvenile population, it was even higher, about 36 per cent. . . . In this regard, it should be noted that dangerous drugs are creating an entirely new class of addicts. In California, the vast majority of narcotic addicts have been in trouble with the law prior to their involvement with narcotics. This does not appear to be the case, however, with dangerous drugs. . . .
>
> It has been asked how dangerous are the dangerous drugs. We consider them very dangerous. Senseless murders have been committed by persons under their influence. There have been armed robberies of pharmacies to obtain them. Automobile accidents have been caused by them. . . . And they are dangerous in this sense: They appeal to and can be obtained by persons who might never try or might never come into contact with heroin or marijuana.

The overall conclusion reached by the conference was that the entire drug field was characterized by misinformation and inadequate facts, and thus there was an urgent need for research to produce reliable data, a structure for efficient dissemination of such data, and a more practical evaluation program for its application to the problem. It also concluded that the apparent increase in abuse of nonnarcotic drugs "has grave future implications if remedial action is not taken now." As for treatment and rehabilitation, all past and current efforts were found to have been unsuccessful "except for promising civil commitment programs . . . in California and New York." The final note was a clarion call "for total involvement of all the Federal, State, and community resources on an interrelated basis."

■ TWENTY-THREE

Advice from a Commission

■ AFTER the White House Conference there was once again a lull. Brown won and Nixon announced his withdrawal from public life, while the Narcotics Bureau under Commissioner Giordano quietly went its own way. Action in Washington centered in the Department of Justice, where Attorney General Kennedy was campaigning spectacularly for new legislation aimed at organized crime in areas other than drug peddling—gambling, extortion, bribery, and the usury racket. It was only after muttering criticism of his apparent lack of interest in the drug problem began to be heard on Capitol Hill, with editorial reflections, that in January 1963 President Kennedy by Executive Order appointed a brand-new Advisory Commission on Narcotic and Drug Abuse.

This Commission, it was announced, would assist the President "in developing a comprehensive program for fighting the drug abuse problem." The press releases made fleeting references to the White House Conference, but the Commission's mandate was to start all over again to review the role of all federal agencies and re-examine all available data. And once more the group was made up mostly of new names and new faces, some of them totally unfamiliar to long-time observers of the American drug scene.

The only member of the 1963 President's Commission who had served on the 1962 Ad Hoc Panel was Dr. Rodger O. Egeberg, a prominent Los Angeles internist who was generally active in California politics and public affairs and subsequently served

240

President Nixon as an Assistant Secretary of HEW. A retired District of Columbia judge of great eminence was named as chairman, and the other members included a San Francisco businessman, a college president, an ex-FBI agent, the New York City Welfare Commissioner, and one of the country's leading penologists, Austin MacCormick. The roster of consultants to the Commission similarly mixed a few prominent authorities and public officials with a spate of unknowns—and included, naturally, Governor Brown, Attorney General Mosk, and a contingent of twenty-two Californians.

To glance backward for a moment, in 1961 during the first session of the 87th Congress, while pros and cons of the White House Conference were being debated behind the scenes on Pennsylvania Avenue and Governor Brown seemed to be calling the shots with the President, New York's powerful senators, Jacob Javits and Kenneth Keating, had launched a play of their own in Congress (which, incidentally, accounts for Mayor Wagner's sudden appearance in the forefront with Brown). Calling for a new approach to the narcotic-drug problem, they introduced a package of four bills which quickly picked up bipartisan support and put further pressure on the Administration to do *something* or risk losing the initiative and being upstaged.

One of these Javits-Keating measures called for a large expansion in federal narcotic-hospital facilities, with the latter being made available to the states for treatment of their addicts, provided the states in turn developed adequate follow-up programs for addicts when they returned to their communities after hospitalization. Another established federal civil-commitment procedures by which addicted persons could be turned over to the custody of the Surgeon General for treatment, as an alternative to criminal prosecution in certain offense categories. A third proposed a research program covering the entire drug field, while the fourth remedied the absurd situation in which youthful narcotic offenders had been deprived (by the Boggs and Daniel Acts) of benefits accorded to all other young offenders under the federal Youth Corrections Act.

Early in 1963, when the 88th Congress convened, these measures were reintroduced and their Republican sponsors began attacking the administration in earnest for its inaction and neglect. In March, Senator Javits told the New York Academy of Medicine:

> Few social problems in our nation are as grave in their impact on raising the crime rate to dangerous levels as the narcotics and

drug addiction problem. Yet, there appears to be almost no prospect of early action on a Federal level to deal adequately with the problem in modern terms. It is time we faced frankly the fact that we are in a state of seemingly endless drift on this issue—characterized by indecision, uncertainty and controversy. It is perhaps a classic example of the governmental technique of inaction by continuous study; new studies and new surveys which are designed to clarify the issue instead add up to new excuses for public officials to avoid making the basic decisions. But the facts are in and the evidence is overwhelming.

I believe the situation calls for a historic decision by the President to set the nation on a new enlightened course to deal with narcotics and drug addiction as an illness rather than a crime. In the current muddle, only the President can make this command decision, and I believe this is the time for him to do it.

The President's response to this and similar attacks (the New York Academy of Medicine, for example, called for an about-face in drug policies) was to release on April Fool's day a hastily drafted Interim Report from his Advisory Commission, which began with a disavowal: "None of the views here expressed are based on special independent factual research in depth by the Commission." Not surprisingly, therefore, Recommendation No. 1 was the design of a "Master Plan of Research":

> On many aspects of the problem, we do not have complete or accurate data. The needed research is of many sorts, from laboratory experimentation to community inquiry. In the opinion of this Commission, a master plan is required. It would determine, first, all those needs served by existing projects and, second, those needs for which new projects should be undertaken. A master plan would also facilitate the institution of means to correlate the findings of the various projects. . . .
> The Commission considers this recommendation to be of high priority in any major effort related to drug abuse. Such a master research plan would be a major undertaking, and it should be adequately financed, staffed, and equipped. The task of designing it should be assigned to a Government official or agency at the highest appropriate level.

Also not surprisingly, the Commission said it was convinced that "the greatest possibilities of advance" lay not in legislative enactments but in administrative action—calling on the Attorney General to launch, with an assist from the Secretary of the Treasury, a "massive attack" upon the wholesale illicit traffic in drugs by the creation of a special unit of investigators and lawyers to coordinate prosecutions against the skillful, ruthless, and well-financed overlords of organized crime who were profiting hugely from smuggling and trafficking. (Soon this idea spawned more bird-calls: "strike forces" and "task forces" began proliferating all over the war-on-crime battlefield.)

Another recommendation was for educational efforts—by Health, Education, and Welfare rather than Treasury—to counteract misinformation about drug abuse, and this one deserves mention for the least-in-most-words award:

> A program for the preparation and widespread distribution of accurate information is one of the essentials to material progress towards solution of the problem. This program should cover all appropriate fields, including the general public, educational, legal and medical professions, and the social welfare agencies. It should include material suitable for publication in various professional journals (legal, medical, pharmaceutical, sociological, law enforcement, religious), material designed for popular appeal (full-length books, magazine articles, scripts and films for broadcasting), and material suitable for use at various educational levels.

The Interim Report had *something* about everything: a readjustment of statutory penalties to soften a few of the mandatory minimums, expanded training facilities for narcotic enforcement officers, a Joint U.S.-Mexico Commission on Drugs (the perennial pet project of Texans and Californians), and more Treasury agents operating abroad to control the illicit international traffic nearer its sources.

In a further slap at the Javits-Keating proposals, the Commission stretched the implications of the 1956 Kentucky "blue grass" case—and a very long stretch it was—into a question about the constitutionality of all civil-commitment procedures: the Commission said it was going to ask the Attorney General to give a ruling on constitutionality before it would take any position on the value of civil-commitment measures. To the suggestion that drug problems might have been slighted by the incumbent administration, the Commission responded stoutly:

> It seems to the Commission that the actions of the President in convening the first White House Conference on Narcotic and Drug Abuse, in personally addressing the Conference, and in establishing this Commission amply demonstrate his view that this problem is important and his desire that all Federal agencies involved act accordingly.

But among all this nonsense (the Commission even took a swipe at Anslinger's Single Convention, while simultaneously

avowing that it had insufficient knowledge to reach any conclusions on the subject), there was one statement of real significance and sinister portent, and that was the proposal, officially
promulgated for the first time on behalf of the administration,
that repressive controls be extended to all other drugs in the
"dangerous" category. On this the Interim Report said:

> The Commission is speaking here not of the narcotics—which are
> under Federal control—but of those compounds frequently referred
> to as dangerous drugs. Some familiar examples are the barbiturates,
> the amphetamines, and the so-called tranquilizers. They are manu-
> factured in the United States in increasing quantities and varieties.

Even so, notes of caution were sounded which, had they been
heeded, might have very much changed the developments we
shall be recording in a subsequent chapter. For the Commission
urged expansion of the regulatory powers of the Food and Drug
Administration, rather than turning all power over to a purely
enforcement arm like Treasury or Justice, and referring to these
"dangerous drugs," it warned specifically:

> The Commision is of the view that any scheme of regulation of
> their manufacture, sale, and distribution should not at this time
> parallel the scheme of regulation in present Federal narcotics laws,
> since the more stringent controls of the narcotics laws would
> seriously hamper the legitimate medical use of these drugs.

Moreover, noting that criminal sanctions would probably be necessary to control illicit manufacture and sale, it gave the further
warning: "The Commission is concerned lest criminal penalties
also be visited upon those who are primarily the victims of these
drugs, those who purchase or possess them for their own use
but without a lawful prescription."

The Advisory Commission's Final Report was submitted to
President Kennedy on November 1, 1963, a scant three weeks
before the tragedy at Dallas. The changes it proposed were altered and aborted under President Johnson, but there is no
question that this report was coolly aimed at enlarging the federal prohibition activity, extending the hard-line approach ("war
on dope"), and excluding the Treasury Department from the
limelight in favor of dramatic new powers to be conferred on
the Attorney General.

First, in a quite new proposal (except that it had been made
by the Hoover Commission in 1949), the Advisory Commission
recommended that all enforcement powers be transferred from

Treasury's Narcotics Bureau to the Department of Justice. General supervision over combatting the illicit drug traffic was to be transferred to a Special Assistant for Narcotic and Drug Abuse appointed by the President and attached to the White House. Even the function of disseminating educational material about drugs was to be shifted from Treasury to HEW, and the latter department was also to take over all aspects of the control of the legitimate importation and manufacture of drugs, which was to be recast in a regulatory pattern based on the interstate and foreign commerce powers of Congress instead of on the tax power.

The Final Report stressed the newly discovered dangers of barbiturates, amphetamines, LSD 25, and even ether and airplane glue, lumping them together with the opiates, cocaine, and marijuana as "psychotoxic (mind poisoning)." Going further than any of the pending congressional proposals, and departing from its own interim findings, the Commission now urged that control over the traffic in *all* dangerous drugs, including all the new categories, be taken away from the Food and Drug Administration and turned over (with the similar powers to be taken from Treasury) to the Department of Justice. A "substantial increase" in the number of enforcement officers assigned to drug investigations—attached to Justice and reporting to the Attorney General, of course—was deemed essential, and the report recommended that wiretapping be made liberally available to support federal efforts aimed at international smuggling.

Lip service was paid to the humanitarian notion that drug addicts are afflicted persons rather than criminals, but the conclusion was nonetheless that drug abusers guilty of offenses against society (including drug and drug-related offenses) should be sternly made to face the consequences of their transgressions like anyone else. The Commission's only real concession was that when drug abusers are penalized they should not be penalized "in the spirit of retribution," and ought to be rehabilitated whenever possible.

It was recommended that the federal narcotics hospitals close their doors to all voluntary patients except any that might be needed for research purposes so that their intake would be only by criminal conviction or involuntary civil commitment, and it was urged that the Director of the Bureau of Prisons (again, in the Department of Justice) establish a special treatment program for addicts subject to his jurisdiction. A Permanent Citizens' Advisory Committee was suggested, to advise the Administration and to keep the drug problem prominently in the public view.

Finally, it must be acknowledged in fairness that among the Commission's other recommendations were some that appeared reasonable, moderate, and well focused. On mandatory minimums, for example, the report said that the present sentence structure should be amended "to fit the gravity of the particular offense so as to provide a greater incentive for rehabilitation." Regarding the right of physicians to prescribe drugs, the Commission urged a revision in the federal regulations to recognize that this was a matter of medical discretion and that the profession should be called upon to set standards of legitimate medical treatment for itself. But at the same time it shied away, quite inconsistently, from any suggestion that new federal facilities ought to be developed for treating and rehabilitating addicts, even while endorsing civil commitment as an alternate for (and supplement to) criminal prosecution.

If I have conveyed a tiny inference that drug matters were handled in ways that might have been influenced by political considerations when the two brothers who were soon to be so tragically martyred sat together in the Oval Room, I would not feel I had abused the truth. But something else should be stressed again: remember that it was they also, when they could act quietly without regard to political advantage, who used their offices to open the prison gates with pardons and commutations for Gilbert Zaragoza and dozens of hopeless long-termers who otherwise would still be suffering because of the stupidity and savagery of characters we met in earlier episodes in this saga.

TWENTY-FOUR

Rehabilitation, from Nothing to NARA

■ A SOURCE of confusion which has long served only oppressing forces is the lumping together of drug categories like the opiates, which are truly and powerfully addicting, with substances like cocaine and cannabis, which do not have true addictive properties. The confusion has been compounded recently by adding barbiturates (fearfully addicting) and amphetamines and hallucinogens (nonaddicting). Alcohol, at least in its hold and effects on alcoholics, is worst of all, while tobacco smoke—likely the most toxic substance mentioned in this paragraph—falls on the borderline and probably should be classified as only strongly habituating.

Periodic efforts by authoritative bodies like the World Health Organization—and by White House publicists and congressional phrasemakers—to alter traditional definitions and fabricate new concepts tend only to make the situation worse. In order to get away from the three classic elements of drug addiction (compulsion, tolerance, and withdrawal symptoms), WHO, responding partly to U.S. pressures, has fumbled with a notion of "drug dependence" (dependence of the cannabis type, dependence of the opiate type, etc.), while various promoters have been pushing "habituation," or "abuse," preferably coupled with some vague test like "harmful" (to the drug user himself or to society) or loss of the user's "self-control." And in the last few years, probably as

a result of the White House Conference, a popular distinction
has come to be made between so-called "hard" narcotics and
those which are labeled "soft," which one observer notes is as
fatuous as talking about "hard" and "soft" pregnancy. Even the
word narcotic is properly descriptive only of sedatives and sopo-
rifics, and should never have been applied to stimulants like
cocaine or hallucinogens like marijuana. Heroin and morphine
are *best* described as analgesics.

As elsewhere in our narrative, the person most victimized by
such confusion is the drug user. What chance has he of a fair
shake when lawmakers and law enforcers neither know nor care
about even the most fundamental realities of his condition? In
the patterns that took shape under the Harrison Act after World
War I, the only kind of drug user who needed "rehabilitation" in
any specialized sense was the user of opiates or their synthetic
equivalents. This addict was truly "hooked," especially if he had
been using drugs of good quality over some period of time so as
to build up a substantial tolerance, and it was his plight that led
medical authorities in the 1919–23 period to open the various
clinics which we have already described. The idea was to provide opium (including morphine and heroin) addicts with sustaining supplies of the drugs to which they were accustomed so
they could go on functioning normally and would not be driven
into criminality. But some of the clinics also doled out cocaine,
from which there are no significant withdrawal symptoms and
the continued use of which under nonmedical administration is
unjustifiable. So to this latter extent, at least, Treasury agents who
hounded the clinic operations out of existence must be conceded
a point.

Concerned observers began to take interest in "rehabilitation"
again in the late 1920's, particularly with regard to addicts
trapped in the federal prison system, and this led Congress to
enact the 1929 Porter Act, under which the U.S. Public Health
Service was authorized to establish two "narcotic farms" for confinement and treatment of addicted persons who had been convicted of offenses against the United States. These were the already mentioned institutions, shortly rechristened "hospitals,"
established at Lexington and Ft. Worth in the mid-thirties, which
continued to do fine work, in their limited way, until their demise
in the early seventies. But since they dealt mainly with convicted
federal prisoners and were never provided by Congress with
significant resources for follow-up supervision or treatment of

released inmates, they scarcely made a dent in the total addict population.

At the state level, most legislatures were content to add drug addiction to their already existing patterns for rehabilitating alcoholics or treating the insane, and in fact very little was done for addicts, or about their problems, anywhere. In 1956, as has been noted, the Daniel Committee came out with the ultimate law-enforcement proposal—that all addicts who could not be "cured" should be incarcerated for life in some segregated detention facility. Even President Kennedy's Ad Hoc Panel and Advisory Commission embraced the notion that addicts (still fuzzily confused with *all* drug users) should either be "cured" of their habits or else confined for life like nineteenth-century lepers if they continued to "relapse."

But as will also be remembered from the last chapter, while the President and his Attorney General brother were making moves to concentrate drug-law enforcement powers in the Department of Justice, opposition leaders in Congress began a campaign of their own to keep control of the situation by developing the theme that addicts were really sick persons (and not inherently abnormal) rather than criminals after all, and that what was most needed were more efforts to rehabilitate them.

The Javits-Keating bills quickly picked up co-sponsorship in the Senate and support by parallel introductions in the House in the 87th Congress (1961). Most important was the elaborate civil-commitment measure, under which a defendant accused of a federal crime could, in the discretion of the court, if found to be an addict and if his crime was found to be addiction-related, be offered the alternative of mandatory civil commitment into the custody of the Surgeon General for treatment. If the Surgeon General agreed, and found that the defendant would benefit from treatment, a civil commitment for an indeterminate period up to thirty-six months, plus an additional two-year probationary period, would follow in lieu of the criminal prosecution. The purpose behind this was to hold addicts in hospitals for treatment as long as necessary, then keep them under close supervision in the community for the balance of the indeterminate sentence, and thereafter follow them for the additional probationary period with diminishing supervision. If at any time during the entire term an addict-defendant turned recalcitrant or returned to drugs, the criminal prosecution could be reinstated.

Other bills in the New York senators' package provided, as we have related, for grants-in-aid to states for the construction of narcotic-hospital facilities, with authority vested in the Surgeon General to prescribe standards for state rehabilitation programs; specified in the alternative that drug addiction should be classified as a mental illness so that existing federal grant programs under the Public Health Service Act would be available; and called for massive research.

Almost as important as the substance of these measures were the political battle lines which emerged over them. On Capitol Hill, the New York delegation championed Governor Rockefeller and sought to squeeze maximum advantage from promoting efforts to "cure" the addict. In the executive branch the Kennedy forces, with Governor Brown as their hero, sought to concentrate enforcement action in the Department of Justice and to play up repressive measures, including activities aimed at the new categories of "dangerous drugs." Within this struggle, the New York contingent stood to gain by emphasizing action at the state level, while the forces in control of the administration understandably wanted to hold as much as possible exclusively in the federal domain.

When the 88th Congress convened in 1963, the rehabilitation bills picked up additional sponsorship and momentum in both houses. Senator Javits urged that the medical-commitment approach, coupled with hospitalization, aftercare, and expanded research, was "the only way in which we can come abreast of this critical problem, which has its main impact in an absolutely alarming and sensational increase in the crime rates." Senator Keating pointed out that addiction was becoming "particularly acute among the youths of our cities" and that if probation and aftercare were widely used in lieu of long-term prison sentences, great savings would result, since it cost approximately $2,000 per year to keep an addict in prison whereas an adequate probation program would cost only about $350 per subject.

In this round, Keating also introduced a related measure providing for involuntary commitment of addicts who submitted themselves to the federal authorities on a voluntary basis, to meet the problem encountered by the narcotic hospitals when voluntary patients wanted to leave as soon as they had been detoxified.

Actually, California and New York had pulled slightly ahead of Congress on the civil-commitment front. In California a new law was enacted in 1961 authorizing the California courts to commit any person upon conviction of a misdemeanor or nonviolent felony, and any person turned in by his relatives or friends or volunteering for himself—whether actually addicted or "in imminent danger of becoming addicted"—to the California State Department of Correction for a maximum period of three years, commencing with at least six months of incarceration at a rehabilitation center. In New York, the Metcalf-Volker Act, which became effective in 1963, authorized civil commitment for addicts in similar categories into the custody of the New York State Department of Mental Hygiene, also for a maximum period of three years. By the end of 1963 the California program was under way with slightly over 1,000 patients at the California Rehabilitations Center in Corona and 600 in halfway houses or under supervision as outpatients, while in New York about 400 persons were undergoing detoxification in six state hospitals, with 300 more under outpatient control exercised through aftercare clinics in various facilities designated by the Commissioner of Mental Hygiene.

The Final Report of President Kennedy's Advisory Commission contained a vaguely stated proposal for a federal civil-commitment program—with everything concentrated, naturally, under control of the Attorney General and various Department of Justice agencies such as the Bureau of Prisons and the Federal Probation Service. The report characterized the New York program as undesirable and possibly unconstitutional, and commended the California commitment law as a superior model for other states to follow. Marijuana smokers were included, without any reservation, as proposed candidates for full rehabilitation treatment: "The Commission recommends that a Federal civil commitment statute be enacted to provide an alternative method of handling the federally convicted offender who is a narcotic or marijuana user."

The reshuffling which took place when President Johnson ousted Robert Kennedy from the Attorney Generalship had particularly curious effects on the drug picture, since Kennedy turned up as successor to Keating in the Senate, side by side with the surviving champion of rehabilitation, Senator Javits. As Keating's heir, Kennedy had no choice but to become a co-sponsor of the civil-commitment legislation. President Johnson in turn inherited the administration's position, which had originally been aimed at building up the post of Attorney General, and also inherited the ingenuous pronouncements of the Advisory Commission. In his first law-enforcement message to Congress, Johnson urged enactment of a civil-commitment law in the following terms: "The return of narcotic *and marijuana* users to useful, productive lives is of obvious benefit to them and to society at large. But at the same time, it is essential to assure adequate protection for the general public." (Italics added.)

The rehabilitation bill which Congress finally passed was entitled Narcotic Addict Rehabilitation Act of 1966. We shall analyze it in some detail because, despite Senator Hughes's efforts, Congress has left it virtually untouched since that time (although most of it has been equally neglected by the executive and judicial branches.)

The bill combined provisions for handling addicted persons who had run afoul of certain federal criminal laws with provisions for accommodating addicts civilly commited or wishing to submit to treatment on a voluntary basis. It began with a noble declaration:

> It is the policy of the Congress that certain persons charged with or convicted of violating Federal criminal laws, who are determined to be addicted to narcotic drugs, and likely to be rehabilitated through treatment, should, in lieu of prosecution or sentencing, be civilly committed for confinement and treatment designed to effect their restoration to health, and return to society as useful members.
>
> It is the further policy of the Congress that certain persons addicted to narcotic drugs who are not charged with the commission of any offense should be afforded the opportunity, through civil commitment, for treatment, in order that they may be rehabilitated and returned to society as useful members and in order that society may be protected more effectively from crime and delinquency which results from narcotic addiction.

The definition of "addict" which this measure introduced into federal law was the vaguest catch-all so far: "any individual who habitually uses any narcotic drug . . . so as to endanger the public morals, health, safety, or welfare, or who is so far addicted to the use of such narcotic drugs as to have lost the power of self-control with reference to his addiction." It was, however, tied to the Harrison Act enumeration, so that even though it applies to nonnarcotic substances like cocaine and omits barbiturates, it happily excludes marijuana.

The Act (NARA) was intended to provide rehabilitative treatment in three categories. In the first, individuals charged with offenses against the United States (except crimes of violence, selling or smuggling drugs, and repeating offenders—in other words, except everything but minor first-offenders, of whom there are not many in the federal courts if one excludes the District of Columbia) were given a complicated option to elect so-called civil commitment in lieu of the threatened criminal prosecution. This choice can only be made if permitted in the discretion of a judge, must be made within five days after it is offered, and will only be allowed if the Surgeon General certifies that facilities and personnel are available to treat the addict and finds, moreover, that he is likely to benefit from treatment.

Accused persons passing through all this were thereupon supposed to be committed to a federal Public Health Service institution or a local public or private facility with which the Surgeon General has made special reimbursement arrangements. Incarceration is for a period of not less than six or more than twenty-four months, followed by parole-like supervision on an outpatient basis under the jurisdiction of the Surgeon General so as to complete a total period of thirty-six months within the program. If during this period an individual is found to be no longer amenable to treatment—"cannot be further treated as a medical problem"—or if he misbehaves or begins using drugs again, he is sent back to the court and the criminal charge which has remained in abeyance is revived. If he survives the three years and comes out "cured," the criminal charge is dropped.

The second category under the Act is persons who have been found guilty, by plea or trial, of an offense against the laws of the United States (except, again, any "crime of violence" or any sale or smuggling offense involving drugs *unless it is also found that the offense was committed primarily because of the defendant's own addiction,* and excluding repeaters). Here, once more in the discretion of the court, this *convicted* offender may be turned over to the custody of the Attorney General—if the Attorney General certifies that he is likely to be rehabilitated through treatment, and if adequate facilities and personnel are available—for an indeterminate period of ten years (or the maximum sentence that could otherwise have been imposed, if that is less). A period of at least six months must be served in custody in an institution prior to any conditional release under supervision. The Attorney General is authorized to place addicts released under this program in the jurisdiction of the U.S. Board of Parole or any appropriate public or private agency to whom supervisory responsibility may be contracted.

The third category consists of addicts (within the same sweeping definition of addiction) who submit voluntarily to the program or who are involuntarily committed to it on petition of a relative. After elaborate hearing and screening procedures (and if it is found that federal facilities are available and no appropriate state or other institution can be used), the individual, now called "patient," is committed to the custody of the Surgeon General for incarceration in a Public Health Service facility for not less than six months, followed by three years of supervisory control. If the patient resumes drug use during the supervisory period, he may be recommitted to hospital incarceration for another six-month stretch, and if he tries to escape or otherwise misbehaves while institutionalized he is subject to the same criminal sanctions applied to federal prisoners.

The 1966 Act also included the substance of other Javits-Keating (and subsequently Javits-Kennedy) proposals, such as authorizing the Surgeon General and the Public Health Service to establish outpatient facilities, either directly or by contract with local agencies, and to cooperate with the states and their subdivisions to encourage research and the development of local programs; a limited federal grant-in-aid authorization; and—importantly, at last—a provision slightly loosening the penalty structures applicable to marijuana, so that parole once again became available to marijuana offenders, including those who were already in prison serving long sentences for marijuana convictions. Also—at last—young persons committed under the federal Youth Corrections Act were made fully eligible for applicable benefits under the rehabilitation options. No provision was made in NARA for federal support for the construction or staffing of state treatment facilities, but this was remedied, in a modest way, two years later in the so-called Alcoholic and Narcotic Addict Rehabilitation Amendments of 1968.

As might have been foreseen, the provisions in all three basic "rehabilitation" categories were so complicated and so restricted that they have not been widely used. Even in so-called Title II cases involving convicted offenders, recourse to the Act has been sharply limited on the ground that facilities are not available to the Attorney General to implement its provisions. The Bureau of Prisons provides approximately a hundred beds for convict-addicts at each of four medical centers in Connecticut, Michigan, West Virginia, and California. Aftercare arrangements have been made with a score of local agencies. But only a few hundred persons in the federal prison system have been allowed the benefits of this program since its inception. In the other classes—minor offenders choosing civil commitment instead of prosecution under Title I and addicts volunteering or civilly committed under Title III—from the start the Surgeon General used his prerogatives virtually to nullify the Act by rejecting applicants found unlikely to respond to treatment or for whom it was certified that no facilities were available.

In 1967, to take pressure off the Surgeon General, the National Institute of Mental Health created a new Division of Narcotic Addiction and Drug Abuse, to run the two hospital centers, supervise research grants and projects in the field, and, through its Narcotic Addict Rehabilitation Branch, to oversee the rehabilitation program in both its inpatient and aftercare phases. For a time the program appeared to be expanding: one so-called halfway house began operating in San Antonio in connection with the Ft. Worth hospital, more contracts were let for outpatient facilities and supervision, and six regional field offices were established to monitor future activities. A total of more than twenty local community centers were launched with federal assistance amounting to approximately $10 million per year. A few additional millions from Mental Health Center Act funds found their way into matching grants for constructing and staffing addict-treatment facilities. A few million more are being allocated to research projects (concentrated heavily on marijuana); several training programs for workers in the drug-rehabilitation field were set up; and a flood of pamphlets, posters, comic books, films, and teaching kits were produced and distributed. In 1970 President Nixon himself called for stepped-up educational and training efforts, whereupon $3.5 million were allocated to the Office of Education and an extra $1 million to NIH for these purposes.

But the concept of NARA, besides being buffeted among the three federal arms, suffered fundamentally from another of the great weaknesses of federal systems—namely, that unglamorous responsibilities can be shrugged off by each branch of government upon another. And rehabilitating addicts, as contrasted with trumpeting enforcement "wars" against them, is unglamorous in the extreme. The NIH Division renamed the Lexington hospital "Clinical Research Center," with the avowed purpose of turning it into a research and demonstration center for the guidance of local authorities. Its intake was limited to eligible civil-commitment patients who happened to meet its research needs, plus a flow of candidates for referral to local centers and facilities. In 1969 it was announced that the administration planned to close both the Lexington and the Ft. Worth hospitals altogether; they were kept open by vigorous protests from the Kentucky and

Texas congressional delegations until after the 1970 elections, but Ft. Worth has been closed since then (dumping some 150 addict-inmates on the streets) and the "clinical research" at Lexington has been further restricted.

By mid-1971 only 1,500 patients had gone through the federal treatment program to the aftercare stage, aftercare being provided by over a hundred small-scale contracts in forty states, with emphasis thus dissipated away from such severe problem areas as New York, California, Illinois, and the District of Columbia. An estimated 9,000 patients were in treatment in twenty-three federally funded local centers, and NIMH was predicting that by the end of fiscal 1972 the number of centers might be increased to thirty and the number of patients involved to between 12,000 and 15,000.

Under strong pressure from federal authorities, who supplied a BNDD counsel as reporter for the project, the National Conference of Commissioners on Uniform State Laws is drafting a Model Act, expected to parallel closely the provisions of NARA, for promulgation among the states. If this results in a flood of similar state programs—as it almost certainly will—the federal role will be further restricted in favor of the politically agreeable alternative of merely handing out federal funds to be spent by state and local authorities on "little NARA's."

The most interesting, most promising, and most controversial rehabilitation efforts now being made in connection with addiction to the opiates are those which rely on the administration of methadone, a synthetic equivalent of morphine developed by German chemists during World War II when Germany's access to natural opium crops was cut off. The effects of methadone are very similar to those of morphine and heroin, except that they act a little more slowly and last longer. Also, although methadone is indisputably addicting, withdrawal symptoms are somewhat milder than those of withdrawal from a comparable addiction to the other opiates. Moreover, it is believed to produce a slightly less intense euphoric "high" when administered to addicts and (like any related substance with cross tolerance) it prevents increased euphoria from other opiates taken when it is present at a high level in the system.

It is worth stressing once again that the differences among opium derivatives and their synthetic equivalents are minor. The oft-heard assertion that heroin is notably more dangerous, or *really* much more likely to produce addiction than any of its sister substances, is misleading nonsense. Although heroin is fast-acting and has almost double the strength of morphine for an equivalent volume, the overall effects of comparable dosages are virtually indistinguishable. This is also true of methadone. A long-time addict, who does not know which drug he is receiving, can scarcely judge anything from effects alone. Neither Nalline reactions nor the chromatography processes used in urinalysis will distinguish heroin from morphine; the body metabolizes them identically. And identification of synthetics like methadone in such tests is not easy or certain unless the equipment used is extremely sophisticated.

Methadone was released in the United States in 1947 and soon came into use at Lexington and other hospitals as the preferred drug for administration in small quantities to alleviate the discomforts of withdrawal. It gradually acquired a popular reputation as a "good" narcotic in contrast with the "bad" qualities ascribed to heroin (no more foolish, perhaps, than the "hard" and "soft" categories). This helped make it possible for two courageous New York doctors, Marie Nyswander and Vincent P. Dole, to launch an experiment at Rockefeller University Hospital, commencing early in 1964, in which they administered methadone on a controlled basis, but in large and steady dosages, to heroin addicts. The Dole-Nyswander theory is that by providing an adequate solution for the direct problems of addiction (methadone is administered orally, on a daily basis, and never given out for self-administration when there is any danger of diversion or abuse), their program frees the addict of pressures associated with his quest for drugs and thus enables him to work out other problems such as finding employment, restoring family ties, and making personal readjustments, with psychiatric help if necessary. Only thereafter are efforts made to reduce or eliminate his drug habit, when the patient has readied himself to go free of his dependency.

This first Dole-Nyswander program was undertaken in tacit defiance of the federal Narcotics Bureau and local enforcement authorities in New York, but because of its eminent auspices it was not molested, and it soon began producing good results with a small, carefully selected group. By 1967 more than a hundred patients had survived on stabilized dosages, and by 1969 over a thousand were being managed successfully through three hospital centers in New York City. Attrition to alcoholism and other drugs cut into the program, and dropouts almost invariably went back to heroin. But "cure" in terms of total abstinence was not the primary objective, and the results claimed for maintenance were spectacular:

> We have observed the almost literal return to life of people who have been as far down as it is possible to go—and whose present dignity and personal stature are the equal of many "decent" citizens we know. Visitors to our methadone services are often disturbed by their inability to tell who are patients, who are staff members, and who are both. The ex-addict on methadone is distinguished by only two things—the "tracks" inside his arms, and his new outlook on life.

Attacks were made from all sides on the alleged immorality of furnishing drugs to sustain addiction, and critics pointed out that this was really no more than the perennial error of substituting a new drug for an old one, as morphine had once been given to cure alcoholism and opium eating, and heroin had once been hailed as a nonaddicting remedy for the morphine habit.

But methadone has caught on. It is inexpensive (a few cents per day for an average maintenance dosage) and it has long been available through legitimate channels to persons with authority to prescribe. The ultimate promise of methadone is that it may offer a face-saving retreat from some popular and official exaggerations about heroin. Saying it "alleviates the craving" for heroin and "blocks" the euphoria of heroin highs is a good way to sugar-coat the reality that methadone is substantially a heroin equivalent. Stressing the novelty of methadone "treatment" preserves the fiction that all—or most, or many—opiate users are curable, or motivated to seek an abstinent state, or perhaps curable *before* they are motivated. By talking of methadone "centers" public-health authorities sidestep the ancient clinic controversy. Because the drug is easily and legally manufactured by U.S. drug houses, sinister myths about Chinese tongs, Sicilian criminals, Marseilles laboratories, and malevolent Turkish farmers can be avoided. And out-and-out maintenance of "incurables" can be camouflaged as long-term withdrawal.

At very least, methadone programs are drawing opiate addicts out of the drug culture and away from the peddler-police domain. With urinalysis it is demonstrably easy to hold heroin and other related drug abuse by methadone patients to a minimum—easier, for instance, than keeping illicit drugs out of all but the most secure hospital and prison facilities.

More than three dozen methadone treatment units have been launched in New York since the Dole-Nyswander pioneering. Work with the drug is being carried on in every major urban center where addiction is a problem, including a score of projects sponsored and financed under Title IV (the grant-in-aid provision) of NARA. Private practitioners have taken on addict-patients in some instances, and programs have also been launched on a large scale by militant organizations such as the Black Man's Liberation Army, whose Washington, D.C., centers are reportedly in contact with more than 13,000 users, including some 3,000 nonblacks.

Nonetheless, development of methadone treatment has been harassed and resisted, instead of being encouraged, by some "experts" and authorities who have a stake in the status quo. Private undertakings like the Black Man's Liberation Army were forced to close from time to time by federal authorities who threatened their medical advisors, interfered with their suppliers, and sought to cut off their operating funds. Doctors prescribing methadone have been castigated, menaced, and in a few cases indicted. Accidents and diversions, inevitable in any large-scale program, are publicized out of proportion. Local police have sometimes sought to frighten addicts away from the programs by openly seizing lists of applicants and patients or by infiltrating the centers with undercover agents. Most sadly, some of the liberal and militant groups that should have been foremost in supporting methadone programs have been misled into fighting them by assertions that methadone is merely being used in an evil plot to perpetuate the enslave-ment of minorities (as if *any* enslavement could be more de-grading than that of user to pusher and user-pusher to high-handed "nark").

The methadone dosages used to ease withdrawal symptoms range from five to twenty milligrams daily, depending on the severity of the user's habit. Maintenance doses administered by Dole and Nyswander to stabilize between euphoria or intoxica-tion on the one hand, and drug-starvation symptoms on the other, reach the 100-to-200-milligram range (referring in all cases to oral administration). The only medical problem fre-quently associated with such dosages is a tendency to constipa-tion. But law-enforcement spokesmen, supported by a few com-pliant echoers in the scientific community and by the customary parroting at the U.N. Commission, now take the line that main-tenance dosages are a new, "experimental" use for methadone, requiring restrictive "guidelines" and subject to all the crippling safeguards imposed on testers of new and untried substances.

We shall return to the details of this latest chapter of the methadone story as a final example of cynicism and folly in the American drug saga. Meanwhile let it be noted that while millions are spent on drug-education comic books, on teaching monkeys to smoke pot, and on buying the favor of indifferent Turkish poppy growers, nearly every significant methadone program in the country has a waiting list of desperate applicants trying to survive on the street until they can be admitted.

Other approaches to rehabilitation, sometimes coupled with methadone programs and urine testing but usually nonclinical, are also having modest success. For twenty years an offshoot of Alcoholics Anonymous, calling itself Narcotics Anonymous, worked with addicts in the Lexington and Ft. Worth hospitals and has maintained somewhat fluid chapters in New York, Chicago, and Los Angeles. Its achievements have been comparable to the effectiveness of A.A. in working with alcoholics: while not making large dents in the addict population it has enabled a number of persons who respond favorably to its religion-oriented program to free themselves from the drug habit and remain abstinent.

In 1958 a promising new endeavor was launched in California with the founding of what came to be known as Synanon, a private group organized by addicts and managed by ex-addicts with the assistance of a volunteer medical staff. Addict-candidates are admitted selectively and are subjected to what is called "attack therapy," fighting their problems in an atmosphere in which their fellow addicts will not tolerate weaknesses or self-pity. And this has helped hundreds, at least, to "make it." There are now other Synanon facilities scattered about the country, plus dozens of imitating groups—Daytop, Phoenix, Odyssey, Topic, Dare, Second Renaissance, Rap, etc.—each accommodating small communities of live-in members. Even the NIMH doctors at Lexington have one, called Matrix House. Techniques vary somewhat, with group or "encounter" therapy and individual counseling instead of the tough Synanon program. These ventures have been helped by federal grants and local funding, though on a small scale, and they still number their participants only in dozens or hundreds. Some addicts who have been helped remain permanently and occupy themselves with assisting others; others are able to move back into society with more or less continuing contact and support from the organization.

The U.S. Public Health Service's experimental halfway house at San Antonio has already been mentioned. There are now many similar facilities and programs aimed at easing the transition of treated or imprisoned addicts back into society, especially since the same concept has caught on with respect to rehabilitating prisoners in general. In these, addicts released from incarceration can live under more or less close supervision while at the same time going into the community to seek employment and make readjustments to a drug-free life. With urine testing they can also be effectively policed to prevent backsliding.

In sum, these contemporary efforts to rehabilitate drug addicts—remembering that we are talking only of drug users who have a true addiction problem—cannot be entirely written off, although the purported "cure" of such persons by pushing them involuntarily into rehabilitation programs is scarcely a realistic total solution. Since their inception in the 1930's, the two U.S. Public Health Service hopitals have admitted more than 80,000 addict-patients, and although reliable follow-up studies have been sparse, it is generally agreed that the relapse rate over the years has been no less than a pathetic 90 per cent, and probably considerably higher. Methadone withdrawal, urine-monitoring programs, the use of narcotic antagonists, and supportive group projects like Synanon and Daytop all play their part in salvaging addicts—by the handful—from the drug-using community. But it cannot be fairly concluded that they represent a main line of approach.

The hard-rock limit is that no user can be truly freed from his addiction or his bad habits by therapeutic efforts until he *wants* to be helped. And conversely, when most users become strongly motivated to give up drugs or bring their habits under control it is not much of a strain for them to do so. Most authorities agree that substantial numbers of drug addicts—who, despite periodic hysteria to the contrary, do *not* generally become seriously involved with addicting drugs until they are young adults—have always simply dropped their habits and ceased to be addicts when they mature and move into middle age.

Finally, it might be observed that recently a new motive toward abstinence has been coming into play: the demand for ex-addicts to window-dress new projects and lecture young people so far exceeds supplies that this has itself become a rewarding career for those who can qualify.

■ TWENTY-FIVE

Dangerous Drugs: Here We Go Again!

■ THE EPISODE in which the menace of dangerous drugs was played up (and the concept of "hard" narcotics invented) by the 1962 Ad Hoc Panel—so the ensuing White House Conference would have something new to talk about—was neither the beginning nor, alas, the end of the dangerous-drug story. Here again political phrasemakers took leave of honest etymology, for many *other* drugs, like aspirin and insulin, are highly dangerous too, though let there be no question that some of the newer drugs currently being abused, and especially depressants in the barbiturate category, are dangerous indeed.

Barbiturates are addicting by every definition. Misuse of them causes permanent and severe physiological damage, and their withdrawal syndrome includes violent convulsions and a distinct possibility of death if acute symptoms are not alleviated. Barbiturates are worse than alcohol in these respects, and when combined with alcohol the intoxicating and debilitating effects of each drug seem to accentuate those of the other. Moreover, unlike the drunk, whose stomach will rebel if he indulges beyond a certain tolerance limit, the barbiturate user can easily keep taking pills in his intoxicated state until he has administered a fatal dose to himself. For many years, deaths from barbiturate poisoning have been numbered in the high hundreds and low thousands, with a fuzzy line separating suicides from accidents in this drugged crossing of the fatal line.

262

Drugs in the stimulant categories, such as the amphetamines, also merit the appellation dangerous, although they are not technically addicting and present no major difficulties in withdrawal. The recently widespread practice of ingesting amphetamines by injection—mainlining "speed" and "splash"—appears to produce destructive effects which are more akin to self-inflicted violence than to mere self-indulgence with drugs. Combinations of speed with depressants like the barbiturates or alcohol allegedly sometimes have effects on their users roughly comparable to a good tap from a blackjack or a bruising encounter with a briskly moving motor vehicle. And by all accounts substances like LSD-25 and STP deserve the reputation for eccentric harmfulness which they are acquiring.

But the basic problems posed by drugs in these categories, and by the whole range of tranquilizers, have been with us for a long time. Among them only the barbiturates produce "addicts," so it is illogical to lump them together. It is no more misguided now, and no less, to talk about "curing" or "rehabilitating" users of Benzedrine than it has always been to apply like concepts to smokers of cigarettes and reefers. The difference is that by now we should know better.

Barbituric acid was synthesized in Germany in the 1860's, and the first barbiturate marketed as a sedative was launched under the name "barbital" in 1882. Properly managed, barbiturates are useful in a wide variety of medical treatments, ranging from gently tempering anxiety and menstrual discomfort to total anesthesia and the remarkable "truth serums." They are generally dispensed in tablets but can be produced in soluble compounds suitable for hypodermic injection.

The amphetamines were developed and introduced into medical practice in the early thirties. During World War II amphetamine compounds were widely used in the armed forces, particularly in aviation, to counteract symptoms of extreme fatigue. One result we have already noted—the dumping of surplus stores in both Germany and Japan, which created major drug-abuse problems for their populations during the allied occupations; another was that our own young men and women returned to civilian life with familiarity, if not habituation, in regard to this category of stimulant. In the 1950's amphetamines were sold without prescription in nasal inhalers and sometimes in tablet form for controlling obesity. They also began to be widely used outside of medical practice, including "spree" use in college groups, military camps, and prisons.

Amphetamines increase athletic performance by suppressing symptoms of fatigue which otherwise slow the performer. This is the drug used to dope racehorses, and though no one has ever undertaken formally to prove anything amiss (and no wrong would actually have been involved anyway), it is interesting that in all the history of competition running, since man learned to measure time, no one had ever succeeded in breaking four minutes for a mile until Roger Bannister did it in May 1954. Bannister was a fast runner who happened also to be a medical doctor. Three months later, before one of the largest TV audiences of that era, Bannister did it again, but so did John Landy, who ran second—and Bannister had had a cold while Landy *had a four-stitch gash in his foot.* A year later, on a soggy track in London, a near-unknown Hungarian soldier (who said he was still airsick from his trip to the meet) broke four minutes again, beating two English runners of moderate renown who *also* did it behind him. The record has been pushed down at intervals ever since by runners from drug-saturated nations like the United States and the British Commonwealth (by 1965 nine U.S. track men, including a remarkable high school boy named Jim Ryun, had broken the four-minute barrier, and the feat had been accomplished a total of 156 times by fifty-four athletes from sixteen nations. Herbert Elliott of Australia still led the field with seventeen official under-four-minute runs.)

As far back as the early 1920's a few states had recognized barbiturates to be potentially dangerous enough to be brought within general prescription laws. References to barbiturate addiction began appearing in the medical literature. But for the most part they were identified separately from narcotics by being described as "hypnotics," and there were authoritative (though wholly erroneous) assertions that even severe barbiturate addiction was controllable and produced no significant withdrawal symptoms. By World War II approximately two-thirds of the states had enacted control laws.

In 1945, addiction centers like Lexington, and physicians working with addicts elsewhere, began to encounter barbiturate use in connection with conventional addiction to morphine or heroin, and the severity of this problem soon began to be recognized. In that first postwar year, 965 deaths were definitely attributed to barbiturate poisoning. The popular press began grinding out stories with titles like "Sleeping Pills: Doorway to Doom," "Sleeping Pill Addicts Walk Terror Path," and "Sleeping Pills Can Kill Like a Cobra." And of course politicians began moving in, led by Congresswoman Edith Nourse Rogers of Massachusetts, who in 1947 offered a bill to bring barbiturates under the Harrison Act pattern.

Mrs. Rogers was immediately caught in a crossfire: the Narcotics Bureau, in Treasury, resisted all suggestions that *it* should undertake the policing of sleeping-pill users, and the all-powerful American Pharmaceutical Association wanted no part of any restrictive regulations imposed on its members, while at the same time the Food and Drug Administration (then seated modestly in the Federal Security Agency) kept trying to stir things up, in a bid for more power for itself, by Anslinger-like puffing of the menace and the importance of its own finger-in-the-dike efforts:

A typical [FDA] case was that directed against H. Otis Fadal, who operated Fadal's Square Drugstore, of Waco, Tex. This case was terminated on March 1, 1945, by a fine of $600 and a six months' jail sentence. . . . The investigation at Waco was begun because of a complaint made to us by the juvenile authorities. Two kindergarten children from the same family were discovered by their teacher to be stuporous in class. She found that they were taking medicine. . . . When our inspectors traced the father's source of supply it developed that some 60 addicts were regularly purchasing barbiturates without prescription from Fadal's Drugstore, which derived large illicit profit therefrom.

The information which we acquired leaves no doubt that the problems growing out of the unwise and unsupervised use of barbiturates is progressively becoming more serious. Tragic incidents of broken homes, destroyed health, suicides, and accidental deaths are commonly encountered in these investigations. . . .

The most recently terminated case in a district Federal court involved the Cohen Drug Co. of Charleston, W. Va. This was begun when a local man died in a telephone booth after an overdose of barbiturates. Another death which was discovered in the same community resulted in the acquisition by our inspectors of the package from which the lethal medicine had been taken. The inspector presented the empty box at the drugstore where the medicine had originally been obtained and was unhesitatingly given a refill of the prescription. . . . Upon a plea of guilty the court fined the corporation $1,800 on May 5, 1947.

Soon the campaign picked up momentum in the usual pattern. Other congressmen swarmed to get on Mrs. Rogers' bandwagon. Tales of heinous crimes committed by persons who had taken sleeping pills commenced to fly about. And, naturally . . .

One of the most alarming aspects of the current situation is the fact that addiction is shown to be increasing most rapidly in teenage groups. A 1950 report of the Chicago Juvenile Protection Association states: "The sale of dope to minors and their addiction now presents one of the most menacing and destructive conditions this Association has ever faced." A study of 41 cases reported for the period January 1 through May 31, 1950, shows that the youngest child was 12 years old and thirty were between 13 and 16. By the end of the year, 93 children had been called to the attention of this [family] court as users or being in possession of dope.

But the man who tried most determinedly to ride the barbiturate issue in the 1950's was Congressman Hale Boggs, author of the infamous Boggs Act, which had brought mandatory minimums into the Harrison Act structure. In 1951 Boggs commenced pushing for legislation imposing drastically repressive federal controls. And immediately he encountered head-on opposition from his erstwhile patron and mentor, Commissioner Anslinger. In hearings on drug legislation that year the Commissioner fairly scolded him:

> But now, as to barbiturates, there is no smuggling. There is relatively little interstate traffic, and there is very little peddling. We have no control over the manufacture, and there are literally hundreds who are manufacturing barbiturates today. We would have no control except in the distribution. . . . You can imagine the terrific problem we would have today with the thousands of pounds of non-tax-paid barbiturates that are in the traffic today. I mean not illicit traffic but that are in the channels of legal trade. It would be worse than prohibition. . . . It would take $5,000,000 and take five times as many men as we have, and then you would have conditions that would be similar to prohibition. I think it would become a very unpopular Bureau in this country. . . .
>
> Another thing is that if they put this under the Bureau, then the next thing will be bromides, and probably we will get down to aspirin. We think we are controlling the very dangerous narcotics now, and . . . certainly I do not think we could give it the proper attention that would be expected of us if this drug is to be controlled like morphine and cocaine.

Even the American Medical Association, speaking officially through its president, jumped in:

> The pending bill . . . has been carefully reviewed by our Committee on Legislation. This Committee has concluded that the enactment of this bill by the Congress would represent a continuation

of a trend to confer more and more authority on the Federal Government in matters more properly coming within the jurisdiction of the states. In the viewpoint of the Committee, if this trend is to continue, we may eventually come to a situation where no drug that may be of harm to a patient if used unwisely may be prescribed by a physician without the consent of the Federal Government. . . . It might appear inapropos for a representative of medicine to interject a question of constitutionality, but it seems to me that the Committee might well keep in mind the possible questions that might arise as to the constitutionality of this bill if it is enacted.

These attacks were enough to head off action in 1951. But the Food and Drug Administration kept putting out vignettes about barbiturate seizures and the association of sleeping pills with crime, and soon it began to talk also about the dangers of amphetamine abuse. Anslinger made a telling countermove by utilizing, as usual, his domination over the World Health Organization. He had relied on the absence of international treaty commitments to ground his arguments against the Rogers-Boggs proposals, and now he went to the international forum to buttress his position that these drugs ought to be regulated by tighter prescription controls only, instead of by repression. In 1954 the WHO Expert Committee on Drugs Liable to Produce Addiction recommended that governments should impose prescription controls on amphetamines, and in 1956 it made a similar recommendation as to the barbiturates, with a finding in both cases that such national control measures would be sufficient to deal with the situation. At the same time, the U.N. Commission on Narcotic Drugs insisted that both categories be excluded from the proposed Single Convention, leaving each government to take appropriate measures individually on its own behalf.

In 1955–56, as we have seen in an earlier chapter, the limelight was pre-empted by Senator Daniel and his far-ranging Subcommittee, which concentrated primarily on stiffer penalties and compulsory rehabilitation for persons connected with the conventional "narcotic" traffic. Nonetheless during the Daniel hearings one session was devoted to drugs outside the Harrison Act pattern, and this gave Commissioner George P. Larrick of the Food and Drug Administration a forum:

Because barbiturates produce greater mental, emotional and neurological impairment than morphine, informed medical experts expressed the opinion that addiction to them is actually more detri-

mental to the individual and society than morphine addiction. . . .
While other drugs had their dangers, the widespread damage barbiturates can do to society as well as to the individual made us
especially aware of the need for their control.

On this occasion Larrick used a device which was to become
one of his major shock-administrators—tossing out free-swinging estimates of how many hundreds of thousands of pounds of
drug substances were probably being produced annually within
the United States and then converting this figure into a guess
as to billions of capsules and a number representing possible
per capita use by the total population of the country (for 1955,
eighteen doses per person per year).

Larrick's credentials as an expert on drug addiction were less
impressive than Anslinger's. He had started as an FDA inspector
in the field, and had spent most of his life working up through
the enforcement ranks. Yet he told the Daniel Subcommittee:

> Addiction produces a general dissolution of character. We know of
> men who have held responsible positions but gradually became
> derelicts through the use of these drugs. Whole families may be-
> come relief problems when the breadwinner becomes addicted.
> Oftentime housewives begin to use the drug on a doctor's pre-
> scription for a nervous condition; they gradually increase the dosage
> as tolerance and emotional and physical dependence develop.
> They no longer take an interest in the home or children, get dirty
> and slovenly; steal money and sell furniture to get the drug.

Then came another parade of horrible cases: the man who, in a
barbiturate stupor, fell into a gas furnace and burned up before
he so much as knew he was getting hot; the nice old couple in
Colorado who so saturated themselves with amphetamines that
they hallucinated they were FBI agents; the attractive young
lady who became intoxicated on barbiturates and drove her car
over a neighbor's lawn, scaring the neighbor's children; and—
triumphantly—Carl Austin Hall, the then-notorious kidnaper of
Bobby Greanlease, who had confessed in writing that he was an
amphetamine user, and whose manuscript confession was waved
about the hearing room and reproduced in the record.

At this point (we are still in the Daniel Subcommittee hearings of 1955–56) Commissioner Larrick initiated the ultimate
reductio ad absurdum foisted on the American people by public
officials trying to aggravate the so-called drug menace. We have
seen a long parade of nonsense: that the addict is a criminal
per se; that Harrison Act drugs are "poison," and heroin sig-

nificantly more dangerous than the rest; that more severe criminal penalties are the solution; that the "clinics" were a total failure and the British approach to the problem merely a shadow of the U.S. reality; that public education about drugs would be harmful and would only recruit new addicts; that marijuana leads directly to addiction to the opiates.

But none of these approaches the reckless falsity of the major theme on which so-called dangerous drugs came to be principally condemned. That was the theme, echoed endlessly by official spokesmen, that dangerous drugs, and specifically the amphetamines, have been responsible for a substantial number of highway fatalities, mainly because of their abuse by long-distance truck drivers. Commissioner Larrick told the Daniel Committee:

> The use of these drugs indiscriminately, not necessarily among habitués or addicts, may also result in tragedy. The motorist who, attempting to reach a distant destination drives continually for twenty hours, takes the "pep pills" to keep from falling asleep may find that dizziness, confusion or hallucinations cause the unexplained highway accident which changes his destination to the hospital or morgue.
>
> Or the trucker who had driven with the aid of "Benny" (benzedrine) and became so confused that he crawled into the sleeping berth and when pulled from his wrecked truck claimed he and "Benny" were driving and "Benny" was doing such a good job he just let him take over while he took a nap.

When Larrick began to drag, the irrepressible Chairman put words into his mouth:

Senator Daniel. I have a statement from you, made not so long ago . . . and I will ask you if this is correct, and place this in the record, if it is. I am quoting now from a statement attributed to you several weeks ago in a magazine: "There is a definite relationship between the illegal use of these drugs," talking about the amphetamines—"and juvenile delinquency. They are to be sold on doctor's prescriptions, but in every big United States city there is at least one source that violates the law." Then you go on to give an example of a case in Missouri. This is the investigation made at an interview with a 16-year-old girl who was found in a semiconscious state as a consequence of taking amphetamines and beer. Is that a correct statement?

Mr. Larrick. Yes.

Senator Daniel. . . . and the statement which we will include in our record regarding the married truck driver who was accused of seducing a girl, states that he was considerably older than the girl, and he was a chronic user of amphetamines. The report of your inspectors in that area includes stories of young waitresses who have taken amphetamines and traveled with transport-truck drivers; of older people furnishing them to teenagers, and having sex relations with them; thefts by gangs of teenage boys who used these drugs to bolster their courage and keep them sharp; as well as professional peddlers supplying the amphetamine.

Mr. Larrick. Correct.

The hearings from which we have just quoted were held in September 1955. But Senator Daniel was making his headlines primarily with the Harrison Act drugs, so in October 1955, Congressman Boggs—not to be left out of the action—launched another investigation on the House side in which barbiturates and amphetamines were featured. Commissioner Larrick sent a cautious deputy to the first House hearings.

Mr. Karsten. Is the Food and Drug Administration equipped to deal with this problem adequately, assuming you get the increase in force? Do you think you can do the same type of job done by the Bureau of Narcotics, or would that be the proper thing to do?

Mr. Harvey. Congressman, it is extremely difficult for me to give you a completely forthright answer. I will have to say that we have not been able to explore the full effectiveness of the law that we have now. At the same time I have to speculate that the problem goes outside of ordinary drug channels, reaches undercover channels, which is likely to require a kind of approach such as we have not as yet been able to use. I have referred to to the fact that barbiturates can be made almost anywhere, that it is a drug that is very widely manufactured, and it is to be remembered that there is a problem of interstate commerce, or establishing the facts of interstate commerce, in any action which is brought under the Federal law under the Food and Drug and Cosmetic Act. Therefore one may well speculate as to reaching a point where difficulties will arise . . .

Mr. Boggs. The difficulty we find ourselves in is that Mr. Anslinger comes in and says he doesn't want barbiturate jurisdiction. It would highly complicate his enforcement procedure. He has a limited staff, something over 200 people, there is no smuggling involved in the sale of barbiturates, it is a domestic operation, and he doesn't want it. At the same time, by your testimony and the testimony of the Public Health Service people, it is admitted the problem of addiction in this field is just as grave if not worse than it is in the field of these other drugs.

Mr. Harvey. That is right.

However, Harvey, the FDA deputy, told the Boggs Committee that his agency was making a big undercover investigation of the illicit traffic in amphetamines, and on October 25, 1955, the Department of Justice put out one of its all-point press releases relating the following:

> Two Government departments today opened a drive to stamp out the illegal sale of stimulant drugs to truck drivers by cafes, service stations, truck stops, and drugstores. United States attorneys in ten Federal districts and six States simultaneously filed twenty-two criminal actions and requested bench warrants for the arrests of forty-three individual defendants. The actions were announced by Attorney General Herbert Brownell, Jr., and Secretary Marion B. Folsum of the Department of Health, Education & Welfare after a year-long investigation by the Food and Drug Administration in Mr. Folsum's Department. . . .
>
> Highway accident reports and information furnished by safety directors of trucking firms and association led to the FDA investigation.
>
> George P. Larrick, Commissioner of Food and Drugs, said FDA inspectors worked undercover as interstate truck drivers to get evidence. He said that the trucking industry and drug-manufacturing firms had contributed materially to the success of the investigation. Mr. Larrick said: "There is evidence that some truckers using the drugs have lost their own lives and have needlessly risked the lives of others. Use of these drugs by truck drivers is particularly dangerous because they so stimulate the driver that he stays on the job long beyond the point of normal physical endurance. His brain tires, his driving judgment and his vision are finally impaired, and a tragic accident sometimes follows."

Larrick used the old Narcotics Bureau trick of feeding sensational stories to the press and then submitting the resulting clippings to the congressional committee as evidence. One such account, from St. Louis, attributed to the local FDA District Director and entitled "Illegal 'Thrill Pill' Sales Bring Tragic Harvest," went as follows:

> Investigation of what Pruitt termed the "most vicious" case in his files began when a 15-year-old girl was found dead in bed at her home in Southern Illinois. The investigation determined that the girl died from an overdose of "thrill pills," given to her at a party by some older men who had taken several teenage girls to

an apartment. At this same party, one of the men fell from the second story apartment window, and later died from the injuries. It was never established if the fall was an accident or if he was pushed. The investigation established that one of the men had obtained more than 100 "thrill pills" from a druggist without a prescription. The druggist was fined in Federal court.

Another case record is that of a married man in Arkansas, who consumed a large quantity of the pills and went berserk. He abducted a teenage girl, criminally assulted her, then murdered her, the record shows.

When Commissioner Anslinger appeared, he repeated his 1951 insistence that his Bureau wanted no part of this:

> *Mr. Boggs.* Commissioner, I think you and your limited staff do a marvelous job. It is one of the best enforcement jobs in the country. There is one other thing that continues to concern us, and that is the question of barbiturates, or whatever you call them . . .

> *Mr. Anslinger.* Mr. Chairman, I have no quarrel with anyone about the fact that there is too much consumption of barbiturates and that there are abuses. . . . However, we have seen no really illicit traffic as we know the illicit traffic in barbiturates. There certainly is no smuggling. There is no need for smuggling. There is no interstate illicit trafficking as such, although there are abuses in relation to certain firms that are exempt under the Durham-Humphrey Act, where you can send in your own diagnosis of yourself and they will put you on barbiturates. . . . We have never considered this on an international level, although many other drugs have been the subject of discussion at the United Nations. This subject has not been discussed because of the fact that there really is no international problem or no international trafficking. We have tried to confine our efforts to the really very dangerous drugs like the opium derivatives and synthetics and derivatives of the coca leaf. As you know, with our small force we have really a manpower shortage now.

And then Anslinger made what must be conceded to be a point worthy of consideration by his critics and adversaries:

> I should like to point out to you, as to what we feel about this situation, that certainly it is in the hands of the medical profession right now. It is not in the hands of the trafficker. Why should the medical profession not take hold of that situation and bring it under control? Right now we are getting from various facets of the medical profession this statement that the narcotics traffic is too much of a police problem and it should now become a medical problem. I would prefer to see the barbiturates problem remain a medical

problem and see if the doctors cannot keep this stuff in the bottle and control it in that way, rather than to suddenly make it a police problem. I think we would probably be as popular as the Prohibition Bureau if this thing went into effect.

The upshot was that Senator Daniel prevailed with his Narcotic Control Act of 1956, and nothing was done about Boggs's proposals to repress drugs in other categories. They remained subject only to the mild power given the FDA by the Durham-Humphrey Amendments of 1951 to classify substances as either safe for self-administration or sufficiently dangerous to require control by doctors and pharmacists. Anything classified in the latter category was supposed to be marked "Caution: To be dispensed only by or on the prescription of a physician."

TWENTY-SIX

Drug-Abuse Control, 1965

■ COMMISSIONER LARRICK did not give up, however. Periodically the Food and Drug Administration put out alarming new estimates, such as 819,000 pounds of barbiturates, worth $40 million, produced in 1959; more deaths from barbiturates than from any other poison, and a 670 per cent increase in such deaths in Los Angeles; 8 billion amphetamine tablets a year, with at least 50 per cent going into the illicit market . . . etc. (Statements about production in this period were easy to puff because the two largest U.S. manufacturers of barbiturates and amphetamines refused to release any figures; and there is no doubt that a substantial flow of both these drugs *was* finding its way into uncontrolled channels via such perfectly legal devices as export to Canada or Mexico, purchase in those countries, and reimportation into the United States.)

Accidents—an airplane crash in which it was learned that the pilot had been taking tranquilizers, two trailer trucks in a multiple-vehicle melée on the New Jersey Turnpike where fourteen benzedrine tablets were found in one of the truck cabs— were widely publicized, and an "expert" estimate was launched by planting in the United Nations Bulletin on Narcotics a story to the effect that more than 5 million Americans were abusing barbiturates and other sedatives, stimulants, and tranquilizers. In 1960, domestic barbiturate production was officially reported as 852,000 pounds, which was translated into an estimate of 6 billion one-grain capsules, or thirty-three for every man, woman, and child in the country. In 1961 the story was that Americans had ingested 1.4 million pounds of tranquilizers, and it was claimed that tranquilizers were beginning to rival the barbiturates as suicide drugs.

The FDA early found an ally in Senator Thomas Dodd, whose Juvenile Delinquency Subcommittee commenced, in 1958, exploring all forces tending to undermine American youth—pornography, the unregulated sales of guns and other weapons, child abuse, and of course drugs. Dodd soon emerged as an outspoken expert, hammering at the idea that so-called dangerous drugs, unlike opiates and marijuana, were not confined to slum use but were affecting young people in high schools, on college campuses, and in wealthy suburban neighborhoods. He linked barbiturates and amphetamines as "hidden accomplices" with crimes of violence, accidents, and suicides, asserting that they contributed to bizarre sexual behavior among young people. He collected his own horrible cases: two teenagers burned to death in a brush fire that overtook their automobile after they had passed out from an overdose of barbiturates taken as part of a suicide pact; an eighteen-year-old boy who killed a friend at a "goof ball" party while they were joking with one another; three teenage lads who robbed and killed an elderly gentleman in Chicago while they were under the influence of barbiturates —allegedly because he was deaf and did not understand immediately that he was being held up. Apparently in the same case, or at least in the case of a similar old gentleman, a sixteen-year-old fired eleven shots into the body, and when asked why was reported to have answered, "The pills made us do it." A seventeen-year-old, his personality totally changed, according to the Dodd Subcommittee, by the use of Seconal, savagely slashed a cab driver to death in Los Angeles. And a young girl, allegedly under the influence of drugs, ran over her mother and dragged the body more than a mile under the car.

In 1961, Senator Dodd sponsored a series of bills to bring barbiturates and amphetamines under strict federal control, and in 1962 his Subcommittee held hearings in California and New York—which incidentally gave Governor Brown and Attorney General Mosk (and Senator Keating, who was on the Subcommittee) an additional platform from which to urge the White House Conference.

But now momentarily the action shifts to another quarter: Senator Kefauver's Antitrust and Monopoly Subcommittee, battling the drug industry over prices and marketing practices, found not only that it was being out-maneuvered and outmuscled by drug-lobbying forces on Capitol Hill, but also that the FDA itself—and Commissioner Larrick—appeared to be aligned with the very interests they were supposed to be policing. In 1960–61 Larrick had named a Drug Subcommittee of his FDA Citizens Advisory Committee to counsel with him on drug matters, and had loaded it with drug-industry apologists. In the summer of 1962 this Committee issued a report, in its quasi-official status as a policy advisor, urging even more leniency toward the drug industry, to allow the drug interests, in effect, to police and regulate themselves.

So Kefauver turned his guns on the FDA and quickly found a vulnerable target. Dr. Henry Welsh, director of the agency's Division of Antibiotics, was discovered to have been paid nearly $300,000 as "honoraria" for various articles and reports, all from drug companies who were directly affected by decisions which Dr. Welsh controlled in his official capacity. When this broke, in 1962, FDA was badly hurt. Simultaneously, Senator Humphrey's Subcommittee on Reorganization and International Organizations attacked FDA's drug-testing practices, Larrick clumsily offended the Senator, and in the summer of 1962 Secretary Celebrezze began murmuring about pressures on him to accept Larrick's retirement. Then right in the midst of these difficulties the story of Dr. Frances Kelsey and thalidomide broke.

One result of the thalidomide scandal was, probably, to save Larrick's neck, for public shock at revelations about deformed babies threatened not only the Food and Drug Administration but the image of the New Frontier itself, so the White House stepped in and helped turn Dr. Kelsey into a national heroine to divert attention from the inexcusable derelictions of her division. Another result was passage of the Kefauver-Harris drug amendments of 1962, which substantially strengthened the hand of FDA in controlling drugs in terms of their safety and efficacy. And these interacting forces, plus the tragic death of movie idol Marilyn Monroe from an overdose of barbiturates, gave strong new impetus to FDA's drive to repress abuse of the so-called dangerous drugs. Larrick might come out looking like a public savior after all.

If I seem to be stressing too much the emphasis continually placed on the theme that misuse of amphetamines was causing large numbers of accidents on the highways, and particularly among truckers, bear with me; I am doing so because that theme has a final note which is remarkably revealing. In his message to Congress on consumer protection in 1962 President Kennedy said:

One problem meriting special attention deals with the growing abuse of non-narcotic drugs, including barbiturates and amphetamines. Society's gains will be illusory if we reduce the incidence of one kind of drug dependence, only to have new kinds of drugs substituted. The use of these drugs is increasing problems of abnormal and social behavior, *highway accidents,* juvenile delinquency, and broken homes. [Italics added.]

This set the tone of the White House Conference (and if the wording seems vaguely familiar, look back to page 235 where I quoted the President's opening statement to that gathering). The conference, as we have already seen, gave much play to dangerous drugs, and resulted in the report by the President's Advisory Commission (November 1963) calling for new repressive legislation.

Meanwhile, Larrick kept publicizing the heroic efforts of his inspectors against allegedly organized gangs of criminals who specialized in distributing amphetamine tablets to truckers through sinister networks of roadside stops along the nation's highways. The entertainment media commenced featuring episodes portraying a lunch-wagon cook rolling pills across a counter to some burly driver, whereupon the scene fades to a spectacular highway accident, the smoking wreckage of at least one monster truck, ambulances, flares, crowds, police, and trumpet flourishes.

By 1964, the gangbuster aspects of controlling these new categories had received so much emphasis that Senator Dodd revised and reintroduced his bill with new provisions authorizing FDA inspectors to carry guns, make arrests, and seize contraband drugs forthwith. The measure, ambitiously titled Psychotoxic Drug Control Act of 1964, recited as congressional findings that illicit traffic was resulting in extensive sales of drugs to juveniles, who were thereupon led into delinquency and crime, and "to experiment with narcotic drugs, which experimentation may result in narcotic addiction," and further that the use of such drugs "often endangers safety on the highway." The Dodd bill was a hybrid, in that it imposed a pattern of controls similar to that of the Harrison Act, but did so under the federal interstate commerce powers and left administration and enforcement to the Food and Drug Administration. The Secretary of Health, Education, and Welfare was authorized to add new drug categories on a finding that they had potential for abuse.

President Johnson, however, displayed little enthusiasm for thus creating a new federal enforcement domain in the province of "dangerous drugs" (where the crime-busting responsibilities

of Attorney General Kennedy might be extended and enlarged).
So he executed a maneuver often resorted to when the chief
executive wants to take a play away from Congress and dampen
a legislative proposal: in July 1964, with appropriate fanfare, he
called upon all existing agencies in the executive branch to work
harder at remedying the situation:

> Narcotic and other drug abuse is inflicting upon parts of the
> country enormous damage in human suffering, crime, and economic
> loss through thievery. The Federal Government, being responsible
> for the regulation of foreign and interstate commerce, bears a
> major responsibility in respect to the illegal traffic in drugs and the
> consequences of that traffic. That responsibility is shared by several
> departments of the Government and by a number of divisions,
> bureaus, etc., within them. I now direct those units to examine into
> their present procedures, to bring those procedures into maximum
> activity, and wherever necessary to put into effect additional pro-
> grams of action aimed at major corrections in the conditions caused
> by drug abuse. I desire the full power of the Federal Government
> to be brought to bear upon three objectives: (1) The destruction
> of the illegal traffic in drugs, (2) the prevention of drug abuse,
> and (3) the cure and rehabilitation of victims of this traffic.

When such a move is made from the White House, spokesmen
for the administration thereupon go to Capitol Hill and urge
Congress to hold off with legislation on the ground that the
matter is being studied and that better coordination of executive
efforts may make additional legislation unnecessary. Accordingly,
although every concerned agency in the executive branch had
already expressed approval of the Dodd bill, official support
from that quarter now slackened. The Senate passed the bill
anyway, whereupon it was stopped in the House by a lobbying
campaign on behalf of the Pharmaceutical Manufacturers Association and the American Medical Association, which was such
a show of strength that the measure—now also lacking administration support—would probably have been abandoned altogether without an unexpected miracle.

But the miracle was forthcoming (surrounded by a slight mystery, enduring to this day, as to whether Larrick or someone
else in Washington originally promoted it). A CBS newsman
named McMullen set up a mail-drop office in New York, printed
some letterheads identifying himself as "McMullen Services,"
and succeeded in buying, from a dozen drug manufacturers,
over a million barbiturate and amphetamine tablets, valued in
retail drug prices at $50,000 and of an estimated worth on the

black market of as much as $500,000—at a cost to McMullen Services of $628. When CBS broke this, against the background of juvenile victims and highway crashes, public excitement seethed and members of Congress crowded forward once again to call for tighter controls and a tough new federal law.

However, when the 89th Congress convened in January 1965, there had been another change, as has been remarked: former Attorney General Kennedy was now sitting in the upper house as Senator Kennedy, and this accounted for a shift in strategy by all concerned. One of President Johnson's first messages (January 7, 1965) exhorted the lawmakers to rush through "legislation to bring the production and distribution of barbiturates, amphetamines, and other psychotoxic drugs under more effective control" and at the same time to give federal law-enforcement agencies "authority to seize counterfeit drugs at their source." A bill for this purpose—including the counterfeit provisions—had already been introduced, as H.R. 2, on January 4, the first day of the session, by Chairman Oren Harris of the House Interstate and Foreign Commerce Committee. Senator Dodd put in his bill again on the Senate side, with eight co-sponsors, including Senator Kennedy, but from the outset the action centered around H.R. 2 and was dominated and controlled by the House proceedings.

H.R. 2 was entitled Drug Abuse Control Amendments of 1965, and differed from the prior Dodd versions in a number of significant respects. It covered all "depressant and stimulant" drugs plus any other substance that the HEW Secretary found to have "a potential for abuse" on account of its depressant, stimulant, or *hallucinogenic* effects, thus giving the Secretary broadened authority. It commenced with a sweeping declaration of policy, including, of course, a reference to our old friends, the truck drivers:

> Congress hereby finds and declares that there is a widespread illicit traffic in depressant and stimulant drugs moving in or otherwise affecting interstate commerce; that the use of such drugs when not under the supervision of a licensed practitioner, often endangers safety on the highways (without distinction of interstate and intrastate traffic thereon) and otherwise has become a threat to the public health and safety.

Although departing from the Harrison Act pattern by relying on Congress' powers over interstate commerce instead of the constitutional power to tax, H.R. 2 imposed a registration, in-

spection, and record-keeping pattern, covering everyone concerned with the controlled traffic, which closely paralleled the
Harrison requirements. Penalties were lighter than for opium,
cocaine, and marijuana offenses, and no mandatory minimums
were provided, but mere possession without a license or prescription was made a federal crime, and medical practitioners
were exempted in the same tricky phrasing that had given so
much trouble in all the prior decades, i.e., "while acting in the
course of their professional practice."

An effort was made to soften the impact of possession offenses
somewhat by placing a special burden on the government to
prove that the possession in question was not merely for personal use of the possessor or some other member of his house-
hold. The penalty for possession was a maximum of $1,000 or
one year's imprisonment, unless the offense was committed "with
intent to defraud or mislead" or unless the offender had been
convicted previously, in which event the maximums jumped to
$10,000 and three years.

The powers of FDA inspectors were increased substantially
more under H.R. 2 than in the Dodd version. Besides being
authorized to carry firearms, serve warrants, seize contraband
drugs and everything related to their production forthwith, and
in certain circumstances to arrest without warrants, they were
to be brought under the special protections extended by the
Federal Criminal Code to U.S. marshals, FBI agents, and other
federal officers primarily engaged in criminal-law enforcement
activities.

But the most important innovation was the quite new—and
more than slightly irrelevant—section inserted into H.R. 2 to
deal with *counterfeit* drugs. One reason this section turned up
in the bill is obvious: the Pharmaceutical Manufacturers Association, backed by the AMA, had shown enough power in the
House of Representatives the year before to kill Senator Dodd's
bill with ease, and it was plain that legislation like H.R. 2
would have little chance of passing if it were not somehow
given the blessing of these powerful drug and medical lobbies.
The counterfeit provision (first publicly referred to in President
Johnson's message of January 7, 1965) was the price of this
blessing. But it was also slightly more, which leads us into a
diversionary story going all the way back to 1962 and the ill-
fated Bay of Pigs expedition.

First, let there be no doubt about how much this provision
really gave the drug industry. Marketing proprietary drugs and

compounds which sometimes cost only pennies to produce and yet are priced in dollars, the drug houses were (and are) uniquely vulnerable to competitors who produce perfectly pure and wholesome equivalents but usurp their brand names or otherwise break into their monopolies. The drug lobby had fought with desperate energy—and total success—to avoid any semblance of a requirement that manufacturers disclose production costs or pricing practices in connection with the Kefauver-Harris Amendments, but they were still concerned about the competitive challenge of counterfeiters, especially because ordinary trade-infringement litigation would require exposure of their mark-up practices. Obviously if they could make drug counterfeiting a *criminal* offense and turn policing over to the FDA or the Department of Justice, they would have a more satisfying solution to this problem than anything that had ever been accorded to anyone else in the whole history of private enterprise in America.

And that, as it turned out, is what they got. Even luck was on their side: it is unlikely that if the two arch-enemies of the drug monopolists had remained in their Senate seats the counterfeit provision of H.R. 2 would have escaped bitter attack, and it is quite possible that the provision might have been lost; but Senator Humphrey had been moved out of the action by his election as Vice President, and Senator Kefauver had died suddenly in the summer of 1963.

Even then it is not likely that other critics of the drug industry could have been so meekly silenced if the concession had been no more than a sop for passage of the bill. But the pharmaceutical houses had another claim for this great favor from their government as well, and that is where the Bay of Pigs comes into the narrative.

Early in the spring of 1961, 1,200 members of the U.S.-backed assault force that came to such grief in the attempted landing in Cuba were made prisoners by Fidel Castro. The then-brand-new Kennedy administration was of course painfully embarrassed. And when Castro opened negotiations for their release on payment of a suitable ransom, the administration and Congress were caught together in a position which was politically vulnerable from both sides: they could not heartlessly leave the victims of the action rotting in Cuban prisons if there was any way to secure their release, yet they could not appear to be "soft" with Castro, or to waste taxpayers' money in paying any such humiliating tribute to him. But after delicate and protracted negotiations the problem was solved by a remarkable compromise in which Castro agreed to accept as ransom some $50 million worth of drugs and medical supplies, *which were to be donated gratis by U.S. drug manufacturers.*

It has been speculated that because part of the deal was allowing the manufacturers to take credit for the donations as tax-deductible gifts (at wholesale prices, without disclosure of their costs), they may well have made awesome profits out of their patriotism and philanthropy. But be that as it may, by thus getting everyone off the spot they put themselves in a position to ask for a whopping return favor from leaders in both branches of government whose faces they had so neatly saved.

Their price was the counterfeit drug ban.

When H.R. 2 was introduced it contained the following recital:

> The Congress finds and declares that there is a substantial traffic in counterfeit drugs simulating the brand or other identifying mark or device of the manufacturer of the genuine article; that such traffic poses a serious hazard to the health of innocent consumers of such drugs because of the lack of proper qualifications, facilities, and manufacturing controls on the part of the counterfeiter, whose operations are clandestine; that . . . the controls for the suppression of the traffic in such drugs are inadequate . . . and that these factors require enactment of additional controls with respect to such drugs without regard to their interstate or intrastate origins.

And the controls it imposed were controls indeed! Nowhere else had criminal sanctions ever been attached directly to mere trade infringements. If, for example, some ambitious manufacturer of film should start putting out his product in a familiar-looking yellow box with a famous word like K-d-k on it, the Eastman Company would have to hire lawyers, commence a civil proceeding, and be content—at most—with an injunction plus whatever damages could be shown to have been caused directly by the infringement of its rights (at the end of which proceedings the infringer might risk wrist-tap punishment if he defied the injunction).

But if the same eager manufacturer decided instead to put out some perfectly pure and efficacious aspirin with a word like B-y-r impressed on the tablets, by the terms of H.R. 2 as it became law he has committed a federal crime for which he can be fined (if he intended to defraud or mislead) $10,000 and imprisoned three years; the gun-toting drug inspectors will go out and seize all his product wherever they can find it; *and even the plant and equipment he has used for the manufacture of the aspirin may be condemned and forfeited to the United States.* Small wonder, then, that the drug lobbyists turned up this time working right along with the proponents of H.R. 2—though even so, an unsuccessful attempt was made to tie the Secretary's hands by an amendment which would have required him to rely on an industry advisory committee, endowed with real powers and following elaborate procedures to facilitate foot-dragging, in the classification of new drugs before they could be added to the dangerous category.

H.R. 2 was rushed to hearings in record time. Supporting testimony reached crescendos of alarm about the new dangers to American youth and the sinister nature of the newly dis- covered illicit traffic. But I forgo further repetitions of these themes, since they sound strikingly like identical outcries heard at intervals ever since 1918, and also since this is the long- awaited point where the death-on-the-highway catechism had, momentarily at least, its tragi-comic comeuppance.

When the hearings were well along, a spokesman for the American Trucking Association asked to testify, and after care- fully disclaiming that his industry had any intention of ques- tioning the bill as such, he explained somewhat diffidently: "We have a problem . . . the use of amphetamines by truck drivers. In our experience we have found it to be a health problem far more than a safety problem." Then he gave the Committee some interesting "hard" data:

> *The Chairman.* You say you do have a problem. From your reports of industry, are you in a position to indicate whether the reports that we get that the truckdrivers use, to a very large extent, these stimulant drugs is correct?

> *Mr. Fort.* We have made very serious attempts to find out, Mr. Chairman. Specifically, we wrote in a formal inquiry to the Interstate Commerce Commission last year in preparation for our Senate testimony on a similar bill then, and asked the ICC whether they could specify how many amphetamine-connected truck accidents had occurred in the past 10 years.
> The Commission Chairman replied that they had seven years' records and that of the 7 years' records, with approximately 25,000 truck accident reports being filed every year, they felt that they had 13 provable accidents involving amphetamines, and 40 in which amphetamines were indicated to be involved.
> So it was, in effect, 13 out of 25,000 a year over a 7-year period. They had 13 in which they felt there were provable con- nections between amphetamines and the accident. This is the only statistic we have been able to arrive at.

Moreover, when pressed on the point, this witness put into the record summaries of the reports on each of the thirteen alleged drug cases (actually fourteen), and it turned out that in nine the record only showed some kind of pill to have been found in the *possession* of a driver involved in an accident. So the net number in which actual drug intoxication was so much as observed faded away to five in that seven-year period (and among official reports of *175,000 accidents*).

This glimpse of reality had little effect, however. Chairman Harris and his Committee challenged the witness before he left the stand:

> *The Chairman.* You may file your statement, Mr. Fort, with the Committee. The Committee will be glad to consider it. However, from your brief presentation today, I understand that you are generally in accord with the proposed bill that is before you?
>
> *Mr. Fort.* That is correct sir. . . .
>
> *Mr. Younger.* That is a statement that is hard to understand, Mr. Fort, because if it is a health problem and involves the health of the driver, certainly it would have something to do with the accidents. If he is a sick man, he probably cannot react as sharply as a well man.
>
> *Mr. Fort.* The use of amphetamines as I understand them, sir, doesn't make a person sick in the accepted sense of the word, in that it dulls his reactions or facilities. In fact, their intended use, as I understand them medically, is just the opposite. They are designed to sharpen a person's reaction for a period.
>
> *Mr. Younger.* Then why do you say it is a health problem?
>
> *Mr. Fort.* Continued use of them is very bad for the health, I am told.
>
> *Mr. Pickle.* My comment, more than a question, is that it is surprising to me that, if this is a health problem, that you would say that the statistics are exaggerated or that your industry as such has not done something concretely to find out the source of these pills.

On the *same day* that this testimony was given, the Interstate Commerce Commission performed an agile kowtow by getting out an open letter to the Harris Committee (holding the H.R. 2 hearings, but which happened also to have primary Congressional jurisdiction over the ICC):

Dear Chairman Harris:

In response to your request . . . I am authorized to submit the following comments with respect to H.R. 2 on behalf of the Commission's Committee on Legislation. . . .

In the discharge of [its] duty the Commission has investigated many serious accidents involving motor carriers and also has inspected numerous motor carriers while enroute. These investigations and inspections reveal that on numerous occasions amphetamine drugs have been found in the possession of truck drivers. I know you are aware how difficult it is to establish conclusive proof that drugs have been used by commercial drivers involved in accidents. Rarely is it possible for the Commission to be at the scene of an accident or to initiate an investigation until sometime after an accident has occurred. We necessarily depend heavily on the investigation made at the scene by State and local officers, many of whom may not be aware of the significance of the problem. Despite these limitations, our experience convinces us that the use of such drugs by drivers of motor carriers is extensive and is frequently the cause of accidents which result in serious injury or death.

The Commission is convinced that the use of stimulant and depressant drugs by drivers of motor carriers is increasing, and that misuse of these drugs creates a grave threat to highway safety. We believe that there is an urgent need for more effective control over the manufacture and distribution of such drugs.

And the stream of testimony by members anxious to have their full share of headline credit continued:

Almost daily, Mr. Chairman, and in almost any newspaper we can read about the devastating effects of the easy availability of barbiturates, amphetamines, and other dangerous drugs—crimes of violence and depravity, widespread delinquency among the young, increased traffic accidents, the graduation into addiction to the hard narcotics, the ruined lives of countless individuals, the misery and heartbreak and dislocation of innocent and helpless families. The evidence is overwhelming. Local law enforcement agencies in my own State and in other highly populated areas of the country report an alarming spread in the abuse of the stimulant and depressant drugs, especially among teenagers and in middle and upper-middle-class neighborhoods where drug addiction previously has not been a major problem. . . .

I can testify from firsthand knowledge of the alarming extent of the use of these dangerous drugs by young people in my own area of northern New Jersey. There have been a number of tragic cases which substantiate the findings of Senator Dodd's subcommittee that the use of these drugs is more and more prevalent among the so-called white-collar youths who have never had prior delinquency or criminal records. The traffic in these drugs is heavier than ever, and vigorous action must be taken to prevent the further toll in ruined lives and serious crime. . . .

I greatly appreciate your giving me this opportunity because I am interested in this type of legislation, and I consider it of vital importance—vital in the literal sense that our lives are in danger from the continued widespread illicit traffic in barbiturates, amphetamines, and the related central nervous system depressant or stimulant drugs. We know that many of the head-on crashes on our super-highways, where a car or truck will suddenly careen across the median strip and plow into a car going in the other direction, wiping out entire families, can be attributed to more than just fatigue on the part of one of the drivers. As the work of the Food and Drug Administration has demonstrated, illicit sales of the so-called pep pills at highway stops are so common that the use of such drugs constitutes a real and present danger to everyone who ventures out on a highway. . . .

Irrepressible Chairman Harris had the last word: "We had testimony last week from both the Commission and a representative of the American Trucking Association that such occurrences were rather rampant all over the country."

The House Committee rushed out a favorable report on H.R. 2, the House passed it in record time (402 to 0) with little debate, and the Senate followed precipitously. No further hearings were held in the upper chamber, the reporting committee merely offering generalities about drug abuse and juvenile delinquency, drug abuse and the rising crime rate, and of course drug abuse which "has contributed to the rising accidents on the highways." The Senate acted in June 1965 without dissent, in a final flurry of oratory:

Today, the dangerous drugs are popular among people in all walks of life, ranging from truck drivers to students to suburban housewives. But they have made their greatest impact in the ranks of our teenage population. These white-collar youths have taken to these drugs by the tens of thousands. And the number increases every year. . . .

The dope fiend was a myth in the past, but it is becoming a real threat today in the person of the habitual user of dangerous drugs.

The addicted sex fiend was a myth as related to the sexually passive user of opiates, but this type of deviate is becoming a reality among the young people hooked on the amphetamine and barbiturate drugs. . . .

Thus, we are faced today with a crop of crippled people in the

most vital productive segment of our population and they are helping to mutilate and undermine our society and our most basic
standards of behavior.

Signing the bill, on July 15, 1965, President Johnson said: "We
know all too well that racketeers in this field are making easy
victims of many of our finest young people. The Congress hopes,
and I hope, that this Act will put a stop to such vicious business."

There were those who thought when this law first took effect
that it might be a step in the right direction at least to the extent that nominally the Food and Drug Administration in the
Department of Health, Education, and Welfare was a science-
oriented agency, not as narrowly devoted to law-enforcement as
Anslinger's Narcotics Bureau (then being run along the same
lines by his successor Commissioner Giordano). But it soon became apparent that this was not to be the new direction. Commissioner Larrick began recruiting gun-slinging agents, including a substantial number pirated from Giordano, and tough
regulations were promulgated, with emphasis on the new order
of things in which everyone who did not carefully toe the line
risked prison. FDA district directors went about warning audiences of affected persons:

> It is now a criminal offense under the Federal Food, Drug and
> Cosmetic Act to fail to prepare or obtain, and maintain, complete
> and accurate records as required by Section 511(d) and it is also
> a criminal offense to refuse to permit access to or copying of any
> records required by that section. In addition, it is interesting to
> note that any drugs with respect to which adequate records have
> not been prepared, obtained, or maintained are subject to seizure.
> Any equipment used in the manufacture, compounding, or process-
> ing of such drugs is also subject to seizure if the violation was
> committed by the manufacturer, compounder, or processor.

Steps were soon taken to add sixteen drugs other than amphetamines and barbiturates to the controlled category, including not only LSD and several chemically produced synthetics,
but also mescaline and peyote, "except when used in bona fide
religious ceremonies of the Native American Church."

Some of the FDA medical people, directed to beat the drums
for the new Act, hedged a little. Consider, for instance, this
from an FDA doctor to a group of student personnel adminis-
trators:

> I would guess that the undergraduate student is likely to use
> stimulants probably about the time of final examinations. . . .
> There is no scientific evidence indicating that this type of usage is

seriously harmful to the subject's health or level of performance if it is not carried to an extreme. On the other hand, the use of sedatives or stimulants to augment the pleasure-producing effects of alcohol, such as might occur at an unsupervised social gathering, could lead to automobile accidents, or impulsive sexual assaults. Incidents such as these are not documented in the scientific literature, and one must depend largely upon rumor and lay reporting to gain some insight into this aspect of the drug problem.

But the agency itself was not troubled by faint-heartedness. In a widely circulated 1965 Fact Sheet it trumpeted its claims:

> Abuse of drugs has become one of the major health and social problems of our times. The non-medical use of certain drugs is contributing to a rising death toll on the highways, juvenile delinquency, violent and bizarre crimes, suicides and other abnormal and antisocial behavior. . . .
>
> The traffic in heroin and other narcotics is being overshadowed by the peddling of barbiturates, amphetamines, and other depressant and stimulant drugs, such as LSD-25 and some tranquilizers. There is evidence that such traffic has become an even more serious problem than the narcotics evil. . . . Organized rings bootleg barbiturate and amphetamine drugs on a large scale. Some of these rings cover many states and deal in millions of tablets and capsules. . . .
>
> Growing abuse of drugs by teen-agers is one of the most tragic and disturbing aspects of the entire drug abuse problem.

FDA speech kits, prepared for use by its inspectors before school and civic groups and anyone else who would listen, spread the alarming word:

> Mr. ——— Mrs. ——— has told you what I'm going to talk about (today) (tonight). There you see it on the heading of the exhibit—"The Drug Habit: Big Problem."
>
> Perhaps your immediate reaction was "problem? to whom? Oh, maybe in some distant, unhappy places! But not here in our (town) (city) (school)! Certainly not to our children."
>
> Are you sure? Perhaps the parents of two West Virginia boys I want to tell you about felt as you do—safe from the drug abuse problem. Yet in 1964 these boys, 18 and 21 years old, began a crime spree that took them across five states and ended with their being sentenced to die in the electric chair. They had been using amphetamines continuously for three months prior to their crime spree. . . .
>
> In February, 1965, three youths, two aged 16 and one 17, assaulted a 66-year-old man on a Chicago street and fired eleven bullets into his body. The motive was robbery. They found $11.

When apprehended, they admitted being under the influence of barbiturates. They explained that the money was needed to buy more pills.

These are the kind of problems I'm going to talk about (today) (tonight). Not narcotic addiction. That we hear a great deal about. We hear less about another form of the drug problem—the abuse and misuse of the stimulant and depressant drugs—the amphetamines and the barbiturates. . . . Even though you may have heard less about it, this problem is even more widespread than narcotics addiction and *just as tragic in many instances*. . . .

Some truck drivers have used them to stay awake on long night hauls, although this is forbidden by commercial trucking firms. . . . Tragic highway accidents have followed their use. . . . The concern of many parents is expressed strongly in a letter written recently by a worried mother who stated, in part: "I am the mother of two little girls and the thought of sending my children to college, after doing my best to raise them decently, only to have them constantly exposed to drugs that undermine logic, morals, intelligence and health, is absolutely terrifying." . . .

[Photo caption] Truck stops and bars are prime sources of the illegal sale of these pills and FDA has had to use undercover agents posing as truck drivers in the detection and prosecution of peddlers. This picture portrays the story of an FDA inspector who is checking on some of the 3,000 Bennies he bought from the pill pusher, shortly before the arrest was made.

[Photo caption] In this accident, a tractor-trailer had crossed over the double white lines. The trailer slammed into an oncoming post office truck. Drivers of both vehicles were killed instantly. Three workers sorting mail in the postal van were also killed. Total number dead—5. Bennies were found in the stomach contents of the tractor-trailer driver and more tablets were found in the wreckage of his cab.

[Photo caption] After too many Bennies, you begin to see things that aren't there, and often you don't see what really is there; this is a sample of what can happen. This driver, trapped in his cab, ran into a freight car. Two hours after this picture was taken, he died—it took almost two hours to cut him out of the cab. The autopsy showed that he had taken more than a dozen Bennies. . . .

This exhibit does not show all the consequences of drug abuse. Other results are seen in terms of crime, delinquency, school dropouts, disruptive family quarrels, inability to hold a job, broken health, progression to marijuana and hard narcotics, and ultimately perhaps confinement to a hospital or mental institution.

In the bootstrap pattern we saw half a century earlier when the Prohibition Unit launched its war on drug users, Commissioner Larrick soon began claiming that the effectiveness of his agents was raising the black-market prices of dangerous drugs so much that the illicit traffic was obviously attracting more predatory peddlers. Result? Why, FDA would need larger appropriations, more manpower to make more arrests, and tough enforcement policies to deal with "big-time criminals."

But Larrick was personally riding for a fall. His resignation was accepted at the end of 1965, and he passed into retirement just before the new Drug Abuse Amendments took effect.

■ TWENTY-SEVEN

And Now, D-Men

■ UP TO this point I have been able to identify moving forces behind most of the important developments in this narrative. But since 1965 less clear motivations have come into play—or perhaps the observer is simply too close to the action. It is hard to understand why Commissioner Larrick was eased out by HEW Secretary Gardner just at what seemed to be his moment of triumph. And it is puzzling that his successor was by no stretch what most observers expected, a nominee of the powerful drug industry. The new FDA Commissioner, Dr. James L. Goddard, was a medically oriented career physician from the U.S. Public Health Service, holding the rank of Assistant Surgeon General when he was appointed to Larrick's post.

Under Dr. Goddard it began to appear that the crime-busting aspects of the 1965 Drug Amendments might be played down after all. FDA's newly established Bureau of Drug Abuse Control continued to recruit and train agents to bring its field staff up to the 200 figure authorized by Congress, but it began putting them through courses in the cultural and social aspects of drug abuse, teaching them the pharmacology of drugs, and stressing restraint in the use of their authority. Goddard said of them:

> These men are enforcers, true. But we are giving them as much information on the psychology and sociology of drug abuse as we can gather together and as they can absorb. For enforcement is not the sole answer. We are dealing with medical and psychological

291

problem areas; we are dealing with phenomena that rise out of a broad spectrum of social or economic stress; we are dealing in areas that are as complex sociologically as some of the drugs are pharmacologically.

A separate Division of Drug Studies and Statistics was created in the new FDA Bureau to coordinate with Goddard's former associates in the Center for Studies of Narcotic and Drug Abuse, which he had helped establish at the National Institute of Mental Health, in wide-ranging research on drug abuse problems.

Instead of regaling congressional committees with stories about the fast-draw exploits of his agents, Goddard was cautious:

> I believe, Mr. Chairman, you will be interested in the philosophy that will guide the new Bureau of Drug Abuse Control. In order to find out where we are going, we must first clarify what has always been an illusive, shadowy picture. To plan, with some measure of accuracy, a program to eliminate drug abuse to the maximum extent possible, we must first determine the magnitude of the problem.

Goddard proposed calm analysis at the outset. He stressed public education about drug abuse as probably his first-priority approach; he put persuasion directed at obtaining full cooperation from the drug industry and the affected professions in second place; and he ranked criminal law enforcement third.

When he struck out at rebels like Timothy Leary and Lisa Bieberman, who had appeared on the scene in the early sixties to extoll the virtues of drug abuse as a positive form of self-expression, his attacks were notably different from the lumbering crudities which had so long characterized pronouncements by police spokesmen from the Anslinger camp:

> Let me explain that the Food and Drug Administration is not engaged in tracking down the users of these dangerous drugs. But we are actively engaged in closing down the manufacturers, counterfeiters, wholesalers, and peddlers of these drugs. To the user, we hold out a compassionate hand: we are ready to aid the drug abuser to find his way back to reality with the help of proper medical expertise.
>
> I believe that the job we have is far greater in scope than the one which the Government has waged thus far against the hard narcotics: cocaine, morphine, heroin, and the opiates. The FDA's efforts take in thousands of drug manufacturers, jobbers, distributors, repackers, and dispensaries where illegal diversion of the controlled drugs may take place. . . .

Above all, our professional people—doctors, teachers, government officials, the clergy—these and others must come forward and strike at the great lie of drug abuse, that drugs provide a "kick" and a "thrill" and a quick, safe way to run away from trouble. That is just not so. And those who know it is not so—as we do—must take up their share of the responsibility to prevent any further erosion of our national strength.

The Learys and the Biebermans and the other apostles of drug abuse are wrong in their science, wrong in their ethics, wrong in their sense of social responsibility. It is a wonder that, by now, after so much confessed ingestion of potent drugs, that they are not all dead wrong.

With respect to the headline potentials of LSD, however, Congress did not leave Goddard alone very long. Dr. Leary's insistence that hallucinogenic drugs were less harmful than alcohol and tobacco had embroiled him first with Harvard University, which fired him from his teaching post, then with zealous local police officers who took to harassing his research headquarters in New York by midnight raids and rowdy searches, and finally with a federal judge in Laredo, Texas, who sentenced him to thirty years on a set-up charge of possessing marijuana. And as might have been expected, these events quickly drew the federal lawmakers back into the act.

Although LSD had been among the first drugs brought under control by the FDA early in 1966, and although possession of it for all purposes except personal use was already a crime, Commissioner Goddard and his associates soon found themselves before a special Senate Subcommittee to give testimony on the unique dangers of the drug and what Congress ought to do about increasing penalties and imposing more effective controls.

And here we encounter once more an old friend. Although the chairman of the Subcommittee (Subcommittee on Executive Reorganization of the Senate Committee on Government Operations, and jurisdictionally a little remote from drug abuse) was Senator Ribicoff, and although its senior Republican member was Senator Javits, both these elder statesmen merely sat by (in a manner most uncharacteristic of elder senators) and deferred to Javits' junior. The presiding senator throughout the proceedings was Robert F. Kennedy.

The Ribicoff Subcommittee had announced in April 1966 that it was going to make a study of how the federal government was providing services for handicapped persons, but a month later Senator Kennedy announced an abrupt change:

Since that time, widespread public attention has been focused on a problem which is a prototype of the problems we will examine in our hearings on the handicapped, a problem which raises many of the same questions that we will be asking as the weeks pass. I refer, of course, to the controversy over the use and abuse of the drug LSD. It has been the subject of cover stories in national magazines and news documentaries on network television, of widespread public debate, and new legislative action among the states. . . .

If LSD has slipped away from us, other new discoveries might be misused and other social dangers might be created, because we pay too little attention to an interlocking design for our programs. One has only to think of how close we came to tragedy in connection with thalidomide to realize the seriousness of the problem.

So the problem we discuss in these hearings is a classic example of the relationship of Government and science. The issue we examine is as broad as our fight against mental illness and our efforts to aid the handicapped generally. We must have a decision-making process about research and new discoveries that work. We must, as Government, weigh the social implications of the research we encourage and heed the warnings of reputable people about the dangers of any particular course of action. And we must be properly organized to do the job and to make and carry out public policy in this important area.

Ribicoff's opening, following Kennedy's, was a little less wordy and a little more blunt:

Only when you sensationalize a subject matter do you get reform. Without sensationalizing it, you don't. That is one of the great problems. You scientists may know something, a Senator may know something, but only when the press and television come in and give it a real play because it hits home as something that affects all of the country, do you get action.

When Commissioner Goddard appeared to testify, he was accompanied by Dr. Stanley F. Yolles, director of the National Institute of Mental Health, and a team of lesser stars, including Dr. Frances Kelsey. Whenever the witnesses seemed to be too conservative, or made qualified statements, the senators pressed them for newsworthy material. For example, when Dr. Yolles described impending breakthroughs in the development of new drugs to treat mental illnesses and estimated that there might be a hundredfold increase in the number and types of such drugs over the next few years, he was interrupted:

Senator Kennedy. May I ask in connection with that: When you talk about the fact that there will be a hundredfold increase in drugs that will deal with the mind, do you include LSD as a drug that deals with the mind?

Dr. Yolles. Yes, sir. . . .

Senator Kennedy. What we are dealing with now is not just a question of LSD but LSD as a symptom of what is to be developed in the scientific world all over the country?

Dr. Yolles. Yes, it is a prototype of the drugs that are being developed, and the possible problems that may develop in connection with them.

Senator Kennedy. We talk about the fact that there will be a hundredfold increase in drugs like LSD. Can these other drugs be as equally dangerous to the mind as LSD?

Dr. Yolles. Quite so. That is quite possible.

When Dr. Yolles described a 1960 study involving 25,000 administrations of LSD to 5,000 subjects, wherein adverse reactions were experienced by only .4 per cent—or twenty persons—the following transpired:

Senator Kennedy. May I interrupt for clarification? This study was based on 25,000 administrations of LSD. I gather that these were under medical supervision?

Dr. Yolles. Yes, sir. . . .

Senator Kennedy. You don't have an answer in your statement on what has been the result of adverse effects on those who have taken the drugs without medical supervision?

Dr. Yolles. That is quite right. We don't know as yet. Studies are going on now.

And Dr. Goddard's reluctance to provide sensational anecdotes was soon overruled:

Senator Kennedy. What about the suicidal or other violent tendencies?

Dr. Goddard. There is no question that there have been suicides that have occurred when the person was under the influence of LSD. Those suicidal tendencies I would suppose probably existed prior to taking the drug, in latent form.

Senator Kennedy. Does LSD stimulate those tendencies?

Dr. Yolles. I would feel that it allows these latent impulses to come out even though in perhaps masked form. The individual, think-

ing he can fly, walks out of an open window. This may be interpreted as a suicidal intent on the part of the person.

Senator Kennedy. Would it be possible for you to furnish us with
some of the case studies which you have covering all of these
categories?

Dr. Goddard. We will be happy to do so.

Senator Kennedy. I would like some regarding violence and some
regarding injury to an individual over a period of time.

Goddard and his team went on to become the most popular
performers of the 1966 congressional season. After the Kennedy
hearing, they were called before the Juvenile Delinquency Subcommittee of the Senate Judiciary Committee to tell their story
again:

Some of our investigations have confirmed the tragic results of
LSD use by juveniles and young adults. . . . We are not prepared
to say that these bizarre and often pathetic cases are representative.
We do not have sufficient data to determine how often such cases
occur. Nor do we have statistical evidence concerning how many
people are experimenting illegally with LSD. There are indications
that the illegal use of the drug is expanding, particularly around
educational institutions.

Then the Subcommittee on Intergovernmental Relations of the
House Government Operations Committee put them through
their paces. And Goddard personally remained in demand every
time there was a plausible excuse for taking another look—with
accompanying press releases and television coverage—at the
hallucinogens and LSD.

Whether cause or effect, the popular media kept doing their
fair share to stir up excitement. It availed Goddard little to point
out again and again that everyone was short on facts. Sunday-
supplement stories ran off the scale chronicling exotic horrors
associated with LSD. Agents of Goddard's new Bureau of Drug
Abuse Control (who made ninety-four arrests in connection with
hallucinogens in the first year of their operation) were dubbed
"Be-daks" and glamorized shamelessly in popular accounts:

Professionally nondescript, their faces as anonymous as their
Bureau of Drug Abuse Control, the Be-dak men waited for him to
start production again. Then, walkie-talkies crackling softly, four
young agents with a warrant eased in, grabbed their quarry as he
stepped out of the door. . . . Coats off, sleeves rolled, more Be-

daks moved systematically into a 5-hour search of the biggest underground lab ever busted.

"Every LSD user is a potential suicide," argues Jan F. Larsen. "People get these delusions of grandeur. They even think they can fly. A kid in Los Angeles was going to throw his girl off the roof when the cops caught him. After one trip, you may freak out again years later."

He's not trying to put you on. Coming out of a hippie pad or acid lab, Larsen makes straight for the nearest washroom. He scrubs his hands. The procedure is standard for agents in the Bureau of Drug Abuse Control, who guard against getting a trace of LSD in the mouth, on a cigarette, or toothpick. "If one of our men went on a trip," says Larsen, "we couldn't trust him anymore —and he carries a gun."

As was to be expected, state legislators also came crowding into the limelight. Led by New York and California, more than thirty states enacted dangerous-drug laws, frequently with penalties more severe than the federal model, including prison terms for all unauthorized possession.

The White House at first kept pace merely by press statements and Executive Orders calling on federal agencies to coordinate their efforts in the face of this new menace. But when the 90th Congress reconvened in 1968, a presidential election year, President Johnson jumped in all the way:

> In no area of law enforcement is there a greater need for a concentrated drive than in dealing with the growing problem of narcotics and dangerous drugs. These powders and pills threaten our Nation's health, vitality and self-respect. . . .
>
> Penalities for improper use of these substances are inconsistent— and in the dangerous drug field, too weak. The illegal sale of LSD, a powerful hallucinogen, is only a misdemeanor punishable by a maximum prison term of one year for the first offense. There is no penalty at present for possession of LSD for personal use. Possession of marijuana, another hallucinogen, is punishable by a minimum term of two years and a maximum of ten for the first offense. Illegal sale is punishable by a minimum of five years. These inconsistencies have seriously hampered law enforcement—for drug and narcotics peddlers do not observe bureaucratic niceties.

The bill introduced by the administration, with a scramble of co-sponsors, identified LSD by name in the same category as regulated stimulant and depressant drugs; made possession of any drug in this category a misdemeanor (one year and $5,000 fine);

increased the penalty for all sales transactions to five years and $10,000; and provided that any sale by a person over eighteen to a minor should be punished as a special offense (ten years and $15,000 on the first conviction, and fifteen years and $20,000 thereafter).

As a sop to medical and scientific spokesmen who had urged more emphasis on educational programs, the administration bill contained a ringing exhortation (devoid of any new statutory authority or all-important appropriated funds):

> It is the sense of the Congress that, because of the inadequate knowledge on the part of the people of the United States of the substantial adverse effects of misuse of depressant and stimulant drugs, and of other drugs liable to abuse, on the individual, his family, and the community, the highest priority should be given to Federal programs to disseminate information which may be used to educate the public, particularly young persons, regarding the dangers of drug abuse.

But now for a second time events unfolding in this era are affected by a personal and national tragedy: on June 5, 1968, Senator Robert Kennedy was shot down in Los Angeles, and he died the next day. Initiative with respect to the new penalty bill thereupon shifted to the House, where it was favorably reported on June 12, 1968, and passed in July. The Senate acted in October, and President Johnson signed on October 24, 1968.

But while this scramble to toughen the laws was taking place, another major development was impending, and with reference to it also I confess puzzlement about moving forces. It is simply not clear why anyone would have wanted to shake up the entire federal drug-enforcement structure so soon after the creation of the new Bureau of Drug Abuse Control in the Food and Drug Administration, and when, thanks to men like Dr. Goddard, there appeared to be developing, for the first time, an extensive and fruitful interplay among medical and scientific officials, enforcement agents, and the lawmakers. But nonetheless the federal structure was radically altered early in 1968, simultaneously with the LSD hearing and the move for stiffer penalties. And what happened—transferring virtually all authority over drug repression and drug-law enforcement to the Department of Justice—already seems not only to have been precipitous and unwarranted, but a large step in precisely the wrong direction.

The Department of Justice, headed by the Attorney General, is the federal arm most narrowly charged with firing-line police work and the prosecution and conviction of persons who commit crimes against the federal sovereign. The FBI is a bureau within this department. So is the federal Bureau of Prisons. The U.S. attorneys who prosecute federal cases throughout the country are answerable to it, as are enforcers of the antitrust laws, policers of the Internal Revenue Code, and other hard-fisted guardians of public order. Scientific resources at Justice have been limited to the remarkable FBI crime laboratories and a few experts qualified to identify substances like alcohol when a bootlegger or moonshiner is brought to book.

Yet presently *everything* pertaining to nonmedical drug use and abuse is centered in this Department in a fledgling Bureau of Narcotics and Dangerous Drugs directed by a former North Carolina police chief, John E. Ingersoll, who has developed a thousand-plus force of agents patterned after the FBI. Ingersoll, like Hoover, answers only to the Attorney General. Former Commissioner Giordano and his entire Bureau of Narcotics were moved over from Treasury; the short-lived Bureau of Drug Abuse Control in the Food and Drug Administration, and its director, John Finlator, were moved in from the Department of Health, Education, and Welfare. Giordano and Finlator became Associate Directors under Ingersoll in the new Justice Department setup, although pharmacist Giordano soon went on to greener fields and Finlator has since departed.

Since FDA retained its responsibilities with respect to many other drugs and chemicals in medicinal categories, most FDA inspectors stayed there, whereas Giordano brought his whole agency with him, so the new Bureau was loaded with men who got their training under Anslinger—though curiously, sadly, and as a final commentary on the quality of the old Bureau, nearly a hundred veteran narcotic agents resigned precipitously or were exposed in various kinds of flagrant corruption when the new Justice regime took over, and some forty have been indicted for bribery, perjury, or illegal dealings in the drugs they were supposed to be repressing.

It has already been noted that the suggestion to place responsibility for actual drug-law enforcement in the Justice Department rather than in Treasury traces back at least to 1949 and the Hoover Commission. Such a transfer was urged again in 1956, when the small band of Anslinger critics who were resisting the Daniel Committee proposed it in a last-ditch attempt to head off the extreme enforcement provisions which became law that year. A similar proposal, suggesting also the transfer of other law-enforcement functions of the Food and Drug Administration, made its appearance in the Final Report of the President's Advisory Commission on Narcotic and Drug Abuse in 1963, somewhat surprisingly since it had not been so much as mentioned in the preceding White House Conference or in the work of the 1962 Ad Hoc Committee.

There has always been an element of logic in these proposals, especially when they were addressed to the police functions of the Treasury unit, for the work of Anslinger's Bureau, through all the years it dominated the scene, had very little to do with drug control (as opposed to prohibition) and less with bona fide tax collection. The case made by the Advisory Commission in 1963 was a good one:

> The Bureau of Narcotics is an anomaly in the Department of the Treasury. . . . The Bureau is not a revenue-collecting unit. . . . Taxation is in fact only a guise for law enforcement and regulation.
>
> The primary functions of the Treasury Department concern fiscal and monetary matters. In these vital affairs, the country looks to the Treasury. To the extent that its top officials must give time and energy to a major criminal problem outside the realm of fiscal affairs, the attention given the prime responsibilities of the Department must necessarily be diluted. . . .
>
> The investigation and prosecution of the illicit traffic in narcotics and marijuana is no minor task. This illicit traffic is one of the major areas of concern at all levels of law enforcement in this country, and it is one of the principal activities and primary sources of income of organized crime. Yet the Department of Justice lacks direct command over the agency primarily responsible for investigating this illicit traffic.

But as already suggested, the real force behind this logical argument when it was made in 1963 was probably that it would bring a large additional area under the control of then Attorney General Kennedy, thus further enhancing his public image as a crime fighter.

Kennedy's successors, brought in when President Johnson took the reins, appeared to have no such concern about their images or those of their Department. On the contrary, both Attorney General Katzenbach and Attorney General Clark played significant roles in developing the Narcotic Addict Rehabilitation Act which, in direction at least, somewhat offset the naked enforcement role; and both encouraged the emergence of the new Food and Drug Bureau, which promised better medical and scientific orientation because of its association with the medical forces of the Department of Health, Education, and Welfare.

In July 1965, when President Johnson created his blue-ribbon Commission on Law Enforcement and Administration of Justice to make a sweeping new study of the nation's crime problem "and the depth of ignorance about it," the Commission in turn set up a Task Force on Narcotic and Drug Abuse which assembled a formidable array of consultants and advisors. In February 1967 the Commission released its final report with separate volumes containing the annotations and working papers of its Task Forces, and it is noteworthy that as of the latter date the idea of wiping out the Narcotics Bureau, or turning any aspects of drug enforcement over to the Justice Department, had apparently been abandoned.

Yet in January 1968 the President made a complete about-face. Goddard had incurred the enmity of powerful forces in Congress by dragging his feet on LSD, marijuana, and the drug menace in general. But his Bureau had scarcely gotten organized, and had certainly not been given a fair chance to demonstrate what it could do. On the Treasury side, Giordano's program as successor to Anslinger had been notably like that of his predecessor. There appeared to be no good reason for rocking the boat.

But perhaps the obvious answer is the true one: it was an election year, and the issue might simply have been too attractive to be let alone. Perhaps (as happens more often than one might wish in Washington) the moving parties were merely under a compulsion to do *something*, instead of nothing. Be that as it may, on February 7, 1968, the President sent a message to Congress stating in part as follows:

> In my first Reorganization Plan of 1968, I call for the creation of a new and powerful Bureau of Narcotics and Dangerous Drugs. With this action, America will serve notice to the pusher and the peddler that their criminal acts must stop. No matter how well-organized they are, we will be better organized. No matter how well they have concealed their activities, we will root them out. . . .
>
> In many instances, we are confronted by well-organized, disciplined and resourceful criminals who reap huge profits at the expense of their unfortunate victims. The response of the Federal Government must be unified. And it must be total. . . .
>
> This Administration and this Congress have the will and the determination to stop the illicit traffic in drugs. But we need more than the will and the determination. We need a modern and efficient instrument of Government to transform our plans into action. That is what this Reorganization Plan calls for.

Under the President's power to reorganize executive departments this proposal required no legislation. Instead, the Reorganization Plan had merely to be submitted to Congress and allowed to lie for a period of sixty days, after which it took effect automatically unless the lawmakers expressly intervened in the interim.

Needless to say, this plan was not ignored when it reached Congress. Several representatives introduced a disapproving resolution, and a new committee, with virtually an all-new cast of participants, commenced hearings in March 1968: "We are all aware that serious social and criminal problems have developed from the use and abuse of narcotics and dangerous drugs, particularly among our young people. We all are searching for proper answers to these vexing problems."

Much of the testimony evoked from spokesmen for the affected agencies is doubletalk, for they dared not oppose the proposal openly, coming as it did from the head of their executive branch, though it meant the total liquidation of some of their prime dominions. But they put their best feet forward. Food and Drug sent an Assistant Secretary of HEW who told how in its brief two-year life the Bureau of Drug Abuse Control had carried out 2,000 criminal investigations resulting in 1,300 arrests, had seized forty-five clandestine laboratories, had completed 300 criminal prosecutions, and had seized various drugs capable of providing an estimated 600 million dosage units; then he (Assistant Secretary Lee) made his mild pitch:

> In summary . . . we believe that drug abuse is a serious problem in our society; it requires an effective and efficient program of law enforcement to adequately deal with the illicit traffic in drugs. We must maintain a broad-based program of research related to narcotics and the problems of drug abuse. These efforts must be combined with programs of public education, prevention, treatment and rehabilitation for the victims of narcotic addiction and drug abuse.

Before this witness was through, Dr. Goddard was dragged in again:

Chairman Blatnik. Mr. Edwards.

Mr. Edwards. Thank you, Mr. Chairman. I suppose somebody has to ask the question that has been frequently asked lately and I might as well. Is Dr. Goddard going to testify?

Dr. Lee. On this reorganization?

Mr. Edwards. Yes, sir.

Dr. Lee. No, sir. But he reports directly to me and he fully supports this proposal. As a matter of fact, he was one of the people who originally made this suggestion.

Mr. Edwards. Is there any reason why he is not here today?

Chairman Blatnik. I can answer that. There is no reason at all. It wasn't necessary. . . .

Mr. Edwards. Dr. Goddard has been rather outspoken on this subject generally. I just thought perhaps his testimony might be of some value to us. I am concerned about this business of enforcement and regulation in the Justice Department. One of you gentlemen mentioned a moment ago the subject of cops and robbers. I had already made a note about cops and robbers. Justice is the Federal cop and I am not convinced that the Justice Department is the place for business regulations, health measures and social reforms as well as enforcement. So I would like for you to explain a little more clearly if you can where this dividing line is going to be. . . . I am mindful of the fact that Dr. Goddard testified before another Subcommittee of this Committee not too long ago, that the coordination between Justice and FDA was good, and that in the area of organized crime, there was a good interplay, good relationship between the agencies. Now, we are told that this is better. And yet in listening to you folks, it is awfully confusing as to just who is going to do what in whose laboratory and who is going to tell whom how to do it. Break it down a little better, if you can, on the question of regulation and enforcement.

Dr. Lee. I might make a general statement to somewhat restate your position and then ask John [Finlator] to give you additional details. From our point of view, the real reason for the transfer is because of the organized criminal elements involved in the trafficking in dangerous drugs. This appears to us to be—and John can comment on this in more detail—perhaps an increasing problem. . . .

Mr. Finlator. First I would like to say, Congressman, I don't believe we have really claimed there would be any savings. I did mention there might be some possible or probable savings and that could be where you have two organizations with the administrative setup that each one has, an amalgamation of that obviously can cut down on the overhead, where you have two units doing the same thing, one can do it. It won't cut down on the number of agents. As a matter of fact, we hope we will have more agents. . . .

Mr. Edwards. What would be the philosophy and the objectives of the Department of Justice in the enforcement of narcotics and dangerous drug laws?

Mr. Finlator. I think it is going to a tough one.

Mr. Edwards. Do you think they will take a hard line?

Mr. Finlator. Well, you are going to take a hard line when you deal with any criminal, I hope.

After the congressmen finished with him, Dr. Lee was taken to task by minority counsel for the Committee, who badgered him into a revelation of some infighting:

Mr. Copenhaver. To go one step further, Dr. Lee, did you recommend in the last year or two that the enforcement of the marijuana laws be transferred to HEW?

Dr. Lee. Did I recommend this? No.

Mr. Copenhaver. In a memorandum . . .

Dr. Lee. It has been discussed.

Mr. Copenhaver. In a memorandum of August 14, 1967—does that refresh your recollection . . .

Dr. Lee. Did I sign that memorandum? I don't recall this. This subject has been discussed with the Treasury Department, with the Bureau and with the Department of Justice within the past year. I don't personally recall sending such a memorandum or submitting such a recommendation to the Secretary.

Mr. Copenhaver. Or did you recommend it to be a part of Health, Education & Welfare, and that the Attorney General and the Treasury Department would have to reach agreement at the Cabinet level on needed changes in the law, budget modifications, and the possible transfer of trained enforcement personnel from the Bureau of Narcotics to the Drug Abuse Control?

Dr. Lee. I don't recall. But if it is in a memorandum I signed, and you have a copy of it, I perhaps did so, but I do not recall forwarding such a memorandum to the Secretary.

Even the 1963 Advisory Commission had had no thought of transferring *all* functions pertaining to federal control of drug abuse to the Attorney General. It recommended only that enforcement of the purely criminal laws should be entrusted to the FBI, and that regulatory functions vested in Treasury—governing manufacture, distribution, record keeping, etc.—be transferred to the Food and Drug Administration, along with the scientific responsibilities of the Secretary of the Treasury in classifying and exempting new preparations. This would have been a substantial wrench nonetheless, to the extent that it put the FBI directly into the business of enforcing tax laws.

But the 1968 Executive Order went further, calling for the transfer of *everything*—scientific analysis, education about drugs and drug abuse, classification of new substances, and even the international aspects based on treaty obligations—lock, stock, and barrel into an entirely new enforcement arm under the exclusive control of whoever happened to occupy the post of Attorney General. Administration spokesmen finally made this clear:

> *Chairman Blatnik.* You still haven't clarified how these functions will be related to each other, how they will be balanced off, with all the emphasis on enforcement. Is enforcement the major primary source of coping with the drug problem?
>
> *Mr. Hughes.* The purposes of the plan are, I think, twofold, really, Mr. Chairman. One of them is to consolidate and thereby improve the enforcement machinery, the drug control machinery. The other purpose, other direct purpose, is to strengthen the Department of Justice's hand and the Attorney General's hand in dealing with problems of crime and particularly of organized crime.

The only thing that was split, and which remained in part under the jurisdiction of the Food and Drug Administration, was the regulation of counterfeit drugs other than drugs in the controlled categories. The Executive Order made no change in the provisions of the counterfeit drug sanctions, but specified that counterfeiting would be policed jointly by the two agencies, FDA and Justice, depending on what category the counterfeited article might fall into.

President Johnson withdrew as a candidate for renomination on March 31, 1968, at the climax of the Reorganization Plan fight. The resolution disapproving it was defeated in the House only two days later, on April 2, by a margin of ten votes. But nonetheless the President moved fast. On April 8 the FDA and Treasury Bureaus were disbanded, and the new Justice Department Bureau was established, with an announcement that recruiting would commence at once to build up a new force of agents. Early in May a separate section was established in the Criminal Division of the Department to centralize prosecution functions arising out of the new Bureau's enforcement efforts, and early in July Ingersoll was named director.

When President Nixon brought in Attorney General Mitchell to replace Ramsey Clark, the new Bureau of Narcotics and Drug Abuse was still being organized. Though weighted with Anslinger-trained enforcement agents, the Bureau also contained a sprinkling of FDA men with solid scientific orientation. But Mitchell made it clear at once that he intended to run the Department as, in his own words, "an institution for law enforcement, not social improvement." His speeches and press releases puffed the menace of addiction, and especially addiction to so-called hard narcotics, in the ranks of adolescents and school-children.

In the summer of 1969 lines were recast so as to emphasize the Department's involvement with marijuana, the federal authorities announced they were concentrating on drug importers, and the highly publicized weekend raid on the Mexican border dubbed "Operation Intercept" was carried out (with few direct results except a temporary inflation of the black-market price of pot, plus a shortage which was claimed by some knowledgeable observers to have actually facilitated the sale of more heroin and other "hard" narcotics in the vacuum created by this brief interruption of a main marijuana supply channel).

So now it has come to pass that after fifty years of tolerating an illogical and unreasonable situation by virtue of the over-emphasis on drug-law enforcement in the Treasury Department, America is proceeding under a new arrangement which threatens to be worse. Justice gets exaggerated authority, funds, and headlines by promoting its dramatic attacks on the traffic. The National Institute of Mental Health carries on research projects in a relationship openly subordinated to the purposes of the Attorney General. And preventive education in the drug field has fallen under the uncoordinated control of the Department of HEW, whose competence and dedication in the field are by no means well established and whose first head in the Nixon cabinet, Secretary Finch, became embroiled in a feud with Mitchell that will leave bitter traces and impair cooperation for a long time.

In sum, after all these years during which the drug problem has been distorted and aggravated by a small bureaucratic tyranny entrenched at Treasury, in this current phase the whole story may well be repeated from the beginning by a new Bureau, equally inappropriately located in and dominated by the Department of Justice.

TWENTY-EIGHT

The 1970 Act: Don't Sit There, Amend Something

■ THOSE WHO ASSUME liberal and enlightened motives on the part of Ramsey Clark as Attorney General—an assumption acceptable to many—might explain his support of the 1968 Executive Order which brought federal drug policies under his control in the Department of Justice as a move to wind down excitement and modify enforcement excesses. It had of course always been true that top-level federal policy makers could have changed the picture overnight. A no-nonsense order from any incumbent Secretary of the Treasury to Mr. Anslinger, directing him *really* to concentrate on big-time smugglers and traffickers instead of bullying little people in the street, would have done it. A forthright ruling by an Attorney General that the Supreme Court meant what it had said in the *Linder* case, so medical authorities could resume active control of the addict population, might have sufficed. Even pressure to bring the quality of federal drug-law enforcement up toward the incomparably high standards of the FBI would have made a great difference over the years.

Attorney General Clark had guiding authority for such moves, in some of the recommendations of the 1962–63 White House Conference, in the 1967 findings of the President's Commission on Law Enforcement and Administration of Justice, and in the good work then being done by the National Commission on Reform of Federal Criminal Laws (commissioned by Congress in 1966 to develop a new federal penal code).

In any event, the contemporary picture would certainly have been different if Clark had carried over, or if more moderately oriented leadership had come to Washington in 1969. The nation's addict population was then officially tallied at 63,000, new patterns in marijuana use and the abuse of other substances were not yet firmly set, rehabilitation efforts and experimental programs such as methadone maintenance hung in the balance, and, in short, the situation was characterized by much fluidity and little panic. Even the Supreme Court had intervened again, in Dr. Leary's appeal, to invalidate most of the basis for federal possession penalties in marijuana cases.

But Clark was immobilized from the beginnings of the 1968 campaign as one of the major targets for attack. When his mentor in the White House announced that he was not going to seek re-election, Clark was left to stand virtually alone against Nixon and Mitchell in resisting their blandishments about law and order, and combatting their simplistic theme that the former should be mainly an instrument for imposing the latter by force.

When Attorney General Mitchell assumed control of the Department of Justice, and hence of federal drug policies, something like a renaissance-in-reverse was predictable. He was soon talking about drug offenders in the metaphors of war:

> The battle against narcotics is an integral part of the Administration's anti-street crime program. A narcotics addict may need $70 or $80 a day to satisfy his habit. Thus, he turns to robbery, mugging and burglary in order to obtain money. It was recently estimated that in New York City alone $2 billion a year is stolen by narcotics addicts and that a substantial proportion of violent crimes are committed by narcotics addicts.
>
> . . . persons who live in ghetto areas, which have substantial numbers of narcotics addicts, literally bar the doors of their apartments at night. They are attacked in broad daylight on the streets. They are terrorized by the knowledge that the heroin addict who needs a fix will commit the most vicious crime in order to obtain a TV set for resale or a few dollars. Even our high school children are beginning to use hard narcotics. . . .
>
> Finally, and perhaps most importantly, we cannot succeed with this war on drug abuse until we enlist the active assistance of every citizen. Young people themselves can and must play a key role in this war. It is a time for synthesis between the generations, a time to harness the dynamism and energy of youth and the experience of their elders for the tasks that lie ahead.

Mitchell's second in command for criminal enforcement, former Texas Attorney General Will Wilson, put it baldly:

> Clark's trouble was that he was philosophically concerned with the rights of the individual. Our concern is more an orderly society through law enforcement. Clark put too many restraints on the law-enforcement agencies. He was like a football coach warning his players not to violate the rules, when he should have been telling them to go in there and win. I'm not opposed to civil liberties, but I think they come from good law enforcement.

In July 1969 the President himself moved into the limelight, warning that drug abuse had recently grown from "essentially a local police problem" into a "serious national threat to the personal health and safety of millions of Americans." He said the general welfare of the United States was menaced, that the number of addicts in the United States had grown to where it had to be estimated in hundreds of thousands, and that several million American college students were involved with other substances like marijuana, hashish, LSD, amphetamines, and barbiturates: "It is doubtful that an American parent can send a son or daughter to college today without exposing the young man or woman to drug abuse. Parents must also be concerned about the availability and use of such drugs in our high schools and junior high schools."

To deal with this alarming situation, the President proposed a ten-point program. Eight of the items were rhetorical exhortation: more international cooperation, better work by the Bureau of Customs ("a major new effort"), suppression of national trafficking (with "special forces" and "action task forces"), and more education, research, rehabilitation, training, and liaison with local enforcers. But in the other two points the President sought to arouse federal and state lawmakers, announcing that the Attorney General was preparing a comprehensive new measure "to more effectively meet the narcotic and dangerous drug problems at the Federal level" by combining all existing federal laws in a single new statute, and also revealing that the Department of Justice would draft a comprehensive model law for adoption by all the fifty states. Referring to the federal proposal, the President concluded: "I am confident that Congress shares with me the grave concern over this critical problem, and that Congress will do all that is necessary to mount and continue a new and effective Federal program aimed at eradicating this rising sickness in our land."

In thus proposing a single statute to restate what was already in federal laws, President Nixon borrowed an Anslinger stratagem: it will be recalled that when the Commissioner seemed to be running out of new moves on the international front in the 1950's, he launched the Single Convention, a combination of all prior drug treaties and conventions with the double advantage of trapping nations that had theretofore refused to ratify some, while at the same time slipping in new terms that would never have been accepted alone, such as the universal undertaking to outlaw marijuana. The so-called Controlled Dangerous Substances Act, which the Nixon forces sent to Capitol Hill in July 1969, pulled together everything Congress had done in the drug field since the opium-smoking curbs of 1887, and it, too, provided cover for some highly dubious innovations. (One of these was noted in the marijuana chapters—the neat reverse twist of tying U.S. federal law directly to international treaty obligations, so that marijuana is now illegal, regardless of anything else about it, precisely because of the Single Convention ban.)

The two cardinal precepts of good statutory drafting are simplicity and precision. With respect to criminal laws, moreover, the Constitution itself gives every citizen a right to know exactly what conduct may be penalized; vague criminal enactments have often been struck down by the courts on this ground. The monumental Lindbergh Kidnapping Act, as a fair example, was written into the federal Penal Code in only seventeen lines. Even the Mann Act, which pioneered a new field in 1910 to outlaw trafficking in females, stands on the books in a scant two pages. By contrast, the administration drug bill, as introduced by Senator Dirksen, ran to ninety-one pages. A dozen statutes and more than a score of code sections were repealed or radically altered. The entire tax basis for federal authority was scrapped, and in its place the bill opened with elaborate findings that all aspects of trafficking in all potentially dangerous drugs adversely affected interstate commerce, thus arrogating to Uncle Sam the broadest conceivable hold on everything from the manufacture of "precursors," which are raw materials capable of being made into prohibited drugs, to ultimate personal possession of any disapproved substance.

As just noted, the federal authority was also expressly based on international treaty obligations of the United States, and this highly unusual statutory recitation, besides locking marijuana into the pattern, may have the further result (depending on an ambiguity that crept into the final version) of tying *future* drug classifications arbitrarily to whatever may be done hereafter, at U.S. instigation or otherwise, under international instruments like the Single Convention.

Everything about this new measure focused on repression. The Attorney General told Congress:

> The passage of this bill will greatly aid the Federal Government in its determined efforts to protect our citizens—particularly our youths—from the physical and psychological tragedies of drug addiction and abuse. Passage of this bill will especially benefit our poorer citizens who may be induced to use drugs as a temporary escape from the bleakness of ghetto life.

It was promised that under the Act the Department of Justice would be able forthwith to launch an enforcement program to bring about the conviction of the "top ten" narcotics wholesalers in each major metropolitan area, provided the Bureau of Narcotics and Dangerous Drugs was also given more agents (increased from a total of 760 in 1969 to 900 in 1970 and 1,150 by 1971).

It was during the ensuing year, as the administration measure worked its way through the legislative processes with steady pressure from Mitchell and the White House, that Senator Hughes and others made their unsuccessful fight for a moderate approach stressing education and rehabilitation, the episode noted in the opening chapter. The signing ceremony at BNDD headquarters on October 27, 1970, signaled total victory for the proponents of repression and set a pattern which gives federal enforcers unassailable control of the whole field.

The final enactment was entitled Comprehensive Drug Abuse Prevention and Control Act of 1970. The token concessions made to Senator Hughes were added as a four-page Title I, called "Rehabilitation Programs Relating to Drug Abuse" and consisting of amendments to the Community Mental Health Centers Act and the Public Health Service Act to broaden small-scale programs already under way by adding "drug abuse and drug dependence" to the definition of "narcotic addiction." Additional funds were authorized to be appropriated for the latter programs, and the National Institute of Mental Health was directed to become a focal point to act as coordinator and technical adviser on health aspects and to develop educational and teacher-training projects, with authorized funding of $3 million, $12 million, and $14 million for 1971, 1972, and 1973 respectively.

The bouquet of powers conferred on the Attorney General and

the Department of Justice was unlike anything official Washington could remember, even recalling bureaucratic czardoms of World War II. Regulatory provisions and criminal penalties were keyed to an elaborate drug-classification system in which, remarkably, the Attorney General makes decisions on whether each substance has an "actual or relative potential for abuse," whether there is "scientific evidence of its pharmacological effect," the state of current scientific knowledge about it, whether it involves any risk to the public health, and what its "psychic and physiological dependence liability" may be.

The Secretary of Health, Education, and Welfare must be consulted on classifications, and he is given a cumbersome veto on bringing new substances under control (if he makes his recommendation in writing and "within a reasonable time"). But all rules, regulations, and controls governing registration, record keeping, and disciplinary actions involving manufacturers, distributors, and dispensers are left to the Attorney General, including power to deny and revoke registration. The *Linder* holding was wiped out; prerogatives of the medical profession are permanently subordinate to political control by a provision that "appropriate methods of professional practice" are to be determined by the HEW Secretary "after consultation with the Attorney General."

Manufacturing and import quotas are set by the Attorney General. Order forms are prescribed and issued by him. He has authority to impose marking and packaging requirements, and the issuance of export permits are left to his discretion. Not only is the shipment of drugs in specified categories restricted to countries which have adhered to the Hague, Geneva, and Single Conventions, but even *then* they may only be shipped if the Attorney General "deems adequate" the system of import controls maintained by the destination country.

Senator Dirksen's original version gave the Department of Justice control over educational and research programs "necessary for the effective enforcement of this Act." This was slightly modified by an amendment confining the Attorney General's jurisdiction to six general categories, but the categories are so broad that in effect the nation's chief law enforcer still ends up in possession of most of the education and research terrain.

The classification system itself is set forth in five schedules, spelled out in some thirteen pages of lists and text. By this device, factors appropriate in classifying for regulatory purposes and quota fixing, but irrelevant in grading penalties, are applied indiscriminately to both. For example, a drug substance falls in Schedule I (the most restricted and penalized) or Schedule II (the next classification downward) depending on whether or not it has "currently accepted medical use in treatment in the United States" and whether it has or lacks "accepted safety for use . . . under medical supervision." Other criteria are so vague as to be virtually meaningless: a "high potential for abuse" rates Schedules I or II, while "less" potential falls in Schedule III and "low" goes to IV or V; substances which are safe under medical supervision (a criterion having little to do with safety in illicit misuse) fall in Schedule II if they lead to "severe" dependence, in Schedule III if dependence is "moderate or low," and in Schedules IV or V if dependence liability is "limited."

But if the schedules call to mind Alice and her Wonderland, the enforcement provisions, accounting for eleven pages, suggest Kafka and de Sade.

In the Department of Justice draft as it was sent to Senator Dirksen, the most objectionable penalty features of the old laws—mandatory minimums and ineligibility for suspended sentences, probation, or parole—were retained in exaggerated form. Unauthorized transactions at any level with Schedule I or Schedule II substances (and remember that marijuana was locked into Schedule I) were to be punished by not less than five years' imprisonment, up to a maximum of twenty years, with a fine up to $25,000, and no suspension or probation. Mere possession in these categories called for a two-to-ten-year sentence and a fine of up to $20,000. Transactions involving persons under eighteen could draw ten to forty years, and repeated offenses doubled the penalties in some circumstances, making possible a *minimum* of twenty years (and maximum eighty) for a single act, with no suspension, probation, or parole. Even violations of regulatory provisions in the bill were punishable by up to three years and a $30,000 fine.

But although Mitchell continued to make tough-sounding public statements, he passed the buck when he addressed himself to Congress:

Title V sets forth criminal violations and sanctions which parallel as closely as possible penalties available under existing Federal law. Provision for lengthy sentences is retained in the penal structure as a deterrent to the illicit drug trafficking. However, the determination of the optimum sentence structure for drug offenses involves many complex and often conflicting considerations. . . . I expect the Congress, in considering this proposed bill, to devote special attention to the sentence structure and to seek and receive the valuable assistance of the National Commission on Reform of Federal Criminal Laws, the American Bar Association, the American Law Institute, and others.

With the onus thus placed on them, the lawmakers made substantial changes, while introducing some new complexities. In the final version, mandatory minimums were removed from most categories, subdivisions were added to adjust penalties within the system of schedules, and something called a "special parole term" was added. Thus any transaction (and mere *possession* if it is with intent to manufacture, distribute, or dispense), and any activity involving a counterfeit drug, draws a maximum sentence of fifteen years and a fine of up to $25,000 for a first offense, which double for succeeding offenses, if the substance involved is a narcotic classified in Schedule I or Schedule II. For the same offenses in the same schedules if the substance is not a narcotic drug, the penalties are maximum five years and $15,000, again doubling for repetitions.

The special parole term, required to be added to whatever term of imprisonment is imposed under the above provisions, is three years for a first offense in the first category with six years for repetitions, and two and four years, respectively, in the second category. In case of a parole revocation during the special parole term, the parolee must serve the balance as if it had been part of the original sentence. For substances in Schedules III, IV, and V the degrees of punishment descend: five years/$15,000; three years/$10,000; and one year/$5,000.

For any infraction of a regulation by a registrant, civil penalties of up to $25,000 for each occurrence may be imposed on top of any applicable criminal sentence and fine. Anyone who uses the mails or a communication facility such as a telephone or a radio in the commission of a felony offense under the Act thereby commits a separate, additional offense, carrying a penalty of four years and $30,000 (doubling to eight years and $60,000 for repetitions) for every such separate use. If a transaction involves one person under eighteen and the other is at least three years older, the penalties for the latter, including special parole terms, double for the first offense and treble for any subsequent repetition.

To these more or less straightforward provisions Congress added two new sanctions that verge on fantasy. If the government can prove that a felony defendant was engaging in "a continuing criminal enterprise" involving drugs, the penalty jumps to a minimum of ten years and a maximum of life with a fine of up to $100,000 *plus forfeiture of "the profits obtained by him" and any interest, claim, property, or contractual right "affording a source of influence" over such enterprise.* No suspension, probation, or parole is possible with this conviction, and in case of a repetition, the penalties jump to a minimum of twenty years, a maximum fine of $200,000, and the same forfeitures. In order to engage in a continuing criminal enterprise one must be an organizer, supervisor, or manager of a group including at least five other persons and must obtain "substantial income or resources" from it.

The second special penalty category is called "Dangerous Special Drug Offender," and takes five pages to spell out. This is a status offense, imposed as a special sentence following a felony conviction, and provable by the government on a mere preponderance of evidence instead of in compliance with the usual criminal requirement of proof beyond a reasonable doubt. If the prosecution does not like the outcome, the *prosecution* may appeal. Defendants who are curious whether they might fall into this category have only to glance through the following:

(e) A defendant is a special drug offender for purposes of this section if—

(1) the defendant has previously been convicted in courts of the United States or a State or any political subdivision thereof for two or more offenses involving dealing in controlled substances, committed on occasions different from one another and different from such felonious violation, and punishable in such courts by death or imprisonment in excess of one year, for one or more of such convictions the defendant has been imprisoned prior to the commission of such felonious violation, and less than five years have elapsed between the commission of such felonious violation and either the defendant's release, on parole or otherwise, from imprisonment for one such conviction or his commission of the last such previous offense or another offense involving dealing in controlled substances and punishable by death or imprisonment in excess of one year under applicable laws of the United States or a State or any political subdivision thereof; or

(2) the defendant committed such felonious violation as part of a pattern of dealing in controlled substances which was criminal under applicable laws of any jurisdiction, which constituted a subtantial source of his income, and in which he manifested special skill or expertise; or

(3) such felonious violation was, or the defendant committed such felonious violation in furtherance of, a conspiracy with three or more other persons to engage in a pattern of dealing in con-

trolled substances which was criminal under applicable laws of any jurisdiction, and the defendant did, or agreed that he would, initiate, organize, plan, finance, direct, manage, or supervise all or part of such conspiracy or dealing, or give or receive a bribe or use force in connection with such dealing.

A conviction shown on direct or collateral review or at the hearing to be invalid or for which the defendant has been pardoned on the ground of innocence shall be disregarded for purposes of paragraph (1) of this subsection. In support of findings under paragraph (2) of this subsection, it may be shown that the defendant has had in his own name or under his control income or property not explained as derived from a source other than such dealing. For purposes of paragraph (2) of this subsection, a substantial source of income means a source of income which for any period of one year or more exceeds the minimum wage, determined on the basis of a forty-hour week and fifty-week year, without reference to exceptions, under section 6(a)(1) of the Fair Labor Standards Act of 1938 for an employee engaged in commerce or in the production of goods for commerce, and which for the same period exceeds fifty percent of the defendant's declared adjusted gross income under section 62 of the Internal Revenue Code of 1954. For purposes of paragraph (2) of this subsection, special skill or expertise in such dealing includes unusual knowledge, judgment or ability, including manual dexterity, facilitating the initiation, organizing, planning, financing, direction, management, supervision, execution or concealment of such dealing, the enlistment of accomplices in such dealing, the escape from detection or apprehension for such dealing, or the disposition of the fruits or proceeds of such dealing. For purposes of paragraphs (2) and (3) of this subsection, such dealing forms a pattern if it embraces criminal acts that have the same or similar purposes, results, participants, victims, or methods of commission, or otherwise are interrelated by distinguishing characteristics and are not isolated events.

(Congress has recently matched this in other nightmarish "omnibus" enactments in the crime field, likewise consisting mostly of old measures warmed over with catchy public relations titles.)

The 1956 requirement that anyone addicted to drugs, and everyone having a past conviction for a drug offense, must register and report upon crossing a border into or out of the United States, was repealed. But this was not much of a concession in view of the discretion conferred on the Attorney General to "promulgate and enforce any rules, regulations, and procedures which he may deem necessary and appropriate for the effective execution of his functions." And a new provision which is in some ways even more severe and unusual was written in: it is now a crime for *anyone,* anywhere in the world, to manufacture, grow, or sell Schedule I and Schedule II substances, such as the opiates, cocaine, and marijuana, either intending or knowing that they are to be imported unlawfully into the United States. Congress explains: "This section is intended to reach acts of manufacture or distribution committed outside the territorial jurisdiction of the United States." To be punished under this provision, a person would have to be caught in U.S. territory or in some special situation (such as traveling on an American flag carrier or being kidnapped by foreign-based BNDD agents); but if caught and convicted he would face a possible fifteen-year/$25,000 punishment, if the substance was a narcotic, and five years/$15,000 for nonnarcotic drugs—in either case with the additional "special parole term" innovated in this Act.

Slightly offsetting the severity of these provisions, which purport to show Congress' firm resolve to scare traffickers out of business, the penalty for simple possession of *any* drug, on first conviction, was reduced in the final version to a mere one year, with a fine not exceeding $5,000 (both doubling for any subsequent conviction). In the case of a first-offense defendant, moreover, the sentencing judge may, in his discretion, impose up to a year's probation, and if the terms of the probation are complied with no final judgment of guilt is entered. If the first offender was less than twenty-one years old at the time of his offense and fulfills probation terms, all records of the matter (except a nonpublic file in the Department of Justice to be used only if the offender later commits another crime) are expunged.

The latter provisions may be availed of only once, and as a practical matter this seeming concession (and the 600-word section that sets it out) is mostly window dressing, because a year's imprisonment in the sole discretion of the convicting judge is still an awesome threat and disproportionate penalty, and, besides, a prosecutor who wants to upgrade the charge can still invoke the fifteen-year/$25,000 provisions (when narcotics are involved) merely by alleging that the possession was coupled with an intent to distribute or dispense.

So although Congress thus modified some of the savagery of Attorney General Mitchell's original punishment proposals, the Act which finally emerged is still one of the most exaggerated composites of overlapping criminal sanctions ever written into a federal law. Nor is that all, because on top of the naked penalty provisions Congress piled virtually every enforcement power and supplementary civil sanction ever entrusted to a federal official.

The Attorney General is given all the policing options developed for the Food and Drug Administration. His BNDD agents are also designated "inspectors." He may hold administrative hearings, subpoena witnesses to testify, and compel the production of documents. He may confer immunity in order to overcome pleas of Fifth Amendment privilege. He is given authority to conduct administrative inspections, execute inspection warrants, seize and impound materials, and demand access to books and records (though in the latter connection, hypersensitive drug lobbyists exacted the same concession they always insist upon— that no inspection may extend to financial data or anything pertaining to their sales figures or the pricing of their products).

As in the case of anti-trust laws and security regulations, the Attorney General may enforce provisions of the Act by civil proceedings for injunctions or the imposition of civil fines (assessed separately from criminal fines and not mutually exclusive). An unusual device borrowed from the Food and Drug Act permits the Director of BNDD to notify any person against whom he is about to start criminal proceedings and give him "an opportunity to present his views," thus extending to the maximum the Director's power to intimidate, and, if he feels like it, to bluff.

The Department of Justice may use Treasury funds to hire informers, pay for incriminating information, and make purchases of contraband substances, with any sum or sums the Attorney General "may deem appropriate." All property connected in any way with a violation of the Act (including, it will be recalled, merely counterfeiting someone else's trademark), such as raw materials, processed substances, factory and laboratory equipment, packing and shipping containers, and aircraft, vehicles, or vessels used for transportation, are subject to seizure by the Attorney General and forfeiture to the United States. And in addition to the powers usually conferred on federal law enforcers, drug agents may act as compliance inspectors, make arrests for *any* offense against the United States, seize on sight any property they regard as contraband or forfeitable, and execute search warrants at any time of the day or night, with the controversial new "no-knock" procedure if a judge has authorized it.

The purpose of the no-knock warrant is to let searching agents smash their way in without identifying themselves, and the rationale is that such entry is necessary when there may be danger that contraband substances will be concealed or destroyed before they can be seized. As a practical matter, from the very nature of drug substances this danger is indisputably present in connection with virtually every drug raid, so no-knock entries are becoming standard procedure. But breaking into people's homes without warning or identification in gun-happy America is so dangerous that the agents tend to go in shooting. There have already been dozens of tragedies and near-tragedies on this account, including raids at wrong addresses and cases of mistaken identities—enough to suggest the possible need for a new category in compiling statistics on "drug-related" deaths.

Finally, the Attorney General and his men are given power and authority to prowl about the countryside looking for poppies, coca bushes, and marijuana plants (any plant from which any Schedule I or Schedule II substance may be derived), and to cut, harvest, carry off, or destroy such plants wherever they may be found.

In short, passage of this comprehensive federal drug law in 1970 overreaches Commissioner Anslinger's furthest aspirations. Where he manipulated drug prohibition for so many years from his minor tax-collecting bureau in the Treasury Department, his cause has now become a major commitment of the nation's chief law enforcer. His old bureau is well on its way to catching up with the FBI in notoriety and power if not in size, proponents of "soft" attitudes toward drug abuse have been routed, and the new federal drug police force has been given every armament and prerogative that could conceivably be conferred on a peacetime domestic agency. Small wonder that in loosing this assault Congress felt obliged to write a rattling disclaimer into the definition of "controlled substance": "The term does not include distilled spirits, wine, malt beverages, or tobacco."

While the comprehensive federal law was being pushed on Capitol Hill, the Department of Justice also pushed the other project promised in President Nixon's 1969 message, drafting a virtually identical measure for adoption by the states and pressuring the National Conference of Commissioners on Uniform State Laws to sponsor it. The Commissioners are an independent and prestigious body of delegates from each state who have traditionally rendered great service in preparing "uniform" and "model" laws in areas where the states have common interests. In eighty years they have produced nearly 150 Acts, many of which have been universally accepted by state lawmakers.

It will be recalled that a Uniform Narcotic Drug Act was promulgated by the Commissioners in 1932, approved by the American Bar Association the same year, and quickly adopted all over the nation. Subsequently, this Act was modified from time to time by innovations such as the addition of a prohibition against marijuana, and in 1966 the Commissioners sponsored a separate Model State Drug Abuse Control Act to bring local jurisdictions into line with the then-new federal campaign against so-called dangerous drugs.

These measures have long been the backbone of state statutory patterns. To scrap them in toto and push the administration's federal bill down the throats of both the Conference of Commissioners and its constituency of state legislators was an ambitious undertaking. But it has been substantially accomplished already. A draft Uniform Controlled Substances Act, based on the Dirksen bill, was prepared by the Department of Justice in the fall of 1969 and widely circulated with vigorous administration sponsorship. BNDD spokesmen lobbied for their project in meetings and conferences set up to reach representatives of the Commissioners, state officials, and interested groups such as the American Bar Association. When the Commissioners, following their usual practice, set up a committee to prepare the official text and commentary, a BNDD counsel who had done most of the actual drafting in the Department of Justice became its reporter.

This was another case where proponents of repression were able to use both the tactic of overwhelming their opposition with the claim that they alone were "experts" and the bootstrap stratagem of using two parallel agencies to generate pressure on each other: the Commissioners were urged to rush their deliberations on the Justice measure to keep in step with Congress, while the federal lawmakers were asked to hurry passage of Senator Dirksen's bill for the reason, among others, that the states were about to revise their enforcement patterns. In August 1970 the Commissioners approved and recommended the new Uniform Act (the federal counterpart had passed the Senate in January, cleared the House in September, was settled in conference in October, and was signed by the President on October 27, 1970). The American Bar Association officially approved the state measure in February 1971.

An unusual power conferred on the Attorney General by the federal Act, along with a provision making it the "duty" of all federal agencies and instrumentalities to render assistance at his request, is authority to "cooperate in the institution and prosecution of cases . . . before the licensing boards and courts of the several states." This contemplates continuation of the long-standing practice under which federal enforcement officials have made use of state prosecutors and state courts in drug cases whenever circumstances suggest things may go harder for the defendant if they do so. To the same end, the prefatory note approved with the uniform state measure recites:

> This Uniform Act was drafted to achieve uniformity between the laws of the several States and those of the Federal government. It has been designed to compliment the new Federal narcotic and dangerous drug legislation and provide an interlocking trellis of Federal and State law to enable government at all levels to control more effectively the drug abuse problem.

Because, as has been noted, President Nixon and Attorney General Mitchell wanted no expansion in rehabilitation programs, the Justice draft for the uniform state act had no equivalent of even the meager rehabilitation provisions that emerged in the final version of the federal law (although preliminary drafting of a new uniform rehabilitation measure for the states has since been undertaken). Similarly, the functions of education and research were merely brushed over in exhortative paragraphs.

It would be imposing too much on my readers to analyze the state act as carefully as we went through the federal law. It is drafted with notably more skill and restraint (running, nonetheless, to approximately thirty pages of text), but it follows the federal provisions and subordinates state activities to federal policies at every important juncture. The same cumbersome system of schedules is prescribed (with marijuana similarly locked into Schedule I), and it is provided that the state authorities must designate, reschedule, or delete substances whenever notified of such federal action unless they invoke an elaborate notice-and-hearing procedure to resist the federal ruling—and even then the state act stipulates that a decision to disagree "shall be final unless altered by statute," an invitation to state lawmakers to meddle if state authorities ever presume to act independently.

Registration, record keeping, prescription practices, and special order procedures are spelled out, in each instance with a provision that appropriate compliance with federal requirements shall be deemed sufficient under the state act. The commentary explains: "Since the criteria for Federal and State registration are virtually identical, nothing would be served by requiring a registrant under Federal law to go through a similar procedure in registering under the State law. Wasteful duplication would be the only result." But this being so, the only *other* result is a duplication of enforcement powers and penalties.

Criminal sanctions are elaborated in a complex structure similar to the federal pattern. Forfeitures are provided, as well as authority to seek injunctions, make civil seizures, and conduct administrative inspections. The innovation of punishing producers of "counterfeit" substances is included: even mere possession of "any punch, die, plate, stone, or other thing" designed to reproduce the trademark or identifying mark of a competitor falls into one of the more serious felony categories.

Twenty states, Guam, and the Virgin Islands have already adopted the new Uniform Act. President Nixon has personally pressed for it at his White House Governors' Conferences. The Department of Justice sends emissaries to lobby for it with attorneys general and lawmakers in state capitols during legislative sessions. With no substantial opposition, the measure is likely to be adopted throughout the U.S. sooner or later.

There has always been overlapping and duplication among federal, state, and local drug-law enforcers. But this new pattern, conceived by Mr. Mitchell's Justice Department and thus firmly set as America enters the 1970's, promises to carry the trend further than ever before. It seems safe to predict that the federal forces will not be pushing to expand their empire for a while. There is simply not much left on any frontier for them to conquer.

TWENTY-NINE

The Bad Scene Today

■ TOBACCO and alcohol owe their important places in American life to two interacting forces. One is the demand created by millions of people who have learned that using these substances makes them feel good. The other is a supply pressed on the market by promoters whose motive is an eagerness for profit. No matter that neither product has redeeming value as nutrient or medicine. No matter that the ravages attributed to both are well known. Feeling good and avoiding feeling bad are among America's most highly esteemed objectives. After all, our noblest declaration of national purpose begins with a reference to "the Pursuit of Happiness."

Some of the drugs (*other* drugs, remember) which so alarm Americans are much better producers of good feelings and better suppressers of pain and anxiety than anything in the liquor or nicotine lines. Most are also less dangerous. Several are widely relied upon in legitimate therapy. Thus it is inevitable that many people who learn about them one way or another will become users, given the chance, and will be willing to pay enough for their desirable effects to make large profits for suppliers. Consumer prices for tobacco products are inflated one or two times over production costs by taxes, while in the case of beverage alcohol the inflation is nearer fivefold. The competing purveyor of illegal substances, on the other hand, *keeps* his profits, at least while he remains uncaught, to the last penny. The only thing he must somehow manage to do without is the agricultural subsidy paid to tobacco and grain suppliers directly out of federal tax-payers' pockets.

But besides popular attraction and exaggerated profit incentives, the illegal drug market responds to a third force that tends more to perpetuate it than to disrupt or suppress—and that is precisely the stake of law enforcers in their *raison d'être* and office holders in their *cause célèbre*. When, as was the case under Prohibition, and as is unquestionably now the case with drugs, an immeasurable flow of bribes, graft, and cleaner-smelling political money is weighed in, this third force appears formidable indeed.

Specifying the amount of outright corruption that floats the drug traffic in America today would be as speculative as—and not much more speculative than—guessing the number of pot smokers or computing the volume of undetected heroin smuggling. But an impressive and impartial authority has spoken recently on the subject:

> There are, as we all know in broad general terms, two kinds of crime—(1) organized crime and (2) individual crime. In dealing with the first it is my firm belief that organized crime can never exist to any marked degree in any large community unless one or more of the law enforcement agencies have been corrupted. This is a harsh statement, but I know that close scrutiny of conditions wherever such crime exists will show that it is protected. . . .
>
> The narcotics traffic of today, which is destroying the equilibrium of our society, could never be as pervasive and open as it is unless there was connivance between authorities and criminals.

That is Chief Justice Earl Warren, speaking from twenty years' experience as a prosecutor and district attorney, and eleven years' service as a governor before his accession to the Court, in an address given on November 13, 1970.

Parties to gambling and drug and vice "arrangements" have so much common stake in protecting one another that—if the arrangements include people with power and authority—their ranks are almost always impenetrable. What everyone on the street knows no one above the street level dares report or challenge. But once, in 1952, the situation in one jurisdiction was brightly, if briefly, illuminated in full. A U.S. Senate Subcommittee investigating crime and law enforcement in Washington, D.C.—never a notably corrupt city—stumbled onto several big-time pushers who were serving long sentences after the police lieutenant for whom they worked had let them be sacrificed because their activities could no longer be ignored by Anslinger's men. The Subcommittee found that the lieutenant (in a department where most senior officers were mysteriously much wealthier than they could explain by reference to legitimate income) had been working in active partnership with the peddlers for several years:

> The protection payment was fixed at $500 per month. [Lieutenant] Carper returned to pick up the first installment that same evening. Soon thereafter James Roberts became a major distributor of narcotics, handling as much as $60,000 worth of cut heroin, pure heroin, and cocaine per month, and making regular payments on the first of each month to Carper. After a few months the monthly payment was increased from $500 to $1,000. Sometimes Roberts would fold the money into a newspaper and drop it on the floor of Carper's police car when the latter drove up to a prearranged meeting place. At other times payments were delivered to Carper at his country club. On some occasions the money was handled through Carper's subordinate, Detective Sgt. William L. Taylor.
>
> Roberts received more than immunity. He was warned when informers were active, and sometimes was given descriptions or photographs of undercover men to protect himself and his people from the danger of making sales to them. When peddlers who worked for him were arrested, he could usually arrange for their release and also for the return of the narcotics which had been taken from them by the police. Carper used the threat of arrest and prosecution to force peddlers to buy their "goods" from Roberts. And on one occasion in the summer of 1948, when the conspirators feared that their New York source was under surveillance, Lieutenant Carper himself went to the National Airport in Virginia, received and paid for a $9,500 shipment of narcotics, and brought it to Roberts' apartment. For each of these "favors" Roberts was obliged to make additional payments.
>
> This conspiracy was of such long standing that its inconceivable to the subcommittee that other members of the police force could have remained in ignorance of it.

On other occasions the police warned their pusher-protégés of impending raids, sold addict-informers drugs for their own use (paid for with money furnished to the informers to make "buys"), and claimed to have disposed of large quantities of seized drugs by "flushing them down the drain" without troubling to keep any records.

Illegal drug selling, like illegal bookmaking, is a retail business, depending on frequent, continuing, and widespread contacts with customers. In the case of addicting drugs, seller and buyer must meet at short intervals, without any interruptions whatsoever in the distribution channel. When to these considerations is added the fact that in urban centers where drugs are common the traffic always concentrates in a few small areas, and the fact that enforcement agents are supposed to *arrest* when they observe crime being committed (not merely guess what a jury might do long afterward), the pressure toward a single conclusion is overwhelming: not merely much but *most* drug peddling is known to the authorities and—for one reason or another—tolerated.

Now and then in centers like New York and San Francisco a determined officer or team of officers has actually appeared on the scene to "bust" everyone who can be observed trafficking. If this kind of boat-rocking and the resulting embarrassments and "panic" are not dealt with by reprimand or transfer, they may be strongly discouraged: "We only make cases against Mr. Big"; "Don't jeopardize our undercover men and their operations"; "Don't bring 'em in when we can't get convictions"; "Leave that stuff to the feds—or the locals."

I strain this inference? I overrate the force of acute demand and cupidity-motivated supply? Consider one more item and one more contemporary event. With the possible exception of the U.S. Public Health Service hospitals at Lexington and Forth Worth in their heyday, where a visitor with greasy hair might expect to have his hair tonic analyzed to make sure it did not contain drugs in solution and no incoming body cavity was below suspicion, there is almost certainly not a custodial institution in the United States where drugs are not available for a price. Some regularly have their share of hepatitis epidemics and drug-related deaths. Several each year attract fleeting attention following some embarrassing break, and then lapse quickly back to normalcy. If prison environments thus defy control, what can be expected of open streets and open cities?

The contemporary event occurred on June 25, 1971. On that day, Senator Hughes, whose acquaintance we have already made, took three other Senators—Javits of New York, Williams of New Jersey, and Schweiker of Pennsylvania— on a tour of Harlem, accompanied by a small crowd of staff aides, local guides, newsmen, and photographers. At 137th Street and Lenox Avenue this conspicuous mini-army was able to watch, from overlooking windows, while a sixteen-year-old boy who looked young for his age bought packets of heroin from a pusher lounging in a candy-store doorway. Then at 49 West 137th Street the whole party walked in on six addicts who were cooking and shooting heroin— and who were very belligerent when a newsman turned on some lights to see better what was going on.

At the other end of the scale from agents and patrolmen on the street who observe without seeing, there are more subtle kinds of corruption. In illegal gambling, for example, it is credibly speculated that something like one-third of the promoters' net goes into bribes and contributions; the figures are: "handle," $20 billion; "take," $7 billion; and "ice" or "juice," $2 to $3 billion. Even discounting such boxcar figures somewhat, that kind of money, passing in cash outside channels where it might be traced or taxed, obviously cannot all be absorbed in Cadillacs for commissioners and tuition payments for police captains' children. I believe the truth is that proceeds from "tolerated" criminal enterprises are helping finance the elective process through practically the whole range of American political life.

There is much to suggest that no aspirant wins a high elective office today without depending, directly or indirectly, knowingly or not, on crime-generated funds. With national campaigns costing upward of $25 million per candidate and contested seats in important states going for upward of $5 million (and winner and loser alike requiring money in lavish amounts), for the past twenty-five years it has nonetheless been a federal felony for any individual to contribute more than $5,000 to one campaign, and for any corporation or labor union *to contribute anything.* No one questions that the resulting hypocrisy—among upright people who blanch at the very idea of tempering marijuana penalties—long served to mask crude exchanges of quid for quo in the upperworld. But it obviously also provided cover for manipulations by criminal entrepreneurs. And though dope money is often regarded as dirtier than the proceeds of other kinds of crime, there is so much of it around that it must inevitably have augmented the flow from time to time.

As I have suggested all through this narrative, deliberately distorting and exploiting a social problem as important as this one is a form of corruption too, and on this score there is little good to be said for President Nixon and his administration. Saddling the nation with the 1970 Drug Abuse Prevention and Control Act, subordinating everything to repressive prerogatives for the Department of Justice, playing heavily on popular fears, and downgrading education and rehabilitative efforts at every turn—these are not policies calculated to win plaudits from the likes of Drs. Linder or Ratigan or Kolb or Howe, or Congressman Coffee, or Professor Lindesmith, or others among my protagonists.

But in the interim since this work was commenced, things have gone from bad to worse. No other occupant of the White House has ever *personally* played the drug theme so hard. Be-

sides lobbying with Congress and with state governors for passage of Mitchell's law-and-order statutes, the President has repeatedly said and done things that seem to purport little concern
for cool-headedness or even respect for the realities of the situation.

In 1969, two weeks after Art Linkletter's daughter tragically
committed suicide six months after an allegedly bad LSD trip,
other pressing matters in Washington were put aside while senior
congressional committee chairmen were summoned to the White
House for a bipartisan leadership conference with Mr. Linkletter
and the President, who began with this statement:

> This is, as I was indicating earlier, an unusual procedure, but
> from time to time, we are trying to bring to meetings of this type
> people from outside of government who have an understanding of
> the problem, particularly when the problem involves massively one
> of education.
>
> In this field, Art Linkletter, who is an old personal friend and
> of course known to everyone around this table, can speak, I think,
> with great knowledge and great eloquence.

Even this far removed, I am hesitant about intruding on a
father's grief to make a point, and unsympathetically. But Mr.
Linkletter was a volunteer, and if someone is to be faulted for
lack of tact or taste it surely cannot be I at this distance from the
occasion. He told the assembled leaders that he was not an expert or authority on drugs, but that he was resolved to alert the
nation, concentrating on parents and young children as his special field:

> That this was a shock to the family and to the nation goes with-
> out saying. I made the decision that this tragic death would not be
> hushed up, it would not be covered over as is the case with so
> many prominent children and people, but that I would seek out to
> shock the nation into the realization that this is not happening to
> other people's children in some poor part of the town, but that it
> can happen to a well-educated, intelligent girl from a family that
> has traditionally been a Christian family and has been straight. . . .
>
> So I am using this platform of my personal tragedy, number one,
> to alert every parent in America that it not only can happen to
> their child, but it probably will happen to their child.

At the end of this conference Mr. Linkletter gave the President
an inspiration:

> *The President.* Art, let me ask you one question about the media
> in another field. Among the most popular programs, of course,

on television, apart from soap operas and all the other things and sports, are programs like the FBI Story; in other words, investigative programs, people like mystery.

Has television done, is it doing, an adequate job, not from the standpoint of public service? We all understand that the public service aspects of television are somewhat exaggerated despite what they may claim because they have to be in it for the money, for the ads and so forth.

Mr. Linkletter. It is an advertising media.

The President. I am speaking now in terms of sometimes making a virtue out of necessity here. Would it not be possible for television not to put on a dull educational program about the evils of marijuana, heroin, speed, LSD, and so forth? It would seem to me that some exciting programs on this could have an enormous educational impact on the country.

Is it adequately being done and is anything being planned?

Mr. Linkletter. I don't think it is adequately being done. But I think it is being planned. . . .

The President. You think there are possibilities?

Mr. Linkletter. Yes, especially since the networks have in recent months been very painfully and sensitively aware of violence and so they are going to have to get into the more intriguing aspects of crime.

One of them certainly is this field rather than the shoot 'em up cops and robbers which we all know is just a dramatic smoke and flame and the real crime occurs in many other areas where it is deep and insinuated into our fabric of our civilization.

The upshot of this was that on April 9, 1970, the nation's more serious business was again put aside for a day while the President and four cabinet officers entertained forty-eight producers of TV adventure shows in the Cabinet Room. To spokesmen for *Dragnet, Hawaii Five-O, The Storefront Lawyers, I Spy, Zig Zag, Felony Squad, Silent Force, The Name of the Game, The FBI, Dan August, Dial Hot Line,* and *Room 222,* the President said, "The power in this room can make the difference on dope. . . . I think of my own children, tuning out the commercials; tuning out the documentary, to go to the entertainment." Urging the assembled performers to use a "soft sell," the President added: "We will turn the tide only if we can get to them through the media that has their eyes and their ears."

For this group the President also connected drug abuse with the fall of great civilizations—China, Southeast Asia, and the

Middle East. In America, he said, drugs are "weakening the character of a strong and great people." Attorney General Mitchell added that drug abuse in this nation in our time had gone far beyond crisis proportions, reaching down into the grade schools, and had "no parallel in history."

On October 14, 1970, radio producers and disc jockeys were given the same message at the White House:

> I want you to know that I chose this particular forum because I just wished that I could sit down with each of you individually and express my own concern with this problem and how much I think you can contribute toward its solution. . . .
>
> We had a meeting a few months ago with television producers. As a result approximately 20 television programs throughout the country are going on this fall dealing with the drug problem in one way or another, and dealing with it not in the way of just a straight-out sermon but in terms of that subtle, far more effective method of approach where a story is told and the individual, and usually the young individual, watching the program becomes interested in the story and, therefore, they get the message.
>
> Now we come to radio. As you may know, in the campaign of 1968 I made a great deal of use of radio, which indicated that I thought the radio was still here and here to stay. I did make great use of it because I have found that while naturally the primary emphasis these days in terms of any public relations program and any political program is on television because of the huge impact that it has, the radio audience is first a very large audience and a very significant audience; second, it is a growing audience. All of your advertising is, too. And, third, it is particularly a large audience in the teenage group. . . .
>
> First, I do not think it is proper for Government to come to people in the private sector and say you must do this or that for the public good. . . . On the other hand, I think that all of you would agree that it is the proper province and responsibility of your national leaders, and particularly in the Government, when there is a great national issue to try to present that issue. Then in the event, in your own judgment and in your newsrooms and in your programming, you feel that you could cooperate in your interest and in the national interest, we ask you to do so.

Early in 1971 the President did it again, this time with clergymen. He told them:

> In the final analysis, if there is an answer to the drug problem, you have it. . . . The worst thing that can happen to a young person is to have no faith. . . . Some sense of faith would have a greater effect than all else that is being done about drugs. You're beginning at the heart of the problem. . . . I very deeply believe this.

The White House has also entertained such key performers as Sammy Davis, Jr., for indoctrination about the drug campaign, and the Department of Justice has financed (with HEW funds) and conducted similar briefing sessions for less well-known groups, such as painters and sculptors.

By mid-1971 official estimates of U.S. opiate addicts had jumped to 250,000, and a new note of alarm was sounded: as many as 36,000 GIs had become heroin addicts while in service in Vietnam. President Nixon went on the air to declare a "national offensive" on this problem, with stepped-up national programs on four fronts: cutting off sources by working with foreign governments ("including the Government of South Vietnam"); prosecuting pushers; treating addicts ("insofar as veterans are concerned . . . before releasing them"); and a "massive program of information for Americans." But the next day the Pentagon countered that the President's words about holding GIs in service to treat them "should not be taken too literally."

On June 17, 1971, the White House announced a "new all-out offensive" on drug abuse, which the President now termed "America's Public Enemy Number One." He requested a special appropriation of $155 million from Congress, announced that he was creating a Special Action Office for Drug Abuse Prevention in the White House, to be headed by a Special Consultant to the President for Narcotics and Dangerous Drugs, appointed Dr. Jerome H. Jaffe to the post, and disclosed that this new offensive was going to be "world wide."

By mid-1971 two young doctors had emerged conspicuously ahead of most of their contemporaries (with Dole and Nyswander) as activists on the rehabilitation front. One was Dr. Robert L. Dupont in Washington, D.C., whose work with methadone has won respect and support in all quarters there. The other was Dr. Jerry Jaffe in Chicago. Jaffe had started slowly with conservative Dr. Brill in New York, but in 1968 he went to Illinois to combine research at the University of Chicago with the development of a program for the Illinois Department of Mental Health, and by 1971 he was perhaps the most-respected and coolest-headed practitioner of methadone therapy, in a variety of experimental approaches, in the nation. He was also one of the few authorities speaking out against the use of slipshod estimates to arrive at inflated numbers in the addict population (an accepted current basis is 200 addicts for every drug-related *death*, about which we shall have more to say in a moment).

Pulling Dr. Jaffe out of his working program in Illinois to

bring him to Washington to be a White House publicist was
somewhat like drafting Dr. Salk to drop everything in the middle
of his polio research to devote his energies to playing Dr. Kildare.

The first thing the President had Dr. Jaffe do was go to Vietnam and look around and then return to the U.S. and hold a
press conference. Excitement about addiction in Vietnam had
not been generated initially by the White House. In April 1971 a
House committee reported that "20 percent of our military personnel may be marijuana users, and upwards to 10 percent of our
personnel in Vietnam could be using hard narcotics." The press
immediately applied the 10 per cent ratio to 250,000 troops and
came up with a figure of 25,000 heroin addicts. A month later
a rival House committee found "the best estimates available are
that 10 to 15 percent of all U.S. troops currently in South Vietnam are addicted to heroin in one form or another." In some units
the percentage might be 25—and "5 to 10 percent of these inject."

The press then talked of 30,000 to 40,000 hard-drug addicts on
active duty, the President said the problem had "assumed the dimensions of a national emergency," and it was revealed that
Pentagon officials "suspect, but have not yet proved in public,"
that the whole thing was "part of a new infectious chemical war-
fare program instituted by the Communists."

In one way, this new flurry of hysteria throws some unintended
light on the whole subject of heroin addiction and America's
unique fixations about it. Beyond doubt Saigon *was* full of good
heroin and considerable amounts of it were sold to and used by
GIs. It is generally accepted that some of the most exalted leaders
of our ally-nations had part of the traffic sewn up for their own
profit. Indeed, no one can fairly expect Americans themselves
to be less moved by a fast dollar abroad than they are at home.
*But so far as we know, this drug-saturated army of 250,000 was
doing its duty day in and day out with never a hint of impairment
of its normal functioning.* Every night the folks at home watched
on their TV sets as all these alleged dope fiends performed quite
normally in and out of combat. *And the only way their officers
can find them even now is by making each man urinate into a
sophisticated testing machine.* Imagine how different the situation would have been if 5 or 10 or 15 per cent had become seriously addicted to Yankee alcohol!

Anyway, Dr. Jaffe reported that the percentage of heroin users
was really much lower—4½ per cent, and many of those probably were not really hooked but used heroin only occasionally.

(*That,* by the way, coming from such an authority, seems to have interesting implications too.) He said it was thus perfectly safe for U.S. employers to hire Vietnam veterans. He recounted how he had talked to General Abrams and General Wyant about the President's policy of no punitive action against GI addicts, and predicted that soon "this feeling will find its way to all levels of command."

> Finally, we have big problems. I told the President that our treatment programs over there, as opposed to the screening test, very frankly, are still rather primitive. It is not lack of dedication or interest or sincerity. It is a lack of skill, experience, and specialized facilities.

How it is proposed to "treat" young men who are healthy and stable enough to have completed honorable tours in 'Nam and who return with an appetite for pot, or a heroin habit they do not *want* to kick, is still unclear. The pot smoker is like the man who returns to civilian life a habitual user of cigarettes, except that he can probably give up pot with less effort. The GI addict is simply an addict, accustomed, perhaps, to better drugs and easier sources of supply, but in all likelihood strongly compelled to go on using. The only logical and humane program (again, for those who do not presently have enough personal motivation to manage giving up drugs) would be maintenance or a very long withdrawal regime using methadone in the manner that Dr. Jaffe himself helped pioneer.

But instead an evil new chapter has just been written in the methadone story. Methadone (and related equivalents) are as safe and easy to handle as morphine—which is very safe indeed when administered by a trained person. Since the Germans put methadone into general use in World War II it has been used by countless millions of human subjects all over the world.

Methadone is no more honestly an "experimental" drug in the seventh decade of this century than cow's milk is an experimental food, and more is actually known about its actions than is known about aspirin or insulin. It is true, of course, that people have been killed by methadone in accidental overdoses and clandestine abuse, but its record is exemplary compared with similar episodes involving either of the other last-mentioned remedies. And blaming it for what happens when it (or some adulterated simulation) gets into illicit channels is as illogical as blaming milk for what Chicago suffered because of Mrs. O'Leary's cow.

We have recounted how local methadone programs have always encountered resistance, harassment, and sometimes starvation from various official quarters. That has continued. A number of substantial operations have been ended by the arrest or threatened arrest of their medical personnel—in one case suddenly dumping several thousand addicts back into the street heroin market where prices immediately jumped.

Moreover, the conservative medical establishment began laying the groundwork for an even more cynical and serious attack on methadone *maintenance* as far back as 1968, when Dr. Nathan Eddy, incoming chairman of the U.N. WHO Expert Committee on Drug Dependence, evoked the following sour evaluation (then aimed principally at Drs. Dole and Nyswander) from his colleagues:

> On the basis of data now available, the Committee was of the opinion that methadone maintenance for drug dependence of morphine type remains experimental, and that it is not suitable for utilization by individual physicians. It requires for its operation the full support of a multidisciplinary medical service to effect the therapeutic, social and rehabilitation measure that may be necessary and to check for possible relapse or multiple drug use, and also to provide data for scientific evaluation and other research.
>
> The Committee believes that despite verified reports of dramatic improvement in patients with a history of repeated treatment failures, methadone maintenance has not yet been adequately evaluated. The techniques of well-designed clinical drug trials, including scientifically controlled series and/or comparison groups, are required.

This position was then echoed in a joint statement issued by the National Research Council and the American Medical Association, which begins:

> 1. Methadone maintenance programs should include at least the following elements in order to constitute proper medical practice:
>
> a. adequate facilities for the supervised collection of urine and for frequent and accurate urine testing for the presence of morphine and other drugs,
> b. general medical and psychiatric services,
> c. hospital facilities as needed,
> d. adequate staff,
> e. rigid controls of methods of dispensing methadone to prevent diversion to illicit sale or to possible intravenous use.

The statement then goes on to insist on "continued evaluation of the long-term effectiveness of methadone programs for persons who are stabilized," training for staff members "in an established effective program," and continuing research. It concludes:

> Methadone maintenance is not feasible in the office practice of private physicians. The individual physician cannot provide all of the services for the various therapeutic needs of the patient. The individual physician also is not in a position to assure control against redistribution of the drug into illicit channels, to maintain control of doses, or to establish the elements for proper evaluation of the treatment.

Thus once again seniors in the medical profession sounded the retreat, still resisting any suggestion that their colleagues should accept addicts as patients or seriously invade the domain of pusher and drug-cop.

Then, early in 1970, the Department of Justice and the Food and Drug Administration began playing up a similar theme with even more sinister implications. It began to be officially insisted that the use of methadone for maintenance programs, as opposed to brief detoxification procedures, was *legally* "experimental," thus coming under the severe requirements of federal law written after the thalidomide scandal and designed to restrict the use of new, untried, and unproven substances on human subjects.

In June 1970 the blow fell. According to the press announcement, FDA and BNDD were promulgating new regulations "in order to clarify the ambiguous position of methadone today under current laws, to establish responsible medical-legal guidelines for its use and to facilitate controlled scientific research in methadone programs." The two agencies concurred in the following jurisdictional finding:

> There is widespread interest in the use of methadone for the maintenance treatment of narcotic addicts. Though methadone is a marketed drug approved through the new-drug procedures for specific indications, its use in the maintenance treatment of narcotic addicts is an investigational use for which substantial evidence of long-term safety and effectiveness is not yet available under the Federal Food, Drug and Cosmetic Act standards for the general marketability of new drugs. In addition, methadone is a controlled narcotic subject to the provisions of the Harrison Narcotic Act and has been shown to have significant potential for abuse. In order to assure that the public interest is adequately protected, and in view of the uniqueness of this method of treatment, it is necessary that a methadone maintenance program be closely maintained to prevent diversion of the drug into illicit channels and to assure the development of scientifically useful data. Accordingly, the Food and Drug

Administration and the Bureau of Narcotics and Dangerous Drugs conclude that prior to the use of methadone in the maintenance treatment of narcotic addicts, advance approval of both agencies is required.

Advance approval meant that before anyone could administer methadone further in an *existing* program he would have to file a Notice of Claimed Investigational Exemption for a New Drug, have it reviewed and approved by the FDA, and also get permission and approval from Mitchell's enforcement forces in the Department of Justice.

Among requirements spelled out for qualifying for an approved exemption were the following: naming proposed suppliers and assuring the FDA that all drugs used would meet "adequate specifications"; furnishing names, addresses, and a "summary of scientific training" for each individual who will be monitoring or evaluating; describing the hospital, institution or clinical laboratory facilities available "to perform the required tests" to FDA's satisfaction; describing the research protocol proposed to be followed; assuring both FDA and BNDD that adequate records will be kept and will be continuously available for inspection by both agencies; and undertaking to make detailed annual reports to the FDA.

The proposed regulation suggested protocol details that would be deemed acceptable, and specified limitations that would have to be observed. These were so rigorous, and so patently inappropriate in the light of what was already being done in existing methadone programs, that large numbers of individual doctors and other scientists, several professional societies, and even spokesmen for the AMA filed protests.

Nearly a year then elapsed while the two federal agencies heard objectors, but the upshot was that the Regulations were finally put into effect (on April 2, 1971) without much change, and most operating methadone projects were thereupon given interim approval without immediate regard for protocol requirements. The resulting situation is that methadone is still being used for maintenance programs on a limited scale (approximately 300 currently approved), in most cases by suffrance extended in the absolute discretion of Commissioner Edwards' bureaucrats at FDA and Mitchell's law-enforcement forces at BNDD. The new Regulations, if and when they are strictly enforced, would require every methadone dispenser in the nation to provide facilities and employ techniques that virtually none, and certainly none who work with ghetto addicts, could command.

The Regulations require all participants to notify FDA promptly of any "hazards, contraindications, side effects and precautions pertinent to the safety of the drug," and specify that each addict admitted to a methadone program must be given "an accurate description of the limitations as well as the possible benefits which the addict may derive from the program." Every new applicant must also be warned that drugs are going to be used on him "for investigational purposes" and must give his "informed consent" to serving as a research subject.

Nearly all existing methadone programs have waiting lists. Some have already been severely curtailed for want of operating funds. Federally controlled grants are flowing elsewhere. Misinformed and misguided activists have even been encouraged to stir up resistance to maintenance programs on the ground that this is really a sinister plot against minorities, and that the pathetic enslavement of some of their brothers to "connections" and "narks" is somehow a more ennobling alternative. Even the threadbare and foolish Anslinger protest that any program involving therapeutic maintenance is bound to encourage prospective addicts to get themselves hooked is being trumpeted again. In short, this most promising of new approaches is being maneuvered into jeopardy and subjected to a campaign patently intended to restrict and discredit it.

Simultaneously, the President and his Washington enforcement spokesmen have increased their emphasis on the *least* realistic line of attack—a reversion to the 1912 Hague Convention notion that inbound supplies of drugs for the U.S. market can be curtailed at their sources. First Mexico was pressed into highly publicized joint efforts like "Operation Intercept" and "Operation Cooperation," and provided with money and equipment to search out marijuana patches. In May 1970 Attorney General Mitchell, announcing that this had been a great success, released a telegram from Attorney General Vargas describing the burning of thirty-six tons of marijuana (the yield of a few dozen acres) in "a public demonstration with the help of civil and military authorities, also radio, television, local and foreign representatives."

Then President Nixon broadened the play, announcing that it was clear to him "that the only really effective way to end heroin production is to end opium production and the growing of poppies." This was when BNDD somehow discovered that 80 per cent of all the heroin reaching U.S. markets (80 per cent, that is, of the undetected and uninterrupted flow) was coming from Turkish poppy growers, and that most of this Turkish opium was being processed into heroin by French chemists in Marseilles. Thereupon Attorney General Mitchell negotiated and signed a solemn protocol binding France to do more about the situation, which the Americans hailed as "another noble chapter in the history of comradeship between our two countries." Yet four months after this ceremony—on June 4, 1971—BNDD Director Ingersoll publicly "expressed regret that French authorities, despite a greatly stepped-up effort, have not seized a clandestine laboratory in the more than two years."

Meanwhile, as already related, Turkey had been provided with an AID loan to encourage her to substitute less profitable crops for poppies, plus U.S. equipment and training for her enforcement officials. In September 1970 American spokesmen called a special meeting of the U.N. Commission to pressure the Turks and other wayward sovereigns more into line:

> But surely, it is callous disregard for humanity to tolerate illegal production or such loose controls over legal production that a product intended to alleviate pain and suffering is turned instead into the cause of human misery and wretchedness. Everyone with human compassion would certainly agree that the legions of opium victims cannot be sacrificed to the economic advantage of the producers. . . . Humanity has a right to expect that opium-producing countries will cooperate fully with the international community in restricting the supply of opium, even if that causes an economic loss to the government responsible and to the farmers who plant the poppy.

When the Administration in Washington began being increasingly embarrassed by stories of heroin in Saigon—which could not be traced to Turkey and some of which *was* clearly traceable through U.S. allies to Laos, Thailand, and Burma—diversionary publicity about Turkey was stepped up. Secretary Laird offered $5 million to buy up the whole Turkish poppy crop. Every press announcement about a heroin seizure re-emphasized the Turkish-French source. Members of Congress began calling for an end to foreign aid unless the Turks cooperated better, and numerous bills calling for this and other sanctions were introduced.

On June 30, 1971, President Nixon personally announced that Prime Minister Nihat Erim had agreed to end legalized growing of opium poppies in Turkey, a step which he hailed as "by far the most significant breakthrough that has been achieved in stopping the source of supply of heroin in our world-wide offensive against dangerous drugs. . . . This very courageous and statesmanlike action deserves the appreciation of all the people of the world, and the people of the United States." Secretary of State Rogers elaborated:

> As the President indicated, this is a very significant act on the part of the Turkish Government. It is a milestone in international cooperation, because for 400 years the farmers in Turkey have grown poppies. They use the seeds and oil and other products of the poppy for many domestic reasons. They do provide a good deal of the opium that is necessary for medicinal purposes, and the people in Turkey do not use heroin at all.
>
> So the Prime Minister of Turkey has taken this action, which obviously will present him with serious domestic problems because it is eliminating a culture that has been part of Turkey's history, for the good of the international community.

Turkish farmers are believed to grow about one-tenth of the world's current poppy crops, though no one, including Turkish authorities, knows how much is grown in remote mountain areas of the country. And BNDD Director Ingersoll conceded on the same occasion: "We must also remember that Turkey is not the only source of opium used for illicit purposes, and our effort to bring about adequate controls or eliminations of production in many of these countries may be vastly more difficult than in Turkey."

Perhaps this whole U.S. campaign, to achieve throughout the world what cannot be accomplished in small drug-traffic sections of American cities, might be put in perspective by an analogy: if, let us say, the Turkish government decided to try to protect its own people from the unquestionably injurious effects of rice-paper cigarettes, it would have an equivalent chance of doing so by pushing other nations into line with such a domestic objective. And continuing the same analogy, the promise of one prime minister to mend his poppy-growing ways is like the assurance of a North Carolina governor that he will take his state out of tobacco production forthwith for the good of Turkey and the rest of mankind. (Or—another irresistible analogy—imagine substituting bourbon whiskey for opium in Director Ingersoll's exhortations to the U.N. ["callous disregard for humanity"], and then proclaiming them as an ultimatum in Kentucky.)

Supplementing the President's efforts to induce entertainment media to play up the evils of drugs (curiously, and to their great credit, the only group who smartly declined to fictionalize on the subject was the association of comic-book artists), BNDD and the National Institute of Mental Health have flooded the nation with pamphlets, films, tapes, leaflets, and "training" material.

Training centers and programs for teachers, social workers, and other professionals and "paraprofessionals" have been lavishly funded. Additionally, grants have been handed out through half a dozen federal agencies to subsidize private projects aimed at the same targets. In 1970 Congress passed a new Drug Abuse Education Act, authorizing additional appropriations of $10 million for that year, $20 million for 1971, and $28 million for 1972.

Even private foundations, led by Ford, have come on the scene at last, sharing support for a new Drug Abuse Council with lavish resources and timid aims. The Council will make a long-term effort (ten years at a minimum), not to support on-going programs but to "obtain the factual information necessary to underpin sound policy, and to disseminate to the public and to persons in key policy positions the best knowledge available in the field and the best analysis of this knowledge as it pertains to current problems." Difficulties to date have been due to lack of effective leadership; the new Council will fill this void by establishing "professional and public credibility," and through "excellence of staff and product." With emphasis on "interdisciplinarianism," the consortium of foundations promises to provide "a kind of center for policy study in the drug field, to which researchers, legislators, educators, policy-making officials and the lay public will turn for nonpartisan analysis and information."

Nonetheless, most of this outpouring does little more than perpetuate the myths and fictions that have misled Americans for so many decades past: marijuana still induces crime and leads to "hard stuff" . . . the sinister peddler still lurks about, ready to "hook" young and innocent passers-by . . . the most heroic figure on the scene is still the police agent—still pitted against evils of satanic dimensions. Publicity handouts and presentations that come through foolishly, or with patent dishonesty, invite disrespect for *all* authority in the field. And no one knows for sure whether exaggerated portrayals in the name of education may not be having exactly an opposite—promotional—net effect.

There are also new distortions, and one of the worst is the recently invented death-count, usually associated with the image of heroin as a "killer drug." In mid-1971, in the course of his long message proclaiming that drug abuse had "assumed the dimensions of a national emergency" and announcing his Special Action Office for Drug Abuse Prevention to deal with it, President Nixon said more people in the fifteen-to-thirty age bracket in New York City die as a result of drug abuse than from any other cause, and that between 1960 and 1970 the city's "narcotic deaths" had risen from 200 to over 1,000 (a rate, incidentally, of only 0.13 per thousand as against the national death rate for all age groups from all causes of 9.5 per thousand). Heroin, the President said, is "deadly poison in the American lifestream" and "a fact of life and a cause of death among an increasing number of citizens in America."

A massive overdose of pure heroin (or, equally, any other opiate such as morphine or a synthetic like methadone) *would* be capable of producing death by slowly depressing respiration and cardiac action. But virtually none of the claimed heroin fatalities are attributable squarely to this, and apart from such acute opiate poisoning *there is no reputable record in the annals of medicine of any physiological damage caused directly by this category of drugs.* What has happened is that medical authorities, with New York leading the way, have commenced lumping together as "heroin deaths" cases where hepatitis or other infections from unsterile injection procedures lead to death, cases where impurities or toxic foreign substances appear to have been at fault, multiple-drug casualties, and even cases like that of a burglar who, surprised by the police while rifling an apartment, jumped out a window to his death and was found by autopsy to have had opiates in his bloodstream.

The coeds and young athletes reportedly sometimes found dead with syringes at their sides are almost certainly not heroin fatalities in the honest sense that it was the drug which took their lives. Puncturing the skin with anything can be mortally dangerous unless one uses antiseptic precautions. Putting anything impure directly into the bloodstream, so that it courses immediately through the lungs and heart chambers, is reckless in the extreme. And this is what can cause sudden death. Recently in New York, for example, sophisticated pushers have reportedly been adding antihistamine powders along with, or instead of, milk sugar to cut their heroin, in the belief that this intensifies and prolongs euphoric effects. But a significant number of people are fatally allergic to antihistamines. And if "mainlined," the same may be true of quinine, aspirin, baking soda, baby talc, and tooth powder.

So the truth is that heroin the killer rarely—*very* rarely—kills. The soothing opiates are among the safest drugs in the whole inventory of modern medicine. Nalline, as noted earlier in this narrative, is an effective antidote for opiate poisoning, if administered properly and in time. Even the coroners and medical examiners who build up these new death statistics consistently acknowledge, if pressed on the point, that neither their autopsy examinations nor the analyses of syringes and packets found around the bodies of drug victims has ever suggested that high concentrations of pure drugs are turning up often in the retail end of the illicit traffic. Street heroin is invariably cut to below 10 per cent, for compelling economic reasons, and tragedies among users are blameable on other causes and not on the drug. Desperate addicts "burn" their fellows by selling fake substances. Pushers allegedly poison with an intentional "hot shot" overdose, or some lethal substitute. Since the favorite current method for estimating addict-populations is the utterly ridiculous application of a ratio (100 or 200 to 1) to drug deaths, and since all addicts are vulnerable and some drug police are fanatics, it is even believed in some quarters that deadly strychnine-laden stuff could be originating from undercover plants and turncoats.

This new distortion from morgues is being reinforced by old fictions. A best-seller on organized crime, after avowing that the Dallas assassination was engineered by a Mafia overlord to clear the way for murdering the Attorney General, goes on to credit the masterminds of evil with an ingenious promotional campaign:

> . . . all reports indicated that marijuana is continually reaching greater numbers of users and filtering down into younger age brackets. And all of these pot smokers are potential buyers of the syndicate's stronger stuff a few months or years hence. . . . As if to substantiate this theory, narcotics officials are currently checking the suspicion that, in some cases, heroin is being mixed into marijuana by the pushers to "hook" people who might otherwise not go on to the stronger stuff.

This same work then goes on to credit the American drug problem simultaneously to another villain, "a real Chinese interest in narcotics can almost certainly be found in the mind of Red China's ruler, Mao Tse-tung, whose heroin factories are turning out the white powder in wholesale lots."

Hyperboles flow from other quarters. Here is Governor Reagan, telling his constituents about the situation in California:

> I want to talk with you today about an epidemic—an epidemic that has infected Californians in every walk of life and has reached into nearly every community from Siskiyou County in the north to San Diego in the south. The epidemic of drug abuse. . . .
>
> Drugs can be bought easily at high schools in the cities, in the suburbs and even in the smallest of towns. The facts are that it is almost as easy in many places for kids to buy pills and pot as it is for them to buy soda pop. This is no longer a problem restricted

to high school students. Addiction and drug abuse has spread to the junior high schools and even the elementary schools.

Although Attorney General Mitchell asserts what every drug enforcer since Harry Daugherty has claimed—"Our goal is not the occasional user. It is the large-scale professional trafficker"—nonetheless 1970 FBI figures show 346,412 drug arrests for the year, with 52.9 per cent (183,310) under the age of twenty-one *and 25.3 per cent (87,907) under eighteen.* Eighty-eight thousand major drug traffickers under eighteen?

Even Mrs. Martha Mitchell has joined the action, summoning 200 administration wives to a day-long symposium on drugs which her husband keynoted:

> I cannot overestimate to you the threat that narcotics and dangerous drugs pose to the mental and physical health of the nation—especially to our young people who are, in frighteningly increasing numbers, turning to marijuana, hard narcotics and other dangerous drugs as a way of life.

And finally, the Commissioner of Internal Revenue, under BNDD pressure, has used Treasury's rule-making power to wipe out the *Linder* decision once and for all, by decreeing that "professional practice" now cannot include *any* administering or dispensing "to narcotic drug dependent persons for the purpose of continuing their dependence" except only in approved methadone-experiment programs, and that "the prescribing of narcotic drugs is not authorized for any such purpose."

It is admittedly unrealistic to hope for some sudden triumph of enlightenment on this subject. Fifty years has set the pattern too firmly, and the current momentum is too great.

Though by early 1972 it appeared that no new excess could top what I have just recounted as high-water marks of law-enforcement zeal, on January 28, 1972, President Nixon and Mr. Mitchell did it again. They announced that they had pulled another first-rate man—Myles J. Ambrose, Commissioner of Customs—away from his work to become a White House "consultant" with Dr. Jaffe, and at the same time to head a new Office of Drug Abuse Law Enforcement in the Department of Justice (with 250 agents, 150 attorneys, nine field offices, and operating in twenty-four U.S. cities), all suddenly established right on top of Director Ingersoll's BNDD. This was necessary, they said, to hold state and local enforcers more in line by establishing "a Federal presence at the local level." Noting that "the most despicable crime is that of the drug pusher and trafficker because the result of his act is that the life of the individual is destroyed," the President assured a press conference called for the purpose: ". . . the states want this Federal activity."

Nor is the end in sight. But perhaps if nothing else has been accomplished in the telling of this tale to date, its essential features might cast light on other areas of larger importance to the nation. Seeing how a great government can err thus in one narrow field where the stakes are in some ways so trifling might induce citizens to ponder how much greater the possibility of missteps where graver issues are faced—and where those who might wish to deceive and mislead have far more at stake, and incomparably more strength, than the shabby consortium of underworld pushers, self-aggrandizing enforcers, and irresponsible publicists.

■ THIRTY

So, What's Right?

■ HAVING BEEN so free with criticism all through this work, it is no less than fair now to say plainly what I think *is* the truth, and what might eventually head us back toward the right path. Problems in this area are not, after all, as complex as the great issues of preserving peace, upgrading education for all, or dealing with crises in depletion, pollution, and over-population. One day Americans might simply wake up—as they did about Prohibition—and begin to concern themselves with more important things.

But let there be no mistake on one point: nothing I have said is intended to be an unreserved apology for drugs or drug users, or for indiscriminate distribution of toxic substances to anyone. I have no quarrel with the conclusion that even useful medicines like heroin and morphine are hurtful when taken habitually for nontherapeutic purposes, while poisons with little medical value, like cannabis, caffeine, coca products, tobacco, and beverage al-cohol, may indeed be seriously damaging to the health of in-dividuals who abuse them (no question as to the latter cate-gories) and should not be promoted in our society—and, above all, not under any circumstances permitted to be exploited for commercial profit.

So there is nothing wrong with the end-purpose of the Ameri-can approach to addiction and abuse—discouraging individual self-injury with drugs. If the choice lay only between presently misguided repression on the one hand, and on the other a so-ciety in which prime time was allotted to selling hard narcotics and college magazines were filled with seductive ads for pot, we would be better off with the status quo. (Recently some of the high-pressure huckstering of nonprescription nostrums to relieve tension and induce sleep *do* sound as if their makers are either deliberately promoting new addictions or else perpetrating shameful frauds on the public.)

The most important single verity about the American drug problem is that it has so long been magnified out of perspective. The nation is not in peril because a minuscule handful of misfits (300,000 addicts among 200 million citizens is .15 per cent) are dependent on chemical gratifications that a majority happens to disapprove. Our youth would not be lost to us if Attorney General Mitchell had been able to report the arrest of 890,000 of them, instead of 89,000, mostly for having had some sort of fling at pot. There is no reason to tolerate further the out-of-sight values put on drug seizures by enforcement authorities, or reckless estimates by "experts" like the current 200-addicts-per-drug-death ratio. Cool facts are obtainable and we are entitled to them.

Yet on the other hand no one can blink the gravity of the current situation. When we ruin tens of thousands of young lives, and squander directly and indirectly resources that must honestly total nearly a billion dollars each year, something *is* amiss. Moreover, it is not open to much question that drug problems are on the increase virtually everywhere. If we do not find better ways to reverse present trends, there may yet come a time when the ravages of drug abuse, taken all together, may live up to today's hyperboles and begin to compare meaningfully with the harm done by other indulgences and self-imposed afflictions such as—to give tobacco and alcohol a rest—poverty, inflation, highway carnage, runaway birth rates, or our benighted mini-wars.

True addiction and other forms of drug abuse are not only not identical, they are not even closely related. Efforts to obscure this distinction by equating addiction with "losing one's power of self-control" have caused much trouble. Nothing currently in use by drug users produces addiction except three categories: the opiates, the barbiturates, and alcohol. Persons "hooked" on these substances must have a continuing supply to avoid withdrawal symptoms, and should usually have medical attention when withdrawal is undertaken. In all other categories, excepting unusual individual cases, the relationship between user and drug is merely that of habituation, and in few other instances is the continuing compulsion to use the drug as strong as that which develops in a person heavily dependent on nicotine. Honest acceptance of this fact makes a good deal of the discussion about drug problems irrelevant in relation to most. The worst present distortion on this account is in popular and official attitudes toward marijuana. No "treatment" has significance in discouraging pot smoking, while no sanctions are necessary to induce a motivated person to forsake the drug—nor demonstrably appropriate against moderate users.

Other habituating substances ought to be sorted out on a sensible descending scale. Cocaine is strong, injurious, and susceptible to reasonable controls because coca is not grown here. Amphetamines are strong, injurious (but more valuable medically than cocaine in today's practice), and not susceptible to such tight controls because they are too easy to make. Hashish and THC (cannabis essence) are strong hallucinogens, less controllable than cocaine but not as easy to produce as amphetamines, probably less injurious than either, not used in medicine, and classifiable a grade or two above marijuana (to which they are closely related). LSD is a dangerous fad, for which we can thank a few Dr. Learys and promotion by the public media, and which will in all likelihood be happily forgotten one day soon; peyote (mescaline) is probably a fad too, destined to be left to the Indians again when popular attention turns away from it. Glue sniffing, banana skins, morning glory seeds, and nutmeg have practically run their courses—though someone may now discover gasoline whiffing as a successor, and then we may have to put up with D-men skulking around garages and gas stations for a while.

In short, abuses of nonaddicting substances merit passing notation and some passing concern. Abuse of a particular category can explode into undesirable fad proportions if it is sufficiently promoted and publicized. Some controls are desirable in controllable instances, and no such substance should be freed for open commercial exploitation of its abuse potential. But "dangerous" is a misnomer for most of them; they do not belong in the same rubric with the addiction producers; and they should be differentiated at every turn when we address ourselves to proposed reforms. As a first step, all of them ought to be removed from the so-called hard-drug pattern.

With further specific regard to marijuana, which may now involve half a million habituated users and several million occasional or experimental smokers, it should be recognized and classified *right now* as a toxic substance closely akin to tobacco, without any further stalling in the name of additional research. Then as we move toward more vigorous restrictions on cigarette marketers, we should be progressing simultaneously from the other end of the scale toward less stringent measures affecting cannabis. Possession should be removed forthwith from all criminal categories—and may heaven preserve us from ever falling into the comparable error of making it punishable to be caught with a cigarette, or tobacco shreds, in one's pocket. If the federal government must concern itself further with this poor weed, control from Washington should be exercised only by appropriate taxation at a level consistent with bona fide revenue collection. Although everyone talks about the "alcohol model" of federal and local controls as a guide for holding pot promotion and pot abuse in check, there is a better one (if maximum discouragement is desired), and that is the web of taxation, licensing, regulations, and restrictions with which butter lobbyists have strangled margarine for most of the past century.

Jumping from this to my most radical observation and suggestion, *ultimately* it must be recognized that the federal government has no rightful place in the drug-*use* picture at all.

And there is actually a close precedent for that, because it is exactly what the national authorities acknowledged with respect to alcoholic beverages after Repeal. Federal controls would still be asserted in a regulatory capacity under the Food and Drug Act, to protect quality and so forth, and the machinery of tax enforcement might still be employed—precisely as it was originally intended to be employed by Mr. Harrison in 1914—to keep the flow of drugs in observable channels, with appropriate records required at each stage of production and distribution. But the management of drug-abuse problems, to the extent that it is a legitimate function of *any* government, is properly the concern of local jurisdictions only.

Remember that when our grandparents first talked themselves into the experiment of outlawing alcohol, it was accepted without question that a full-blown constitutional amendment would be required to permit the federal government to curb consumption of that most popular of drugs. And when our fathers saw what folly the Eighteenth Amendment had been, it took another amendment, the Twenty-first, to knock it out.

Yet we have seen how, simultaneously, a mere handful of Treasury agents, acting without any constitutional mandate and without even any honestly conferred statutory authority, managed to launch a national prohibition campaign against opium and cocaine which has been carried on relentlessly ever since.

The U.S. system is, after all, a *federal* system. The Tenth Amendment says that powers not expressly delegated to the national government under the Constitution are reserved to the states or to the people, and for the first hundred years after the founders set this pattern Congress honored it scrupulously by staying out of local law enforcement. Except for a few special areas like treason and counterfeiting, how each individual citizen behaved himself was left strictly to state lawmakers and city fathers. Again with a few exceptions for specialties such as collecting the customs and policing federal territories, there were virtually no federal enforcement officers in Uncle Sam's service until after the turn of the twentieth century.

Congress first departed from his hands-off policy in the Lottery Acts of 1890 and 1895, banning lottery materials from the mails and from transportation across state lines. The provocation was great: lotteries had grown so out of hand during Reconstruction that no local power was a match for their greedy and fraudulent promoters. And the federal sanctions worked. Quickly the problem began to diminish. Lottery abuses, though still with us locally in one guise or another, have never since been much of a threat to the national welfare.

Thereafter Congress passed a cautious series of laws in support of other local enforcement, each time responding to some special situation where criminal activity had outgrown city limits and state lines: carrying poached game from one state to another (1900); robbing trains (1902); the Mann Act, aimed at white slavery (1910); the Dyer Act, stolen vehicles (1916); the Lindbergh Act, kidnaping (1932); and bank robbery, extortion, and interstate transportation of stolen property (1934).

Without exception, in every one of these instances federal intervention had immediate and salutary effects: the criminal activity at which Congress took aim shrank in importance or sometimes virtually disappeared. There have been only two areas where Uncle Sam's intrusion has had the opposite result: Prohibition, the soon-acknowledged mistake, and drug-use suppression. So today it is in the drug field alone that federal enforcement efforts go on from failure to failure, and where the national community is more burdened and more threatened than it was before Congress stepped in more than half a century ago.

Without a constitutional amendment the underlying bases of federal police authority in this field are questionable. Poachers and kidnapers who skip across state lines are understandably regarded as threats to the national welfare. They also fall squarely within reach of the interstate commerce power. But it is hard to make any similar identification with respect to individuals who merely choose to ingest or inject some vegetable or chemical substance, selected voluntarily by themselves, into their lungs, alimentary tracts, or bloodstreams. Quite to the contrary, it is hard to imagine any area in the whole range of human activity where there would appear to be *less* federal concern and *less* possibility of attaching legitimate federal importance, especially bearing in mind that the only touchstone of power over all these years, until the 1970 Act, was Congress' right to lay and collect taxes.

The omniscient founders had something to say about this kind of incursion too, at least as some authorities read the great charter they wrote. One of these days more attention may be paid to the Ninth Amendment, which has lain in the Bill of Rights without attracting much notice, but which provides: "The enumeration in the Constitution, of certain rights, shall not be construed to deny or disparage others retained by the people." If people have no freedom to make such choices as cannabis over nicotine for their preferred lung irritant, what *did* the Constitution leave to them?

My other most sweeping proposal—that anyone truly addicted be supplied with drugs through medical or public health channels—also has a close precedent, being the principle on which Great Britain has always operated. British attitudes can hardly be characterized as a separate philosophy, for persons who have addiction problems in England are calmly regarded as medical patients, "cured" by being induced to withdraw entirely from drug use if possible and otherwise "treated" by being furnished an appropriate source of their drug of addiction. The small number of British addicts who end up on stabilized dosages cause no more excitement in England than diabetics being maintained on insulin cause in the United States. (Pursuing the matter of attitudes a little further, since the *crime* of addiction and the *disease* of addiction have been the subject of so much embattled controversy in America, it would perhaps be helpful to promote a different concept, more accurately descriptive than either: the *accident* of addiction. Viewing the chronic drug user as a product of a social accident would be a long first step toward focusing on his real situation and true needs.)

Now confining the discussion narrowly to genuine addiction,

which means principally the problems surrounding opiates, why *not* furnish these drugs rather freely to confirmed users? The foolish notion that morphine and "H" cause antisocial conduct and turn people into "fiends" has been dispelled. No one really believes any longer that society must protect itself by withholding such drugs from individual members, so the hard truth is that all the efforts, and energies, and sacrifices, and most of the disagreeable conditions I have described in this long narrative relate solely to protecting drug addicts from the personal consequences of their own weaknesses. And we have *never* been able to do that successfully. A true addict cut off from his source of supply for a few days "kicks" his habit and ceases to be physically hooked, so by definition the addict population is made up of people *who have always been receiving an adequate and uninterrupted flow of drugs.* Why not knock the peddler out completely—and scrap most of our drug-police apparatus, and put an end to drug-induced crime—by providing such a flow ourselves?

Even the extreme expedient of allowing all adult persons whose addiction is medically established to have unrestricted access to drugs for their own use through medical channels would be more rational than our present efforts to save these afflicted souls from themselves via the criminal-enforcement route. The out-and-out sacrifice of a few thousand, or even a few hundred thousand, addict-citizens, who might at worst nod away their lives in harmless euphoria, seems to me to compare favorably with sending them out in everlasting torment to keep raising tribute solely for the benefit of the odious pusher. One might argue that America has been known to tolerate sacrifices of this magnitude, and of more deserving individuals, in the pursuit of less sensible objectives.

But this approach need not involve such extremes. Current experience with methadone has already exemplified some of its possibilities, and with excellent initial returns (doubtless one of the reasons the federal enforcement agencies have made such a crude attack on it in their IND—experimental drug—regulations). Many individuals, freed of the compulsion to spend their lives hustling for the next fix, may be able then to deal with other problems, such as finding jobs, readjusting their family and social relationships, or resuming interrupted educations. Some, with a helping hand, will assuredly free themselves from drugs altogether. Contemporary studies suggest that drug users often drift out of addiction as they approach middle age, even after long and severe involvement. This hopeful trend could be encouraged in a broad-scale maintenance program.

In any event, following the English precedent would still mean concentration on withdrawal and drug-free rehabilitation, holding out the ultimate, permitted access only as a sort of carrot-on-the-stick to motivate cooperation. In the present order of things most American addicts have only two points of contact, the pusher who exploits them mercilessly on the one hand, and the policeman who is their relentless nemesis on the other. They bargain so unequally with these two that if they were provided a third alternative it might be possible to exact rather large concessions in return.

Specifically, if there were a way in which the addict could approach medical or public-health authorities to seek help with the management of his affliction, he might, in many instances, pay a substantial *quid pro quo* for relief—especially if the relief included, at the end of the line and if all else had failed, a secure supply of drugs. This is essentially what was demonstrated when addicts flocked to the so-called clinics of the early twenties, and it is why most of today's methadone programs have been so stormed with applicants that they are forced to maintain long waiting lists.

An addict applying for relief would first be screened to make certain his problem was indeed an established addiction (thus weeding out the stereotyped "youthful experimenter" and other borderliners); he would then be put through examination and diagnosis covering his physical condition, psychiatric state, and social circumstances as far as might be necessary; thereafter he could be given whatever was available in the way of counseling, therapy, job placement, or hospitalization or location in some facility outside his usual haunts; he would be subjected to periodic urine testing, to control possible abuse of drugs outside the program; and of course he would be held to the most important rule of all—namely, no drugs released into his possession, and accordingly no temptation to sell to others or to "picnic" by accelerating his intake from a supply intended for future consumption.

Everything just described now characterizes the best of the methadone programs—and would apply as well to morphine or heroin maintenance if foolish notions about these natural opiates were dispelled. By controlling input, psychiatric counseling and hospital and resident facilities could be used effectively and to capacity, instead of being alternately starved and inundated depending on the haphazard workings of compulsory "commitment" machinery. It is true that persons currently in these programs are sometimes found to be supplementing their intake by obtaining drugs from illicit sources—specifically, in methadone maintenance, by shooting cocaine to get something of the "high" which is difficult to achieve under methadone saturation (and this allegedly accounts for part of the notable renaissance of cocaine use, after the drug had all but disappeared from the illicit traffic).

But such problems should diminish proportionately as an adequate program reached out to make contact with more and more addicts in the community. A few holdouts could not sustain much of a black market. And once the police were induced to stop harassing the centers (which is almost universally the case with methadone programs today, and which raises some ugly implications about police attitudes), and to turn instead to cooperating by running down the sources from which abusers might still be getting additional supplies, the situation could reverse for the better very quickly.

Finally, as already indicated, this approach faces realistically the fact that there are some individuals in our society who prefer being drugged to being abstinent, and who, once addicted, are going to go on saturating themselves with these substances no matter what we do about it. The best solution for them, and for society, is controlled permanent administration. Again assuming a program which is effectively handling the problems of most addicts, this last-resort maintenance regime would raise few problems and could probably eventually be freed of burdensome supervision. Details such as unforgeable identification, limiting prescriptions to one pharmacy or one prescribing authority, and spot checks have been worked out many times and could almost certainly assure that drugs were not diverted by these cases. And on the so-called moral issue, to paraphrase one of Dr. Kolb's observations, anyone who goes about looking skyward to invoke divine wrath against giving addicts access to their chosen nirvana had better take care lest he break his neck stumbling over one of the nation's insensible gutter drunks.

The three main things I have urged so far—throw non-addicting drugs out of the pattern, limit federal involvement to tax collection and quality policing, and treat confirmed addicts as accident victims or patients along the British line—would quickly cool the drug scene. But although methadone may be a faltering start toward British permissiveness, the trend is to *add* controlled substances instead of restricting the "dangerous" list, and federal drug authorities seem more entrenched and aggressive than ever.

So, being realistic, let us consider lesser adjustments.

Something that should have been done long ago, and should now be given priority, is the abolition of all possession offenses, in every category, coupled with an amnesty-release for everyone now confined as a result of a possession conviction. Unless possession of drugs is surrounded by circumstances which indicate that it is incidental to pushing, in which case the charge should be the latter offense, penalties attaching to it serve only to punish victims of the traffic. In reality, the main purpose has always been to allow agents and police to force drug users caught in possession to serve as informers or betrayers of their associates. The argument that possession convictions can be used as a shortcut to incarcerate people who are actually guilty of unprovable offenses in more serious categories is as unworthy in this context as in any other; many policemen would *like* to have power to put away anyone they thought might be an offender, but as a basis for the exercise of real authority to arrest and convict this is a dangerous power indeed. Buyers who come into possession of adulterated food and recipients of counterfeit bills are not harassed or prosecuted; the law enforcers start up the line to find out who manufactured, or sold, or passed. That should be the limit of the law-enforcement reach with respect to contraband drugs too. Punishing mere possession by *addicts* is also objectionable in the extreme because it usually amounts to imposing sanctions for being addicted; the compulsion to take drugs compels its victim equally to possess before taking.

Another step imperatively needed is the reduction of drug-offense penalties to moderate levels, with no minimums in any category, no status offenses, and maximums graded in a range below five years, or certainly not above ten, plus reinstatement of eligibility for probation, parole, youth-correction programs, and other benefits generally available to all convicted persons. This should be done with retroactive application, to put prisoners now serving time for drug offenses into a more endurably fair relation with their fellow inmates atoning for such crimes as murder, rape, and treason.

Of course no one can disagree that whenever we catch prototypes of Mr. Big, supposedly elegant white overlords of the traffic who are neither addicted themselves nor ever touch the stuff, who sport names ending in Sicilian vowels and very likely boast important connections with cops and political figures, they should be severely punished. Even traffickers with less gloss, not themselves addicted and who reap profits from extorting such high prices in the addict community, are indefensible predators.

But there are few of these important criminals behind the bars. And anyway what deters them is not how severely they might be punished if caught, but whether they are likely to be caught at all. It is the swiftness and certainty of criminal justice that makes the difference; excessive severity is a good theme for spellbinders, but is not a solution for enforcement problems and can actually upset the evenhanded administration of justice. In the drug field, juries have been known to bring back obviously incorrect verdicts of not guilty, and judges have defied their statutory obligations in imposing sentence, simply to avoid the severity of harsh mandatory terms in borderline cases.

Retention of the special law-enforcement prerogatives which have come to be associated with drug prohibition over the years seems unjustified. Making money loosely available so that agents can make "buys" and bribe informants for information should end forthwith. So should the practice of rewarding informers with a percentage of fines collected or of the value of drugs seized (and sometimes, as has been suggested, with some of the drugs in kind). There is no reasonable need to give drug agents overbearing powers such as making arrests and seizures without warrants, the serving of warrants at night, granting limited immunity in return for compelled testimony, or even the carrying of firearms in the ordinary discharge of their duties as mere regulators and tax collectors. Above all, the controversial "no-knock" authorization, currently being pushed as a new police prerogative justified by the danger that people with drugs in their homes are likely to destroy them if they are given warning when the police come to the door, is a hysterical overreaction which cannot be abandoned and forgotten too quickly.

The best change short of withdrawing federal authority altogether would be to remove nearly everything from the jurisdiction of the Attorney General and the Department of Justice. Responsibility for scientific evaluation and classifications should go back to the Food and Drug Administration and the National Institutes of Health. The counterfeit provisions, if they cannot be wiped out, ought to go to FDA also, or to the Federal Trade Commission. Remaining tax-collection authority should be returned to Treasury, but placed with the Alcohol Tax Unit for bona fide enforcement instead of being turned over to anything like another Drug Bureau. If further international maneuverings are warranted, they should be handled by the State Department; dealing with smugglers belongs entirely in the jurisdiction of Customs; educational efforts, if the federal government insists on continuing its intrusions in this field, belong in the Department of Health, Education, and Welfare; and such research as is deemed necessary ought to be conducted or controlled through the National Institutes with no strings attached by Justice or other agencies.

On the critical question of what constitutes good medical practice in the prescribing and administering of drugs, we should, after all these years, do what the British did in 1924 and let the medical profession itself lay down standards by which the laws are to be interpreted. This could be done through the organized medical societies or by a special federal commission of some kind, charged with responsibility for proposing appropriate regulations. The same thing could probably also be undertaken by any state, with the effect of pre-empting the federal prerogative. If, for example, the New York State legislature asked the New York Academy of Medicine to prepare something like the British Rolleston Rules, and then enacted the result as governing policy binding on licensed physicians in New York State, this would probably be binding likewise on federal agents despite contrary notions in the U.S. Treasury or the Department of Justice.

Education about drugs, in moderation and aimed only at audiences where it is directly relevant, seems in order, but only if the educators are honest and enlightened on the subject. Heroin must be stripped of its mythical terrors and returned to the pharmacopoeia. Free-swinging distortions and alarms about marijuana must be quieted. Fads must be damped. And we should not expect too much from educational campaigns. Every American schoolchild for several generations has been exposed to propaganda about the evils and dangers of alcohol, yet no one has ever demonstrated that the result has been a single abstinent person who might otherwise have developed a drinking problem.

Taking the situation as it is today, there is a greater need for narrowly targeted enlightenment, verging toward counseling, than for broadcast education. Accurate knowledge must be made available about specific conditions in such communities as New York City's Manhattan, where addiction and abuse problems are concentrated, so that troubled parents, puzzled users on the threshold of being hooked, and anyone else who may be directly affected can understand and cope with their own situations. In some instances where doctors, public-health authorities, or private groups have sought to have this kind of service provided, the greatest single difficulty has been police harassment. Unless the doctor-patient, lawyer-client, or clergy-penitent privilege is available and invoked, narcotic-squad officers try to find out who comes for counseling, to get at advisors' records, and sometimes to entrap participants. This is of course inexcusable and ought not to be tolerated anywhere.

On the international scene, it is time the United States put aside all notions of controlling its unique problem by forcing other nations to do its bidding in curbing their own drug production or oppressing their own citizens with Yankee-type laws. Fifty years of bullying and cajoling the world community in this fruitless campaign is more than enough. This does not mean that present routines to reduce the smuggled inflow of prohibited drugs should be abandoned—only that U.S. international efforts should be drastically reduced to the same level as present activity in connection with other kinds of smuggled contraband.

While looking at the international scene, and approaching the end of this discussion, I am impelled to note a related suggestion along quite a different line: perhaps the U.S. government could be induced to take the lead in pressing for international outlawry of the official use of drugs to subjugate, oppress, and torture. Not forgetting how scornfully I have reported charges along the way that America's enemies are plotting to undermine the United States with drugs, I venture nonetheless to suggest that there is something a little different that *does* merit alarm and international action. That is the use of drugs to enslave or destroy individuals under oppressive political control. The Nazis reportedly used depressants in the food of concentration-camp inmates to make it possible for small numbers of guards to keep the upper hand with thousands of otherwise desperate and resourceful prisoners. The Greeks are now said to be neutralizing certain political dissenters by shattering their minds with heavy dosages of some hallucinogen like LSD, administered continuously for a week or two. Scopolamine can make a joke of the constitutional rights cherished as safeguards for accused persons in the Western world. And a variety of other chemicals are now at hand to enable an oppressor to incapacitate and render submissive the oppressed, which seems to me to do more violence to human integrity than any of the lethal gases or prior conditions of slavery from which we recoil in horror. U.S. spokesmen could begin trying to persuade political

authorities everywhere to renounce this dreadful possibility under all circumstances in the future.

Lastly, the single concentration of effort which would do more
than any other to break up the existing illicit drug traffic, without changing present enforcement patterns, would be some truly
effective assault on corruption in all its degrees and nuances. In
many areas, current circumstances suggest that someone may be
looking the other way. And where authorities are tolerating drug
activities, it is inevitable that someone is also taking bribes or
receiving other benefits from the traffic. Diligent enforcement of
bribery laws, aggressive internal policing of the drug police,
rigorous scrutiny of all sources of political funds—and perhaps
even a new federal statute to bring errant local enforcers more
directly under the jurisdiction of the incorruptible FBI—such
measures could do much to further real prevention by repression,
so long as we are going to cling to that approach anyway.

So there it is. The implications of this discourse are not so insignificant, in truth, when viewed against today's background
of unrest and pressure on the one hand, and a measureless flood
of new drug substances commencing to inundate us on the
other. It seems important simply to start trying very hard to be
right about drug problems, and to look at the situation realistically and with less emotion. We must induce Uncle Sam to
get the monkey off *his* back altogether if we can. We must re-
lax more about the few poor souls who won't or can't kick their
addiction, and try to help the rest escape instead of hounding
them deeper into drugs and crime. It is time to face the fact
that we are never going to succeed pushing our prejudices onto
the rest of the world. And if we cannot cool the ardor and soften
the powers of law enforcers, at least we must strive to keep them
honest and incorruptible.

Chronology, References, Citations, and Sources

This appendix serves four purposes: it gives a rough chrono-logical outline of the story, following chapter arrangements; it sets forth general references and authorities, the best of which are marked with an asterisk, together with supporting annotations for main points and sources for important quoted material; it fur-nishes citations leading directly to the texts of key treaties, legis-lative proceedings, statutes, and cases; and it provides, at the end, a list of contemporary sources for additional firsthand information.

CHAPTER 1
(Introductory Background and the 1970 Drug Act)

General appraisal of the 1960's

> Brown, Thorvald T., *The Enigma of Drug Addiction*, Thomas, Springfield, Ill., 1961
> *Chein, Isadore, and others, *The Road to H*, Basic Books, New York, 1964
> *Cohen, Sidney, *The Drug Dilemma*, McGraw-Hill, New York, 1969
> *Einstein, Stanley, *The Use and Misuse of Drugs*, Wadsworth, Belmont, Calif., 1970
> Eldridge, William B., *Narcotics and the Law* (2nd ed.), Ameri-can Bar Foundation, Chicago, 1967
> Fort, Joel, *The Pleasure Seekers*, Bobbs-Merrill, Indianapolis, 1969

Geller, Allen, and Boas, Maxwell, *The Drug Beat*, Cowles, New York, 1969

Knowlis, Helen H., *Drugs on the College Campus*, Anchor Books, New York, 1968

Kolb, Lawrence, *Drug Addiction*, Thomas, Springfield, Ill., 1962

°Lindesmith, Alfred R., *The Addict and the Law*, Indiana University Press, Bloomington, Ind., 1965

Louria, Donald B., *The Drug Scene*, McGraw-Hill, New York, 1968

°Louria, Donald B., *Overcoming Drugs*, McGraw-Hill, New York, 1971

°Maurer, David W., and Vogel, Victor H., *Narcotics and Narcotic Addiction* (3rd ed.), Thomas, Springfield, Ill., 1967

O'Donnell, John A., and Ball, John C., *Narcotic Addiction*, Harper & Row, New York, 1966

°Strauss, Nathan III, *Addicts and Drug Abusers*, Twayne, New York, 1971

Taylor, Norman, *Narcotics: Nature's Dangerous Gifts*, Dell, New York, 1963

October 27, 1970: Drug Act signed

"Comprehensive Drug Abuse Prevention and Control Act of 1970," P.L. 91–513, 84 Stat. 1236

Congressional Record, January 23–28, September 23 and 24, October 7 and 14, 1970

U.S. House Committee on Ways and Means, "Controlled Dangerous Substances, Narcotics and Drug Laws," Hearings, July 20–27, 1970, Government Printing Office, Washington, D.C.

U.S. House Committee on Interstate and Foreign Commerce, Subcommittee on Health and Public Welfare, "Drug Abuse Control Amendments—1970," Hearings, February 3 through March 3, 1970, Parts 1 and 2, Government Printing Office, Washington, D.C.

U.S. Senate Report 91–613

U.S. House Report 91–1444 (Parts 1 and 2)

1970 Hughes Subcommittee hearings

U.S. Senate Committee on Labor and Public Welfare, Special Subcommittee on Alcoholism and Narcotics, "Federal Drug Abuse and Drug Dependence Prevention, Treatment and Rehabilitation Act of 1970," Hearings, Parts 1–3, March 16 through April 25, 1970, Government Printing Office, Washington, D.C.

CHAPTER 2
(Ancestors and Prohibitionists)

Seventeenth and eighteenth centuries: the China traffic

Collis, Maurice, *Foreign Mud*, Knopf, New York, 1946
International Anti-Opium Association, *The War Against Opium*, Tientsin Press, Tientsin, 1922

1898–1901: U.S. control of the Philippines

Kritikos, P. G., and Papadaki, S. P., "The History of the Poppy . . . ," *U.N. Bulletin on Narcotics*, XIX (July–September, 1967), 17

*Taylor, Arnold H., *American Diplomacy and the Narcotics Traffic, 1900–39*, Duke University Press, Durham, N.C., 1969

U. S. War Department, Bureau of Insular Affairs, *Report of the Philippine Opium Commission*, Government Printing Office, Washington, D.C., 1905 (also U.S. Senate Document 59–265, 1906)

March 3, 1905: Philippine Tariff Revision Act (with opium-prohibition section)

P.L. 58–141, 33 Stat. 928, 944

CHAPTER 3
(Antecedents of the Harrison Act)

c. 1806: morphine isolated by Serturner (codeine, 1832)

c. 1845: hypodermic developed by Wood

1861–65: widespread use of opiates in U.S. Civil War

1880's: moderate concern; abuse by nostrum promoters; beginnings of local regulation

Kolb, *Drug Addiction*, see Chapter 1
Kolb, Lawrence, and DuMez, A. G., *The Prevalence and Trends of Drug Addiction in the United States and the Factors Influencing It*, U.S. Public Health Service (39 Pub. Health Rep. 1179), Government Printing Office, Washington, D.C., 1924
Kremers, Edward, and Urdang, George, *History of Pharmacy* (3rd ed.), Lippincott, Philadelphia, 1963
*Musto, David, *Narcotics and America: A Social History*, Yale University Press, New Haven, Conn., 1972

*Terry, Charles E., and Pellens, Mildred, *The Opium Problem* (for Bureau of Social Hygiene, Inc.), Haddon Craftsmen, Camden, N.J., 1928

1883: cocaine isolated

1898: heroin from morphine base

February 9, 1909: Act prohibiting importation of opium for non-medicinal use

P.L. 60–100, 35 Stat. 614

1909: Shanghai Opium Conference convened by President Roosevelt

Buel, Raymond L., *The International Opium Conferences*, World Peace Foundation (Pamphlets, VIII, Nos. 2 and 3), Boston, 1925

*Eisenlohr, Louise E. S., *International Narcotics Control*, Allen Unwin, London, 1934

Renborg, Bertil A., *International Drug Control*, Carnegie Endowment, Washington, D.C., 1947

Taylor, *American Diplomacy and the Narcotics Traffic*, see Chapter 2

1912: Hague Opium Convention

38 Stat. 1912, 1930

December 17, 1914: Harrison Narcotics Act

P.L. 63–223, 38 Stat. 785; amended February 24, 1919, by P.L. 65–254, 40 Stat. 1057, 1130
U.S. House Report 63–1196
U.S. Senate Report 63–258

CHAPTER 4
(Toward Hysteria)

Mrs. Vanderbilt's campaign; Prohibition; war scares

Lindesmith, Alfred R., *Opiate Addiction*, Indiana University Press, Bloomington, Ind., 1947

18th Amendment (January 29, 1919) implemented by Volstead Act, P.L. 66–66, 41 Stat. 305

New York Times, January 22, 1914; April 1914; December 1915; April 1917; December 1917; April 2, 1918; August 20, 1918; April 10, 1919; *et passim*

U.S. Treasury, Special Narcotic Committee, *Traffic in Narcotic Drugs, Report of Special Committee of Investigation*, Government Printing Office, Washington, D.C., 1919

CHAPTER 5
(The Medical Profession's Role)

1920–23: the clinic controversy

Congressional Record, January 13, 1922; June 30, 1922; June 15, 1938; *et passim*

Lindesmith, *The Addict and the Law*, see Chapter 1

New York Times, April, July, and August 1919; March 3 and 7, 1920; June 23, 1920; February 25, 1921; *et passim*

Terry and Pellens, *The Opium Problem*, see Chapter 3

Williams, Henry S., *Drug Addicts Are Human Beings*, Shaw, Washington, D.C., 1938

Treasury enforcement of the Harrison Act as a prohibition law

American Medical Association, *Narcotics Addiction: Official Actions of the A.M.A.*, American Medical Association, Chicago, 1963

Anslinger, H. J., and Tompkins, William F., *The Traffic in Narcotics*, Funk & Wagnalls, New York, 1953

Bishop, E. S., *The Narcotic Drug Problem*, Macmillan, New York, 1920

Lindesmith, Alfred R., "Dope Fiend Mythology," *Journal of Criminal Law and Criminology*, 31 (1940) 199

New York Times, September and October 1923

Schmeckebier, Laurence F., *The Bureau of Prohibition*, Brookings Institute, Washington, D.C., 1929

CHAPTER 6
(The Supreme Court Intercedes)

1919: constitutionality of Harrison Act upheld, 5 to 4
United States v. Doremus, 249 U.S. 86

1919–22: doctors' right to prescribe severely limited
Webb v. United States, 249 U.S. 96
Jin Fuey Moy v. United States, 254 U.S. 189
United States v. Behrman, 258 U.S. 280

1925: Dr. Linder vindicated in prescribing to addict
Linder v. United States, 290 Fed. 173, rev'd, 268 U.S. 5

1928: Harrison Act again upheld, 6 to 3
Nigro v. United States, 276 U.S. 332

CHAPTER 7
(Dr. Ratigan)

Sources

> *Seattle Times,* May–July 1934; October 9–14, 1934; April
>   1935; August 1936; June 17 and 18, 1937; *et passim*
> *Symposium, Narcotics, Law and Contemporary Problems,* XXII
>   (Winter 1957), Duke University, Durham, N.C., 1957

CHAPTER 8
(Congressman Coffee and Others)

Sources

> Bishop, *The Narcotic Drug Problem,* see Chapter 5
> *Congressional Record,* May 20, 1938 (App., 2075); June 14,
>   1938 (App., 2706); September 19, 1940 (App., 5767)
> Lindesmith, *The Addict and the Law,* see Chapter 1
> Stevens, Alden, "Make Dope Legal," *Harper's,* November 1952
> Terry and Pellens, *The Opium Problem,* see Chapter 3
> Williams, *Drug Addicts Are Human Beings,* see Chapter 5

*January 19, 1929: Act authorizes federal narcotic "farms," later U.S.
Public Health Service hospitals*

> P.L. 70–672, 45 Stat. 1085
> U.S. House Judiciary Committee, "Establishment of Narcotics
>   Farms," Hearings, April 26–28, 1928, Government Printing
>   Office, Washington, D.C.
> U.S. House Report, 70–1652
> U.S. Senate Report, 70–1353

CHAPTERS 9, 10, 11, 12
(Anslinger and Marijuana)

Sources

> Anslinger, H. J., and Oursler, Will, *The Murderers: The Story
>   of the Narcotic Gangs,* Farrar, Straus & Cudahy, 1961
> Meisler, Stanley, "Federal Narcotics Czar," *Nation,* February 20,
>   1960

*June 14, 1930: Act creating Bureau of Narcotics in the Treasury De-
partment*

> P.L. 71–357, 46 Stat. 585

August 2, 1937: Marijuana Tax Act

P.L. 75–238, 50 Stat. 551

Anslinger, H. J., and Cooper, C. R., "Marijuana: Assassin of Youth," *American*, July 1937

Merrill, F. T., *Marijuana: The New Dangerous Drug*, Foreign Policy Association, Washintgon, D.C., 1938

U.S. House Committee on Ways and Means, "Taxation of Marijuana," Hearings, April 27, 1937, Government Printing Office, Washington, D.C.

Walton, Robert P., *Marijuana: America's New Drug Problem*, Lippincott, Philadelphia, 1938

The role of the Rowells

Lindesmith, *The Addict and the Law*, see Chapter 1

Rowell, Earl A., *Dope Adventures of David Dare*, Southern Publishing Association, Nashville, 1937

Rowell, Earl A., and Rowell, Robert, *On the Trail of Marijuana, the Weed of Madness*, Pacific Press, Mountain View, Calif., 1939

1939: Mayor La Guardia's study

Mayor's Committee on Marijuana, *The Marijuana Problem in the City of New York: Sociological, Medical, Psychological and Pharmacological Studies*, Cattell Press, Lancaster, Pa., 1945

Taylor, Norman, *Flight from Reality*, Duell, Sloan & Pearce, New York, 1949

*Solomon, David, ed., *The Marijuana Papers*, Bobbs-Merrill, Indianapolis, 1966 (containing the La Guardia text)

Additional references re marijuana

Advisory Committee on Drug Dependence, *Cannabis*, H.M. Stationery Office, London, 1968

Bloomquist, E. R., *Marijuana*, Glencoe, Beverly Hills, Calif., 1968

*Blum, Richard H., and Associates, *Society and Drugs*, Jossey Bass, San Francisco, 1969

Grinspoon, Lester, *Marijuana Reconsidered*, Harvard University Press, Cambridge, Mass., 1971

*Kaplan, John, *Marijuana—The New Prohibition*, World, New York, 1970

President's Commission on Law Enforcement and Administration of Justice, *Task Force Report: Narcotics and Drug Abuse*, Government Printing Office, Washington, D.C., 1967

Rosevear, John, *Pot: A Handbook of Marijuana*, Lancer Books, New York, 1967

Snyder, Solomon H., *Uses of Marijuana*, Oxford University Press, New York, 1971

U.N. Commission on Narcotic Drugs, *Report of 23rd Session,* United Nations, New York, 1969

U.S. Senate Judiciary Committee, Subcommittee to Investigate Juvenile Delinquency, "Juvenile Delinquency" (Part 19, "L.S.D. and Marijuana Use Among Young People"), Hearings, March 4–6, 1968, Government Printing Office, Washington, D.C.

Wolff, Pablo O., *Marijuana in Latin America,* Linacre Press, Washington, D.C., 1949

1968: Supreme Court invalidates some marijuana penalties

Leary v. United States, 395 U.S. 6

June 30, 1970: "Marijuana and Health Reporting Act"

P.L. 91–296 (Title V), 84 Stat. 352

U.S. Department of Health, Education, and Welfare, *A Report to the Congress—Marijuana and Health,* Government Printing Office, Washington, D.C., 1971

CHAPTER 13
(The Kefauver Hearings and the Mafia)

Congressman Boggs's (1951) hearings

U.S. House Ways and Means Committee, "Control of Narcotics, Marijuana, and Barbiturates," Hearings, April 7, 14, and 17, 1951, Government Printing Office, Washington, D.C.

Senator Kefauver's (1951) hearings

U.S. Senate Special Committee to Investigate Organized Crime in Interstate Commerce, "Organized Crime in Interstate Commerce," Hearings, Parts 1–19, May 26, 1950, through August 7, 1951 (with composite index), Government Printing Office, Washington, D.C.

U.S. Senate Report 81–2370 (Interim)

U.S. Senate Report 82–141 (Second Interim)

U.S. Senate Report 82–307 (Third Interim)

U.S. Senate Report 82–725 (Final)

Kefauver, Estes, *Crime in America,* Doubleday, New York, 1951

The Mafia

Allen, Woody, "A Look at Organized Crime," *The New Yorker,* August 15, 1970

King, R., "Wild Shots in the War on Crime," *Journal of Public Law,* XX, No. 1 (1971) 85

O'Callaghan, Sean, *The Drug Traffic,* Blond, London, 1967

Reid, Ed, *The Grim Reapers,* Regnery, New York, 1969

Siragusa, Charles, *The Trail of the Poppy*, Prentice-Hall, Englewood Cliffs, N.J., 1966

Washington Post, July 23, 1970; March 25, 1971

November 2, 1951: Boggs Act increases penalties with mandatory minimums

P.L. 82–255, 65 Stat. 767

CHAPTERS 14, 15, 16
(The Daniel Subcommittee and the 1956 Act)

Queries and criticisms of the era

Advisory Council of Judges, *Narcotics Law Violations: A Policy Statement*, National Council on Crime and Delinquency, New York, 1964

Berg, Roland H., "We're Bungling the Narcotic Problem," *Look*, February 1953

Berger, Herbert, "To Dispel the Nightmare of Narcotics," *New York Times Magazine*, July 8, 1956

Berger, Herbert, and Eggston, Andrew A., "Should We Legalize Narcotics?", *Coronet*, June 1955

DeMott, Benjamin, "The Great Narcotics Muddle," *Harper's*, March 1962

Gerrity, John, "The Truth About the Drug Menace," *Harper's*, February 1952

Howe, Hubert S., "A Physician's Blueprint for the Management and Prevention of Narcotic Addiction," *New York State Journal of Medicine*, February 1, 1955

Kobler, John, "The Narcotics Dilemma: Crime or Disease?", *Saturday Evening Post*, September 8, 1962

Kolb, Lawrence, "Let's Stop This Narcotics Hysteria!", *Saturday Evening Post*, July 28, 1956

Lindesmith, Alfred R., "Dope: Congress Encourages the Traffic," *Nation*, March 16, 1957

Meisler, "Federal Narcotics Czar," see Chapters 9–12

*Murtagh, John M., and Harris, Sara, *Who Live in Shadow*, McGraw-Hill, New York, 1959

Rosenthal, Herbert C., "How Much of a Menace Is the Drug Menace?", *Pageant*, October 1952

Sondern, Frederick, Jr., "This Problem of Narcotic Addiction— Let's Face It Sensibly," *Reader's Digest*, September 1959

Stevens, "Make Dope Legal," see Chapter 8

Senator Daniel's hearings

U.S. Senate Judiciary Committee, Subcommittee on Improvements in the Federal Criminal Code, "Illicit Narcotics Traffic,"

Hearings, Parts 1–10, June 2 through November 25, 1955 (with composite index), Government Printing Office, Washington, D.C.

U.S. Treasury, Interdepartmental Committee on Narcotics, *Report to the President*, February 1, 1956, Government Printing Office, Washington, D.C.

Senator Kefauver's (1956) hearings

U.S. Senate Judiciary Committee, Subcommittee to Investigate Juvenile Delinquency, "Treatment and Rehabilitation of Juvenile Drug Addicts," Hearings, December 17 and 18, 1956, Government Printing Office, Washington, D.C.

Congressman Boggs's (1956) hearings

U.S. House Committee on Ways and Means, "Traffic In, and Control of, Narcotics, Barbiturates, and Amphetamines," Hearings, October 13, 1955, through January 30, 1956, Government Printing Office, Washington, D.C.

The New York session for dissenters

U.S. Senate Judiciary Committee, Subcommittee on Improvements in the Federal Criminal Code; see Senator Daniel's hearings, cited above, Part 5, 1303–2110, September 19–21, 1955

The Daniel Reports and the 1956 Act

U.S. Senate Report 84–1440
U.S. Senate Report 84–1850
"Narcotic Control Act of 1956," P.L. 84–728, 70 Stat. 767

CHAPTER 17
(State Laws and Policies)

June 30, 1906: Food and Drug Act

P.L. 59–384, 34 Stat. 768
Kremers and Urdang, *History of Pharmacy,* see Chapter 3
Rhodes, Lynwood M., "The Battle for the Nation's Health," *Today's Health,* April 1969

1932: National Conference of Commissioners on Uniform State Laws adopts Uniform Narcotic Drug Act

9B Uniform Laws Annotated 415 (amended 1942, 1952, 1958)
Eldridge, *Narcotics and the Law,* see Chapter 1
U.S. Senate, *Laws Controlling Illicit Narcotics Traffic,* Document 84–120, supplemented by Document 84–145, 1956

1963: Supreme Court holds statutes punishing addiction per se unconstitutional

Robinson v. California, 370 U.S. 660

1966: National Conference of Commissioners on Uniform State Laws adopts Model State Drug Abuse Control Act

1970: National Conference of Commissioners on Uniform State Laws adopts Uniform Controlled Substances Act

CHAPTERS 18, 19
(ABA-AMA and NIH)

The Reports

Joint Committee of the American Bar Association and the American Medical Association on Narcotic Drugs, *Narcotic Drugs—Interim Report* (unbound), Grosby, New York, 1958

Lindesmith, Alfred R., ed., *Drug Addiction: Crime or Disease?*, Indiana University Press, Bloomington, Ind. 1961

U.S. Treasury, Advisory Committee to the Federal Bureau of Narcotics, *Comments on Narcotic Drugs—Interim Report of the American Bar Association and the American Medical Association on Narcotic Drugs*, Government Printing Office, Washington, D.C., 1958

New York Times, April 30, 1961

Washington Post, March 18, 1960; April 19 and 21, 1961

The Symposium

Livingston, Robert B., ed., *Narcotic Drug Addiction Problems* (Public Health Service Pub. No. 1050), Government Printing Office, Washington, D.C., 1963

CHAPTER 20
(The British and Others)

Sources

*Deedes, William, *The Drugs Epidemic*, Barnes & Noble, New York, 1970

Larimore, G. W., and Brill, Henry, "The British Narcotic System: Report of Study," *New York State Journal of Medicine*, January 1, 1960

Lindesmith, *The Addict and the Law*, see Chapter 1

Report to the United Nations by Her Majesty's Government in the United Kingdom of Great Britain and Northern Ireland on the *Working of the International Treaties on Narcotic Drugs*, United Nations, New York (annual)

*Schur, Edwin M., *Narcotic Addiction in Britain and America*, Indiana University Press, Bloomington, Ind., 1956

1920: Dangerous Drugs Act

10 and 11 Geo. V c. 46

Departmental Committee on Morphine and Heroin Addiction, *Report*, H.M. Stationery Office, London, 1926

1951: Dangerous Drugs Act

14 and 15 Geo. VI c. 48

Dangerous Drugs Regulations, *Duties of Doctors and Dentists under the Dangerous Drugs Act*, H.M. Stationery Office, London, 1956

Report of the Interdepartmental Committee, *Drug Addiction*, H.M. Stationery Office, London, 1961

1964: Drugs (Prevention of Misuse) Act

12 Eliz. II c. 64

Second Report of the Interdepartmental Committee, *Drug Addiction*, H.M. Stationery Office, London, 1965

1965: Dangerous Drugs Act

13 Eliz. II c. 15

1967: Dangerous Drugs Act

15 Eliz. II c. 82

Advisory Committee on Drug Dependence, *The Rehabilitation of Drug Addicts*, H.M. Stationery Office, London, 1968

National Health Service, *Dangerous Drugs (Notification of Addicts) Regulations*, H.M. Stationery Office, London, 1968

1971: Misuse of Drugs Act

19 Eliz. II c. 70

London Times, May 20, 1971

May, Edgar, "Drugs Without Crime," *Harper's*, July 1971

New York Times, March 12 and 30, 1970; December 30, 1970; January 24, 1971; May 20, 1971

Periodic U.N. reports

Session Reports, Commission on Narcotic Drugs

Summary of Annual Reports of Governments

Summary of Laws and Regulations Relating to the Control of Narcotic Drugs (English translations)

CHAPTER 21
(International Efforts)

Sources

Eisenlohr, *International Narcotics Control*, see Chapter 3
Renborg, *International Drug Control*, see Chapter 3
Siragusa, *The Trail of the Poppy*, see Chapter 13
Taylor, *American Diplomacy and the Narcotics Traffic*, see Chapter 2
Willoughby, Westel W., *Opium as an International Problem*, Johns Hopkins Press, Baltimore, 1925

July 13, 1931: Geneva Limitation Convention

48 Stat. 1543

March 30, 1961: Single Convention on Narcotic Drugs

18 U.S. Treaty Ser. 1407

February 21, 1971: Convention on Psychotropic Substances

New York Times, October 3, 1970; January 17, 1971; March 30, 1971; July 1, 1971
U.N. Bulletin on Narcotics, XXIII (July–September 1971) 1
Washington Post, July 23, 1970; November 12, 1970

CHAPTERS 22, 23
(White House Conference and 1963 Commission)

Sources

Ad Hoc Panel on Drug Abuse, *Progress Report*, The White House, Washington, D.C., September 7, 1962
Los Angeles Times, May 30, 1962
President's Advisory Commission on Narcotic and Drug Abuse, Interim Report, The White House, Washington, D.C., April 3, 1963
Ibid., *Final Report*, Government Printing Office, Washington, D.C., 1963
White House Conference on Narcotic and Drug Abuse, *Proceedings* (with *Report of Ad Hoc Panel* appended), Government Printing Office, Washington, D.C., 1962

CHAPTER 24
(Rehabilitation)

Sources

Brill, Leon, and others, *Rehabilitation in Drug Addiction* (Public Health Service Pub. No. 1013), Government Printing Office, Washington, D.C. (revised, 1964)

Casriel, Daniel H., *So Fair a House: The Story of Synanon*, Prentice-Hall, Englewood Cliffs, N.J., 1963

Goodman, Walter, "The Choice for Thousands: Heroin or Methadone?", *New York Times Magazine*, June 13, 1971

*Nyswander, Marie, *The Drug Addict as a Patient*, Grune & Stratton, New York, 1956

Warshofsky, Fred, "Methadone: A Drug to Lick a Drug?", *Reader's Digest*, May 1970

Yablonsky, Lewis, *The Tunnel Back: Synanon*, Macmillan, New York, 1965

Senator Hennings' Hearings

U.S. Senate Committee on the Judiciary, Subcommittee to Investigate Juvenile Delinquency, "Juvenile Delinquency—Enforcement of Federal Narcotic Laws," Hearings, Part 7, January 22 and 26, 1960, Government Printing Office, Washington, D.C.

Senator Dodd's hearings

U.S. Senate Committee on the Judiciary, Subcommittee to Investigate Juvenile Delinquency, "Juvenile Delinquency," Hearings, May 9 through September 21, 1962, Parts 11, 12, and 13, Government Printing Office, Washington, D.C.

Ibid., "Juvenile Delinquency," Hearings, March 4, 5, and 6, 1968, Government Printing Office, Washington, D.C.

Ibid., "Narcotics Legislation," Hearings, September 15 through October 20, 1969, Government Printing Office, Washington, D.C.

Senator Hughes's hearings

See citations for Chapter 1

November 8, 1966: "Narcotic Addict Rehabilitation Act"

P.L. 89–793, 80 Stat. 1438

U.S. House Committee on the Judiciary, Subcommittee No. 4, "Treatment and Rehabilitation of Narcotics Addicts," Hearings, June 23 and 30, 1971, September 21–30, 1971, Government Printing Office, Washington, D.C.

CHAPTERS 25, 26
(Dangerous Drugs and the 1956 Amendments)

Sources

Blum, Richard, and Associates, *Utopiates—The Use and Users of LSD-25*, Atherton, New York, 1964

Geller and Boas, *The Drug Beat*, see Chapter 1

Harris, Richard, *The Real Voice*, Macmillan, New York, 1964

Mintz, Morton, *By Prescription Only*, Houghton Mifflin, Boston, 1967

Russo, J. Robert, ed., *Amphetamine Abuse*, Thomas, Springfield, Ill., 1968

Taylor, *Narcotics: Nature's Dangerous Gifts*, see Chapter 1

July 15, 1965: "Drug Abuse Control Amendments"

P.L. 89–74, 79 Stat. 226

U.S. Senate Committee on Labor and Public Welfare, Subcommittee on Health, "Control of Psychotoxic Drugs," Hearings, August 3, 1964, Government Printing Office, Washington, D.C.

U.S. House Interstate and Foreign Commerce Committee, "Drug Abuse Control Amendments of 1965," Hearings, January 27 through February 10, 1965, Government Printing Office, Washington, D.C.

U.S. Senate Report 89–337

U.S. House Report 89–130

Senator Robert Kennedy's hearings

U.S. Senate Committee on Government Operations, Subcommittee on Executive Reorganization, "Organization and Coordination of Federal Drug Research and Regulatory Programs: LSD," Hearings, May 24–26, 1966, Government Printing Office, Washington, D.C.

October 24, 1968: Act increasing penalties for hallucinogen offenses

P.L. 90–639, 82 Stat. 1361

U.S. House Committee on Interstate and Foreign Commerce, Subcommittee on Public Health and Welfare, "Increased Controls over Hallucinogens and Other Dangerous Drugs," Hearings, February 19 through March 19, 1968, Government Printing Office, Washington, D.C.

U.S. House Report 90–1546

U.S. Senate Report 90–1609

Congressman Pepper's hearings

U.S. House Select Committee on Crime:

"Crime in America—Views on Marijuana" (October 14 and 15, 1969)

"Crime in America—Drug Abuse and Criminal Justice" (September 25 and 26, 1969)

"Crime in America—Illicit and Dangerous Drugs" (October 23–27, 1969)

"Crime in America—Why 8 Billion Amphetamines?" (November 18, 1969)

"Crime in America—The Heroin Paraphernalia Trade" (October 5 and 6, 1970)

"Crime in America—Heroin Importation, Distribution, Packaging and Paraphernalia" (June 25–30, 1970)

Government Printing Office, Washington, D.C.

U.S. House Report 91–978 (Marijuana)

U.S. House Report 91–1807 (Amphetamines)

U.S. House Report 91–1808 (Heroin)

CHAPTERS 27, 28
(D-Men and the 1970 Act)

Sources

President's Commission on Law Enforcement and Administration of Justice, *The Challenge of Crime in a Free Society*, Government Printing Office, Washington, D.C., 1966

National Commission on Reform of Federal Criminal Laws, *Final Report (Proposed New Federal Criminal Code)*, Government Printing Office, Washington, D.C., 1971

Ibid., Working Papers (Report on Drug Offenses), Vol. II, 1059–1165 (1970)

April 8, 1968: Reorganization Plan No. 1 of 1968 creates new Bureau in Justice Department

33 Federal Register 5611 (April 11, 1968)

Congressional Record, April 2, 1968

U.S. House Committee on Government Operations, "Reorganization Plan No. 1 of 1968," Hearings, March 19–21, 1968, Government Printing Office, Washington, D.C.

U.S. House Document 90–249

U.S. House Report 90–1214

October 27, 1970: 1970 Drug Act signed

See citations in Chapter 1 and under Senator Dodd's hearings in Chapter 24

CHAPTERS 29, 30
(Contemporary Scene and Future Outlook)

The armed forces

U.S. House Armed Services Committee, "Alleged Drug Abuse in the Armed Services," Hearings, September 20 through December 15, 1970, Government Printing Office, Washington, D.C.

Ibid., "Inquiry into Alleged Drug Abuse in the Armed Services" (Report of Special Subcommittee), April 23, 1971, Government Printing Office, Washington, D.C.

U.S. House Committee on Foreign Affairs, "World Heroin Problem: Report of Special Study Mission," May 27, 1971, Government Printing Office, Washington, D.C.

New York Times, May 13 and 17, 1971; June 6, 23, and 24, 1971; August 15, 1971; *et passim*

The senators' New York adventure

New York Times, June 26, 1971

The District of Columbia police scandal

Healy, Paul F., "They Got the Goods on Washington's Cops," *Saturday Evening Post,* September 27, 1952

U.S. Senate Report 82–1989

The 1971 methadone restrictions

Notice re proposed rule-making, 35 Federal Register 9014, 15 (June 11, 1970)

Regulation and "Guidelines," 36 Federal Register 6075 (April 2, 1971)

The 1971 restriction on physicians' rights to prescribe

Treasury Decision 7076, 36 Federal Register 6081 (April 2, 1971)

April 24, 1971: comprehensive BNDD regulations for registrants

36 Federal Register 7776–7826 (April 24, 1971)

December 3, 1970: "Drug Abuse Education Act of 1970"

P.L. 91–527, 84 Stat. 1385

U.S. Senate Committee on Labor and Public Welfare, Special Subcommittee on Alcoholism and Narcotics, "Drug Abuse Education Act," Hearing, August 27, 1970, Government Printing Office, Washington, D.C.

U.S. House Report 91–599

U.S. Senate Report 91–1244

June 17, 1971: creation of Special Action Office for Drug Abuse Prevention

U.S. House Document 92–131

Executive Order No. 11599, 36 Federal Register 11793 (June 19, 1971)

January 28, 1972: creation of Office of Drug Abuse Law Enforcement

Executive Order No. 11641, 37 Federal Register 2421 (February 1, 1972)

The foundations

Report, *Dealing with Drug Abuse,* Praeger, New York, 1972

Contemporary evaluation

*Brecher, Edward M., and others, *Licit and Illicit Drugs: The Consumers Union Report,* Little Brown, Boston, 1972

Duster, Troy, *The Legislation of Morality,* Free Press, New York, 1970

*Packer, Herbert L., *The Limits of the Criminal Sanction,* Stanford University Press, Stanford, Calif., 1968

Schur, Edwin M., *Crimes Without Victims,* Prentice-Hall, Englewood Cliffs, N.J., 1965

Skolnick, Jerome H., *Coercion to Virtue,* American Bar Foundation, Chicago, 1968

MISCELLANEOUS SOURCES
(For Direct Inquiries)

Addiction Research Foundation
33 Russell Street
Toronto 4, Ontario, Canada

Addiction Services Agency
71 Worth Street
New York, N.Y. 10013

American Bar Association
and
American Bar Foundation
1155 East 60th Street
Chicago, Ill. 60637

American Medical Association
535 North Dearborn Street
Chicago, Ill. 60610

Baywood Publishers
1 Northwest Drive
Farmingdale, N.Y. 11735
    Publication: *Drug Forum* (quarterly)
              Journal of Drug Education (quarterly)

British Information Service
845 Third Avenue
New York, N.Y. 10022

Capitol Region Drug Information Center
179 Allyn Street
Hartford, Conn. 06103

Commission of Inquiry
into the Non-Medical Use of Drugs
100 Metcalfe Street
Ottawa, Ontario, Canada

Community Organization
for Drug Abuse Control (CODAC)
4 Aldwyn Center
Villanova, Pa. 19085

Drug Abuse Council, Inc.
1828 L Street, N.W.
Washington, D.C. 20036

Drugs Branch, Home Office
Romney House
Marsham Street
London SW1, England

Haight-Ashbury Free Medical Clinic
558 Clayton Street
San Francisco, Calif. 94117
Publication: *Journal of Psychedelic
Drugs* (semiannual)

Institute for the Study of Drug Addiction
680 West End Avenue
New York, N.Y. 10025
Publication: *The International Journal
of the Addictions* (quarterly)

International Council on Alcohol and Addictions
Case Postal 140
1001 Lausanne, Switzerland

Lower East Side Service Center
46 East Broadway
New York, N.Y. 10002

National Association for the Prevention
of Addiction to Narcotics (NAPAN)
175 Fifth Avenue
New York, N.Y. 10010

National Clearinghouse
  for Drug Abuse Information
5600 Fishers Lane
Rockville, Md. 20852

National Commission on Marijuana
  and Drug Abuse
801 19th Street, N.W.
Washington, D.C. 20006

National Conference of Commissioners
  on Uniform State Laws
1155 East 60th Street
Chicago, Ill. 60637

National Coordinating Council
  for Drug Abuse Education
1211 Connecticut Avenue, N.W.
Washington, D.C. 20036

National Council on Crime and Delinquency
44 East 23rd Street
New York, N.Y. 10010

National Institute of Mental Health
Division of Narcotics and Drug Abuse
Rockville, Md. 20852
  Publication: *Drug Dependence* (periodical)

New York State Narcotic Addiction
  Control Commission
1855 Broadway
New York, N.Y. 10023

Office de la Prévention et du Traitement
  de l'Alcoolism et des Autres Toxicomanies (OPTAT)
Ministry of Social Affairs
969 Route de l'Eglise
Quebec 10e, Quebec, Canada
  Publication: *Informations* (bimonthly)

Office of Drug Abuse
Department of Health and Rehabilitative Services
Tallahassee, Fla. 32301

The Office of Narcotics and
  Drug Abuse Coordination
915 Capitol Mall
Sacramento, Calif. 95814

Society for the Study of Addiction
  to Alcohol and Other Drugs
Wellcome Foundation
Euston Road
London, N.W.1, England
    Publication: *The British Journal*
              of Addictions (quarterly)

Student Association for the Study
  of Hallucinogens (STASH)
638 Pleasant Street
Beloit, Wisc. 53511
    Publications: *STASH Journal* (semiannual)
            STASH Capsules (bimonthly)

Superintendent of Documents
Government Printing Office
Washington, D.C. 20402

United Nations
Publications Office, Room 1059
New York, N.Y. 10017
    Publication: *U.N. Bulletin on Narcotics*
          (quarterly)

U.S. Bureau of Narcotics and Dangerous Drugs
1405 I Street, N.W.
Washington, D.C. 20537

U.S. Public Health Service
5454 Wisconsin Avenue
Chevy Chase, Md. 20015
    Publication: *Crime and Delinquency Abstracts*
         (periodical)

Index

(Page numbers of quoted material in italics)